SCIENCE IN THE ELEMENTARY AND MIDDLE SCHOOL

Donna M. Wolfinger
Auburn University, Montgomery
Montgomery, Alabama

LONGMAN

An imprint of Addison Wesley Longman, Inc.

New York • Reading, Massachusetts • Menlo Park, California • Harlow, England
Don Mills, Ontario • Sydney • Mexico City • Madrid • Amsterdam

To my father,

George Wolfinger

Editor-in-Chief: Priscilla McGeehon
Acquisitions Editor: Virginia L. Blanford
Marketing Manager: Drew Mitty
Full Service Production Manager: Denise Phillip
Project Coordination, Text Design, Electronic Page Makeup, Art Studio: Thompson Steele, Inc.
Cover Designer/Manager: Nancy Danahy
Cover Illustration/Photo: PhotoDisc
Senior Print Buyer: Hugh Crawford
Printer and Binder: R.R. Donnelly & Sons Company
Cover Printer: Coral Graphics Services, Inc.

For permission to use copyrighted material, grateful acknowledgment is made to the copyright holders on p. 461, which is hereby made part of this copyright page.

Library of Congress Cataloging-in-Publication Data

Wolfinger, Donna M.
Science in the elementary and middle school / Donna M. Wolfinger.
    p.   cm.
    Includes bibliographical references and index.
    ISBN 0-8013-2058-5
    1. Science—Study and teaching (Elementary)—United States.
    2. Science—Study and teaching (Middle School)—United States.
I. Title.
LB 1585.3.W65   2000   99-24131
372.3'5044—dc21   CIP

Please visit our website at http://www.awlonline.com

ISBN 0-8013-2058-5

12345678910—DOC—02010099

BRIEF CONTENTS

CONTENTS

LIST OF ACTIVITIES

PREFACE

I remember my first real science lesson. We opened our books and began to read about two children who were learning about sound. As we read about what they did as they played with various kinds of musical instruments, we learned about pitch, volume, vibrations, sound waves, wind instruments, percussion instruments, and stringed instruments. We never saw any of the instruments the children in the story played with except in the pictures. We never heard any of the instruments played. That was science: reading about what others did.

I remember another science lesson. It was high school chemistry. We followed the directions in the lab manual, watched as the dark reddish orange powder in the test tube turned bright orange, as a ring of silver appeared, and as a smoldering wood splint burst into flame when it was inserted into the test tube. We wrote down what we saw. We handed in our lab reports. The next day we went back to the classroom and a lecture. That was science: doing experiments divorced from the real content of the course.

I also remember the last science lesson I had. It was in graduate school. After spending hours outside, hanging to rock faces above highways collecting fossils, documenting the evidence collected, measuring the depth of the various strata, reading journal articles about the time period, and generally becoming immersed in the Devonian era, the course instructor gave us the directions for the final project: Write a paper using the data collected and other sources describing the area we had investigated as it would have been during the Devonian era. That was science: skinned knees and knuckles, data collection, journal articles, and long days trying to make sense out of the information.

Which of these three lessons gave the best image of the nature of science? The first lesson showed science as reading. The second showed science as activity. The third showed science.

The purpose of this book is to help preservice and inservice teachers learn how to teach science to elementary and middle school students. As such it is based on three premises:

1. Good science teachers are able to defend their instructional decisions on the basis of an understanding of the nature of science, the latest thinking on the science curriculum, and the characteristics of the students they teach.

2. Good science teachers have a repertoire of instructional strategies designed to demonstrate all of the facets of science and designed to reach all of the students.

3. Good science teachers know how to present science to all children using appropriate instructional strategies, good questioning techniques, and good evaluation strategies.

Using these three premises as a basis, this text is divided into three parts.

Part One "The Child and the Science Curriculum" looks at the nature of science and the characteristics of children from preschool through eighth grade. The nature of science as a combination of content, process, attitudes, and values is first discussed. This sets the stage in terms of the components of science and the components of the science curriculum. From there the text looks at how these components of science are considered in reform documents: *Project 2061, Standards for Science Education,* and *Benchmarks for Science Literacy.* After looking at the nature of science, the nature of students is considered, first from a Piagetian prospective. However, Piaget alone is not enough to fully describe our students and how they learn. Consequently, the theories of Vygotsky and of Gardner are also discussed. It is not enough for a science teacher to know what to teach. Good science teachers know who they teach and are able to make decisions about the science content they will teach as well as about the teaching strategies they will use.

Part Two "The Processes of Science" is a unique aspect of this text. In this section the basic, causal, and experimental processes of science are fully defined and developed. In addition, the processes are considered from a developmental prospective including which processes are appropriate at the various grade levels, the sequence of process skill introduction, and the use of processes within investigations and experiments. No other text gives this detailed attention to the process skills.

Part Three "Constructing Science with Children" is unique in many of its components. First, multiple teaching strategies are developed. Rather than one strategy that may or may not be appropriate to particular content or teaching situations, everything from expository teaching to Learning Cycle to field trips is considered, including how to plan for teaching in the strategy, when to use that strategy, and what kinds of problems may be encountered when the strategy is used. In addition to the multiple strategies, the chapter dealing with teaching strategies considers them within the context of unit planning so the relationship of long- and short-range planning is developed. Also unique to the text is the extensive information on integrated and interdisciplinary teaching with a differentiation made between the two curricular concepts and specific strategies for planning in both formats included. Topics such as questioning skills, handling sensitive topics within the classroom, inclusion, reading in science, technology, and evaluation are all considered in Part Three.

Almost as important as what is in this text is what is not in this text. First, this text does not contain an extensive review of science content information. Students entering their professional courses should already have developed their background knowledge. Those students needing to review or extend their understanding of science content can be directed to appropriate books: chemistry, physics, biology, geology, and so on. Second, this text does not contain an extensive collection of simple activities for pre- and inservice teachers to take into the classroom. Activities for teaching science to children can be found anywhere. Activity books abound. There is no shortage of activities for science teaching and learning. But there is a shortage of knowledge about how to present activities effectively. The purpose of this textbook is to assist pre- and inservice teachers in learning to use this plethora of activities purposefully, appropriately, and effectively in the classroom.

I would like to thank the teachers and children who have used the techniques and strategies included in this text. I would also like to thank my own students for their feedback on the activities used in classes. Only in the real world—elementary schools, middle schools, high schools, colleges, and universities—can the effectiveness of teaching strategies be tested. In addition, I would like to thank my colleagues at Auburn University, Montgomery, for providing information on those topics unfamiliar and yet important to the ever-changing view of science teaching at the elementary and middle school levels. And, finally, I would like to thank the following reviewers for the long hours spent reviewing the manuscript. Their comments and suggestions were more than appreciated.

Joel Bass, Sam Houston State University
Robert Boram, Morehead State University
Barry Brucklacher, Mansfield University
Nancy Davis, Florida State University
Norman Dee, Lesley College
Kevin Finson, Western Illinois University
Richard Green, Rhode Island College
Mark Guy, University of North Dakota
Marlysue Holmquist, Bethany College
Lawrence Kellerman, Bradley University
Marylin Lisowski, Eastern Illinois University
Robin McGrew-Zoubi, Sam Houston State University
Faye Neathery, Southwestern Oklahoma State University
Eric J. Pyle, West Virginia University
Diana Rice, University of South Carolina—Aiken
William Rieck, University of Southwestern Louisiana
Anita VanBrackle, Kennesaw State University
Melissa Warden, Ball State University
Dana L. Zeidler, University of South Florida

Donna M. Wolfinger

CHAPTER ONE

SCIENCE IN THE ELEMENTARY AND MIDDLE SCHOOL

Chapter Objectives

Upon completion of this chapter you should be able to:

1 define the terms *content, process, attitude,* and *value* as they pertain to science and science education.

2 identify the role played by science content, processes, attitudes, and values in the science curriculum.

3 discuss how calls for reform in science education were met in the past.

4 discuss current factors affecting the science curriculum.

5 discuss *Science for All Americans, Benchmarks for Scientific Literacy,* and the *National Science Education Standards.*

6 discuss the integration of science content, processes, attitudes, and values into the total elementary and middle school science curriculum.

1

Introduction

In Utah, a group of men and women carefully chip away the rock surrounding the enormous thigh bone of a dinosaur. In Zaire, a team of doctors works on identifying the disease organism that decimated a village in only a few days. On a university campus, men and women watch as the equations leading to a new source of energy unfold on a chalkboard. In the Pacific Ocean off Australia, a team of divers searches for the identifying fins of a great white shark, then enter the water to observe the great predator in its habitat. In the desert of Israel, men and women carefully uncover the traces of an ancient village, collecting shards of pottery and bits of charcoal from long dead fires. And, in an observatory, a young woman pores over the latest Hubbell Telescope photographs of the distant reaches of space searching for clues to the origins of the universe.

Dinosaurs, disease organisms, equations, sharks, pottery, and stars: all different and yet all similar in one way. All are objects of study, objects that arouse curiosity and a desire to understand in men and women from many nations and cultures, a curiosity that leads those men and women to try to understand the past and the present so they can contribute to the future. In each case, whether digging out a dinosaur or attending to the equations of physics, these people are actively engaged in the pursuit of information, in the pursuit of understanding. They are engaged physically with rock hammers and brushes, scuba equipment and cameras, chalk and photographs. But this is not just physical activity, it is also intellectual activity. These scientists gather information, interpret that information, and work toward understanding.

Whatever the field of endeavor, zoology, astronomy, archaeology, medicine, physics, paleontology, or many others, the people who engage in the active investigation of some aspect of the world around them are called scientists and their generalized field of endeavor, science.

Scientists are those men and women in every nation who attempt to extend understanding of our universe through active investigation. **Science,** then, may be defined as an active pursuit of understanding. However, everyone who pursues information cannot be considered a scientist, nor can every pursuit of understanding be considered science.

What separates science from other endeavors that seek understanding? What identifies a scientist as a seeker of understanding? In this chapter we consider the nature of science and the most recent suggestions for reform of science teaching and learning at the elementary school level.

The Nature of Science: Values, Attitudes, Processes and Content

What is science? Ask most people, and they'll tell you the answer is easy. Science is what you learn from your science textbook, a popular science magazine, or a science program on television. Science is information about plants and animals, stars and planets, rocks and minerals, body systems and oceans. Science is facts and definitions and theories and laws and principles. Science is knowing that $E = mc^2$, knowing the names of all nine planets in their order from the Sun, being able to correctly identify the tibia and femur, and knowing that a whale is a mammal not a fish. Although every one of these answers is correct, every one of these answers is also incorrect.

How can an answer be both correct and incorrect? The reason is simple. Even though all of these typical answers define science, they define it in a limited way. Science is far more than learning the bits and pieces of information you and I memorized in school. If we really want to talk about science, then we need to go beyond vocabulary, facts, and equations, and also talk about attitudes, values, and methods. In the following sections, we consider what is meant by scientific values, attitudes, processes, and content.

Scientific Values

We all have values. Usually we tie those values to religious beliefs, family background, and cultural identity. The values we develop help us make choices. They help us decide how to behave in certain situations. And they help us know how to react in new situations. Just as we have values to guide our behavior, scientists also have values to guide their behavior.

Unlike our personal values, scientific values are not tied to a particular culture or a particular belief system. Instead, scientific values are tied to the idea that science is a search for understanding. These values form the basis for science. If children at the elementary and middle school levels are going to understand how scientists think and behave, then they need to understand the values on which scientists base their behavior. **Scientific values** then, might be thought of as the principles common to the behavior of scientists and which govern that behavior.

As reflected in Kitchner (1984), Project 2061 (American Association for the Advancement of Science, 1989), and the National Science Education Standards (National Research Council, 1996), the scientific values considered here are these:

1. longing to know and understand
2. questioning of all things
3. search for data and their meaning
4. demand for verification
5. respect for logic
6. consideration of premises
7. consideration of consequences

Longing to Know and Understand.   Scientists want to learn; they want to know how the universe operates. They want to determine the laws and principles governing the universe. They want to develop the theories that explain how the universe works. A scientist without the desire to know and understand could not function as a scientist. And so, the first of the scientific values is **longing to know and understand.**

As scientists pursue this desire to know and understand, some of the information they gain is practical and immediately useful in society. When Edison discovered how to make a light bulb and a phonograph, he developed information that was immediately useful to society. This kind of information with its immediate, practical application is called **applied science** or **technology.**

But not all scientists want to make light bulbs and phonographs. Many scientists are simply interested in finding out more, more about galaxies, more about atoms, more about giraffes. The information these scientists gain may have no practical use. It may not even be interesting to anyone other than scientists. But no matter how many people are interested, the information is still important. It is important because it contributes to our understanding of the universe. Pursuing information for the sake of finding out, pursuing knowledge for the sake of knowledge is called **pure science.**

Pure science and technology are not, however, completely separate. Pure science may lead to application. Scientists trying to find out how an atom is constructed, how the parts interrelated, how the nucleus stayed together were pursuing pure science. Using that pure science to construct nuclear power plants or create new cures through nuclear medicine came after the knowledge but was not the purpose for gaining an understanding of the atom. In this case pure science led to technology, but the technology was not the original goal.

Questioning of All Things.   How did the universe begin? Do really cold materials conduct electricity better than warmer materials? How do gorillas behave in the wild? How did human beings evolve? What is the effect of vitamin C on cancer?

Every one of these questions has been asked by a scientist. In fact, one of the main activities of scientists is to ask questions. Questions lead to experiments and observations. Experiments and observations lead to answers. There are, however, two big differences between the kinds of questions scientists ask and the kinds of questions most people ask. First, scientists not only ask questions about things they don't know but also about those things everyone appears to know. They want to know if the information everyone accepts is correct. If no one had ever questioned, we would still believe, as did Aristotle, that we think with our hearts rather than our brains. Scientists challenge the status quo in an attempt to increase understanding. They challenge the authority figures of their areas of study. And, second, the questions scientists ask differ from our own because they ask questions about anything and everything. Scientists ask questions about the origins of religious belief. Scientists ask questions about human reproduction. Scientists ask questions about race and culture. For scientists, no areas are taboo, no areas cannot be questioned or studied; they are **questioning all things.**

Search for Data and Their Meaning.   Average temperatures around the world have been increasing. Is there a reason for this? Pandas are disappearing from the wild. Why? The galaxies farthest from us are moving faster than those close to us. What can this tell us about the early universe?

Information is vital in science. Such information is generally termed **data** and is usually made up of observations and measurements. One of the aims of data collection is to be as accurate and thorough as possible. Why is accuracy and thoroughness important? Because scientists base their theories, hypotheses, and conclusions on that data.

Scientists not only collect data, but also interpret it; that is, they **search for data and their meaning.** They try to find out what the data mean. By finding out what data mean, they can then answer questions about speeding galaxies and disappearing pandas. And sometimes they run into problems. Everyone knows the trouble Galileo got into suggesting that Earth moved around the Sun rather than the Sun around Earth. His data and his conclusion challenged what was generally believed to be true. This type of problem, however, is unusual. A different type of problem may be more common. Scientists, like everyone else, have their own beliefs. Those beliefs may deal with the scientific area they study or may be personal. When data conflict with beliefs, something has to change. What changes is the mind of the scientist as he or she accepts the new information and its meaning.

Demand for Verification. Trying to be healthy can be very difficult. One day we are all eating oat bran muffins to lower cholesterol, and the next day we are told our bran muffins are not helping at all. One day we are eating our margarine and feeling good about not consuming the saturated fat of butter, and the next day we find out the fat in margarine may be even worse than the fat in butter. One day we are told drinking any amount of alcohol is bad for health, and the next we are told a single drink a day may actually help us live longer. And one day we are being told to exercise for 20 minutes a day three times a week, and so on. Actually, that last one seems to still be effective.

Why so many changes? Do scientists really change their minds like that? Although they do change their minds when they get new data, scientists do not tend to change so quickly or so frequently as it often seems. Sometimes changes occur because there has been no **verification,** or confirmation, of the results.

Demand for verification simply means that someone else, or perhaps a great number of someone elses, have repeated the same experiment in order to check the results and be certain they are accurate. Only after the results have been repeated, or **replicated,** can they be said to be accurate and acceptable to scientists.

In some cases this value becomes difficult to practice. News media, eager to present new results, sometimes present information to the public that has not yet been verified. In other cases, new discoveries in science may result in financial gain for the discoverer and the new discovery may be announced prior to verification in order to assure the originator will receive credit and so the financial success as well.

Respect for Logic. Charles Darwin saw changes in animals from one island to another in the Galápagos, and Alfred Russell Wallace saw the same thing in the Malay Archipelago. They considered their data and drew a logical conclusion from that data. A **respect for logic** forms the foundation for interpreting data.

This is not to say intuition plays no role in science. Intuition can result in a new theory, a new way of testing a hypothesis, or a new piece of equipment to allow more accurate measurements. But when that new theory is tested against reality, intuition takes a back seat to logic.

When logical reasoning proceeds from the specific to the general, we say **inductive reasoning** is being used. Darwin and Wallace were using an inductive form of reasoning as they interpreted their data and drew their conclusions. On the other hand, reasoning may begin with a generalization, with a theory, and move to the collection of data through hypothesis testing to the collection of facts to support the theory. For example, a paleontologist may intuit that dinosaurs were possibly warm-blooded and then begin to look for ways of testing that hypothesis. In this second case, **deductive reasoning** is being used. In the true working of science, both are used nearly simultaneously or in succession in order to interpret data.

Consideration of Premises.   The first time I tried to grow a pineapple plant from the green top of a pineapple, a neighbor told me it would never become a pineapple unless I put an apple in the pot with the pineapple top. How was I to do that? Easy. Plant the pineapple top in a big pot. Place a whole apple, a Macintosh worked best according to the neighbor, on top of the dirt and just watch. The reason this worked was that "pineapple" had the word *apple* in it and placing an apple near it would somehow coax the plant into making a pineapple. I have to admit, I did not follow the directions. Why didn't I place an apple in my pot? Because I asked some questions about the information first. Where did you get this information? Who originally developed the information? Were there experiments to test this idea? If they were, were they carefully controlled and replicated? These are the kinds of questions both scientists and laypersons should ask before accepting any information. These questions are considering the premises on which the information is based.

Premises form the foundation on which theories and hypotheses are built. The firmer the foundation, the more likely the theory will be supported. This is one reason why scientists always do a literature search prior to an experiment. That is, they look through scientific journals to find out what has already been done to investigate a particular theory or to test a particular hypothesis. They look at the strength of the data, the methodology followed in the experiment, the logic involved in developing the conclusion—a **consideration of the premises.** The stronger the supporting foundation, the stronger the new theory.

Consideration of Consequences.   What is matter composed of? What are molecules? What are the parts of atoms? How do atoms hold together? How are matter and energy related? Scientists worked to discover the nature of matter to probe into the atom and to release its secrets. One of those secrets was the fantastic energy source contained within the atom. What these scientists could not have known when they began searching for an understanding of atoms and of the structure of matter was that the energy of atoms would first be used to create a devastating bomb.

Scientists do try to consider the consequences of their discoveries; they do look at how new information could affect the environment, could affect society—a **consideration of the consequences.** The difficulty lies in the fact that the impact a

Table 1.1

The Scientific Values

Longing to know and understand

1. Pure science
2. Applied science or technology

Questioning of all things

1. Studying all topics
2. Questioning authority

Searching for data and their meaning

1. Collecting and interpreting data
2. Changing one's ideas on the basis of evidence

Demanding verification

1. Accepting experimental results only after they have been replicated

Respecting logic

1. Inductive reasoning
2. Deductive reasoning

Considering premises

1. On what information is research based

Considering consequences

1. Consider the future ramifications

discovery could have in the future is often not known at the time of the discovery. A consideration of consequences of research may not always be possible at the time of the original research.

The scientific values, summarized in Table 1.1, are the basic, underlying beliefs held by scientists as they practice their art. Scientific values may take a lifetime to develop, to be incorporated into the behavioral structure of an individual. Although the scientific values may take a lifetime, the scientific attitudes can be developed and manifested in the elementary school child.

Scientific Attitudes

Scientific attitudes are the behaviors that can be seen in children as they investigate in the science classroom and beyond. The scientific attitudes guide the thinking skills of children as they search for meaning in the world around them. In essence, the scientific attitudes are derived from the scientific values. The scientific values of longing to know and understand and questioning of all things are seen in the scientific attitude of curiosity. The value of questioning of all things results in the attitudes of skepticism and willingness to suspend judgment. The search for data and their meaning result in the scientific attitude of honesty. The demand for verification asks that students be willing to suspend their judgment until they have all of the evidence. A respect for logic manifests itself in the scientific attitude of lack of

Table 1.2

The Scientific Attitudes

1. Curiosity

2. Honesty

3. Willingness to suspend judgment

4. Skepticism

5. Objectivity

6. Positive approach to failure

7. Respect for the environment

8. Lack of superstition

superstition. And finally, the scientific attitude of respect for the environment results from a consideration of consequences. Scientific attitudes and their development are more fully considered in Chapter 6; however, Table 1.2 shows a full listing of the scientific attitudes.

The pursuit, collection, and interpretation of data, of information, are the result of both the scientific values and the scientific attitudes. However the collection of accurate data does not come automatically because a student is curious or objective or willing to suspend judgment. The collection of accurate data results from applying the scientific processes.

Scientific Processes

Science as inquiry "requires that students combine processes and scientific knowledge as they use scientific reasoning and critical thinking to develop their understanding of science" (*Standards,* 1996, p. 105). **Scientific processes,** therefore, are used to investigate the physical world and to allow students to develop concepts in a direct, personal, and active manner. Science processes involve children in using the methods of science to gain an understanding of the physical world. Through observation, inference, conclusion, classification, and experimentation, both scientists and children collect data and look for meaning in that data. **Process,** therefore, can be defined as the techniques or methods used by scientists as they gather, interpret, and disseminate information. Processes are also the methods used by children as they work with direct, hands-on science activities to gather, interpret, and disseminate information. Although the specific processes and their development are discussed in Chapters 3, 4, and 5, Table 1.3 shows a complete listing of the science process skills discussed in this text.

For children, process skills such as observation, prediction, conclusion, measurement, and communication are used to actively investigate the environment. Through active investigation, children begin to confront their current ideas and beliefs, to refine those ideas when they are inaccurate, to change those beliefs when there are misconceptions or errors of understanding. The final result of this active

Table 1.3

The Scientific Processes

Basic processes

1. Observation
2. Communication
3. Classification
4. Using numbers
5. Using space/time relations
6. Operational questions

Casual processes

1. Inference
2. Prediction
3. Conclusion
4. Cause and effect
5. Interaction and systems

Experimental processes

1. Controlling variables
2. Hypothesizing
3. Experimenting
4. Interpreting data
5. Operational definitions

investigation is that children construct meaningful concepts rather than simply memorize information read in a book or told to them by the teacher.

In their most powerful form, processes involve scientists in using controlled experiments in which a single factor, perhaps out of hundreds, is manipulated so that its effect is found. Isolating a single food as the cause of an allergy, testing water to determine why fish are dying and isolating a single pollutant, or identifying a particular virus as the cause of a disease, all show how experiments can be used in solving problems typical in daily living.

As children confront their world through science process skills, they gather data. Those data are interpreted, and conclusions are drawn. Those conclusions may give students new concepts or may modify previously held concepts. Either way, students are learning science information. That science information is termed science content.

Scientific Content

Scientific content is the stuff of science. It is all of the information contained between the covers of biology, chemistry, physics, astronomy, geology, meteorology, and astronomy books. It is exactly what most people think about when asked what science is. Simply comparing science textbooks from a hundred years ago to science textbooks of today is enough to give insight into one of the major characteristics of science content: It changes. Science content changes as new experiments lead to new information, which leads to new questions and then to new experiments in a cycle that is unlikely to ever end.

Scientific content constantly changes because of new, more accurate information, but the process of change requires many years, even when the experimental evidence is overwhelming (Kuhn, 1970). But once the evidence accumulates and change does occur, the once strongly supported ideas of yesterday may become the myth of today. In fact, controversy and change within a particular area of science are generally considered to show the strength of that area, rather than an indication of weakness or problems, because they mean active investigation (AAAS, 1989).

Science content includes five areas. The traditional science textbook or curriculum includes information from three: the biological sciences, the earth-space sciences, and the physical sciences. **Biological science** includes information on the five kingdoms of living organisms: monera, protista, fungi, plants, and animals. It also includes information dealing with ecological principles. The **earth-space sciences** include geology, astronomy, and meteorology; students study rocks and minerals, stars and planets, weather and climate. Finally, students are involved in the study of matter and energy through the **physical sciences.** Table 1.4 summarizes the areas of science content from the viewpoint of scientific disciplines.

In addition to these three traditional areas of study, two other areas should be included as a part of the content of the science curriculum (AAAS, 1989). The first is mathematics. **Mathematics** is included within the content of science, not only because it is considered a science in itself, but also because of the role it plays in supporting science through measurement, modeling in terms of equations, and statistics. "Because mathematics plays such a central role in modern culture, some basic understanding of the nature of mathematics is requisite for scientific literacy. To achieve this, students need to perceive mathematics as a part of the scientific endeavor, comprehend the nature of mathematical thinking, and become familiar with key mathematical ideas and skills (AAAS, 1989, p. 33).

Finally, the content of the science curriculum should include technology. The curriculum should demonstrate the contributions of science to technology and of technology to science. In terms of the content of science, **technology** refers to "our abilities to change the world: to cut, shape, or put together materials; to move things

Table 1.4

Areas of Science Content as Viewed by the Scientific Disciplines

Biological sciences	Physical sciences
1. Botany	1. Physics
2. Zoology	2. Chemistry
3. Ecology	
4. Genetics	**Earth-space sciences**
5. Human physiology and anatomy	1. Geology
	2. Astronomy
6. Paleontology (also included under earth-space sciences)	3. Meteorology
	4. Paleontology

Figure 1.1

The Relationship Among Content, Process, Attitude, and Value

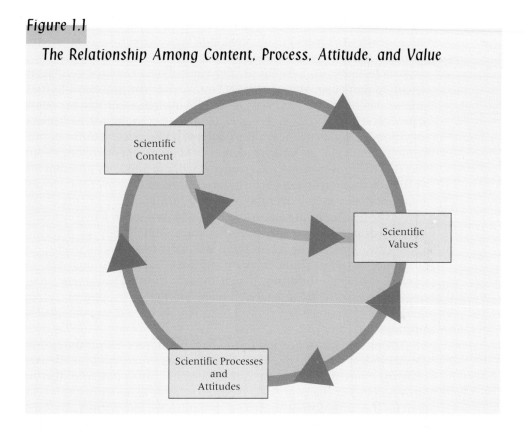

from one place to another; to reach farther with our hands, voices, and senses (AAAS, 1989, p. 39). In addition to showing the interactive role of science and technology, the effects of technology on society and how decisions on the use of technology can be made should also be developed in the science curriculum. Figure 1.1 shows the relationships among content, process, attitude, and value.

Integrating Values, Attitudes, Process, and Content into the Elementary and Middle School Curriculum

According to the *National Science Education Standards* (1996), the content of science as found in the elementary school curriculum should include physical science, life science, earth-space science, technology, social perspectives on science, the history and nature of science, as well as science as inquiry. The problem is that these five areas include everything in science. Trying to teach everything at every grade level would be absurd, and so decisions have to be made about which topics from each of these areas should be included at each grade level. Most school systems have already made these decisions. State courses of study for science, local curriculum guides, and textbooks or programs selected for your school and grade level tell you the content to teach. As a teacher you have little control over the content areas taught at a particular level.

As a teacher you have far greater control over how the content information is taught. In particular, you have great control over the process skills that the students in your classroom use. This is true even if your school or school system has a listing of process skills for your grade level because you, as the teacher, select the learning activities you will use to teach the content. If you select hands-on, minds-on investigations to challenge your students through problem solving, you will also be selecting the process skills your students will use and your program will emphasize. As the classroom teacher, you will have more control over the processes your students use than you will over the content information presented.

As the teacher in the classroom, you will have complete control over two of the areas of science: the scientific attitudes and values as they are presented to children in the classroom. As the teacher you will have total control over these two aspects of science because attitudes and values are taught through the actions of the teacher, through **modeling.** If you model curiosity, skepticism, logical thinking, consideration of consequences, respect for the environment, questioning of all things as you conduct your science classes, then your students will develop those attitudes and values.

The picture of science as a fusion of content, process, attitude, and value should govern how science is approached in the elementary and middle school. Without knowing content, children cannot understand the grandeur of the universe; without engaging in the processes, children cannot experience the excitement of the search, and without encountering the attitudes and values of scientists, children cannot begin to value the knowledge gained. A complete elementary and middle school science program should permit children to encounter the world directly on a level where understanding can develop. If children are to learn science, they must experience it in all of its facets.

Activities 1.1 and 1.2 are designed to have you investigate the elementary or middle school science curriculum for its inclusion of science content, process, attitudes, and values.

Science Curriculum Activities

Activity 1.1

Purpose   To interview practicing teachers about their views of the nature of science.

Procedure

1. Arrange to interview at least three teachers at different grade levels. In your interview include, but do not limit yourself to the following questions:

  a. What is science?

  b. What is meant by the term *scientific attitude?*

  c. What is meant by the term *scientific value?* What do you think some of the scientific values are?

  d. What kinds of things do you emphasize when you teach science to your students?

  e. How important do you think it is to have students do hands-on investigations in science? What are you trying to teach when you do this kind of investigation?

2. Consider the responses of the teachers to each of your questions. How are the teachers' views of science similar to and different from those presented here?

3. What effects could these teachers' views of science have on how they teach science to the children in their classrooms?

Activity 1.2

Purpose   To investigate children's understanding of science.

Procedure

1. Arrange to work with three small groups of children from three different grade levels and from the same classrooms as the teachers interviewed in Activity 1.1.

2. Begin with the following question, and then use additional questions to probe the children's understanding of what science is. Do not try to teach the children a definition or to change their own ideas.

3. Questions: What do you think the word *science* means?

4. After the students have finished with their ideas of what science is, use the following question to have them summarize:

  a. If you were going to tell someone who was not here today to listen to everything we were saying, what would you tell them science was?

5. Analyze the answers given by the children interviewed. How does their concept of science change from one grade level to another?

6. Compare the responses of the students to the perceptions of science shown by their teachers.

  a. How have the perceptions shown by the teachers influenced the perceptions of the students?

  b. How do the perceptions of the students in each classroom reflect the concept of teaching through modeling?

Science Curriculum in Today's Elementary and Middle Schools

Why is our science curriculum like it is? Why are we hearing calls to reform that science curriculum? If we are going to answer these questions, we need to look into the past. Although we could go back as far as the 1850s and the nature study movement (Comstock, 1911), to the 1920s and the work of science educator Gerald S. Craig (Craig, 1927), or to 1964 and the National Science Teacher's Association's position paper "Theory into Action in Science Curriculum Development" (1964), the latest call for reform can be more purposefully considered by going back only about 30 years to the 1960s and projects for reform that began in that decade and were considered in the 1970s. See Boxes 1.1. 1.2, and 1.3 for a summary of major events in science education in the United States to the 1960s.

Reform in Science Education: Projects of the 1960s and 1970s

A variety of projects for teaching elementary school science appeared during the 1960s and influenced science teaching during the decades of the 1960s and 1970s. These elementary school science projects were distinguished from the textbooks of

---

Box 1.1   A Brief Overview of Science Education in the United States

1. The colonial period: Science was not a part of the school curriculum.

2. The period between 1830 and 1880

   a. In 1830 suggestions were made for specific courses such as botany and geology. Science was taught in order to develop an understanding of God and the Bible, to strengthen the mind, and to show practical applications. Science was mainly for the wealthy.

   b. In 1850 Johann Pestalozzi introduced the object lesson. Students made observations, analyzed their observations, and developed generalizations.

   c. In 1880 science appeared in the elementary school curriculum.

   d. In 1890 the nature study movement, consisting mainly of the study of nature outside the classroom, dominated.

3. The period from 1890 through 1960

   a. In 1910 Henry Armstrong advocated the use of discovery teaching for school science.

   b. In 1927 Gerald S. Craig developed a list of science topics for use in the elementary school. See Box 1.2.

   c. In 1957 Sputnik's launch initiated calls for reform in science education.

   d. In 1964 Theory into Action in Science Curriculum developed themes for science education. See Box 1.3 for a list of themes.

Box 1.2   Topics for Elementary Science Content: Gerald S. Craig

1. Health and nutrition
2. Living things
3. Conservation and the balance of nature
4. Rocks and soil
5. Atmosphere and weather

6. Chemical and physical changes
7. Motions, mechanics, and technology
8. Electricity, magnetism, and technology
9. Energy from the Sun
10. Earth and sky

---

the previous decades by being child oriented, activity oriented, and process oriented. In the view of the science curriculum shown by these projects, textbooks were out, and kits, hands-on experiences, and projects were in.

Three of the projects developed during the 1960s are considered prime examples of the thinking and of the teaching methods advocated during this time: *Science—A Process Approach (SAPA)* (AAAS, 1975), *The Science Curriculum Improvement Study (SCIS),* and the *Elementary Science Study (ESS)* (1978). Although not extensively used in classrooms, these three programs were, along with many others of the period, highly influential in changing the nature of textbooks and the nature of science teaching in the elementary school. Although the three projects were developed during the same period of time and had the same goal, major differences in the projects existed.

SAPA focused its attention on the development of science process skills rather than on science content. *SAPA*'s lessons developed 12 science process skills through

---

Box 1.3   Curricular Themes from Theory into Action in Science Curriculum

1. All matter is composed of elementary particles that may under certain conditions be converted into energy; energy may also, under certain conditions be transformed into matter.
2. The particles of matter interact with each other.
3. Because matter exists in time and space, and because the particles of matter interact, changes must occur in time and space.
4. Matter exists in a variety of forms, arbitrarily classified by their complexity.

5. The distribution and behavior of matter in the universe is often best studies statistically.
6. The interactions of matter tend toward equilibria in which available energy is least and random distribution of energy is greatest; total matter-energy in a closed system is constant.
7. Motion of particles of matter is one of the major forms of energy.
8. The processes of the past are those of the present and the future.

sequenced lessons beginning at the kindergarten level and moving upward to the sixth grade level. The lessons were highly structured and sequential.

By the time students had completed the *SAPA* program, they were expected to show certain characteristics. Children were supposed to (1) apply the scientific method of thought to a wide range of problems including social problems, (2) distinguish facts from inferences, and (3) identify the procedures required to obtain verification of hypotheses and problem solutions.

By the end of sixth grade, children were supposed to be able to read a written account of an experiment and then identify the question being investigated, the variables being manipulated, controlled, and measured, and the hypothesis being tested; show how such a test related to the results being obtained; and determine if the conclusion could be legitimately drawn from the data. *SAPA* students were also expected to be able to design and carry out an experiment that would test a hypothesis relevant to a particular problem. And, finally, *SAPA* students were expected to show an appreciation of and an interest in the sciences by choosing science topics for reading, entertainment, and other kinds of leisure-time pursuits.

In the *SAPA* classroom, the program carefully controlled the science curriculum. The lessons contained explicit instructions for the teacher to follow. The teacher, in turn, controlled exactly what the students did during the lessons. And, in the end, the *SAPA* program determined how the students would be evaluated after a particular lesson was taught. Although this may sound like a rigid approach to science teaching, the structure was needed in order to assure the sequence required for developing the process skills (*SAPA*, 1979).

SAPA 's approach to science teaching made process the content of the program. *SCIS*, the *Science Curriculum Improvement Study* (Palady, 1978), in contrast, saw process, content, skills, and attitudes as equally important in the development of a scientifically literate individual. The primary emphasis of the *SCIS* program was on developing concepts, but attention was also given to developing attitudes, abilities, and skills such as making observations, methods for recording observations and experiences, discrimination of differences, and recognition of similarities, along with the ability to obtain quantitative data and to use appropriate vocabulary. Each grade level from kindergarten through sixth grade had only two units of work: one biological science and one physical science. Each of these units was designed not only to engage children in science learning at a particular grade level but also to provide a foundation for the unit taught at the next grade level. The *SCIS* units at each grade level developed more depth and used more abstract concepts than those of the previous level, so that the program moved from the simple to the complex and from the concrete to the abstract.

Within the *SCIS* program was a technique for presenting content known as learning cycle. **Learning cycle,** more fully discussed in Chapter 8, consisted of three phases: exploration, invention, and discovery. During **exploration,** children were free to explore the materials without the constraint of learning a particular concept. Rather, the children had the opportunity to familiarize themselves with new materials and to identify problems that could be investigated in later lessons. In **invention,** children were introduced to new concepts. The teacher provided experiences through which the children would be able to develop an understanding of a concept. They developed a concrete definition of the concept with the aid of materials, demonstrations, textual materials, and audiovisual materials. Also in the invention stage, the children reviewed and discussed the validity of the applications of the concept being developed. At this stage, the concept was given a verbal label in order to help with communication and to ensure stability for the concept. In the final phase, **discovery,** the children tested the concept they had learned during the invention stage through experimentation and explanation. The purpose of the experimentation was to test the consequences of the concept in a variety of situations. The majority of any *SCIS* unit was spent in the discovery phase. In general, the children, rather than the teacher or the program materials, controlled *SCIS*. The children in a class had the opportunity to identify their own questions, analyze their own information, and interpret their own data (*SCIS,* 1970, 1980).

Although both *SAPA* and *SCIS* approach the teaching of science in a sequential manner, *ESS*, the *Elementary Science Study*, was far more open in its approach. Scope and sequence were of importance in the *ESS* program, but the developers also recognized there was no way to know what content would be of importance in the future. Consequently, they did not attempt to predict the future by establishing a program of specific content all students in all schools should learn. The developers of *ESS* saw it as the prerogative of individual schools and teachers to determine an appropriate curriculum.

So that schools and teachers could develop a school or classroom appropriate curriculum, *ESS* (Romney, 1971; Rogers and Voelker, 1970) prepared more than fifty units for grades kindergarten through 9. Although the majority of the units were developed for fourth, fifth, and sixth grades, there were still many units appropriate for other grade levels. In addition, *ESS* had a feature unique to the three programs examined here. Many of the units were designed for multiple grade levels rather than for a single grade level. As a result, the units showed great variety in their approaches. Some units were process oriented, some content oriented, some oriented toward the development of thinking skills. Some of the units were designed for use by the entire class at the same time and some for use by small groups or individuals. By selecting from the units and approaches available, a teacher could develop a program unique to his or her classroom situation. And, once that program was developed, the teacher had an opportunity to play a different kind of role.

The *ESS* teacher was a consultant, a guide, and a catalyst rather than an authority figure relaying information to the children. The teacher advised, listened, diagnosed, and gave aid when children were unable to do something alone. When using the *ESS* program effectively, the teacher turned control of learning over to the children. The *ESS* program was firmly in the hands of the learner rather than the teacher.

The curriculum projects of the 1960s and 1970s sought to reform science education by making science learning more hands on and more attuned to the true nature of science. They did not, however, have the final word in reforming science education.

Influences on Science Education Reform in the 1980s

During the 1980s several factors influenced science education. Concerns about declining test scores led to the back-to-the-basics movement. Environmentalists, creationists, animal rights activists, parents concerned about the influence of drugs and alcohol on children, advocates and nonadvocates of sex education, along with many others, all attempted to influence the elementary school curriculum and the science curriculum specifically. Advocates of organizing science curricula around technology and society developed the science-technology-society movement. And the American Association for the Advancement of Science took a close look at science education and reemphasized the need for a scientifically literate society.

Back to the Basics.   In education, the period of the 1980s was most strongly characterized by the back-to-the-basics movement that emphasized reading, language, and mathematics to the detriment of other subject matter areas. In most situations, science and social studies were not seen as basics in elementary education. As a consequence, most of the science teaching done during this period was from a reading perspective. Indeed, 90 percent of science teachers reported teaching from a textbook 90 percent of the time. Even though discovery-oriented teaching strategies were advocated, the typical science class was a reading-discussion class (Weiss, Nelson, Boyd, and Hudson, 1989).

Special Interest Groups.   **Special interest groups** are groups that attempt to influence those making decisions. Although the back-to-the-basics movement may be viewed as a special interest group, other groups with narrower interests also attempted to influence the science curriculum of the 1980s. Creation science originally sought to include a biblically based account of the origins of Earth and the universe in the science curriculum as an alternative model to that of evolutionary theory. In addition to the proponents of creationism, environmental groups along with animal activist groups also challenged curriculum developers to add information to the curriculum or to change methods of study, particularly the use of dissection in biology classes and the use of animals in research projects. Additional challenges to the curriculum came from groups advocating various curricula for teaching information on drugs, alcohol, or sex education. In some school systems, controversial topics were simply removed from the curriculum to avoid controversy; in others, topics or viewpoints were added to the curriculum to placate vocal groups. Often the science curriculum grew by accretion without consideration of how best to integrate information into the total program.

One viewpoint on science education during the decade of the 1980s, the science-technology-society movement, did attempt to integrate topics and concepts into a coherent program. This movement strengthened in the 1980s and moved into the 1990s with a strong influence on the curriculum.

Science-Technology-Society.   The science-technology-society (STS) movement was strong in the 1980s and has continued in the 1990s. In 1985 the National

Science Teachers Association (NSTA) published its yearbook *Science-Technology-Society*. According to McInerney (1985), it was necessary "that citizens be educated to deal with the issues at the junction of science and society" (p. 23). How to accomplish this educational focus provided direction for the yearbook and the STS movement. From the STS viewpoint, traditional approaches to science education were not enough because traditional science education emphasized facts and definitions. The STS approach had a different orientation:

> The science education required to prepare citizens for effective citizenship must be more socially oriented. It must eschew contextless content in favor of instruction that addresses not only the nature, capabilities, and limitations of science but also the ways, both obvious and subtle, that science and values are related, especially policy decisions that affect individuals and society at large. (McInerney, 1985, p. 23)

The STS movement did not propose a new science curriculum, but rather a new way of organizing the science curriculum:

> There are no concepts and/or processes unique to STS; instead STS provides a setting and a reason for considering basic science and technology concepts and processes. STS means determining and experiencing ways that these basic ideas and skills can be observed in society. STS means focusing on real-world problems which have science and technology components from the students' perspectives, instead of starting with concepts and processes. This allows students to extend beyond the classroom to their local communities. These activities should be appropriate for the age of the students and be learner-centered. STS should help lay the basis for empowering students so that as future citizens they realize they have the power to make changes and the responsibility to do so (NSTA, 1992–1993, p. 168).

Content remained important. Process skills remained important. Attitudes and values gained in prominence as science was shown as a human activity, useful to society, and often derived from societal needs. In essence, the STS movement leaned toward teaching science as personally and socially relevant in the lives of the students rather than as something found only in the pages of a textbook (Pederson, 1993; Yager, 1993).

Reforming the Science Curriculum (Again): The 1990s

The decade of the 1990s, like the decades of the 1960s and 1970s, has focused once again on reforming science education in the United States. Evidence from international comparisons, as well as from the National Assessment of Education Progress conducted solely in the United States, shows that our children are not receiving an adequate science education. The major impetus to the reform of science education came at the conclusion of the decade of the 1980s and has provided the force behind the reform movement.

Science for All Americans

In 1989 the American Association for the Advancement of Science published *Science for All Americans: A Project 2061 Report on Literacy Goals in Science, Mathematics, and Technology.* This document, according to its authors, "is about scientific literacy. It consists of a set of recommendations by the National Council on Science and Technology Education—a distinguished group of scientists and educators appointed by the American Association for the Advancement of Science—on what understandings and habits of mind are essential for all citizens in a scientifically literate society" (p. 3). Scientifically literate individuals were defined by *Science for All Americans* as those "who are aware that science, mathematics, and technology are interdependent human enterprises with strengths and limitations; understands key concepts and principles of science; is familiar with the natural world and recognizes both its diversity and unity; and uses scientific knowledge and scientific ways of thinking for individual and social purposes" (AAAS, 1989, p. 4).

As a part of *Science for All Americans,* AAAS described the current state of science in education in the United States and in so doing provided a foundation for the call to reform. Among their findings were two of particular importance to elementary and middle school teachers.

> The present science textbooks and methods of instruction, far from helping, often actually impede progress toward scientific literacy. They emphasize the learning of answers more than the exploration of questions, memory at the expense of critical thought, bits and pieces of information instead of understanding in context, recitation over argument, reading in lieu of doing. They fail to encourage students to work together, to share ideas and information freely with each other, or to use modern instruments to extend their intellectual capabilities. (AAAS, 1989, p. 14)

This particular statement is cautioning us, as teachers, against overreliance on science textbooks for teaching at the elementary and middle school levels. Good science teachers go beyond the strategies and methods described in the textbook. Good teachers help their students question, investigate, discover, share, and comprehend information in context. A second important point for teachers to remember is this:

> The present curricula in science and mathematics are overstuffed and undernourished. Over the decades, they have grown with little restraint, thereby overwhelming teachers and students and making it difficult for them to keep track of what science, mathematics, and technology is truly essential. Some topics are taught over and over again in needless detail; some that are of equal or greater importance to scientific literacy—often

from the physical and social sciences and from technology—are absent from the curriculum or are reserved for only a few students. (AAAS, 1989, p. 14)

Science teachers who simply cover the science book from the first page to the last page are not doing their students a favor. Science books contain far too much information for students to learn and in far too little depth for true understanding to develop on the part of students. Good science teachers select from those overstuffed textbooks those topics that are developmentally appropriate to their students, important to the development of scientific literacy, and develop the student's background in a continuous manner rather than continually and unnecessarily repeating topics. In addition, good science teachers show the connections between and among science content as well as between science and mathematics. And, finally, good science teachers present a balanced science program in which content, processes, attitudes, and values all receive appropriate attention.

In addition, *Science for All Americans* (AAAS, 1989) identified six **themes** that appear over and over again throughout science, mathematics, and technology and transcend the boundaries of the individual scientific disciplines. These themes are systems, models, constancy, patterns of change, evolution, and scale.

Systems.   **Systems** are collections of things that have some influence on one another and appear to make up a unified whole. The things can be almost anything, including objects, organisms, machines, processes, ideas, numbers, or organizations. Think about a bicycle. In telling someone about the system that makes up a bicycle, I have to include the frame, handlebars, chain, pedals, and wheels. Less than this and my bicycle will not work. More than this and I may have unnecessary parts. But within the bicycle as a system I also have a subsystem: The pedals, chain, and wheels make up the subsystem. So if I want to describe a system, I have to include enough parts that the relationship of those parts to one another is clear. I also have to realize that there may be subsystems in the total system and one system may be so closely related to another that there is no way to draw a boundary between them. Put the bicycle on a street and a rider on the bicycle, and I have interrelated systems.

Models.   A **model** of something is a simplified imitation that we hope can help us understand the real object or phenomenon better. A model may be an object, a drawing, an equation, a computer program, or just a mental image. The value of a model lies in helping us understand how something works. **Physical models** are things like model engines, model skeletons, model solar systems, or model airplanes. The advantage of a physical model is that it is smaller than the real thing and so may allow for controlled experiments. Working with a full-sized airplane would be impossible for children. Putting a model airplane in a wind tunnel is possible. **Conceptual Models** are analogies or metaphors based on some attribute or similarity to the real thing. Visualizing the human brain as a computer or evolution as a tree can help develop understanding. But using models can cause some problems. Very simple models may not give an accurate picture, and complex models may not be practical to use. In addition, the conceptual model may actually affect how we look at something. A model of evolution as a tree with every branch moving upward gives a different impression than a model of evolution as a bush radiating outward and producing diversity in all directions. **Mathematical modeling** attempts to find a mathematical relationship that allows behavioral prediction without a physical model. Mathematical modeling allows us to send satellites to orbit the moons of Jupiter without recourse to physical models of rockets, planets, moons, or satellites.

Constancy. **Constancy** looks at the ways in which systems do not change. Most physical systems will eventually reach a point where they no longer change. When we start a terrarium, it usually is too wet or too dry. The plants get too big or stay so small they are uninteresting. But eventually, the terrarium reaches a point where it has exactly the right moisture, the plants grow perfectly, and we can let it be. At this point the terrarium, a system, is balanced; it will not change a great deal. This balance is termed **equilibrium** and may mean one of two things. First, it may mean all changes have stopped. Second, it may mean a change in one place is balanced by a change in another. Basically, the terrarium has reached constancy.

Patterns of Change. When we talk about **patterns of change** we are talking about three things: predicting what will happen, analyzing what is going on, and controlling change in the system. Changes can be described as **trends,** moving in one direction and easily described; **cycles,** which are a sequence of changes that happen over and over again; or **chaos,** which is the random component of any change.

Evolution. The general idea of **evolution** is that the present arises from the materials and forms of the past, more or less gradually, and in explicable ways. In evolution, what can happen is limited by what has happened. In evolution, changes may be slow or may have rapid intermediate stages but whether slow or rapid, evolution does not occur in isolation (Ridley, 1996). Instead, while one part of a system is evolving so are other parts of the system around it. For example, the very early Earth had an atmosphere very different from that of today. It was lacking in oxygen. As photosynthesizing organisms evolved, oxygen was added to the atmosphere. And as oxygen in the atmosphere developed, animals were able to move from the oceans to land (MacDougal, 1996). Each part of the system was important to the other parts, and as each part of the system evolved, other parts evolved as well.

Scale. **Scale** refers to size and particularly to the magnitude of size. Scale models and scales in general are useful in helping us understand such things as size, duration, and speed. Scale models in particular are needed because distances within the universe are so vast, time scales dealing with the history of Earth are so long, and sizes within the atom are so small. Scale also can help us understand how greatly a change in one part of a system affects other parts of a system. A small change in one place can result in an enormous change elsewhere. Those changes can often be described mathematically in order to help us understand changes in systems.

The themes common to science, mathematics, and technology can provide a means for organizing the content of the curriculum that is independent of the content area disciplines. For example, the theme of changes can be investigated by looking at how environmental changes cause changes in plants and animals, at how the forces of erosion and deposition change Earth, at how using simple and compound machines changes the work done by human beings, or at how exercise and diet affect animals in general. Rather than study particular branches of science, the students are engaged in looking at changes in a variety of contexts.

Benchmarks for Science Literacy

Science for All Americans provided the foundation for the development of science curricula in the 1990s. The second step in this development came in 1993 with the publication of *Benchmarks for Science Literacy,* a companion volume to *Science for All Americans. Benchmarks* (AAAS, 1993) is a plan to be used by educators in designing a curriculum appropriate to their particular situations. It is not a prescription for science education or for a science curriculum. Instead, *Benchmarks* is a reference work that describes the levels of understanding all students should reach on the way to becoming scientifically literate. *Benchmarks* does not show all of the science, mathematics, and technology goals that should be in the science curriculum. Because students have interests in various areas, school systems have differing goals, and individual schools have students with specific needs, *Benchmarks,* by not showing all of the goals, gives great leeway for the development of curricula.

Within *Benchmarks* are 12 areas in which suggestions, termed benchmarks, are made as to the outcomes that can be attained in science, mathematics, and technology by children in grades kindergarten through 12. The twelve areas are as follows:

1. The nature of science: dealing with the scientific worldview, scientific inquiry, and the scientific enterprise.
2. The nature of mathematics: dealing with patterns and relationships; mathematics, science, and technology; and mathematical inquiry.
3. The nature of technology: dealing with technology and science; design and systems; and issues in technology.
4. The physical setting: dealing with the universe, Earth, processes that shape Earth, the structure of matter, energy transformations, motion, and forces of nature.
5. The living environment: dealing with the diversity of life, heredity, cells, interdependence of life, flow of matter and energy, and evolution of life.
6. The human organism: dealing with human identity, human development, basic function, learning, physical health, and mental health.
7. Human society: dealing with cultural effects on behavior, group behavior, social change, social trade-offs, political and economic systems, social conflict, and global interdependence.

8. The designed world: dealing with agriculture, materials and manufacturing, energy sources and use, communication, information processing, and health technology.

9. The mathematical world: dealing with numbers, symbolic relationships, shapes, uncertainty, and reasoning.

10. Historical perspectives: dealing with displacing Earth from the center of the universe, uniting the heavens and Earth, relating matter and energy and time and space; extending time, moving continents, understanding fires, splitting the atom, explaining the diversity of life, discovering germs, and harnessing power.

11. Common themes: dealing with systems, models, constancy and change, and scale.

12. Habits of mind: dealing with values and attitudes, computation and estimation, manipulation and observation, communication skills, and critical-response skills.

In order to assist schools in developing good science programs, *Benchmarks* shows checkpoints, called benchmarks, for students at four points in their education: kindergarten through grade 2, grades 3 through 5, grades 6 through 8, and grades 9 through 12. The benchmarks indicate what students on the road to scientific literacy should know by the conclusion of each of the named levels of education. For example, in dealing with Earth, the following benchmarks are listed:

Grades Kindergarten through 2: by the end of second grade, students should know:

1. Some events in nature have a repeating pattern, some vary from day to day, but things such as temperature and rain (or snow) tend to be high, low, or medium in the same months every year.

2. Water can be a liquid or a solid and can go back and forth from one form to the other. If water is turned into ice and then the ice is allowed to melt, the amount of water is the same as it was before freezing.

3. Water left in an open container disappears, but the water in a closed container does not disappear. (p. 67)

Grade 3 through 5: by the end of fifth grade, students should know:

1. Things on or near Earth are pulled toward it by Earth's gravity.

2. Like all planets and stars, Earth is approximately spherical in shape. The rotation of Earth on its axis every 24 hours produces the night-and-day cycle. To people on Earth, this turning of the planet makes it seem as though the Sun, Moon, and stars are orbiting Earth once a day.

3. When liquid water disappears, it turns into a gas (vapor) in the air and can reappear as a liquid when cooled, or as a solid if cooled below the freezing point of water. Clouds and fog are made of tiny droplets of water.

4. Air is a substance that surrounds us, takes up space, and whose movement we feel as wind. (p. 68)

Grades 6 through 8: by the end of eighth grade, students should know:

1. We live on a relatively small planet, the third from the Sun in the only system of planets definitely known to exist (although other, similar systems may be discovered in the universe).

2. Earth is mostly rock. Three-fourths of its surface is covered by a relatively thin layer of water (some of it frozen), and the entire planet is surrounded by a relatively thin blanket of air. It is the only body in the solar system that appears able to support life. The other planets have compositions and conditions very different from Earth's.

3. Everything on or anywhere near Earth is pulled toward Earth's center by gravitational force.

4. Because Earth turns daily on an axis that is tilted relative to the plane of Earth's yearly orbit around the Sun, sunlight falls more intensely on different parts of Earth during the year. The difference in hearing of the Earth's surface produce seasons and weather patterns.

5. The Moon's orbit around Earth once in about 28 days changes what part of the Moon is lighted by the Sun and how much of that part can be seen from Earth—phases of the Moon.

6. Climates have sometimes changed abruptly in the past as a result of changes in Earth's crust, such as volcanic eruptions or impacts of huge rocks from space. Even relatively small changes in atmospheric or ocean content can have widespread effects on climate if the change lasts long enough.

7. Cycling of water in and out of the atmosphere plays an important role in determining climatic patterns. Water evaporates from the surface of Earth, rises and cools, condenses into rain or snow, and falls again to the surface. The water falling on land collects in rivers and lakes, soil, and porous layers of rock, and much of it flows back into the ocean.

8. Fresh water, limited in supply, is essential for life and also for most industrial processes. Rivers, lakes, and groundwater can be depleted or polluted, becoming unavailable or unsuitable for life.

9. Heat energy carried by ocean currents has a strong influence on climate around the world.

10. Some minerals are very rare and some exist in great quantities, but—for practical purposes—the ability to recover them is just as important as their abundance. As mineral are depleted, obtaining them becomes more difficult.

Recycling and the development of substitutes can reduce the rate of depletion but may also be costly.

11. The benefits of the Earth's resources—such as fresh water, air, soil, and trees—can be reduced by using them wastefully or by deliberately or inadvertently destroying them. The atmosphere and the oceans have a limited capacity to absorb wastes and recycle materials naturally. Cleaning up polluted air, water, or soil or restoring depleted soil, forests, or fishing grounds can be very difficult or costly. (pp. 68–69)

As you can see from this example, the benchmarks take children from simple concepts that can be directly investigated in a hands-on manner using simple materials to complex concepts that involve the student not only in more extensive investigations but also in concepts which are more abstract and more directly related to the community and the world the student inhabits.

Consult Benchmarks for Science Literacy for the full listing of benchmarks at each grade level and for each of the areas.

National Science Education Standards

In 1996 the National Research Council published the *National Science Education Standards,* which are based on the premise that all students deserve the opportunity to become scientifically literate. The *Standards* "look toward a future in which all Americans, familiar with basic scientific ideas and processes, can have fuller and more productive lives. This is a vision of great hope and optimism for America, one that can act as a powerful unifying force in our society" (p. ix).

Within the *Standards* are standards for science teaching, professional development, assessment, science content, science education programs, and science education systems so that all areas of the science teaching-learning process are considered. As with *Science for All Americans,* and *Benchmarks for Science Literacy,* the *Standards* are directed toward the development of **scientific literacy.**

Scientific literacy, according to the *Standards,* is "the knowledge and understanding of scientific concepts and processes required for personal decision making, participation in civic and cultural affairs, and economic productivity" (p. 22). It includes such abilities as being able to ask and find answers to questions stemming from curiosity about the world. It includes such processes as being able to describe, explain, and predict natural phenomena. And it includes such goals of scientific literacy as being able to read and comprehend articles about science in the popular press as well as being able to identify scientific issues underlying national and local decisions so as to be able to express informed opinions. Scientific literacy also means being able to evaluate the quality of scientific information on the basis of its sources and on the basis of the methods used to generate that information.

The content of the *Standards* is founded on certain principles that then affect the selection of teaching strategies and content information as well as program development. As its first principle, the *Standards* state that science is for all students. All students from all backgrounds should be included in challenging science learning opportunities with specified levels of understanding and abilities that every student should develop. Excellence in science education means all students can achieve understanding of science if given the opportunity.

Second, the *Standards* consider learning science as an active process including both physical and mental activity in a cooperative setting. It is not enough to simply do an activity or experiment in the science classroom. Students also need to engage in thinking, reasoning, and problem solving so they can understand what they have done.

The third of the principles is that school science should reflect the intellectual and cultural traditions which characterize the practice of contemporary science. Students should not only learn the content of science, but they should also learn the methods of scientific inquiry, means for formulating problems and questions, and ways of proposing explanations. Students should understand the nature of science as well as the facts of science, the rules of science as well as the principles of science, the role of science in the world as well as the theories of science.

Using these basic principles as the starting point, the *Standards* then consider the goals for science education. According to the *Standards,* the goals for school science are fourfold. First, school science should result in students who are able to understand the world around them, who can appreciate the richness of that world, and who gain a sense of excitement in knowing about that world. Second, school science should develop in students the ability to use scientific processes and scientific principles not only in investigating and explaining within the science classroom but also in making personal decisions. Third, science in schools should develop individuals who are able to engage in debate and discussion of scientific and technological concerns within their communities and lives. And, finally, school science should produce individuals who are able to pursue careers in which science and scientific reasoning may lead them to increased economic productivity.

If you are beginning to think you have heard all of this before, you have. All of the reform documents, all of the ideas of the nature of science are saying the same thing: Children should experience science as a human enterprise, occurring within the context of society, and including content, process, attitudes, and values. What has not been previously considered, however, is how you as the science teacher fit into the picture.

In terms of the teacher's role, the *Standards* recognize that teachers are central to education. If those teachers are going to do the best for their children, then they need to put more emphasis on (1) understanding and responding to individual students' interests, strengths, experiences, and needs rather than treating all students alike and responding to the group as a single unit; (2) selecting and adapting curricula to meet the needs of particular student populations rather than rigidly following a curriculum; (3) focusing on student understanding and use of scientific knowledge, ideas, and inquiry rather than on the simple acquisition of information; (4) guiding students in active and extended scientific inquiry rather than relying on lecture, text, and demonstration; (5) providing opportunities for scientific discussion and debate among students rather than asking for recitation of acquired knowledge; (6) continuously assessing student understanding rather than testing for factual information at the end of a chapter; (7) sharing responsibility for learning with students rather than maintaining authority and responsibility; (8) supporting a classroom community with cooperation, shared responsibility, and respect rather than supporting competition; and (9) working with teachers to enhance the science program rather than working alone.

As you can be see by this listing, the *Standards* see the teacher not as someone reacting to a curriculum but as someone reacting to the needs of students within the curriculum. The teacher is a co-learner, modeling the kinds of behaviors students should show, assisting students in developing scientific knowledge, and helping students develop scientific inquiry skills.

Appendix A contains a complete listing of the Teaching Standards from *The National Science Education Standards*. Appendix B shows the content strands, and Appendix C contains the Content Standards for grades kindergarten through 8.

Activity 1.3 is designed to have you consider science textbooks in light of the information considered in the preceding sections.

Science Curriculum Activity

Activity 1.3

Purpose   To investigate the inclusion of the latest thought on science curriculum in science textbooks for the elementary school or middle school level.

Procedure
1. Locate three science textbook series for elementary or middle school grades. You will need the teacher's edition including the materials found in the preface of the teacher's edition that describe the series in general.
2. Using the information found in the teacher's edition and the information presented here on the *National Standards, Benchmarks,* and the nature of science, critique the inclusion of the latest suggestions for science education reform as found in the series materials.
3. If the textbooks series indicates in its materials that it adheres to the suggestions of the *Standards, Benchmarks,* or the nature of science, select one chapter from each textbook. Critique the textbook chapter on how well the content of the teaching suggestions and the chapter adhere to these standards.
4. How well do the textbooks you have reviewed incorporate the information from the *National Standards* and *Benchmarks* into their programs? What could you, as a teacher, do to more fully incorporate these documents into the program?

A Total Curriculum in Elementary School Science

Taking into consideration all that has been said here, what should an elementary school science program be like? First, it should be a place of active involvement where children are designing and implementing investigations, discussing and debating results, learning and understanding as a result of their own efforts. Children should be immersed in their learning rather than being subjected to learning imparted from the teacher, textbook, or program.

Second, the science program at the elementary school should be understuffed and overnourished. Each grade level should see a few, carefully selected areas of study rather than a broad spectrum of topics that attempts to consider every possible area of study at varying levels of difficulty. The themes of science as outlined in *Science for All Americans* should provide a foundation for selecting the topics and organizing the curriculum. In this way elementary school science can come to demonstrate the interrelationships among and between the various domains of scientific knowledge. Rather than study plants or animals or magnets or rocks and minerals, learning would come to be organized around the grand themes that pervade science, mathematics, and technology.

Third, children should have time to carry out extensive investigations, to pursue questions of interest to them, to develop concepts rather than vocabulary, to understand rather than to memorize. Exposure to topics in hopes that they will be familiar later in education should give way to study of topics so that children develop understanding at that time and in that place.

Fourth, the elementary school science program should place science learning into contexts that are real to the children and authentic to the subject matter under consideration. The location of the school, the backgrounds of the children, the situation of the community in which the children are growing and learning should be a part of the selection of science content and teaching strategies. The role of technology in science and of science in technology should form a foundation for authentic science education programs.

Fifth, science at the elementary school level should be taught by teachers who are themselves inquirers into science, who are able to model the kinds of processes, attitudes, and values they want their students to exhibit. Teachers should no longer view themselves as authorities to be attended to but rather as models to be emulated. And, finally, the science education program of the elementary school should develop scientifically literate individuals able to apply the content, methods, and thought processes of science to the solution of personal, societal, and global problems.

Summary

Science is often thought of as science content: the stuff found in science books. Science, however, has far more to it than simple content. Science consists of content, process, attitudes, and values. The scientific values are the basis for the enterprise called science and include longing to know and understand, respect for logic, and consideration of premises and consequences. From the scientific values come the scientific attitudes including curiosity, objectivity, and skepticism. When longing to know and understand and curiosity come into play, then the scientist plans investigations. Those investigations require the collection of information, and it is through process skills such as observation, inference, prediction, and conclusion that the information is gained. The total science curriculum should include all four of these areas.

The science curriculum is under constant change and reform. Beginning in the 1960s and continuing to today, many attempts at reform have occurred. During the 1960s the thrust of reform in science education was toward developing curriculum projects such as *SAPA, SCIS*, and *ESS*. More recent reform movements have not focused on the development of programs for use in schools, but rather on guidelines for the development of curricula within school systems and districts. The emphasis is on local rather than national construction of science programs to enable reform in education. Currently the most influential documents in this reform movement are *Project 2061: Science for All Americans, The National Science Standards*, and *Benchmarks for Science Literacy*.

Chapter Vocabulary

The number following each term refers to the page on which the term is first introduced.

Applied science, 4
Biological science, 10
Chaos, 22
Conceptual models, 21
Consideration of consequences, 6
Consideration of premises, 6
Constancy, 22
Cycles, 22
Data, 4
Deductive reasoning, 6
Demand for verification, 5
Discovery, 17
Earth-space sciences, 10
Elementary Science Study (ESS), 15
Equilibrium, 22
Evolution, 22
Exploration, 16
Inductive reasoning, 6
Invention, 16
Learning cycle, 16
Longing to know and
    understand, 3
Mathematical modeling, 22

Mathematics, 10
Modeling, 12
Model, 21
Patterns of change, 22
Physical models, 21
Physical sciences, 10
Process, 8
Pure science, 4
Questioning all things, 4
Replicated, 5
Respect for logic, 5
Scale, 22
Science, 2
*Science—A Process Approach
    (SAPA)*, 15
*Science Curriculum Improvement
    Study (SCIS)*, 15
Scientific attitudes, 7
Scientific content, 9
Scientific literacy, 26
Scientific processes, 8
Scientific values, 3
Scientists, 2

Applying the CONCEPTS

1. As a teacher, you have developed a science program including content, process, and attitude. During a parent conference, one child's parents want to know why you are having your students spend so much time "playing" with levers, batteries, seeds, and rocks instead of teaching them the facts. How would you respond to these parents?

2. Select one of the themes from *Science for All Americans*. Show how you could incorporate content from biological science, physical science, earth-space science, and mathematics to help children develop the concepts shown in the selected theme.

3. As a teacher you are given your state's course of study for science, you school system's curriculum guide, and the textbook for your grade level. As you read through each document, you discover your text does not reflect your local curriculum guide or the state course of study. What would you, as a teacher, do in this situation? How would you defend your decision to your school principal?

4. How is the view of science presented here similar to or different from your own view of science? What do you think caused the differences between your view and that presented here?

5. Calls for reform in science education have been occurring for more than thirty years, but American students still score very low on tests of scientific knowledge. What could be some of the reasons science education reforms have not been successful? What could classroom teachers do to help the current calls for reform succeed?

References

American Association for the Advancement of Science. 1975. *Science—A process approach.* Lexington, Mass.: Ginn.

American Association for the Advancement of Science. 1989. *Science for all Americans: A project 2061 report on literacy goals in science, mathematics, and technology.* Washington, D.C.: Author.

American Association for the Advancement of Science. 1993. *Benchmarks for science literacy.* New York: Oxford University Press.

Bybee, R. W. 1986. *Science Technology Society. 1985 Yearbook of the National Science Teachers Association.* Washington, D.C.: National Science Teachers Association.

Comstock, A. B. 1911. *Handbook of nature study.* Ithaca, N. Y.: Comstock.

Craig, G. S. 1927. *Certain techniques used in developing a course of study in science for the Horace Mann elementary school.* New York: Bureau of Publication, Teachers College, Columbia University, Contributions to Education, No. 276.

Elementary Science Study. 1978. *Elementary science study materials.* New York: McGraw-Hill.

Kitcher, P. 1982. *Abusing science: The case against creationism.* Cambridge, Mass.: MIT Press.

Kuhn, T. S. 1970. *The structure of scientific revolutions.* Chicago: University of Chicago Press.

MacDougal, J. D. 1996. *A short history of the planet earth.* New York: Wiley.

McInerney, J. D. 1986. Scientific progress and public policy: Challenge to traditional values. In R. W. Bybee (Ed.). *Science Technology Society. 1985* Yearbook of the National Science Teachers Association. *Washington, D.C.: National Science Teachers Association.*

National Research Council. 1996. *National science education standards.* Washington, D.C.: National Academy Press.

National Science Teachers Association. 1964. *Theory into action in science curriculum development.* Washington, D.C.: Author.

National Science Teachers Association. 1992–1993. *Science/Technology/Society: A new effort for providing appropriate science to all.* In *National science teachers association handbook (1992–1993)* (pp. 168–169). Washington, D.C.: Author.

National Science Teachers Association Curriculum Committee. 1964. *Theory into action in science curriculum development.* Washington, D.C.: NSTA.

Palady, L. G. 1978. *SCIS II sampler guide.* Boston: American Science and Engineering.

Pederson, J. E. 1993. *STS issues: A perspective.* In R. E. Yager (Ed.) *National Science Teachers Association (1939): The science, technology movement.* Washington, D.C.: NSTA.

Ridley, M. 1996. *Evolution* (2nd ed.). Cambridge, Mass.: Blackwell Science.

Rogers, R. E., and A. M. Voelker. 1970. Programs for improving elementary science instruction in the elementary school; elementary science study. *Science and Children* 8, 1.

Romney, E. A. 1971. *A working guide to the elementary science study.* Newton, Mass.: Educational Development Center.

Science—A Process Approach. 1979. *Curriculum materials.* Lexington, Mass.: Ginn.

Science Curriculum Improvement Study. 1970. *SCIS sampler guide.* Chicago: Rand-McNally.

Science Curriculum Improvement Study. 1980. *Curriculum materials—SCIIS.* Chicago: Rand-McNally.

Weiss, I. R., B. H. Nelson, S. E. Boyd, and S. B. Hudson. 1989. *Science and mathematics education briefing book.* Chapel Hill, N. C.: Horizon Research.

Yager, R. E. (Ed.). 1993. *What research says to the science teacher: The science teacher: The science, technology, society movement* (Vol. 7). Washington, D.C.: NSTA.

CHAPTER TWO

PSYCHOLOGY AND SCIENCE TEACHING

Chapter Objectives

Upon completion of this chapter you should be able to:

1 describe the developmental characteristics of children from the sensori-motor through the formal operational stages of development.

2 discuss the work of Jean Piaget as it applies to teaching and learning science.

3 discuss the work of Lev Vygotsky as it applies to teaching and learning science.

4 describe the seven intelligences as described in the work of Howard Gardner.

5 discuss the work of Howard Gardner as it applies to teaching and learning science.

6 discuss criteria for the selection of appropriate science activities for children at various developmental levels.

7 apply the characteristics of appropriate science activities to the activities found in texts and programs for science teaching.

Introduction

In a third grade classroom, Ms. Kent begins her science lesson with these words: "Take out your science books and open them to page 125. Today we are going to learn about photosynthesis." After waiting a moment for the children to comply, she asks, "What do you think photosynthesis is?" On the first page of the section is a large picture of a flowering plant. One of the children answers that photosynthesis has something to do with plants. With that as the basis, the children begin to read the textbook. Periodically Ms. Kent stops the reading and asks a question:

What gas do plants need for photosynthesis?
What gas do plants give back?
What kind of change is taking place when carbon dioxide and water combine?
Do plants need to have water for photosynthesis?
What are plants making when they photosynthesize?
Is photosynthesis important?

Twenty minutes into the half hour science lesson, Ms. Kent tells the children to answer the questions on page 130. A half hour later, the children hand in their papers and put away their science books. Most of the children have the correct answers to the questions and so Ms. Kent is certain they understood the lesson. However, on Friday, when the unit test is given, not one of the answers to questions about photosynthesis is correct. Ms. Kent assumes the children did not study for the test and goes on to the next chapter in the textbook.

According to the *Science and Mathematics Education Briefing Book* (1989) and *Science for All Americans* (1989) as well as the *Handbook of Research on Science Teaching and Learning* (Gabel, 1994), this type of lesson is found in most science classrooms in the United States. Ninety percent of teachers use the science textbook 90 percent of the time. The vast majority of teachers use reading, lecturing, and questioning to teach. Questions ask children to recall specific facts found in the textbook and rarely ask students to use higher order thinking skills.

If reading, lecturing, and questioning are the most common ways of teaching science, then surely these are also the most appropriate ways to teach science to children. Unfortunately, if we look at the characteristics of children from preschool through middle school, we find these are not really the most appropriate techniques. In this chapter we look at why reading, lecturing, and questioning are not the most appropriate ways of teaching children science. In order to do this we will review the work of Jean Piaget, Lev Vygotsky, and Howard Gardner.

Developmental Stages: A Brief
Overview of Piagetian Concepts

Children think differently from adults. The younger the child, the more different the thought process. As children mature, their thought processes change, finally showing the same kind of thought processes we show as adults. For children's thought processes to move from those of a preschooler to those of an adult, they need to interact with things in their environment as well as with other people.

Jean Piaget effectively showed that children's thought processes not only change, but that they change in a predictable way. These predictable changes, summarized in the four developmental stages for which Piaget is most widely known, are based on the latter assumption.

The Four Developmental Stages

The four **developmental stages,** probably the best known part of Piaget's work, show how children's thought processes gradually mature from birth through to adulthood. Ages are often used to show when children are in a particular stage, but ages are not always a good way of determining the developmental stage of a child. Many factors can influence when a child reaches a particular developmental stage. Consequently, both traditional chronological ages and cognitive markers are given here in defining the four stages.

These stages follow one after another in this order. But just because a child has left one stage for another does not mean that he or she cannot return to the previous stage. Young children may return to preoperational thought when they encounter new situations. Adults in formal operations often return to concrete operations when they meet new material.

The Sensorimotor Stage

The **sensorimotor stage** is most often defined as beginning at birth and ending at about 18 months of age. It can also be defined as from birth to the beginning of language use in children.

In a child care center, a worker tells a 10-month-old to stop banging the blocks against the floor and is frustrated when the child continues to bang. In a grocery store, a young mother tells her 1-year-old to put down the candy bar and looks surprised when the child doesn't do it. And, in a newspaper comic strip, a baby sits in the sunshine and talks to the sunbeam through words in a balloon above her head. Comic strip infants aside, children who have not yet developed spoken language cannot be expected to respond to spoken language. According to Piaget, very young children do not use words in their thought processes (Piaget, 1974).

Instead of words, sensorimotor children think through their actions. As an example of how sensorimotor children think, consider this 14-month-old playing with blocks:

> Eddy brought one block at a time from his bedroom and placed them on the dining room table. After he had four blocks on the table, he began to pile them one on top of another until he had a tower about seven inches high. Eddy went back to his room for another block, piled it on the tower, then went for one more block. This time the tower was too tall for him to reach the top. He looked at the block in his hand, at the tower, then back at

the block once again. He tried to reach the top once more. Then he jumped up and down a few times as well as he was able. Placing the block on the table, he ran to his bedroom and returned with a pounding bench. He placed it on the floor and climbed onto it. He was then able to reach the top of the tower and add the block.

Instead of using words, Eddy thought through the problem in actions using a physical movement, jumping, as the link between the needed height and the bench that was among his toys.

For the most part, the children you teach will not be sensorimotor. Exceptions may occur in the preschool if you have a hearing or speech impaired child who has yet developed the ability to use language.

The Preoperational Stage

Cognitive Factors.   The **preoperational stage** is generally defined as beginning at approximately 18 months and ending at about 6.5 years of age. This may also be viewed as from the beginning of language use, including manual forms of language among hearing impaired children, to the development of conservation of number. Preschool and kindergarten children, along with some primary grade children, are likely to be preoperational.

Although preoperational children do use words in thinking, their thought processes still differ from those of adults. The main ways in which these thought processes differ are egocentrism, conservation, centering, reversibility, transduction, and concreteness.

Egocentrism.   Preoperational children see the world from their own point of view (**egocentrism**) and find it nearly impossible to take the point of view of another person or to accept a point of view with which they do not agree. An egocentric child may tell you "he did it with me" and be perfectly sure you understand the sentence. From an egocentric child's point of view, you have exactly the same information he or she has and so you should understand. As children interact with others more frequently in social situations, they begin to understand that everyone does not know everything he or she knows (Piaget, 1975a).

Conservation.   **Conservation** is the ability to realize that a change in the appearance of an object does not change the quantity of that object. A child who conserves, for example, will realize that a ball of clay flattened into a pancake still has the same amount of clay or that a large glass of juice poured into three smaller glasses still results in the same amount of juice.

The clay ball and the juice both require conservation of substance. In the preoperational stage children see many quantities as changing if the appearance of the object or the conditions change: number, substance, length, area, weight, time, and volume. Because preoperational children have difficulty seeing quantities as unchanging, they are generally designated as **nonconservers.**

Centering. Preoperational children tend to look at one characteristic of an object at a time. They look at the height of a plant without looking at the thickness of the stem. They look at the color of the leaves without looking at the size of the leaves. This tendency to look at one characteristic at a time is called **centering.** When children center, they are unable to shift their attentions from one characteristic to another while still remembering the first characteristic.

Reversibility. **Reversibility** means being able to trace your thought processes backward to the starting point. We can see that water freezes when it is put into the freezer. We can then go backward and infer that ice taken out of a freezer will melt. This ability to reverse thought processes is not available to preoperational children. They need to be able to see the warm water put into the freezer and see the ice come out of the freezer. They need to see the ice in the warm room turn back to water.

Transductive Reasoning. Adults tend to reason from particular facts to general conclusions. Preoperational children, in contrast, reason from specific to specific. Given a list like chicken, bread, brussels sprouts, mashed potatoes, and apple pie, adults will say they are all foods. Given the same list, a preoperational child using transductive reasoning may say, "You can eat chicken, you can eat bread, you can eat mashed potatoes, you can eat apple pie, I don't eat brussels sprouts." **Transductive reasoning** means children find the use of the concept of "all" difficult.

Concreteness. Preoperational children learn best when they can get their hands on the real thing(**concreteness**). They learn what a hole is by digging holes. They learn what a dog is by seeing many real dogs. They learn what seashells are by handling seashells. As they interact with these objects and with other persons, they construct their concepts of holes, shells, and dogs. When we talk about concrete objects and concrete experiences in science classrooms, we are talking about providing these real experiences.

These characteristics give us some idea of how children think. What they do not do is give us an indication of how they relate to one another, a facet as important as their thought processes in letting us know the kinds of science experiences appropriate at the preschool and kindergarten levels.

Social Factors. Preschool and kindergarten age children are preoperational in their thought processes. Their classrooms should be exciting, dynamic places where young children interact with a wide variety of materials, with each other, and with adults. Three-, 4-, and 5-year-olds do not generally categorize information into subject matter areas. Instead they move rapidly from one activity to another, utilizing skills gained in one area to work in a second. In the preschool and kindergarten, science may emerge as children fashion clay animals, listen at story time, or socialize in the playground sandbox.

Language Use. Children of 3 and 4 years of age talk to one another. Listening in on their conversations, however, reveals that their conversations are more likely to be collective monologues than they are to be real conversations. In a **collective monologue,** two or more children seem to be talking to one another but the successive sentences may not actually relate to one another. Collective monologue can make it very difficult to have a group discussion following a science activity. The teacher's questions and the student responses may bear little resemblance to one another. One teacher in a preschool classroom asked about zebras. One of the children responded to the question by talking about bumblebees and a second by describing his new striped shirt. Five-year-olds, however, are better able to use language to communicate their thoughts to one another. Collective monologues are unusual among 5-year-old children. Instead they will talk about an activity. And, frequently, they enjoy working together to plan and carry out activities (Geneschi, 1987).

Questions. Three-, 4-, and 5-year-old children often ask questions. Most of their questions begin with the word *why*. Both parents and teachers spend a great deal of time trying to answer those why questions, often without success. With children of 3 or 4, verbal explanations are generally not understood. Five-year-old children do understand simple explanations. But there are other problems with questions from children. First, the why questions children ask may not be interpreted correctly by adults. When we ask a question beginning with why, we are usually asking for a cause. When preoperational children as a question beginning with why, they are often asking for the purpose for something (Piaget, 1972). An appropriate answer to the question "Why is the sky blue?" may be "because it looks pretty when it's blue." The second problem is that young children have little understanding of cause and effect. Consequently, the explanations their parents and teachers give them about the cause of something may involve cause-and effect-ideas too complex for them to understand.

Working Together. When it comes to working with one another, there are differences among 3-, 4-, and 5-year-old children. Three-year-old children like to play or work near other children, but generally are working with individual activities and their own sets of materials. This is known as **parallel play.** Four-year-old children are beginning to cooperate with one another and to play or work together, but engage in parallel play as well. Realize that children of 3 and 4 frequently decide to end an activity before the point adults see as closure. Young children do not feel the same need to reach a specific end point and so quit when they are satisfied with the effort. In contrast, 5-year-old children enjoy playing and working together. They often cooperate in planning and carrying out an activity, such as building a block house. In fact, 5-year-old children often choose to work in small groups rather than alone. In terms of a science activity, 3- and 4-year-olds at a water table will prefer to work alone trying to see if the object floats or not while 5s will be more likely to want to work with a partner or partners in trying the objects (Goffin and Tull, 1988).

Coordination. Children of 3 and 4 are better able to use large muscles than small muscles. Large muscle activities include running, jumping, hopping, throwing, catching, and skipping. Small muscle skills include using scissors or drawing letters with a pencil or marker. Even when small muscle use may be appropriate, young children tend to use large muscles. Children paint with the whole arm in motion rather than with the fingers and brush in motion.

Among 5-year-olds, both small and large muscle coordination are improving. By 5, children can be expected to walk a balance beam, fold paper on a corner-to-corner diagonal, copy a square, triangle, or design, and draw recognizable letters or numbers. Thus, science activities for young children should allow for large muscle use rather than expecting children to work with small items requiring use of small muscle skills.

Independence. Three and 4-year-old children tend to do best in an atmosphere that provides security, guidance, clear routines, and the opportunity to make decisions in a limited framework. Five-year-olds enjoy more independence. They enjoy planning and starting an activity. At times, however, they will stop an activity before it seems to be complete. A good teacher will not insist that a 5-year-old immediately clean up after leaving an activity because 5s often return to an activity at a later time. Five-year-old children thrive in an atmosphere of activity and freedom. This is an age when children should have the freedom to use and develop their personal abilities. However, 5-year-old children also like to have a routine so that they are able to feel secure within the total situation, secure enough to make choices and to try new things.

The Concrete Operational Stage

Traditionally, the **concrete operational stage** is thought to begin at about 6.5 years and continue to 11 or 12 years. This may also be viewed as from the onset of conservation of number to the onset of conservation of volume. At the first and second grade levels, children may be preoperational or concrete operational, but from third grade through the middle school years, most children are concrete operational.

Cognitive Factors. During the concrete operational stage of development, children develop patterns of thought similar to those used by adults, but still differing in some ways. During the concrete operations stage, children develop the ability to conserve number, substance, length, area, weight, and time. Other characteristics of this period are as follows:

1. the appearance of operations
2. limited ability to use verbal reasoning
3. a decrease in egocentricity
4. the appearance of reversibility

Operations. An **operation** is "an action that can return to its starting point and that can be integrated with other actions also possessing this feature of reversibility" (Piaget and Inhelder, 1956, p. 36). By developing this ability to use operations, to use reversible thought, children also develop the ability to conserve. Now they can see that a ball of clay flattened into a pancake still has the same amount of clay. It can be put back into its original form and nothing was added or taken away.

Verbal Reasoning.   Concrete operational children are better able to use language than the preoperational child, but verbal reasoning is still limited. Reasoning from a premise is still not possible for concrete operational children. Consequently, when presented with a question like, "What would happen if the Sun did not come up tomorrow?" the concrete operational child is likely to answer that the Sun always comes up.

Part of the difficulty that concrete operational children have with this type of question is due to their inability to use language effectively in thinking. This is also evidenced in the difficulty children have in explaining proverbs like, "Still waters run deep." And children at this stage of development still have problems defining words.

In terms of science teaching, this means it will be hard for children to explain verbally how or why something occurs. It also means that defining words using a glossary or dictionary will not necessarily provide understanding.

Reversibility of Thought.   A third change in concrete operational children's thinking processes also demonstrates a distinct difference from the preoperational child. Concrete children have reversible thought. Children can now reason that if warm water froze in a cold location then putting the frozen water in a warm location will return it to a liquid.

Egocentricity.   Concrete operational children no longer view the world egocentrically. Children are now able to shift their viewpoints from their own to those of others. Children are now more able to listen to different sides of an issue and to listen to opinions differing from their own.

Social Factors.   Concrete operational individuals can be as young as 6 and as old as the oldest adult. Consequently, their social characteristics are very much tied to their ages. Primary grade children who are concrete operational behave very differently from concrete operational children who are in the intermediate grades.

Primary Grade Children.   Six-year-old children entering the first grade are very similar to the previous year's 5-year-olds. Physical activity is still highly important and they tend to throw their whole bodies into any activity. Sixes still have difficulty with small muscle activities. And because these small muscles are not well developed and the eyes are not yet mature, fatigue follows prolonged attempts at hand-eye coordination.

Six-year-old children enjoy working with other children. It is difficult, however, for children of 6 to take turns. It is also difficult for them to follow group rules. Children of 6 often withdraw from an activity if they do not get their own way. But even when the child does not withdraw, it is not unusual for a 6-year-old to leave an activity unfinished.

By 6 years of age, children are trying to identify with those children who are older rather than with younger children. This change in outlook causes 6-year-olds to want both the responsibility of increased maturity and the security of an established routine. They are eager to learn new things, especially about the immediate environment, but they are also contented with whatever is occurring at a particular time. They are keenly competitive, yet criticism causes them to wilt. Sixes can best be described as a bundle of contradictory behaviors.

By age 7, about second grade level, many of the contradictions found in the 6-year-old have been eliminated. Sevens are still active and in need of large muscle activity, but they are also better able to use small muscles for tasks like writing than are 6s. Eyes are more mature so that reading is not quite so tiring, but fatigue still follows prolonged eye use. As reading and writing skills develop, so do oral language skills. Sevens are talkative and frequently exaggerate as they tell stories.

Children of 7 are trying to break from the world of little children to the world of adults. Striving for greater maturity, 7-year-olds stand up for their rights but also reach out for the assurance of adults. Because of these traits, guidance is needed, so that the 7-year-old can gain in independence but within a secure environment. In their desire to please adults, however, 7-year-olds can easily become overly dependent on those adults (Dodge, 1986; Dodge, 1983).

When compared to the younger primary grade children, 8-year-olds seem very mature. Their small muscles are better developed and their eyes are mature. Reading is now an important way to get information, and writing is useful as a way of recording information.

At about 8 years of age, the peer group becomes important. Boys and girls start to separate from one another and form same-gender play groups. Increasing identification with the peer group has two important results. First, in cases of conflict, children now side with other children rather than with adults. Second, children really want to belong to a group. Outcasts first begin to develop among 8-year-olds. But even though peers are highly important, children still look to adults for praise and for encouragement (Hartup and Moore, 1990; Howes, 1988).

At about 8 years of age, children begin to get as much enjoyment out of completing a task as out of beginning one. For these children, planning is important, beginning is important, and coming to an end point where the activity is complete is important as well.

Intermediate Grade Children.   Children of 9 and 10, those in fourth grade and early fifth grade, are better able to handle a variety of teachers and teaching techniques than are younger children. They tend to be decisive and responsible, dependable and reasonable. By 9 or 10 children are able not only to plan and complete an activity but also to do both without a great deal of adult supervision.

Many children of 9 or 10 become perfectionists. One result of this desire for perfection is that children can become demoralized if there is too much pressure or discouragement. In addition, perfectionism can also lead to conformity as children try to fit into peer groups by taking on the characteristics of others in the group. Nines and 10s find it hard to accept those who are different, yet they are beginning to realize that a number of differing opinions can exist and that all may be equally valid (Howes, 1988; Ladd, 1988).

Individual differences are quite apparent among 9s and 10s. Physically, girls are more mature than boys. But perhaps more important, their physical maturity is accompanied by differences in interests and abilities. It becomes possible for teachers, parents, and other children to point out the interests of individual children.

Reading for 9- and 10-year-old children can become a source of discouragement for many children. The emphasis of the intermediate school grades is often on gathering information through reading. Children with reading problems, more frequently boys than girls, are put under great pressure when they are asked to learn through reading and they may feel themselves to be failures.

At 9 and 10 children are beginning to show the half-adult, half-child behaviors that teachers find so frustrating. They want responsibility, but also need to be able to fail in their responsibilities without too much reminder that they did fail. These children are able to learn from their mistakes and handle deserved punishment. At this age, too, children strongly resent adults who talk down to them (Coie and Coppotelli, 1982).

The Formal Operational Stage

Cognitive Factors.   Traditionally, formal operations is defined as from 11 or 12 years of age throughout adulthood. The ages of 11 or 12 may be too early to reflect reality. The transition to formal operational thought is more likely to occur at age 15 or later. This may also be considered to begin with the development of conservation of volume and extend throughout adulthood. Children at the fifth, sixth, seventh, and eighth grade levels may be making the transition to formal operational thought. During formal operations, the ability to think logically is developed (Inhelder and Piaget, 1958).

Hypothesizing.   Of particular importance is the development of the ability to develop and test hypotheses logically. This is, of course, the foundation for scientific thinking. The formal operator can look at a set of data and draw from that data all of the conclusions that would be possible. The formal thinker can then logically analyze those conclusions and establish hypotheses and means for testing those hypotheses in order to determine which are valid and which are not.

Propositional Thinking.   The formal thinker in the process of reasoning manipulates either assertions or statements, also called **propositions,** which contain the new data from which the assertions were developed. For a formal operational thinker, responding to a question like "What would happen if the Sun did not come up tomorrow?" can result in a variety of possibilities founded in factual information or reflecting great imagination.

Combinatorial Reasoning.   **Combinatorial reasoning** looks at possible combinations. One example of this would be the ice cream problem. The ice cream problem establishes the fact that an ice cream store has vanilla, chocolate, and pistachio ice cream. It also has strawberry sauce, hot fudge, chopped nuts, and caramel sauce. Ice cream cones have one dip of ice cream and one topping. This is the problem: How many different kinds of ice cream cones can I buy before I have to repeat? For a formal operator, the answer is easily determined in a systematic manner.

Social Factors. Eleven- and 12-year-olds experience the awkwardness of preadolescence and 13- and 14-year-olds experience the awkwardness of early adolescence. The change from child to adolescent can be characterized by such adjectives as awkward, restless, lazy, changeable, overly critical, rebellious, uncooperative, self-conscious, independent, and curious. Children of 11 through 14 are all of these things, sometimes within the same hour. Their very changeableness makes them one of the most challenging and most interesting of age groups to teach.

Children between 11 and 14 begin to experience peer pressure. For the first time, the opinion of the peer group becomes more highly valued than that of adults. The peer group becomes the socializing agent, providing a better gauge of behavior than parental norms can provide for the child.

Peer pressure can also have a negative effect on pre- and early adolescents, causing them to doubt their own judgments and to change from a correct to an incorrect idea in order to conform. Preadolescents and early adolescents frequently go along with the group rather than stand on their own convictions.

The pre- and early adolescent period is also the time when curiosity is high. Curiosity, at this level, is highly correlated with self-esteem. Very curious individuals tend to be more self-reliant, less prejudiced, more socially responsible, and to have a greater sense of belonging. It is possible that students with poor self-esteem do not appear to be curious because they expect to fail. From the opposite side, it is also possible that children who are not curious may not explore their surroundings as much as curious children and so may fail to learn those things necessary to help them gain in self-esteem.

At the pre- and early adolescent level, language begins to take on a function that extends beyond simple communication. These students are making a transition from thought stimulated by concrete objects to thought using abstractions as a basis for thought. This transition to abstract thought permits students to think and to learn in an adult manner. Therefore, children in the **formal operational stage** have a strong need for independence and increased responsibility, for treatment as an adult, and for freedom from condemnation for acting like a child. Both independence and responsibility need to develop in an atmosphere without nagging and among adults who are able to demonstrate affection and a sense of humor. But because these students are not yet adult and are struggling with a combination of childhood and maturity, the teacher needs to be certain that expectations for behavior and learning are appropriate to the students.

In general, the work of Piaget and his followers in detailing how children think shows that we cannot, as teachers, treat children as if they are small versions of adults. It shows that we must adapt our teaching strategies to the developmental level of children. Preoperational children are not going to learn effectively by reading from science books, listening to explanations, or looking at pictures. Their thought processes are far more attuned to hands-on activity and direct experiences with objects so they can develop ideas for themselves. Concrete operational children, even though they may be able to use reading and writing more effectively, are still going to learn more effectively through direct hands-on science experiences from which they derive the content. Students at the preoperational and concrete operational levels are best taught through a constructivist rather than an objectivist approach. Boxes 2.1 and 2.2 show the characteristics of each of these approaches.

Only at the formal operational level will children actually be able to benefit from reading and listening as well as from concrete experiences. However, always keep in mind that one of the main characteristics is the ability to design and carry out experiments. This kind of activity once more requires hands-on experience. Here is the best rule of thumb for the preschool, elementary, and middle school levels: If you can teach a topic concretely, with real objects, with students actively involved in using those materials, then it is probably an appropriate topic for your students.

Activities 2.1 and 2.2 are designed to provide an opportunity to observe the characteristics of students at various grade levels.

Box 2.1   *The Objectivist Approach to Learning*

1. Objectivist strategies are based on the concept that the environment is structured for the learner. Knowledge has a structure of its own.

2. The teacher interprets the environment for the learner and the learner places new information into the context of present knowledge.

3. The teacher gives information and the students are expected to learn that information through practice exercises. The student is assumed to learn the same information exactly as it was transmitted by the teacher.

4. The teacher ignores the inconsistency of the students' own concepts with those being presented. The student is expected to accept new information and learn it.

5. **Strengths:**

a. The teacher controls the learning environment.

b. The subject matter can be sequenced and scheduled according to time frames.

c. Evaluation of students can be easily accomplished through comparisons to others at the same grade level.

d. Students can be grouped according to their current levels of knowledge as compared to the standard curriculum.

6. **Weaknesses:**

a. Assumes the background knowledge of the students makes little difference in the learning process.

b. Assumes all students learn in the same manner.

c. Assumes thought processes in children are the same as those in adults.

d. Assumes that subject matter areas are completely separate.

e. Assumes that standardized evaluations will determine student learning.

Box 2.2   The Constructivist Approach to Learning

1. Constructivist strategies are based on the concept that learners construct their own knowledge based on their perception of the environment.

2. The students develop and test their own explanations as they develop an individual construction of reality.

3. Students revise their rules and their beliefs as they meet new information conflicting with what is already known.

4. The teacher's role is to bring children into conflict with their misconceptions so they can develop more accurate concepts. Teaching in the constructivist viewpoint is providing experience not telling information.

5. **Strengths:**

   a. Learning and teaching are child centered.

   b. The differing backgrounds of the students are used in planning instruction.

   c. Direct experience are provided to encourage learning.

   d. Students develop understanding rather than learning by rote.

   e. Evaluation looks at individual growth rather than at particular norms.

6. **Weaknesses:**

   a. The teacher has little control over the learning process.

   b. Children in the same classroom may be at different points in the learning process requiring additional work for the teacher in individualizing instruction.

   c. Evaluation according to state mandates is difficult.

   d. Subject matter lines are blurred so scheduling is difficult.

   e. More instructional materials are required and time that may not be readily available.

Developmental Characteristic Activities

Activity 2.1

Purpose   To investigate similarities and differences in child behavior among children at different developmental levels.

Procedure

1. Arrange to visit classrooms or group settings at four different, spaced age levels (e.g., 5-year-old, 7-year-old, 10-year-old, 13-year-old). Arrange to observe the children in the setting over a 3- to 4-day period for at least 30 minutes at a time.

2. Observe how the children at each age level interact with one another, listen to their conversations, observe how the children at each grade level interact with the adults in the setting and with any materials in the setting.

3. Compare and contrast the students in each setting, considering in particular the social characteristics of the children.

4. How could you use the social characteristics of children at the various ages in determining how you would teach science? What effects would those characteristics have on the classroom setting?

Activity 2.2

Purpose   To investigate the thought processes of children at different developmental levels.

Procedure
1. Arrange to interview four children at spaced age levels, having at least two years age difference between each pair of students.
2. Investigate the Piagetian tasks used to determine two of the following conservations:
    a. number
    b. substance
    c. length
    d. area
    e. weight
    f. volume
    g. time
3. Develop the materials and the interview that would be needed to test a child for conservation.
    a. Using the same materials and the same interview, test each of the students you are working with for conservation.
    b. Compare and contrast the responses of the children.
4. What effect on learning science could lack of conservation in the areas investigated have? What might you as a classroom teacher do to minimize those effects?

Lev Semenovich Vygotsky

The work of Lev Semenovich Vygotsky adds another dimension to an understanding of children and their learning. Vygotsky's work emphasizes the influence of three areas on cognitive development: the social, the cultural, and the historical. His work also emphasizes the relationship between thought and language, and the greatest area of difference between Vygotsky and Piaget. And Vygotsky's work considers how learning and instruction contribute to the advancement of cognitive development.

Cultural and Social Impact on Cognitive Development

To Vygotsky, children develop cognitively because they develop an understanding and mastery of the world around them. Adults have a great deal of influence on this development, for it is from adults that children learn the language, manners, and customs of their culture. From Vygotsky's point of view, it is impossible to understand cognitive development without understanding the social environment of the child.

Thought and Language

Vygotsky and Piaget differ on the role of language in cognitive development. To Vygotsky, language and thought developed along somewhat different lines. In the beginning, very young children think through nonverbal gestures. For these children, speaking is babbling and crying. When children begin to use verbal language, their first words are used socially rather than for the purpose of thought. Therefore, a young child's use of "bye-bye," accompanied by a wave, does not indicate an underlying process but only a social skill: connecting a sound and an action to a particular situation. Only when children begin to use language to label objects in their environment do language and thought meet. Children pointing to a dog and saying "dog" are using language for thinking (Vygotsky, 1962).

Children often use external objects to help them solve problems. For example, a first grader might use blocks to help add two numbers together. And just as blocks are used as an external means for solving a problem, so is language. This external language that Vygotsky termed **egocentric speech** and others, **private speech** (Berk, 1986, Bivens and Berk, 1990) is used by children to help them solve a problem. So children talk out loud because they see language, like blocks, to be something external to them. All you need to do is listen to children in a first grade classroom, children talking to themselves as they work, to hear this external use of language and see how it is used.

Piaget saw this kind of external language as a part of children's egocentricity. According to Piagetian theory, egocentric language disappears when egocentricity disappears. Vygotsky, in contrast, did not see egocentric speech as disappearing. Instead, he saw egocentric speech as providing a link between social speech expressed externally and internal speech expressing thought processes.

A good indication of the connection between egocentric speech and action in children is found in Vygotsky's investigations. He discovered that egocentric speech increased when children encountered problems. Not only did it increase, but the increase was directly related to the difficulty of the problem. The harder the problem, the more the children talked to themselves. From these observations, Vygotsky concluded that egocentric speech was far more than an accompaniment to children's thinking. Egocentric speech showed the thought processes children were using as they thought. And so Vygotsky stated that children use egocentric speech for four reasons: (1) to direct attention to aspects of the problem, (2) to plan for problem solution, (3) to form concepts, and (4) to gain self-control. Egocentric speech helps children regulate their behavior.

It is rare to hear adults talking aloud to themselves as they work. However, adults do talk to themselves as they work. This talk is internal rather than external. Instead of disappearing with the disappearance of egocentricity, egocentric speech becomes the silent, mental speech of an adult trying to solve a problem. To Vygotsky, this transition from audible egocentric speech to silent, internally directing speech is a fundamental process in cognitive development. Vygotsky termed this internal speech used by adults in thinking, **inner speech** (Berk, 1986; Vygotsky, 1962).

Learning and Instruction

At any point in the child's development there are certain problems a child is on the verge of solving. Although a child may not be able to solve the problem alone, he or she can solve it with the help of an adult. Vygotsky termed this area where a child can solve a problem with help but not alone the **zone of proximal development.** Vygotsky defined the zone of proximal development as "the distance between the actual developmental level as determined by independent problem solving and the level of potential development as determined through problem solving under adult guidance and under the direction of more capable peers" (Dixon-Krauss, 1996, p. 86).

The concept of a zone of proximal development can be applied in the classroom in order to help children learn new skills. In order to apply this concept, children are placed into learning situations where they are asked to accomplish a task just beyond the current level of their ability. The children then need to be guided by explanations, demonstrations, and work with other children to accomplishment. Indeed, within the zone of proximal development, the most effective teachers may be other children who have just learned how to accomplish a particular task. In any learning situation, children should be encouraged to use language to organize their thinking, to talk about what they are trying to accomplish, and to communicate to themselves and others their successful and unsuccessful strategies in learning (Wertsch, 1984).

An additional concept important to Vygotsky's concept of teaching is the idea of **scaffolding.** Scaffolding is done all the time by parents as they teach their children some task. Consider, for example, teaching a child to tie a shoelace. At first a parent helps the child through every step of tying a lace. After a while, the parent helps only when the child is uncertain of what to do next, and finally the parent simply watches and praises the accomplishment. Scaffolding is the idea of gradually removing the prompts or hints a child needs in order to accomplish some task (Dixon-Krauss, 1986; Fleer, 1992). In a science classroom, the same kind of process is often used in helping children accurately find the mass of an object with a balance, learn how to use a microscope effectively, or care for a plant or animal.

Vygotsky's conception of learning as presenting children with tasks that are somewhat beyond their current abilities and then providing assistance, particularly from other students, supports the use of cooperative learning in hands-on situations within the science class. In particular, the use of cooperative learning groups provides the opportunity for children to interact with children just beyond their own level of learning so that one child may help and support another. In cooperative learning, support is also given to the concept of children contributing suggestions for areas of study, for questions to be answered, and for methods of solving problems or answering questions. Children will ask questions or suggest areas of study that are just beyond their current levels of ability or knowledge, thus providing that slight mismatch between what the child is currently able to do and what the child can do with assistance. This places the child into the zone of proximal development.

Concept Development

In Vygotsky's view, words are first used in concept development and then are used as a symbol for the concept. For example, children may hear and know the word *liquid,* but that word may have little meaning. Then the child has experiences with water, milk, soft drinks, and a variety of other liquids. He or she pours, drinks, mops up, and plays with a variety of liquids and the word gains in meaning. Eventually, after many experiences, the word *liquid* becomes meaningful. And so, in **concept develop-ment,** each child constructs a concept around a word. Then, after developing the concept with familiar liquids, the child can use that term for any material that fits the characteristics. Now the word has become a symbol of a category of materials.

Concepts, however, do not appear full blown. Instead, they develop in four stages: heaps, complexes, potential concepts, and genuine concepts. When children begin to label objects in the environment, they tend to group them into random categories called **heaps.** Young children just learning what a "dog" is will create heaps as they put into the same category any kind of animal with four legs and fur. But children do not lump dogs, cats, sheep, and rabbits in the same category for long. As their experience with animals increases, they notice similarities and differences. From those similarities and differences, children develop relationships among and between the objects, relationships that may be unstable and changing. They are called, according to Vygotsky, **complexes.** As children enter school, however, they enter the third stage in concept development. The stage of **potential concepts** begins in the early years of school and lasts into early adolescence. The transition from complexes to potential concepts indicates a transition from concrete to abstract concepts. Finally, children develop **genuine concepts.** These genuine concepts indicate that children have gained the abstract and systematic knowledge common to their culture. Heaps, complexes, and potential concepts generally develop concretely through direct, everyday experiences. Genuine concepts develop through formal schooling as children link words with experiences and finally gain understanding. In developing genuine concepts children need to talk with adults, not just listen to adults. Vygotsky's view demonstrates the importance of scientific vocabulary in helping children develop science concepts. It also shows how important adult-to-child interaction is in the development of understanding, in the development of concepts.

Vygotsky's work in concept development, like Piaget's, emphasizes the need for active involvement in learning. Children construct their own meaning from direct interaction with materials and objects coupled with direct verbal interaction with adults. It is not enough to simply provide materials and opportunities to manipulate those objects. Teachers also need to help children develop the appropriate words for discussing what they see and so help them to develop the concepts embodied in those words.

Howard Gardner and the Multiple Intelligences

The Eight Intelligences

When the word *intelligence* is mentioned, most people immediately have an image of Albert Einstein, Stephen Hawking, or some other academically gifted person. In 1985, however, the book *Frames of Mind: The Theory of Multiple Intelligences* by Howard Gardner challenged this limited idea of intelligence. Rather than consider academic brilliance as the only indicator of intelligence, Gardner suggested that intelligence comes in many forms: interpersonal, intrapersonal, linguistic, spatial, logical, bodily, musical, and mathematical. These are Gardner's **multiple intelligences.**

Interpersonal Intelligence

Interpersonal intelligence is used to understand the feelings, desires, and ideas of others. Children who have a high level of interpersonal intelligence can interact with others in many different situations. These children can understand the beliefs, interests, and desires of others, and because of this, they excel in developing non-threatening ways to solve conflicts. Students showing interpersonal intelligence often volunteer to work with children who are different, include those who are not often included in games, and understand that differences in children do not mean inferiorities. Children with high levels of interpersonal intelligence learn best when information is put into the context of the persons involved in the events.

Intrapersonal Intelligence

Whereas interpersonal intelligence is concerned with others, **intrapersonal intelligence** is more concerned with the self. Intrapersonal intelligence should not, however, be confused with self-centeredness. Children of high intrapersonal intelligence are also concerned with the effect of their values and beliefs on how they behave. Children with high intrapersonal intelligence are self-starters who can complete long-term projects with little or no supervision. In addition, they work independently without difficulty and usually know their own strengths and weaknesses. In learning, children using intrapersonal intelligence often approach learning on an emotional and personal basis using trial and error approaches.

Linguistic Intelligence

Linguistic intelligence focuses on language: writing, reading, speaking. Stories and conversation are the mainstay of this type of intelligence. But linguistic intelligence is more than simply using language to communicate. It also involves enjoying the very sound of language, the playfulness and humor of language, and the ways in which various peoples communicate through language. The focus of this intelligence is on language itself rather than on the message conveyed by the language.

Narratives and stories, particularly those that are rich in colorful language, as well as reading and writing are often used in learning.

Spatial Intelligence

Children using **spatial intelligence,** organize the world through spatial relations. Because they see the world in terms of its physical attributes, they interact with that world through seeing, hearing, tasting, touching, and smelling. This kind of interaction generally results in memories that are stored in the form of images or pictures.

Because art is a visual representation of the world, it is particularly helpful in learning for children of high spatial intelligence.

Logical Intelligence

Logical intelligence involves reasoning including inductive and deductive logic. It includes looking for the validity and reasonableness of connections between and among ideas, identifying patterns that connect seemingly different objects or events, drawing conclusions about the patterns, and making predictions about future events. Using reasoning, developing systems to organize and classify information, and developing logical conclusions according to a systematic set of rules are also a part of logical intelligence.

Children using logical intelligence learn most effectively when their logical processes are used to develop classifications, illustrate relationships among ideas, and recognize patterns.

Bodily Intelligence

Children with high **bodily intelligence** live primarily through their bodies. These children are able to form mental images about how their bodies feel when moving or preparing to move. Children with high bodily intelligence can rehearse the movements of an activity mentally and benefit from this mental rehearsal.

For children with high bodily intelligence, learning is enhanced through activities that allow them to involve their entire bodies: sports, dance, and other movement activities.

Musical Intelligence

Musical intelligence is the ability to think in terms of musical sounds: melody, harmony, countermelody, rhythms, pitches, keys, and chords. Children from cultures where music is not written down easily learn the musical forms of their culture through listening and are able to pass the sounds and rhythms to others through demonstration. Children in cultures where music is written in symbols find those symbols easy to comprehend and translate into sound. But it is not simply the reproduction of music that demonstrates high musical intelligence. Instead, these are the individuals who are able to manipulate the aspects of the music they play and so create new musical forms and compositions.

Learning for the child using musical intelligence is enhanced through a musical context.

Mathematical Intelligence

Mathematical intelligence is defined as thinking about the physical world and its properties. Mathematical intelligence goes beyond the simple ability to use mathematics in daily living to using mathematics to develop a model of the world. To the mathematically intelligent child, mathematics possesses a beauty, an aesthetic, and a humor of its own. Mathematical intelligence encodes information in terms of numbers and symbols that can then be manipulated according to established rules and procedures.

The child with high mathematical intelligence is especially involved in the learning of mathematics and relates to other subject matter areas through the use of mathematical means. Box 2.3 summarizes Gardner's multiple intelligences.

Although each of these intelligences can be separated out and discussed, never think of them as mutually exclusive or as fixed. Most people have more than one area in which they excel. After all, Albert Einstein was not only a great physicist but also a fine violinist. As children mature, the area of greatest ability may change so that the third grade mathematician becomes the ninth grade artist.

We should be careful not to use the various types of intelligence to categorize children or to provide a reason for a one-sided education. Instead, the idea of multi-

---

Box 2.3   Gardner's Eight Intelligences

1. **Interpersonal intelligence:** a high level of ability to understand the feelings, desires, and ideas of others.

2. **Intrapersonal intelligence:** a tendency to be highly aware of one's self and to be introspective.

3. **Linguistic intelligence:** intelligence focusing on the elements of language: writing, reading, speaking.

4. **Spatial intelligence:** intelligence manifesting itself as an interest in the physical attributes of the world and in which memory is often stored as images and pictures

5. **Logical intelligence:** looking for the validity and reasonableness of connections

between and among ideas, identifying patterns, drawing conclusions, and making predictions.

6. **Bodily intelligence:** students with the form of intelligence live primarily through their bodies and are active in such areas of sports and dance.

7. **Musical intelligence:** the ability to think in terms of musical sounds: melody, pitch, rhythms, and key.

8. **Mathematical intelligence:** intelligence that manifests itself through thought about the physical world.

ple intelligences should be used to develop a well-rounded science program in which all children can use their strengths to help them succeed (Gardner, 1993; Gardner, 1991). One way of organizing so that we include activities appropriate for children with a variety of intelligences is the integrated approach to curriculum. An integrated curriculum uses mathematics, art, music, physical education, and language arts as ways of increasing science knowledge. And because children are involved in a wide variety of subject matter areas as they learn science content, they are also involved in a wide variety of activities. The greater the variety, the more likely children will find an activity to match their intellectual strength. Chapter 12 considers the integrated curriculum approach in detail.

Activity 2.3 asks you to consider how the eight intelligences could be incorporated into a science topic at the elementary or middle school levels.

Multiple Intelligences Learning Activity

Activity 2.3

Purpose   To demonstrate how the various intelligences could be purposefully incorporated into a science topic.

Procedure
1. Obtain a science textbook for any grade from first through eighth. Select one chapter from that textbook and read it carefully, including any teaching suggestions.
2. Consider the content of the chapter in terms of Gardner's eight intelligences. How could you, as a teacher, utilize those intelligences to teach the content in the chapter? Note: Do not try to force the eight intelligences into the content, but use only those which are appropriate to the content information.
3. How could attention to Gardner's eight intelligences enhance the chapter? How could attention to Gardner's eight intelligences weaken the chapter?

Appropriate Science Experiences for the Elementary School Years

Children in the elementary and middle school years vary from about 5 years of age to approximately 14 years of age. Their cognitive and social characteristics differ greatly from year to year and grade to grade. Consequently, it is incorrect to assume that the kinds of experiences planned for sixth grade children would be appropriate for kindergarten or first grade children. Instead, the cognitive-developmental characteristics of children should be applied to the selecting of appropriate science content and appropriate science activities for children.

This does not mean, however, that there are no commonalities among science experiences for all children. Indeed, certain things will be true no matter what the grade level or age of the children. First, science experiences for all grades should be coherently organized so that students are investigating the broad themes of science rather than experiencing a variety of unconnected activities. Second, science experiences for all grade levels should include mathematics and technology in authentic ways. Mathematics should be used where it is appropriate in the collection and interpretation of data: from counting how many bean seeds grew in first grade to calculating the mean growth rate of those beans under different conditions in the sixth grade. Third, science activities for all grade levels should focus on direct experiences with materials enhanced by discussion and reading. Fourth, science experiences for all grade levels should allow children to direct their own learning. As students progress from the kindergarten to eighth grade levels, they should have increasing responsibility for selecting topics within a broad framework, for organizing their learning, and for designing their own activities and experiments for solving problems. And, finally, science for all grade levels should be purposeful for the child as a child rather than seek to present topics that may be of use to the individual some time in the adult future. As a teacher you should always ask, "Why are we studying this?" If the answer has to do with student interest, with the importance for a child's understanding of science at that time in life, then the topic is probably appropriate to the grade level. If the answer to the question is "because you'll need this next year" or "because it's on a standardized test," then you might want to rethink the topic or the focus of the topic.

In addition to these commonalities, certain differences also are true of science at the preschool-kindergarten levels, science for primary grade children, and science for intermediate and middle school children.

Science Appropriate for the Preschool and Kindergarten

The natural curiosity of children in the preschool and kindergarten lends itself to an interest in science. The characteristics of preschool-kindergarten children, however, lead to science experiences that differ somewhat from the traditional image of science teaching. In fact, it would be more appropriate to call these science activities rather than science lessons. Science lessons have particular outcomes determined by the teacher, and science activities provide opportunities for children to learn what they are developmentally ready to learn through their interaction with materials. Effective science activities for young children meet the following criteria:

1. *Science activities for young children should allow the child to directly investigate the environment around them.* Science activities should not be based on teacher demonstration, teacher lecture, pictures, films, filmstrips, or other vicarious learning experiences.

2. *Science activities appropriate for young children should be based on the kinds of things children do as they play.* Young children manipulate the environment as they play. They roll cars across floors and down inclines. They bounce balls. They toss beanbags. They pour water and sand. They mix materials together. As they are doing these things, they are learning about their environment. They are constructing their own concepts based on their direct experiences.

3. *Science activities appropriate for young children should allow them to use simple, familiar, safe materials.* The use of science labs and sophisticated science equipment is inappropriate for young children. Children can investigate important science concepts, particularly those from the physical sciences, through everyday materials. Sufficient materials should be provided so that children can choose to investigate alone, in parallel with others, or in small groups. Enough materials should be provided for children to leave a small group and investigate singly.

4. *Science activities appropriate for young children should allow for diversity in action.* The most effective science experiences for young children should not require children to come to a particular conclusion as predetermined by the teacher. Instead, the materials should allow children to investigate a broad generalization in a variety of ways.

5. *Science activities appropriate for young children should be open ended.* Young children should have the opportunity to investigate for as long a period of time or as short a period of time as they wish. Children should be able to quit an investigation when they feel satisfied and to return to an investigation at a later time.

6. *Science activities appropriate for young children should have cause-and-effect relationships that are immediate.* Young children have little concept of cause and effect. They do understand cause-and-effect relationships that meet two criteria. First, the cause and the effect should be immediately related in space and time. That is, the cause should produce the effect right then and there. Second, the child should be active in the cause.

7. *Science activities appropriate for young children should allow them to investigate ideas related to conservation in an intuitive rather than a formal manner.* Preoperational children are not conservers. Consequently, teaching them formal concepts of number, substance, weight, area, time, or volume is inappropriate. This does not mean, however, that these topics cannot form the basis for science activities. Children can investigate weight through placing objects on balances without finding the actual weight or mass of the objects. They can investigate volume and substance through pouring. These are intuitive investigations focusing on actions rather than on units of measurement.

8. *Science activities appropriate to young children allow children to make the connection between words as signs and words as symbols for concepts.* The development of accurate scientific vocabulary is important in the development of science concepts. However, the simple development of vocabulary should not be the goal of a science activity. Rather, activities should allow young children to begin to develop the concepts named by the vocabulary. In order to do this, children should have the opportunity to interact with one another during activities, to share findings and experiences with one another during group sharing, and to interact with the teacher and other adults as they investigate and as they talk about their investigations.

9. *Science activities appropriate to young children should allow children to construct their own conceptions of the world rather than attempting to teach them concepts directly.* The cognitive structure of the young child is far different from that of the adult. Adult explanations are generally based on a complex concept of cause and effect using language as the means of communication. Because the preoperational child has yet to develop a concept of cause and effect, he or she rarely benefits from this type of

explanation. Instead, young children should be provided with experiences that challenge their naive conceptions and will then allow them to develop more sophisticated concepts, to refine those concepts through repeated experiences, and to construct their own understanding of the world.

10. *Science activities appropriate to young children should have their basis in a coherent and organized program.* Children at the preschool and kindergarten levels should be actively engaged in experiences. However, in order for conceptual development to occur, those experiences should be organized around the common themes as developed by Project 2061 rather than a haphazard collection of isolated, disconnected activities.

A Preschool-Kindergarten Science Experience.   The children in a multiage center including 3- through 5-year-old children in the same setting arrived to find the teacher building a tower out of empty plastic milk containers. In addition to many more cartons than were needed to build her tower, the teacher also had empty cans, beanbags, rubber, plastic, and plastic foam balls, toy cars, cylindrical blocks, wooden blocks and boards, and straws. When the children asked what she was doing, she told them she was building a tower so she could knock it down.

She then backed away from the tower she had built and lightly tossed a beanbag at it, missing the tower entirely. "I guess I can't get it to fall down. Can anyone help me?"

Four of the children immediately picked up balls to throw, knocking the tower down and then running to build another one. They soon tired of using the balls and decided to try other items. While they worked at bringing the tower down, others built a ramp out of the blocks and board and were seeing how far they could get a toy car to roll. They began changing how the board was placed in order to see what would happen. Still others picked up straws and began trying to move some of the objects by blowing on them or by poking them with the straws. As soon as the children were involved, the teacher moved away from the area to allow them to pursue their own investigations.

After a few minutes, some of the children left to go to other classroom centers but most remained, trying to find out how to knock down a tower or how to move objects or how to roll a car farther. At one point the children stopped knocking down the tower and started trying to build the tallest tower they could using the blocks, cans, milk containers, and boards.

"Watch this!" one of the 5-year-olds called. He had built a ramp to roll a ball on and could get the ball to drop into one of the cans. Some of those building decided to see if they could do the same thing.

Not until all of the children had moved away from the materials did the teacher gather them together. She focused the discussion around two questions:

What were some of the things you tried?
What did you find out?

As the children answered the questions, describing their investigations, she recorded their ideas on chart paper.

Although the children seemed to be finished with the materials and with the activity, the teacher left the materials where they were. Later in the day, some of the 5-year-old children returned to the activity. They set the milk containers into a single row and attempted to knock them down as if they were bowling. They changed the speed they rolled the balls, the type of ball, the distance, and the angle, thus extending the original activity into new areas.

Activity 2.4 is designed to allow you to put into practice the information considered in this section.

Content Appropriateness Activity

Activity 2.4

Purpose To apply the criteria for appropriate science activities at the preschool kindergarten level to an activity book or curriculum guide designed for this level.

Procedure
1. Obtain a curriculum guide or activity book designed for use at the preschool or kindergarten level.
2. Considering the developmental characteristics and using the ten criteria for appropriate science experiences listed in the text, critique the guide or activity book.
   a. How appropriate are the suggested activities for children of this age? Why do you rate them in this way?
3. How could you, as a classroom teacher, make the activities of the book or curriculum guide more developmentally appropriate for preschool and kindergarten children?

Science in the Primary Grades

The reading interests of children in the primary grades give an indication of the interest in science-related topics that exists at this age level. Nature stories, stories about space and rockets, as well as stories about machines are all enjoyed. Although such stories are read and enjoyed, this interest in reading should not be taken to mean that children at the primary grades should learn science through reading. Science teaching and learning should take place in an atmosphere of purposeful activity, activity directed toward the learning of science content.

The following criteria can be used in helping the teacher to select and develop appropriate science activities:

1. *Appropriate science activities for the primary grades should be multisensory in nature.* The activities should involve the child through as many senses as possible and

should include large muscle activity. Such multisensory approaches not only allow children to investigate in a variety of ways but also allow the various intelligences to be put into play.

2. *Activities for children at the primary grades should be open ended, with the activities becoming more focused toward closure at the third grade level.* Open-ended activities allow for varying abilities and cognitive levels within the primary grade classroom. Children at the preoperational stage of development may choose to end an activity or to change the direction of an activity. Concrete operational children are more likely to come to closure and to follow the directions for a given activity. In addition, open-ended activities allow each child to construct knowledge based on his or her background. Finally, open-ended activities play on children's initiative by allowing them to plan their own courses of action.

3. *Activities for primary grade children should allow for a variety of grouping arrangements.* Younger primary grade children should have individual sets of materials for science activities. This allows the young primary grade child, who is likely to be preoperational in cognitive development, to withdraw from an activity planned as a group endeavor while still continuing with the activity. Later, as children reach the third grade level and show the ability to plan for a large-group experience, a single set of materials can be provided and divided for group use. This should not, however, be taken to mean that all third grade experiences should involve group work. Many experiences in the science area are better handled by children working as individuals or in pairs.

4. *Activities for primary grade children should utilize reading skills in an appropriate manner but not rely on reading skills.* The incorporation of written materials into a hands-on program becomes more appropriate with the use of written materials increasing from first through third grade. The most effective use of reading materials is after students have developed concepts in a hands-on manner, however. A wide variety of selected textbooks and trade books should be made available to primary grade children so that their reading can be directed toward a particular purpose.

5. *Activities for primary grade children should allow them to utilize written communication skills but not be driven by written communication.* The use of journals to record information and to describe the results of activities is an effective means of including writing skills at this level. However, all activities do not need to be recorded in a written format, nor should the teaching of writing be considered part of science teaching. Writing should be included in an authentic and purposeful manner. Worksheets in which students answer low-level questions are inappropriate as a means for incorporating written language into a science program.

6. *When appropriate, collections should be used to enhance science concepts.* The use of leaf collections, rock collections, and other kinds of collections not only play on the child's developing ability to classify but also leads to questions that can be answered through the use of the collections themselves or through the use of additional activities using concrete materials.

7. *Appropriate science activities should allow children to interact directly with materials, to collect data from the use of those materials, and to draw conclusions based on their direct experiences.* Children in the primary grades are in the preoperational and concrete opera-

tional stages of development where the basic prerequisite for the construction of new concepts is direct experience. In addition to the direct experience, however, students need to interact with one another and with the teacher in order to develop appropriate vocabulary and appropriate conclusions. Simply doing an activity is not enough. The teacher and children must then work together to make sense out of the activity and the concepts shown. In all cases, the direct experiences of the students should form a coherent whole rather than a series of isolated activities outside of a conceptual framework.

8. *Activities for the primary grades should increasingly incorporate student interests and student initiative in the development of activities.* As primary children grow in responsibility, independence, and ability to work in groups toward closure, the teacher should work toward more cooperative planning with the class rather than designing the experiences for the class.

A Primary Grade Science Experience. The children in this second grade class were working in a unit on weather. They had observed the weather outside for a week, noting that weather changed frequently. One day it was sunny and warm. The next day it was cloudy and rained. On another day it was cold and windy. On a third day it was sunny and warm. February in Alabama is like that. They decided, however, that it was not enough just to know that the weather changed. They wanted to know how warm it was. How fast the wind blew. How much rain fell in a day. They also wanted to know why the weather changed so much from one day to another. With the teacher's help, they made a list of the questions they wanted to answer as they learned about weather.

What makes the weather different?
What kinds of clouds are in the sky?
How much does it rain?
How fast does the wind blow?
How can a weathercaster tell what the weather is going to be like tomorrow?
Why is the weather different in July and February?
Is the weather in other places the same as the weather here?

By using books in the classroom, the children discovered how to make a wind sock, a rain gauge, and an anemometer. They also found pictures of different kinds of clouds. After finding how to make the various instruments, they came together as a group to decide whether everyone should make the same instruments or whether they should make just one or two of each of the instruments. The group finally decided that it would be better to make only one or two of each type. They divided into groups to construct the instruments they had found as well as to make a barometer from the directions the teacher had found. When the instruments were finished, they decided to take them outside to learn how to use them and to learn more about the weather that day. One group decided it would be the "cloud group" and would draw pictures of the clouds they saw each day. The children decided that because it was not raining that day they would just leave the rain gauge outside.

It rained two days after they began drawing the clouds and collecting information from their weather instruments. All of the information they collected was recorded in their science journal. As they recorded how much rain had fallen, Eric looked puzzled by the amount. "It didn't rain at my house yesterday," he told the class. Some of the children were surprised. Some of them thought he was mistaken.

"How could we find out if it rains the same amount everywhere?" the teacher asked.

After discussion, they decided they would need to make more rain gauges and put them in different places. Four children were selected to take the rain gauges home that week and to bring them back to school if it rained. It rained that night so the rain gauges came back to the classroom the next morning. The school gauge showed a half inch. The one Rosa brought showed an inch. The rain gauges Caleb and LaShaundra brought both had only a quarter of an inch. And Joey's gauge showed no rain at all. The children decided that it didn't rain the same amount everywhere. At that point Terri asked where it rained the most "in the whole world."

They used a variety of sources to determine the answer to Terri's question: science texts, Internet, encyclopedia, and the local weather station. The sources all agreed on the place with the most rain and the place with the least rain.

The study of weather continued for another two weeks including a visit to the weather station at the air base within the city and a visit to a television station to meet the weathercaster and watch a broadcast.

Activity 2.5 is designed to allow you to put into practice the information on appropriate primary grade science as described here.

Content Appropriateness Activity

Activity 2.5

Purpose   To apply the criteria for appropriate science activities at the primary level to a textbook or curriculum guide designed for this level.

Procedure
1. Obtain a curriculum guide or textbook designed for use at the primary grade level.
2. Considering the developmental characteristics and using the eight criteria for appropriate science experiences listed in the preceding paragraphs, critique the curriculum guide or textbook.
   a. How appropriate are the suggested activities for children of this age?
   b. Why do you rate them in this way?
3. What could you do as a classroom teacher to make the activities of the curriculum guide or textbook more developmentally appropriate for children in the primary grades?

Science in the Intermediate and Middle School Grades

It is the nature of the pre- and early adolescent to be both responsible and irresponsible, mature and immature, independent and dependent, cooperative and uncooperative, adult and child. In order to allow for the changeable nature of the preadolescent, the science program needs to be an open and accepting one, where discussion demonstrating a variety of opinions occur and a wide variety of activities can be conducted leading the child toward more adult modes of thought. The following criteria are useful in selecting appropriate science activities for intermediate and middle grade children:

1. *Science experiences for the intermediate and middle grade student should allow for individualization of instruction.* This level is characterized by a wide range of maturity levels and interests. In order to better assure suitability of a program, individualization through student selection of topics and projects within a broad area of study should be possible.

2. *Science experiences for the intermediate and middle grades should allow students the opportunity to plan and carry out activities with a minimum of adult interference.* Pre- and early adolescents need to be given latitude to develop as individuals as well as the freedom to pursue topics of information in supporting one's opinions and ideas.

3. *Science experiences for middle school should develop the ability to collect data, draw conclusions from that data, and discuss the support for a conclusion found within the data.* Among pre- and early adolescents, pressure to conform is so strong that opinions can be changed solely by pressure from other children. Consequently, attention should be given to the collection and interpretation of factual information and the use of that for discussion

4. *Science experiences for intermediate and middle grades should allow students to engage in discussion and debate.* The topics and the structure of these discussions and debates should be such that a variety of opinions can be elicited without any final, absolute decision possible. The pre- and early adolescent needs to become aware of the variety of possible opinions on science-related topics so that the idea grows that it is normal and natural.

5. *Science experiences for intermediate and middle grades should move students toward higher levels of abstract thinking.* Students at the fourth and fifth grade levels are most likely to be concrete operational in their thought processes. Students at the sixth, seventh, and eighth grade levels may be beginning the transition to formal operational thought. It is important that students have the opportunity to develop their abstract thinking processes through use of inductive and deductive logic during activities.

6. *Science experiences for the intermediate and middle grades should focus on the use of hands-on experiences with gradual development of the ability to conduct a true experiment.* The fifth through eighth grade student is developing the ability to conduct a true experiment. However, this type of activity requires the use of formal thought processes, which may not be available to all students. Consequently, there should be the option of returning to activities that do not require the use of hypothesizing, control of variables, or other processes involved in a true experiment.

7. *Science experiences for the intermediate and middle grades should include verbal learning as well as concrete learning.* Although a steady diet of learning through written materials is not appropriate for pre- or early adolescents or to the spirit of science, reading can help middle school children determine how to plan for an experiment by providing background information and supplying missing theoretical information that will allow for a fuller understanding of experimental results. A wide variety of textbooks, trade books, magazines, films, and filmstrips should be available to the 11- through 14-year-old so that the research scientist's need to keep up on current information may be developed in the student. In addition, the use of the Internet can allow students to locate information not readily available to them in the school setting as well as to discuss their projects and ideas with children in other schools, other states, and other nations. The Internet provides a unique opportunity for developing projects that cut across state, national, and international boundaries.

8. *Science experiences for the intermediate and middle grades should develop correct scientific terminology but not be directed by such terminology.* Terms that are new to students must be defined if written material is to be understood and if concepts are to be fully understood in an abstract sense. An effective sequence for the development of meaning provides concrete experiences that will develop the underlying concepts prior to the verbal definition of the term.

9. *Science experiences for the intermediate and middle grades should cultivate and develop the child's curiosity.* Using the interests of the students as a foundation for at least some of the topics considered during a school year provides for the inclusion of the child's natural curiosity. Following up on questions asked by the students also allows the development of curiosity on the part of students. And spontaneity on the part of the teacher for investigating sudden areas of interest to the students can develop and maintain curiosity. Real problems evolving from student interests are more valid for teaching science than are artificial problems found in textbooks, programs, or curriculum guides.

10. *Intermediate and middle grade experiences should build on the student's background experiences and extend those into new areas, particularly into the social applications of science.* Although background experiences are important at all grade levels in the selection of appropriate experiences, the growing ability to think abstractly provides greater opportunity than ever before for using the child's existing information to develop new ideas. Once again, the Internet provides a unique opportunity for extending the preadolescent's learning into new and distant areas.

An Intermediate Grade Science Experience.   These seventh grade students had begun with a unit on natural resources, but as the unit progressed past the definition of a natural resource and what is meant by renewable and nonrenewable resources, the interest level of the students began to decrease. As the teacher listened to the conversations the children were having, however, he noticed they were interested in the environment and how the environment was changing as a result of the activities of people. Rather than look at the topic from the viewpoint of what natural resources are, the teacher decided to change the focus to changes in the environment and what that means in terms of resources.

Because the community itself was changing, it became the focus of the study. One group of students began to study the construction of a new mall in an area that had been covered with trees and underbrush. A second group began to look at how a new apartment complex was going to affect the rest of the community. And the third group began to look at a pond that had been constructed as a part of the school grounds when a new wing had been constructed.

As their study unfolded, the students tested water quality in the pond and in the runoff area near the new mall and at the apartment complex. They tested the water for pollutants and for acidity. They collected soil samples and investigated the materials in those samples and then looked at how well plants would grow in soil from the construction areas as well as from areas where there was no construction. In addition, students began to consider the increase in electric power use and water consumption that would result from the new construction. But as they researched the mall and the apartment complex, they also found that they needed to consider the economic impact on the community.

While the first two groups were investigating the community and the impact on the community of new construction, the third group was considering the pond and how the plants and animals of the pond interacted with one another, how the pond affected the area around it, and how it affected the students and teachers in the school.

The students in this seventh grade class planned their own investigations, seeking help from the teacher as necessary, and included a variety of methods for collecting information. They utilized their science textbooks as well as trade books and encyclopedias. They worked with multimedia programs on the computer and accessed information from the Internet. They interviewed town officials and also persons living in the neighborhoods to see what their views on the construction were. The group investigating the school pond relied more on so-called science methods for gaining information as they conducted water and soil tests, observed plant growth and types of plants, and observed animal behavior. They also collected data on student and teacher perceptions of the pond.

At the conclusion of the unit, each of the groups presented its information to the rest of the class and to other seventh grade classes using charts, drawings, a videotape, and oral as well as written presentation.

Activity 2.6 is designed to help you put into practice the criteria for appropriate science at the middle school level discussed here.

Content Appropriateness Activity

Activity 2.6

Purpose   To apply the criteria for appropriate science activities at the middle school level to a textbook, program, or curriculum guide designed for the fifth, sixth, seventh, or eighth grade.

Procedure
1. Obtain a curriculum guide or activity book designed for use at the middle school level.
2. Considering the developmental characteristics and using the ten criteria for appropriate science experiences listed in the text, critique the guide or activity book.
   a. How appropriate are the suggested activities for students of this age?
   b. Why do you rate them in this way?
3. What could you do, as a classroom teacher, to make the activities more developmentally appropriate for the students at the middle school level?

Summary

Children and adults do not think in the same way. The work of Jean Piaget in partic-ular has demonstrated the differences between adult and child thought. Most chil-dren in the primary grades, kindergarten through third grade, are in the preopera-tional stage of development. Their thinking tends to be concrete, to be egocentric, to be lacking in reversibility, and to show a tendency to center on a single characteris-tic. Children at this stage of thinking work effectively with materials in developing new facts and concepts. Children in the upper elementary school grades tend to be in the concrete operational stage of development. Although their thinking is tied directly to concrete materials, they are no longer egocentric, no longer centered, and have developed the ability to reverse their thought processes. Although most sixth grade children are concrete operational in their thoughts, some are making the transition to formal operational thought processes.

Although the work of Piaget and his followers has had great influence in the elementary school, the work of Lev Vygotsky is becoming more prominent. In par-ticular, Vygotsky considers the development of concepts in learning and focuses on the use of egocentric language as a means for problem solving in children. The zone of proximal development, another important concept of Vygotsky's work, describes an effective time and means for presenting new information to children.

Children do not think like adults, nor do all children think alike or have strengths for learning in the same area. The work of Howard Gardner on multiple intelligences reminds the teacher that a single mode of presentation may not be appropriate for all children, but rather that children may have intelligence in differ-ing areas: interpersonal, intrapersonal, mathematical, spatial, musical, bodily, or linguistic.

Because children change in their thought processes as they develop across the elementary school years, science teaching must also change across the school years. The open-ended activities of the primary grades can slowly become more focused and more student directed as the children progress through the elementary school to the intermediate grades and beyond.

Chapter Vocabulary

The number following each term refers to the page on which the term is first introduced.

Bodily intelligence, 57
Centering, 37
Collective monologue, 38
Combinatorial reasoning, 42
Complexes, 49
Concept development, 49
Concrete operational stage, 39
Concreteness, 37
Conservation, 36
Developmental stages, 35
Egocentric speech, 47
Egocentrism, 36
Formal operational stage, 43
Genuine concepts, 49
Heaps, 49
Inner speech, 48
Interpersonal intelligence, 50
Intrapersonal intelligence, 50
Linguistic intelligence, 50
Logical intelligence, 51

Mathematical intelligence, 52
Multiple intelligences, 50
Musical intelligence, 51
Nonconservers, 36
Operation, 39
Parallel play, 38
Potential concepts, 49
Preoperational stage, 36
Private speech, 47
Propositions, 42
Reversibility, 37
Scaffolding, 48
Sensorimotor stage, 35
Spatial intelligence, 50
Transductive reasoning, 37
Zone of proximal development, 48

Applying the **CONCEPTS**

1. A science fair requires that all projects be experiments involving developing and testing a hypothesis. As a judge for that science fair, you notice that all of the projects submitted by the primary and intermediate children show extensive parental assistance. At the sixth through eighth grade levels, however, the projects show that the children developed the projects for themselves. Why do you think the amount of work contributed by parents changed over the grade levels?

2. You notice that some of the children in your seventh grade class are able to plan and carry out an experiment but that others are still having difficulty. How could you use Vygotsky's ideas of zone of proximal development and scaffolding to assist students in developing their ability to do experiments?

3. The school in which you teach science is a magnet school for children talented in art, music, and dance. As the science teacher, you want to develop a program as appropriate as possible for these

children. How could you use Gardner's theory of multiple intelligences to help you plan appropriate science experiences for your students?

4. You have been asked by your principal to chair a committee to develop a new science curriculum for your kindergarten through sixth grade school. One of the teachers assigned to the committee has sent you a note indicating that the curriculum should have more "meat" and less "play." You find out the teacher means more content and vocabulary teaching and less emphasis on hands-on experiences. How would you respond to this colleague using Piagetian concepts as your basis?

5. Your fourth grade students are having great difficulty learning the science required in the curriculum for your school. Describe how you would use the work of Piaget, Vygotsky, and Gardner first to determine why there are problems, and, second, to help remedy the problems.

References

Berk, L. E. 1986. Relationship of elementary school children's private speech to behavioral accompaniment to task, attention, and task performance. *Developmental Psychology* 22(5), 671–680.

Bivens, J. A., and L. E. Berk. 1990. A longitudinal study of elementary school children's private speech. *Merrill-Palmer Quarterly*, 36, 443–463.

Brooks, J. G. 1990. Teachers and students: Constructivists forging new connections. *Educational Leadership* 47, 68–71.

Coie, J. D., K. A. Dodge and H. Coppotelli. 1982. Dimensions and types of social status: A cross age perspective. *Developmental Psychology* 18, 557–570.

Dixon-Krauss, L. 1996. *Vygotsky in the classroom.* White Plains, N.Y.: Longman.

Dodge, K. A. 1983. Behavioral antecedents of peer social status. *Child Development* 54, 1386–1399.

Dodge, K.A., G. Petit, J. McClaskey, and M. Brown. 1986. Social competence in children. *Monographs of the Society for Research in Child Development* 51, 2, serial number 213.

Fleer, M. 1992. Identifying teacher-child interaction which scaffolds scientific thinking in young children. *Science Education,* 76(4), 393–397.

Fosnot, C. T. 1993. Rethinking science education: A defense of piagetian constructivism. *Journal of Research in Science Teaching* 30(9), 1189–1201.

Gabel, D.L. (Ed.). 1994. *Handbook of research on science teaching and learning.* New York: Macmillan.

Gardner, H. 1983. *Frames of mind.* New York: Basic Books.

Gardner, H. 1991. *The unschooled mind: How children think and how schools should teach.* New York: Basic Books.

Gardner, H. 1993. *Multiple intelligences: The theory in practice.* New York: Basic Books.

Geneshi, C. 1987. Acquiring oral language and communicative competence. In C. Seefeldt (Ed.), *The early childhood curriculum, a review of current research* (pp. 136–151). New York: Teachers College Press, Columbia University.

Goffin, S. G. and C. Q. Tull. 1988. Encouraging cooperative behavior among young children. *Dimensions* 16, 15-18.

Hartup, W. W., and S. G. Moore. 1990. Early peer relations: Developmental significance and prognostic implications. *Early Childhood Research Quarterly* 5, 1–7.

Howes, C. 1988. Peer interaction of children. *Monographs of the Society for Research in Child Development* 53, 1, serial number 217.

Inhelder, B., and J. Piaget. 1958. *The growth of logical thinking from childhood to adolescence.* New York: Basic Books.

Jonassen, D. H. 1991. Evaluating constructivist learning. *Educational Technology* 31(9), 28–33.

Kagan, J. 1980. Jean Piaget's contributions to education. *Kappan* 62, 4.

Ladd, G. W. 1988. Friendship patterns and peer status during early and middle childhood. *Journal of Developmental and Behavioral Pediatrics* 9, 229–238.

Lazear, D. 1991. *Seven ways of knowing: Teaching for multiple intelligences* (2nd ed.). Palatine, Ill.: Skylight.

Perkins, D. N. 1991. What constructivism demands of the learner. *Educational Technology* 31(9), 19–21.

Piaget, J. 1972b. *The child's conception of physical causality.* Totowa, N. J.: Littlefield.

Piaget, J. 1974. *The origins of intelligence in children.* New York: International Universities Press.

Piaget, J. 1975a. *The child's conception of the world.* Totowa, N. J.: Littlefield.

Piaget, J. 1975b. *The psychology of intelligence.* Totowa, N. J.: Littlefield.

Piaget, J., and B. Inhelder. 1956. *The child's conception of space.* London: Routledge and Kegan Paul.

Vygotsky, L. S. 1962. *Thought and language.* Cambridge, Mass.: MIT Press.

Wertsch, J. V. 1984. The zone of proximal development: Some conceptual issues. In B. Rogoff and J. V. Wertsch (Eds.). *Children's learning in the zone of proximal development* (pp. 7–18), San Francisco: Jossey-Bass.

Yager, R. E. 1991. The constructivist learning model: Towards real reform in science education. *The Science Teacher* 58(6), 52–57.

CHAPTER THREE

THE BASIC PROCESSES OF SCIENCE

Chapter Objectives

Upon completion of this chapter you should be able to:

1 discuss the viewpoint of the the *National Science Standards* on inquiry and processes.

2 use the basic processes of science: observation, classification, communication, operational questions, space relations, and number relations to collect data from a science activity.

3 define each of the basic processes of science: observation, classification, communication, operational questions, space relations, and number relations.

4 identify the basic processes as used in a science activity.

5 use the basic processes to develop science concepts through inquiry.

Introduction

Science classrooms should be active places where students use concrete materials to discover facts and concepts on their own. But although science educators have long thought this, their idea of how this activity should take place has changed many times.

One way of looking at process skills and inquiry was found in *Science: A Process Approach (SAPA)*, developed in the 1960s. In this program, processes were the main part of the curriculum and science content was secondary. This was a radical departure from a traditional textbook approach in which the curriculum was organized around the concepts of science. In *SAPA*, process became content. The outcome of the program was students who could use the methods of science to investigate a wide range of problems.

A differing view of science process skills and science inquiry is shown in the textbook series *Concepts in Science* (Brandwein et al., 1980). *Concepts* focused on concept seeking, that is, learning concepts in science through planned experiences. Concept seeking required activity on the part of children. "Their investigations may be of many kinds, ranging through simple discussion, library research, field trips, collection and observation of specimens, and perhaps a laboratory investigation as a culmination" (p. T–18). This quotation shows the general concept of activity, not as the focus of concept development, but as the final aspect of concept development. Rather than inquiry, rather than process use to develop concepts, process and the inquiry were used to verify concepts learned in other ways.

Finally, the *Science Curriculum Improvement Study (SCIS)* demonstrated a third viewpoint on the use of process skills. Within *SCIS*, process skills and inquiry were impossible to separate from the development of content. In fact, the total *SCIS* program was developed around the continual inquiry of children into science content. This view of inquiry of process skills, as indivisible from content development, as an integral part of the process of inquiry is now advocated by the *National Science Education Standards* (NRC, 1996).

The content standards for grades kindergarten through 8 list two items under the heading of Science as Inquiry. As a part of the science program, students should develop:

1. the abilities necessary to do scientific inquiry.
2. understandings about scientific inquiry. (pp. 109–110)

With these as the starting point, the *Standards* then go on to state that the science curriculum should be changed to promote greater emphasis on the following:

1. activities that investigate and analyze science questions
2. process skills in context
3. using multiple process skills—manipulation, cognitive, procedural

4. doing more investigations in order to develop understanding, ability, values of inquiry, and knowledge of science content (p. 113).

What each of these suggestions for change indicates is that science process skills and science inquiry cannot and should not be divorced from learning content information. Children should learn the process skills and develop their ability to inquire as they investigate meaningful science concepts. They should not learn process and inquiry skills in isolation before applying them to activities.

One of our roles as teachers is to assist our students in their inquiries, to help our students develop purposeful activities and experiments, to help our students gain the ability to inquire in a meaningful manner. If we are going to be able to help our students do these things, then we need to be familiar with the science process skills and with the process skills that are developmentally appropriate at each grade level.

The next three chapters are devoted to the commonly used process skills including the developmental appropriateness of those skills. This chapter outlines the basic processes. In Chapter 4, the causal processes are considered, and in Chapter 5 we discuss the experimental processes.

The Basic Processes of Science

The **basic processes** are those fundamental to any science activity: observation, classification, communication, operational questions, using space/time relations, and number relations. Not only are these process skills fundamental to the activity of inquiry, but they are also appropriate for all grade levels from kindergarten through eighth grade. In some cases the way in which the process skill is used varies from grade level to grade level or from developmental level to developmental level. These are considered basic processes because they form the foundation for the experimental processes. Learning to use numbers assists in data collection. Asking operational questions assists in learning to develop hypotheses. Classification is fundamental to the concept of interpreting data. Finally, the basic processes are appropriate for all children. Average children, gifted children, and mainstreamed or included children can all be successful using the basic processes.

Observation

Definition. The ability to observe accurately without first making judgments from those observations is the most basic of all of the science processes. Many of the things we call observations are actually interpretations of what we see, smell, taste, touch, or hear. Consequently, because most individuals almost automatically begin interpreting, making true observations can be difficult at first.

An **observation,** then, is a piece of information learned directly through the senses. An observation is a fact with which it is nearly impossible to argue, and no interpretation of such a piece of information is required. And, vice versa, a fact can be defined as an observation of high probability.

Observations are made through the use of each of the five senses: sight, touch, hearing, taste, smell. Using the sense of sight, students at any grade level can observe color, luster, relative size, surface markings, and object location. Through the sense of touch, students can observe such things as the texture and relative temperature of an object. Through the sense of hearing, students can observe similarities of sounds, considering pitch and loudness as relative ideas. Through the sense of taste, students can observe the sweetness, sourness, saltiness, or bitterness of an object. Finally, through the sense of smell, students can observe the similarity of one smell to another as well as the relative strength of an odor. When we look at the idea of relative size or temperature or at similarities between or among sounds and smells, we see that an observation is frequently preceded by the phrase, "It smells (tastes, etc.) like . . . " The term *like* immediately indicates that the observation is a comparison.

An Example of Observation.   Look at the patterns found in Figure 3.1. It could be an example of rather poor modern art; it could be a page from a coloring book for children that attempts to teach shapes as well as provide entertainment. With a good imagination, one could make this figure represent a dozen or more possibilities. But trying to decide what the page could represent is *not* observing. Look at the observations listed here and notice that no interpretations are involved.

1. There are nine shapes.
2. The shapes have different markings.
3. Three of the shapes are circular.
4. The background is white.
5. There is one striped shape.
6. Each shaded shape has two long parallel sides and two shorter parallel sides.
7. The dotted shape has three sides.
8. The dashed shape is irregular.
9. One cross-hatched shape has four sides, whereas the other cross-hatched shape has three sides.
10. All of the shapes are outlined in black.

There are many more observations we could make of the shapes appearing on the page. We have not even mentioned the smell or the texture of the page or of the proximity of one shape to another.

The main idea is that the observations listed here require no interpretation; they are simply statements of what is seen on the page. It would be impossible to argue that the striped shape is not striped or that there are not two cross-hatched shapes, one with four sides and one with three sides. It is unlikely that new observations will be made that will lead to a change in the observations listed here.

Figure 3.1

Observations

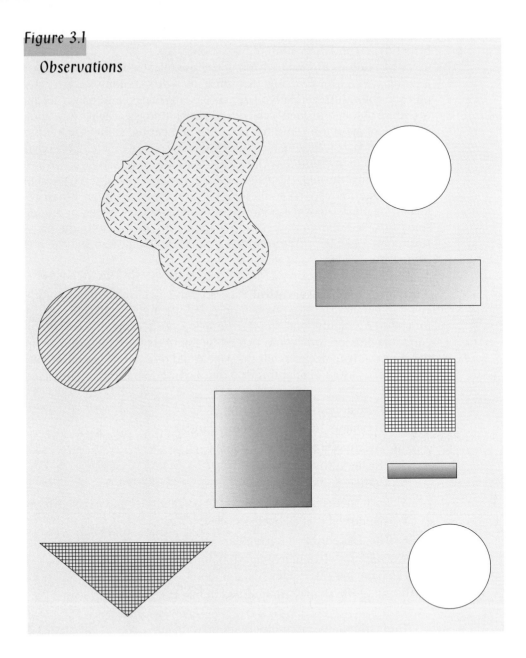

Observation as a Developmental Process.   Observations can be made by students at all grade levels, and, in fact, younger children are often better observers than adults as they try to determine the characteristics of what is in front of them instead of immediately drawing conclusions about what they think an object or event should be. Although developmental appropriateness in the use of observation is not a major concern, teachers should keep two factors in mind when using observation with preoperational children. First, preoperational children tend to center on a single characteristic. It is up to the teacher to help them extend their observations into a variety of characteristics. Recording the observations made by the children on a chalkboard, overhead, or experience chart can help demonstrate the variety of possibilities. Second, children at the preoperational stage are egocentric and so make observations based on their own points of view. If children are working directly with materials and making observations in conjunction with that direct experience, egocentricity should not be a problem. If they are making observations of a demonstration, then egocentricity could influence the ability to make observations. Concrete operational children generally have no difficult in making accurate observations, but students at the sixth, seventh, and eighth grade levels may fall into adult patterns by jumping to conclusions about what an object is before deciding on the characteristics of that object.

Observation and Science Content.   Observation is used in every science activity to gain content information, and the use of observation quickly changes the teacher's role from that of purveyor of information to that of facilitator of learning. Rather than telling second graders the characteristics of plants, the teacher can set up an activity in which those students observe and find the characteristics on their own. Rather than hearing a lecture on the kinds of weather brought by various types of clouds, fourth graders can observe the daily sky and see which types of weather and clouds are associated. Rather than looking at diagrams of the differences between plant and animal cells, seventh graders can look through microscopes and observe those differences for themselves. The process of observation should allow the children to develop their own knowledge from situations determined jointly by the teacher and the children. Other means of gaining information about a particular phenomenon, that is, books, films, filmstrips, or other sources, can then be used to further extend and develop the child's direct observations.

In order to be able to work effectively with observation in a classroom, you, as the teacher, should be able to observe effectively. Also, you should be able to determine how students at differing grade levels observe. Activities 3.1 through 3.4 are designed to help you learn to observe effectively and to assist in investigating observation among children at various grade levels.

Observation Activities

Activity 3.1

Purpose   To develop your own ability to make observations.

Procedure
Describe in as much detail as possible, using all of the appropriate senses, two of the following objects or phenomena. You should describe it so well that, without knowing the identify of the object or phenomena, another person could immediately name it.

1. a sunrise
2. a sunset
3. an animal
4. a flowering plant
5. a cake
6. a storm
7. the ocean
8. a pizza place or other restaurant
9. a forest
10. a cup of coffee, tea, or hot chocolate

Activity 3.2

Purpose   To compare and contrast the observations made by students at different grade levels.

Procedure
1. Prepare the following materials: clear plastic or glass container, club soda, 10 to 15 raisins.
2. Arrange to try the same activity with three children representing different grade levels (e.g., first, third, and sixth).
3. Do the following activity and either record the observations made by the children or ask the children to write down their own observations.
   a. Show the materials to the child and identify any that are unfamiliar.
   b. Ask the child to describe the objects either orally or in writing.
   c. Pour the club soda into the clear container so that it is within 2 cm of the top of the glass.
   d. Put in about five raisins and have the child observe what happens, recording the observations or describing those observations orally.
4. Compare and contrast the observations made by the students at each level. How are those observations similar? How are they different?
5. Knowing the developmental characteristics discussed in Chapter 2, how would these differences and similarities be predictable?

Activity 3.3

Purpose   To investigate the use of observation in textbook activities.

Procedure
1. Obtain at least three science textbooks for three different grade levels (e.g., third , fifth, and seventh).
2. Locate two activities or experiments within each of the grade levels.
3. Read the description of the activity, and if necessary, carry out the activity.
4. How is the process of observation used within each of the activities?
5. How does the use of observation differ from one grade level to another? Are the differences in use of observation from one grade level to another developmentally appropriate?

6. What could be done to extend the use of observation as it is found in each of the activities?

Activity 3.4

Purpose   To develop an activity appropriate to a range of grade levels that could be used to develop the students' ability to observe.

Procedure
1. Select a range of grade levels: kindergarten–second, third–fifth, or sixth–eighth.
2. Examine a textbook for the grade levels in your selection, and determine a content area in common to those grade levels.
3. Develop an activity that could be used to develop the observational abilities of the students at the grade level selected and is consistent with the common subject matter area.
4. Try your activity with a small group of children from one of the selected grade levels. Critique the success of your activity. What changes might you make to improve the activity? What developmental criteria are you applying in suggesting these changes?

Classification

Definition.   **Classification** is the ability to place objects into groups on the basis of the characteristics that those objects either do or do not possess. Classification ability moves from simply placing objects into groups on the basis of a single, easily observed characteristic such as color or texture to hierarchical classification like that used in the biological classification system.

Classification as a Developmental Process.   Through his investigations into the abilities of children to classify objects, Piaget showed that the ability to classify develops through various stages until the child is able to classify in the form of a true hierarchy. Even 2- or 3-year-olds try to order toys, pots and pans, and other items into groups or seriations, showing the start of a classification scheme. It is not, however, until the fifth or sixth grade that children reach the point where they are able to use the more complex forms of classification.

Simple Forms of Classification.   Four-year-old Ashley was given a set of circles, squares, triangles, and rectangles in the colors of red, blue, green, and yellow. Each of the shapes also had one thick and one thin representative. He was asked if he could put them into groups, and immediately he said he could. Ashley picked out all of the circles, then carefully arranged them so the thick yellow circle was on the bottom followed by a thick red circle, a thin green circle, and a thin yellow circle. He looked for another circle, shrugged when he couldn't find what he wanted, and then picked up the blue circle and put it on top of the others. At that point, he said he was done. I asked him to tell me about his group and he sighed as if I should have understood. Then he explained, "The fat yellow circle is white bread, the red circle is bologna, the green one is the lettuce, the skinny yellow one is the mustard, and I couldn't find another white bread so I used whole wheat." The whole wheat was the blue circle. Ashley was typical of many preschool children who were presented with a collection of squares, rectangles, circles, and triangles and asked to put these shapes into groups. Ashley is showing developmentally appropriate behavior according to the work of Piaget. Rather than groups, young children form **patterns** or **pictures** from the shapes and consider those patterns to be groups. Figure 3.2 shows the kinds of patterns and shapes children at the preschool level often use.

Figure 3.2

Classification Through Patterns and Pictures

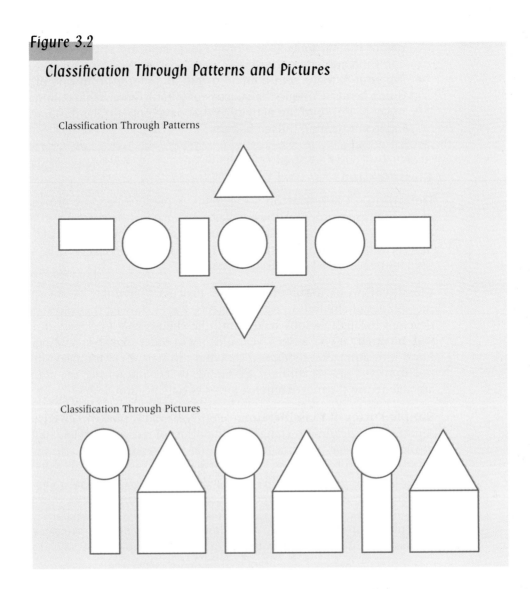

Classification Through Patterns

Classification Through Pictures

According to Piaget, the kind of classification used by children changes as children mature. At about kindergarten level children begin to place shapes or other objects into groups; however, these groups do not have a great deal of stability, and a child frequently changes the characteristics on which the grouping is based. A kindergartner may start gathering triangles but notice that the second triangle is blue; then the child may select the next object after the triangle because it is also blue, but a blue circle. At kindergarten level a child, using **resemblance sorting,** may change the trait with each of the objects or keep the same trait for a few of the objects before changing to something else. Consequently, all of the original pile of objects may end up in a single pile again. A second feature of kindergarten classification is that children may not classify all they are given. This tendency is termed a lack of **exhaustive sorting.** This occurs either because the remaining objects do not readily fit into the current grouping property used by the child or because the child has grown tired of the task.

During first and second grade and usually by the time a child reaches 8 years of age, the groupings he or she chooses have become stable, provided the child is attempting to classify by a single trait. Between 6 and 8 years of age, children are able to choose a single characteristic and to classify on the basis of that characteristic but find it difficult to use more than one characteristic at a time. Primary grade children are usually able to classify on the basis of either color or shape but not on the basis of both color and shape. During this period, the children become able to classify all objects and are said to be able to use exhaustive sorting.

As children move into fourth and fifth grade they are able to classify using two or more characteristics at a time, that is, to use **multiple traits.** Classification at these intermediate grade levels is generally fairly easy and children rarely make errors in their classification. In fact, this is the level at which many children become serious collectors of stamps, baseball cards, toy cars, or rocks and classify those collections into accurate categories with little or no difficulty. When children are able to use multiple traits in classification, the transition to hierarchical classification becomes possible.

Hierarchical Classification.   Only after children have had experience and success using multiple traits in classification should they be expected to use hierarchical classification. **Hierarchical classification** is a sophisticated form of classification involving the use of sets and subsets of categories. The traditional classification system used in biology is a hierarchical system. The system shown in Figure 3.3 could be used to classify the children at the sixth, seventh, or eighth grade level.

A true hierarchical classification system has ten criteria that must be met if the system is to be correct in all ways:

1. All objects must be classified even if a unique object must be placed in a class by itself.
2. No class can be isolated from the rest of the system.
3. A class includes all objects having a certain, specified characteristic.
4. A class can include only those objects that have a certain, specified property.

Figure 3.3

Hierarchical Classification System

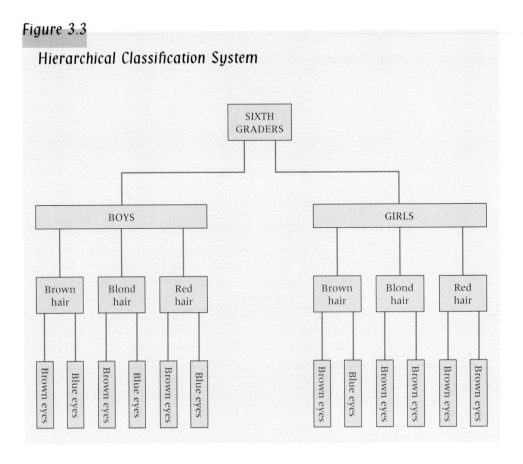

5. All classes of the same rank in the system must be disjoint (detached and distinct).

6. A complementary class has its own characteristics, which are not possessed by its complement.

7. A class is included in each higher ranking class that contains all of its objects.

8. The objects included in a class are the minimum compatible with the defining properties of the class.

9. Similar characteristics are used to distinguish classes of the same rank.

10. Classes must be divided symmetrically (Piaget, 1972).

Figure 3.3 illustrates a classification system that is consistent with these ten rules. Figure 3.4 illustrates a classification system that violates classification rules 2, 5, 9, and 10.

The process of classification develops from a very simple form to a highly complex form. Piaget's work on classification indicates the kinds of classification experiences that children can be given as a part of the kindergarten through eighth grade science program and the kinds of experiences which will allow children to succeed. Likewise, the Piagetian view of classification gives an indication of what can be

Figure 3.4

Hierarchical Classification System Incorrectly Done

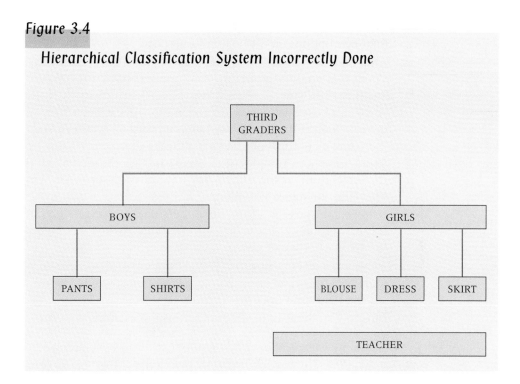

expected of children as they try to understand and use classification to develop the concepts of science.

Using Classification to Develop Concepts. Classification is often used within scientific inquiry as a means for organizing objects and information. In the former case, students involved in investigating soil and soil types may classify the materials found in loam, topsoil, clay soil, sand, and potting soil and then use the classifications as a way of comparing the kinds of soils. In the former case, students may classify the information found through reading or viewing films into categories which allow them to communicate that information more succinctly to others. Students investigating animals, therefore, may classify the information into the categories of body characteristics, diet, habitat, and reproductive method. Such a classification can allow a great deal of disparate information to be organized more effectively.

However, classification can also be used outside of the specific realm of inquiry. In this case, classification can be used in a direct teaching method to develop a particular concept or can be used as a way of introducing a new topic of study.

Classification in Concept Development. Simple classification can be used to help students develop a concept. In general, this involves a nine-step process:

1. Show examples of the concept through pictures or simple demonstrations using only one item at a time.

2. As each item is shown, ask the students to describe what they see. Record their descriptions on the board or overhead.

3. After showing about three items, have the students begin to focus on the similarities among the items. Continue recording their descriptions on the board or overhead.

4. After all of the pictures or demonstrations have been shown, ask the students to look at the things listed on the board or overhead and to pick two of them that all of the items had in common.

5. Show some nonexamples of the items and ask the students if they belong in the same group as the things they have already seen. Ask why they do not belong. Begin a new grouping.

6. Show some "possibles" and have the students decide whether they fit into the first grouping or the second grouping. Always ask students why they belong in a particular group.

7. Name the concept using the criteria decided on by the group.

8. Show examples and nonexamples of the concept and have the students classify the items into the proper group.

9. Have the students brainstorm other examples of the concept.

This strategy was used by a first grade teacher in developing a beginning concept of a mammal. The teacher began by telling the children she was going to show them some pictures. After each picture she was going to ask them what they saw. The first picture was of a raccoon. The children said it had eyes, ears, fur, feet, hands, was brown, and was on a log. The second picture was of a pony. Once again the characteristics were listed on the board as the children itemized them. The third picture was of a cheetah, and again the characteristics were listed. The teacher made a check mark beside characteristics that had been identified once and were voiced again. Before showing the fourth picture the teacher asked the children to start looking for how the animal in the picture was the same as the other animals. She then showed pictures of a buffalo, a lion, a wolf, a baboon, and a mouse. The pictures were set in a group on the ledge of the chalkboard where they could all be seen.

"Joey is absent today. When he comes to school tomorrow what could we tell him about how all of the animals in the picture are alike?" the teacher asked.

The children decided they all had fur and they all had four legs.

The teacher then said she had some other pictures to show them. "I want you to decide if I should put these animals in the same group as the animals we've already seen or if I need a new group." She then showed pictures of a frog, a snake, a seagull, a fish, and a chameleon. The children decided they didn't fit because they didn't have any fur and, in the case of the snake and the fish, they didn't have any legs at all. The seagull was rejected on the basis of fur. But because it had two legs and two wings, they weren't so sure about the other characteristic. At this point, the teacher told them she had three other pictures that were hard to decide on. One was of an emu whose feathers looked rather furry, a spider that looked furry, and a caterpillar which seemed to have hair. The children decided all of these animals had to go into the pile with the fish and frog because even though they seemed hairy or furry they all had the wrong number of legs.

"So we have one group of animals with fur and four legs and another group of animals that doesn't fit these characteristics. Animals like these with fur and four legs are called 'mammals.' Let's see if we can decide which of the animals in these next pictures are mammals and which are not mammals." The children then decided into which category a bear, an elk, an iguana, a robin, a shark, a beetle, a deer, a zebra, a tiger, and a picture of a man with a full beard belonged. They correctly classified the pictures as mammals or nonmammals. When they were finished with the pictures, the teacher asked the children if they could name some other animals that would be mammals. They named dogs, cats, cows, horses, sheep, goats, and themselves.

In this particular lesson, the type of classification used was appropriate to first grade children. They could look at one characteristic at a time, first looking to see if the animals had fur and then looking for and counting the legs. The classification itself resulted in two groups: mammals and not-mammals. Based on the characteristics considered in this lesson, the class could then move on to looking at other characteristics of mammals.

Although this example is appropriate for the first grade level, the same sort of procedure is appropriate for any grade level from kindergarten through eight grade or beyond.

Classification in Introducing a Unit. Students need to have a little bit of information already in their cognitive structures if they are to remember new information in a meaningful manner. David Ausubel (1960) referred to this bit of information as a **cognitive anchor.** Classification can be used at the start of a new unit in order to develop that cognitive anchor and to provide students with an overview of the information they will be learning. In this case, the teacher uses questioning strategies and a hierarchical classification system to organize and present an overview of the unit. In general, the teacher begins with aspects of the information that will be familiar to the children and works toward information which will be least familiar to the students. Figure 3.5 shows a hierarchical system used to introduce a unit on animals as part of a seventh grade biology class.

In using hierarchical classification in this way, the teacher develops the system with the assistance of the students so their experiences are incorporated into the system and therefore into the overview of the unit.

In introducing this seventh grade unit on animals, the teacher begins by placing the word *animals* on the chalkboard or overhead and drawing a box around it. The teacher then tells the class that they already know a lot about one of the groups of animals they will be considering. The teacher than asks the students to run their fingers up the middle of their backs and then asks what they feel. They feel their own backbone. The teacher then draws a new box connecting it to the term *animals* and introduces the word *vertebrate* as an animal with a backbone. At this point the teacher asks students to name some animals. From the animals named, the teacher helps the class to identify the five classes of vertebrates: fish, amphibians, reptiles, birds, and mammals. With each identified class, the teacher asks the students to talk

Figure 3.5

Classification of Animals

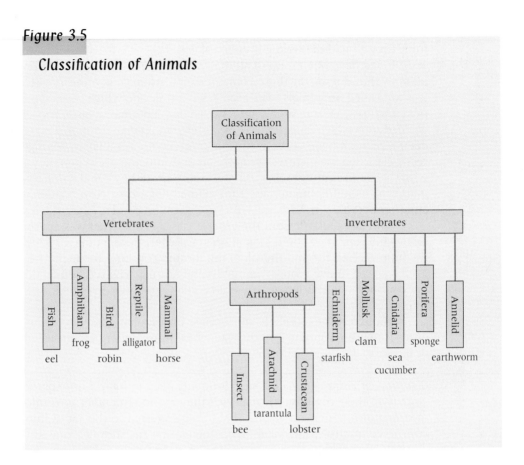

about the characteristics of each of the classes as they are identified. In addition, she asks the students to give some examples of the various classes. The classes and the examples are added to the classification system being developed on the board.

Vertebrate animals are generally familiar to students, but invertebrates are generally not so familiar. The term *invertebrate* is added to the chart and defined for the class as an animal that does not have a backbone. Because the phyla of invertebrates is generally not familiar to students, the teacher needs to begin by giving the children a situation where they are likely to meet up with invertebrate animals. If children are familiar with the seashore, asking them to think about the kinds of animals they often see there is a good starting place. A list of the animals is made. From the list, the teacher then introduces the names of the vertebrate phyla used in the chapter: Arthropoda, Porifera, Cnidaria (Coelenterata), Annelida, Echinodermata, and Mollusca, and then further defines the arthropods into the classes of crustacea, Arachnoidea, and Insecta. As these are defined, the teacher gives ways to recall the various phyla and classes. For example, Porifera can be remembered because it sounds like pores, and sponges have lots of pores. Arthropoda can be remembered because when people have arthritis their joints hurt. Finally, the teacher uses the examples given by the students as examples of each of the phyla and classes. These are added to the classification chart developing on the board. At this point the chart is finished and an overview of the unit has been shown. The overview allows students to see what they will be studying, gives a glimpse of the kinds of works they will be eventually learning, and uses familiar examples, given by the students to elucidate the new groupings of animals. In this way, hierarchical classification activates recall of previously learned material and provides that cognitive anchor which will allow children to incorporate new information meaningfully into the cognitive structure.

Activities 3.5 through 3.9 are designed to put into practice the information considered in this section on classification and will give you an opportunity to compare the kinds of classification used by children at various grade levels as well as to develop a concept development strategy and a unit introduction strategy based on classification.

Classification Activities

Activity 3.5

Purpose   To develop your ability to use various forms of classification.

Procedure
1. List the first 30 objects you see in an elementary or middle school classroom.
2. Look at the list and decide on five or more traits that could be used to classify those objects.
3. Classify the objects on the basis of only one of those characteristics. What problems did you encounter in developing your classification system?
4. Classify the objects on the basis of more than one characteristic at a time. What problems did you encounter in developing your classification system?
5. Develop a hierarchical system that could be used to classify the objects in the classroom. Try to classify those objects to the point that each object is in a class by itself. What problems did you encounter in using this type of classification system?

Activity 3.6

Purpose   To investigate the use of classification in textbook activities.

Procedure
1. Obtain at least three science textbooks for three different grade levels (e.g., third , fifth, and seventh).
2. Locate two activities or experiments within each of the grade levels.
3. Read the description of the activity, and if necessary, carry out the activity.
4. How is the process of classification used within each of the activities?

5. How does the use of classification differ from one grade level to another? Is the type of classification developmentally appropriate?
6. What could be done to extend the use of classification as it is found in each of the activities?

Activity 3.7

Purpose To develop an activity appropriate to a particular grade level and that will teach a concept through the use of classification.

Procedure
1. Select a grade level from kindergarten through grade 8.
2. Examine a textbook for the selected grade level and choose one concept.
3. Develop a strategy for teaching that concept through classification which uses the technique described on pages 77–78.
4. Try your activity with a small group of children from the selected grade levels. Critique the success of your activity. What changes might you make to improve the activity?

Activity 3.8

Purpose To develop a strategy for using classification to introduce a science unit at a particular grade level.

Procedure
1. Select a grade level from fifth through eighth grade.
2. Examine a textbook for that grade level and select one unit.
3. Using the strategy outlined on pages 79–80 develop a strategy for introducing your selected unit through hierarchical classification.
4. Try your activity with a small group of children from the selected grade level. Critique the success of your activity. What changes might you make to improve the activity?

Activity 3.9

Purpose To develop a list of ways in which classification is used in the daily lives of children at various grade levels.

Procedure
1. In order for children to learn to classify with understanding, they should be able to see classification used in ways that are meaningful to them. List five ways in which classification could be shown in the daily lives of children at each of the following grade level ranges:
   a. Kindergarten through second
   b. Third through fifth
   c. Sixth through eighth
2. Describe how you might incorporate your examples into your science teaching in developmentally appropriate ways.

Communication

Definition.   Communication is any means for passing information from one individual or group of individuals to another. All too frequently, communication is considered to be through words, only through words, and preferably only through words on the printed page of a book. For young children, words and symbols for words are the least appropriate means of communication. This does not mean that oral and written communication should or could be avoided, but it does mean that other types of communication should also be available to the child and teacher.

Types of Communication Used with Students.

Pictures.   Pictures are a good means of communication for all students, but particularly for those who tend to use their spatial intelligence. Drawings in paint, pencil, crayon, or any other medium can help the student to get across those ideas that he or she wishes to communicate. For very young children, pictures may not convey much because their drawing skills do not allow for realism. However, even the most abstract pictures can serve as a basis for the child to talk about a picture, so that the teacher can write an appropriate caption. Older students can both draw their own pictures and write their own stories to go along with those pictures. As students reach the sixth, seventh, and eight grade levels, drawings and sketches can be a part of observational and experimental records showing such things as flower parts, arrangements of equipment for an experimental procedure, objects viewed through a microscope, or diagrams of internal organs from a dissection.

Journals.   **Journals** are a means for recording and communicating information that can be used at a every level. Because of the use of written communication within a journal, the child of high linguistic intelligence has a particularly appropriate form of communication. Particularly for young children, journals should not be tied to accuracy of spelling, grammar, or punctuation. Revising and editing can take place in order to further develop accuracy in writing skills. With older students, a science journal can reflect not only a growing understanding of inquiry and concepts but also of written communication forms. At the seventh and eight grade levels, a journal can take on the more formal look of a lab notebook including experimental results and displays of data as well as observations and diagrams, but room should always be available for students to write, to question, and to speculate.

Models.   Closely tied to using pictures for communication is using **models,** or representations. Models can be made from clay, papier-mâché, paper, boxes, straws, toothpicks, or any other readily available materials. Models allow children not only to communicate ideas but also to explore spatial relationships in three dimensions. As such, models are highly appropriate for children possessing spatial intelligence. Models also give the child something to talk about if oral communication is being used. For young children, models should be as similar to the modeled objects as possible, so that the child is not forced, for example, to pretend a balloon is a lung and a glass jar the chest cavity.

As students reach the sixth, seventh, and eight grade levels and begin to make the transition into formal operational thought processes, the use of models can be increased. Models of the internal structure of Earth, the solar system, or of the internal organs of the body can be understood by students who are reaching these more abstract thought processes. And students can create models from items that have little or no relationship to the real components and still understand them. For students at sixth, seventh, and eight grade levels, a model of an animal cell composed of gelatin, macaroni, yarn, and various kinds of beans will have meaning. For younger students such a model would be difficult to comprehend.

Movement.   **Movement** is also an appropriate communication means for children, especially those showing high levels of bodily intelligence. Forming shapes with their bodies, showing how animals behave by role playing, pretending to be growing plants, or demonstrating different types of motions, all allow younger children to investigate the common phenomena of their world with their entire bodies, thus involving them in the large muscle activities so appropriate to their physical development. Somewhat less active, yet still involving movement, are fingerplays, which combine science with language and music. For the most part, movement is more appropriate to younger children, kindergarten through fourth grade, than to students in fifth through eighth grades, but the option should be present for those students who show high levels of bodily intelligence.

Music.   **Music** such as songs can help children with high musical intelligence to relate science to their preferred modes of thinking and other children to relate science to other parts of the curriculum. Including music is especially good if children have the opportunity to write their own words and music. Making instruments as a part of science, decorating them as a part of art, and finally performing the songs written in language arts and music integrate all areas of the curriculum.

Although activities dealing with music seem to be most appropriate for students at the primary grades, music can also be used as a means of communication in the upper grades. Students at seventh or eight grade may have the musical skill to write songs about topics of study, particularly those dealing with environmental and social issues, or to create rhythms that will allow certain facts and terms to be recalled more easily.

Oral Communication.   Oral forms of communication should develop naturally from the activities of the science program. In this way, the child is able to see the purpose for learning appropriate oral communication skills.

Usually, the best way to include oral communication is to make that communication an integral part of the activity, so that language use follows logically from the firsthand, concrete experiences of the child. Such a sequence of **oral communication**—concrete first, language second—allows students at any grade level to have something real to talk about rather than trying to rephrase the ideas contained in a text or story. Questions from the teacher that lead students to talk about the salient points of an activity can be very helpful to the students. Such questions should start with something obvious; in that way all students can answer and all students can experience success. Other questions can then lead the children to make observations they may have missed, to construct inferences, or to draw conclusions about the activity.

In many cases, cooperative learning groups or small groups can be arranged to facilitate communication during and before activities and experiments or as a reading and discussion strategy for sharing information gained through research.

Activities 3.10 through 3.14 focus on applying the process of communication at various grade levels.

Communication Activities

Activity 3.10

Purpose To investigate the use of communication in preschool- and kindergarten-level children.

Procedure
1. Collect the following materials: yellow and blue finger paint, white paper, water, sponge, plastic or newspaper to cover a table. Have enough materials so that groups of three or four children can work with the finger paints.
2. Have the children work freely with the fingerpaints to create pictures and to find out what happens when the colors are mixed.
3. After the children have had ample time to work with the finger paints and to make a number of pictures, make an experience chart with them. Use large paper with lines about 2.5 cm apart placed where all of the children can see the words as they are written. Use the children's exact words on the chart and attempt to have all of the children contribute to the chart.
4. If the children can read, have them read the chart to you and to the others in the group when it is finished. If the children cannot read, read the chart to them.
5. How would you characterize the communication of these children? What problems did you encounter in creating the chart? How might you overcome these problems?

Activity 3.11

Purpose To investigate the use of communication among kindergarten through second grade children.

Procedure
1. Collect the following materials: 10 to 15 pictures of mammals; a living hamster, guinea pig, or mouse; and 10 to 15 pictures of nonmammals.
2. With a group of about five children, use the pictures and the animal to develop the concept of a mammal.
3. Have the children draw a picture of a mammal and a picture of an animal that is not a mammal. Have the children write a description of their picture and of what they think a mammal is.

4. Collect the children's pictures. (You may need to assure the children that you will return their pictures at another time.) Review the pictures and writing.
5. What generalizations can you make about the use of pictures and writing as means of communication for children at the chosen grade level? What could you do to overcome some of the problems of using these forms of communication?

Activity 3.12

Purpose To investigate the use of communication among third through fifth grade children.

Procedure
1. Collect the following materials: paper, chalk, metersticks. Have enough materials for five children.
2. Find a sunny location where children can work outdoors safely. Four or five times during the day, have the children go outdoors to the same location and measure the length of their shadows. This can be done most easily by having one child stand still while a second draws a chalk line the length of the first child's shadow. Each child should measure the length of all the shadows cast: his or her own as well as those cast by the other children. Each child should keep a record of the measurements of each of the shadows. Do not provide the children with a chart to use.
3. After the last measurements have been made, discuss with the children what they learned about shadows and have them write a description of what they learned. Collect the papers on which the description and the measurements were recorded.
4. How well do you think the children understood the idea that shadows change in size during the day? How do the descriptions written indicate an understanding or lack of understanding?
5. Look at the data sheet collected. How systematic was the collection of the data? What are some of the problems you see? How could you overcome those problems?

Activity 3.13

Purpose To investigate the use of communication among sixth through eighth grade students.

Procedure
1. Collect the following materials for each group: two metersticks, tennis ball, Ping-Pong ball, golf ball, rubber ball.
2. Have the students work in groups of four with at least two groups. Present the groups with the following challenge: How could you find out the best conditions to get a ball to bounce the highest?

3. Allow the students to work in groups to develop a procedure, carry out their activity, and record and interpret their results. Have the students keep a written record of their entire activity.
4. While the groups work, eavesdrop on their discussions and make notes about the kinds of comments made by the students.
5. When the students finish the activities, have each group present its activity and discuss its results.
6. Prepare a paper describing the communication used among and between students at the selected grade level. Include in your paper a description of the written records kept as well as the deliberations as the students developed their activities.

Activity 3.14

Purpose   To develop a strategy for including communication within a lesson and then to critique the strategy.

Procedure
1. Involve a group of five children from any grade level in an activity you have developed to alert them to one of the following environmental problems: water pollution, air pollution, acid rain, decreasing number of rain forests, endangered species.
2. Following the activity, have the children communicate to you what they learned in a way that is appropriate both to the activity and to the grade level.
   a. What level or age of children did you choose?
   b. What concept did you teach?
   c. What was your activity?
   d. What method of communication did you try? What reason did you have for choosing that method?
   e. Did the students learn what you expected them to learn?
   f. What did they do to indicate that they had learned? What did they learn that you had not expected them to learn?
   g. What errors in their learning did you find? How might you account for those errors?
   h. What problems did you encounter with the kind of communication you chose to use? What could be done to overcome these problems?

Operational Questions

Definition.   An **operational question** is, first of all, a productive question and one that when asked can be answered through hands-on investigation by the child or children who first asked the question. An operational question has the following characteristics:

1. It does not begin with why. "Why" generally requires a theoretical or philosophical answer.
2. It cannot be answered with a simple yes or no.
3. It has inherent in the question a means for investigating the question and so providing an answer through inquiry.
4. It can be investigated through the use of simple materials.
5. It allows for a variety of changes in some factor.
6. It is asked and investigated by students.

Here are some examples of operational questions:

1. What would happen to the number of times the pendulum swings if the length of the string were changed?
2. How does the kind of liquid you use change the shape of the drops you get?
3. How does the surface affect the height to which a ball will bounce?
4. What happens to light when it goes through liquids other than water?
5. How does the weight of a paper airplane affect the distance it flies?
6. In what kind of soil will radish seeds grow best?

Questions Asked by Children.   Questions frequently seem to make up the bulk of child-to-adult conversation. These is almost no difficulty getting children to ask questions. The problem comes, of course, in answering those questions.

By trying to answer all of the questions our students ask us, we do a disservice to our students. Helping students to answer their own questions, however, helps develop problem solving and research skills. Although attempting to answer every question asked by a group of children may not lead teachers to insanity, it often leads teachers to feelings of inferiority or, at least, of inadequacy in the area of science. Faced with a question like, "Why aren't there any dinosaurs today?" teachers have a number of options:

1. Use words the child does not understand and give an answer: "Archaeosaurs became extinct because of macroclimatic variation in the biosphere."
2. Give a simple answer and hope for no further questions: "They died."
3. Tell the truth: "I really don't know." The trick in this response is *not* to follow it up with a qualifier:
   "I'll try to find out for you."
   "Why don't you find out and let me know."
   "You'll learn about that in seventh grade."
   "We're studying plants, *not* dinosaurs."
4. Ignore the question entirely.
5. Refer the child to the librarian to find a book.

In each case, the questioning student has little or no involvement in answering the question. In some cases, there is no answer given, and the student's curiosity is left unsatisfied. The question, "Why aren't there dinosaurs today?" is a nonproductive question. It is also typical of the kinds of questions asked by children encountering new science phenomena. When children ask questions, they frequently begin with "Why" or "What."

"Why does a seed sprout?"
"Why is the Moon round?"
"What makes a battery work?"
"What makes light turn into a rainbow when it goes through a prism?"
"Why is Tommy taller than Jane?"

These questions all call for highly theoretical or very complex answers. And, just as with the question about dinosaurs, these answers can be found only by reading or by asking an authority. In any case, few children are able to benefit from the answers that they receive because they simply do not have the cognitive structures or the experiential backgrounds to understand.

Children at any grade level can be helped to ask productive questions that involve them directly in finding answers and develop the experiential background necessary for later understanding of complex theories. These questions are called *operational questions*—a term originally coined by Dorothy Alfke—and are productive questions.

Developing Children's Ability to Use Operational Questions.   Children do not automatically use operational questions, but they can learn to ask them with some ease. Activities can be planned to elicit questions from students. Some unusual or interesting phenomenon can be shown and the children given the opportunity to ask any questions they have. These questions can be recorded on the chalkboard and then reworded as operational questions that the children can investigate through the use of concrete objects. Once the children understand the basic idea of an operational question, whenever they ask questions they can be helped to rephrase those questions as operational questions that can be investigated.

In addition to recording and revising nonoperational questions into operational format, a second means of helping students to learn to ask and investigate operational questions is for the teacher to model this type of question. For example, if children are investigating objects which sink and objects which float and find out that clay will sink, the teacher could model operational questioning behavior by asking children, "What do you think would happen if you changed the shape of the clay?" In working with solubility, the teacher could model operational questions by asking, "What do you think would happen to the amount of salt that will dissolve if you change the temperature of the water you're using?"

Once the teacher has modeled operational questions and the children are encouraged to investigate to find the answers, children will begin to ask similar questions and to develop investigations spontaneously.

Of course, other kinds of questions can be asked and investigated. Some questions and topics do not lend themselves to rewording as operational questions. It would be very difficult to ask an operational question about dinosaurs, Moon trips, nuclear energy, or endangered species. Consequently, operational questions are only one of the many ways to gain information that children should be encouraged to use.

Activities 3.15 through 3.17 are designed to engage you and children in the use and investigation of operational questions.

Operational Question Activities

Activity 3.15

Purpose   To investigate kinds of questions asked by children in kindergarten, first, and second grade.

Procedure
1. Arrange to work with groups of children from two of the three grade levels.
2. Collect the following materials so that each child in a group of five or six children has a set to work with: liquid detergent or commercial bubbles, straws, paper tubes, bubble pipes and other objects that can be used to blow bubbles, paper towels, newspaper or plastic, paper cups, water.
3. Pour about an inch of detergent or bubble liquid into paper cups so that each child has a cup. If using detergent, add a little water to the cup. Use the straws or bubble pipes to blow some bubbles for the children to watch. Talk about bubbles for a few minutes, and then have the children blow bubbles. Use the newspaper or plastic to cover the area and contain the resulting mess.
4. While the children blow bubbles, as they talk to one another, and following the activity, keep a record of the questions the children ask. Write the questions just as the children phrase them. You might ask, after the activity, what questions about bubbles the children have.
5. Review the list of children's questions. Classify the questions as operational or nonoperational and rewrite as operational questions any of the questions that are nonoperational.

Activity 3.16

Purpose   To investigate the use of operational questions with children in third through fifth grades.

Procedure
1. Select two of the following grade levels to work with: third, fourth, fifth.
2. Collect the following materials: clear plastic cups, warm water, ice, red, blue, and yellow food coloring, water at room temperature. Plan an assort-

ment of these materials with more than enough for a group of five children.

3. Collect the following materials for *your* use: two quart glass jars, hot water, ice water, blue food coloring. Fill one jar about half full of hot water and the other half full of cold water.

4. Place both of the jars on the table in full view of the children. Have the children touch the outside of the jar with the *cold* water to establish the fact that the water is cold. Do not allow the children to handle the jar with the hot water, but do tell them it is hot.

5. While the children watch, place a few drops of food coloring in each of the jars. Discuss with the children the differences in the rate at which the color spreads through the two jars of water.

6. Ask if they have any questions about what happened. Collect the questions. With the children, rewrite some of the questions into operational questions. Have the children use the materials to find the answers to one or more of their questions.

7. Considering each group separately: What problems did you encounter in working with the children using this method? How might you overcome those problems?

8. Compare and contrast the two grade level groups. How where they similar? Different?

Activity 3.17

Purpose To investigate the use of operational questions with children in sixth through eighth grades.

Procedure
1. Select two of the following grade levels to work with: sixth, seventh, eighth.

2. Collect the following materials: two quart jars with lids, rubbing alcohol (three pints), ice cubes, water, marker. The alcohol and water should be at room temperature. Prior to working with the children, fill one jar about two-thirds full of alcohol and label it A. Fill the other jar about two-thirds full of water and label it B. Put the lids tightly on the jars. Have the ice ready.

3. Place the jars on a table in front of a group of five or six students. Have the students observe the two jars and write down their observations. Discuss the observations. Then, as the children watch, place two or three ice cubes in each of the two jars, quickly replacing the lids so that the odor of alcohol does not reach the students.

4. Have the students make observations again. Then have them ask questions about what happened. As each questions is asked, have the students reword them until you have an operational question that can be investigated using the materials available. Try to draw a conclusion about the activity.

5. Compare and contrast the questions by each of the two grade levels. Compare and contrast the development of the operational questions between the two groups.

Space Relations

Definition. **Space relations,** as a process, uses three major geometric concepts: solid geometric forms, plane geometric forms, and measurement as a part of data collection. In general, geometric forms and measurement skills need to be approached prior to their use in science activities.

Solid Geometric Forms. **Solid geometric forms** is the first area of space relations. The preschool, kindergarten, and first grade child should already have experiences with those solid shapes that are common to their environment: sphere, cube, rectangular solid, pyramid, prism, cylinder, cone. Such shapes are commonly seen in the child's environment as balls, boxes, blocks, tents, ice cream cones, and cans. Sixth, seventh, and eighth grade students should be thoroughly familiar with these shapes and may even have experience with determining volume through calculations using a formula.

Plane Geometric Forms. As children gain familiarity with the solid shapes, and beginning about the first grade, the second concept, that of plane geometric shapes, can be introduced. The **plane geometric forms** may first be considered in relation to the already known solid shapes: cylinders show circles as their bases, the sides of rectangles, a pyramid has triangular sides. Other common shapes like the pentagon, hexagon, and octagon, as well as the parallelogram and rhombus, can be introduced in terms of objects in the environment. Snowflakes are hexagons. A stop sign is an octagon and some of the tables found in classrooms are trapezoids. By the end of the third grade, the child should be familiar enough with both plane and solid shapes so that he or she can use them in making observations.

Once again, by sixth, seventh, and eighth grade, students should have a good grasp of concepts such as perimeter, area, and, in the case of circles, diameter and circumference.

Teaching Young Children Geometric Forms. The following procedure for teaching both plane and sold geometric forms tends to work very well. It is particularly designed for introducing young children to the various shapes.

Step 1. Introduce one shape at a time using familiar concrete objects.

Step 2. Allow the children to work with the shape until they have developed a concept of the shape and can recognize it in the environment. The objects should be freely handled by the students.

Step 3. Through questions, concrete objects, and semiconcrete examples, help the children discover the characteristics of the shape. Have the children use observation rather than telling the children the characteristics.

Step 4. After a concept of the shape has been developed, have the class compare it with other shapes in the environment, so that the children begin to know what the shape is as well as what it is not.

Step 5. Each time a new shape is introduced, preface the lesson with a review of each of the previously learned shapes.

Measurement. The third concept used in space relations is measurement. **Measurements,** such as length, area, weight, and volume, are all part of space relations. These concepts, however, require more complex cognitive understandings than does the recognition of plane or solid shapes. For a true understanding of these concepts, the child needs to have attained conservation. According to Piaget, conservation of each of these measurement concepts is attained at approximately the following ages:

conservation of length—about 8 years

conservation of area—conceptually after 8 years and computationally at about 11 years.

conservation of weight—about 10 years.

conservation of volume—conceptually after 11 years and computationally after 15 years.

Consequently, in working with space relations, those relations that involve measurement should be introduced at about the third grade level. Prior to the third grade level, informal means of measurement can be used to develop needed background information.

With students in the sixth, seventh, and eighth grades, measurement should form an integral part of science activities and experiments. Derived measurements such as density and specific gravity can also begin to be included. However, even at this level, the concept of volume has not fully developed, and so it is not a good idea to simply rely on the calculation of volume by formula. Instead, have a concrete means for determining volume of objects as well as a computational format.

Informal Measurement. Children can use **informal measurement** to measure by placing shoes end to end and counting how many shoes long a room is or by pacing off the length of the room and counting the number of steps taken, or measurements can be made using hands, body lengths, paper clips, strings, or any other uniform objects that children can lay end to end and count. At first, it is a good idea to have enough objects so that the entire length or width under consideration can be covered; this will eliminate the problem of moving the object and remembering not only the original position but the number of times the object was used. After using such informal means of measurement, children should be conceptually ready to develop the more formal concepts of measurement consistently used in the sciences.

Formal Measurement. **Formal measurement** uses a particular standard as well as specific devices for measuring. Because of its simplicity and common usage in science, the metric system is probably the best formal measurement system to use in the elementary science program.

An appropriate sequence in teaching the metric system is to begin with the meter, using the meterstick to teach not only how to measure length but also the standard prefixes of the system. Once the children are able to use the meter to comprehend the use of the prefixes, move to the use of the liter as a measure of liquid volume. Finally, work with the gram and kilogram as measurements of mass. Practice with measuring devices and with direct measurement of length, mass, and volume should occur before the children are expected to use the metric system in their science classes.

If both the metric system and the English system are known to the children or are being taught simultaneously, use only one system consistently in the science program rather than both. Consistency in the choice and use of a method of formal measurement may help prevent confusion of units.

At upper grade levels, students can begin to look at the relationships existing between mass and volume within the metric system and can also utilize derived measurements such as the newton, acceleration due to gravity, or erg.

Using Space Relations.   Once the various shapes are known and the ability to measure informally or formally has been developed, the process of using space relations should be considered an aspect of observation. Children should be encouraged to describe objects in terms of the various solid and plane shapes as soon as they are familiar enough with these shapes for them to be meaningful. Measurements, both formal and informal, should also be taken as soon as children are able to understand them.

Number Relations

Definition.   Using number relations involves more abstract concepts than do any of the previously considered processes. **Number relations** is the process of using numbers to describe the outcome or ongoing occurrences of an activity. This includes the use of graphs. According to Piaget, children do not typically conserve number until approximately 6.5 years of age, so the process of number relations should probably be delayed until late first or second grade levels.

Sequencing the Use of Number Relations: Numerical Forms.   The kind of number relation used in a science activity should be matched to the mathematical level of the children. In general, children should be introduced to the mathematical skill they will be asked to use outside of the activity, in the mathematics class, and then helped to apply that skill to science activities.

Counting.   **Counting,** both ordinal and cardinal, should be the first use of number relations encountered by children. Collection of data like the following can form the child's first encounter with quantification in science activities:

1. How many seeds did you plant?

2. How many ways did you find to classify the stones?
3. How many children like vanilla ice cream best?

Questions like these ask the child to count concrete objects, that is, to give a cardinal number to a set of objects. Once children are able to count with meaning and accuracy, then counting can be extended to comparing groups: which has more, which has less, which groups are the same.

Computations. Once children are capable of using the basic counting skills to describe activities and experiments, other forms of numerical usage should be used purposefully in activities. The use of computations should follow from the activity and be a direct, integral part of the activity rather than an artificial something added to include the process of number relations. Children can use addition, subtraction, multiplication, and division—**computations**—to quantify science activities as soon as they understand these computational skills through their mathematics program. The use of computational skills in the science program can make arithmetic more meaningful by showing that arithmetic can be used outside of the mathematics class. The purposeful use of computation in collecting data in science activities also begins to develop a concept of the relationship between science and mathematics.

Numerical Relationships. Using **numerical relationships** involve two steps. Finding the average height of a group of fifth graders while studying the human body or determining the growth rates of various plants while investigating various fertilizers are science activities that naturally use numbers. Such computations use the numbers derived from these activities, and the endpoint of the calculation is a number that can be used to describe the activity results or to compare different aspects of the activity—as when two rates of growth for plants are compared. There is, however, still another step in the use of number relations: finding numerical relationships that exist within collected data for purposes of developing a law or extrapolating from the data.

For example, the data in Figure 3.6 were collected during an activity using a first-class lever and various masses. Eighth grade students placed blocks of differing

Figure 3.6

Levers

| Trial | Left Side | | Right Side | |
	Mass	Distance	Mass	Distance
1	1 g	50 cm	2 g	25 cm
2	5 g	17 cm	9 g	10 cm
3	20 g	9 cm	60 g	3 cm
4	100 g	10 cm	500 g	2 cm
5	15 g	27 cm	45 g	9 cm
6	27 g	31 cm	54 g	70 cm

masses on either side of the fulcrum and moved the blocks until the lever balanced. The distance from the fulcrum to the center of each of the blocks was then measured.

Through questions, these eighth graders were guided to see that the heavier mass is always closer to the fulcrum. With this rule developed, students were guided, through attention to trials 1, 3, and 4, to derive the relationship that exists between mass and distance to the fulcrum: if one side is twice as heavy as the other, then the heavier mass is half as far from the fulcrum. Finally, the formula, $mass_1$ x $distance_1 = mass_2$ x $distance_2$, was developed. With this formula, students can determine that trial 6 is not accurate and can also calculate placement of other masses on the lever. Rather than simply calculating a number, these students used their mathematical skills to develop a relationship between numbers, a formula they can use in other situations.

As children use their mathematical abilities to determine relationships within data and to apply the formulas they derive to other situations, the hand calculator is a useful tool. By using the calculator children can concentrate on the data rather than on how to do division. When the numbers grow larger than those found in their books, children find that the calculator can provide an extra edge of confidence. In particular, the calculator can help the nonmathematical child compete on an equal basis in science with the child whose main ability is in mathematics.

Formulas. The final step in the use of numerical forms involves the use of formulas. The discovery of a **formula** is a highly abstract use of number relations. This degree of abstraction would not be appropriate before the fifth or sixth grade levels and most appropriate at seventh and eight grade levels, when children are making or have made the transition to formal operational thought processes. All students, even at the eighth grade, will not have reached this level of cognitive development, and formulas should be used sparingly.

Sequencing the Use of Number Relations: Charts. A second aspect of the use of number relations involves the use of charts for the collection and organization of data. In general, **charts** provide children with an easy way to record information that they collect during an activity. A chart also allows for systematic collection of data, so that children can easily find their data for later discussion. Problems arise, however, when children are suddenly confronted with an activity and told to collect certain pieces of information, yet do not know how to go about the actual collection. To help children develop their ability systematically to collect information, the teacher can follow five steps. These steps assume that child has had no previous experience with data collection; however, it is not necessary to begin at step 1 if children do have some experience.

Step 1. Rather than giving each child a chart, use the chalkboard or an overhead projector and collect the data for the entire class. Children can either fill in a section of the chart themselves or can call out information to the teacher. In this step, children must be informed of exactly what information they will need to collect as they work, and they must be guided as they fill in the chart.

Step 2. Each child is given an individual data chart to use in data collection, but a similar chart is displayed either on the chalkboard or overhead projector. The students watch as the teacher fills in a sample section of the chart, they fill in the corresponding section of their own charts, and then they work on their own with the rest of the data collected.

Step 3. By this step, children should be well acquainted with the use of a chart and can simply be given a chart, with some general instructions; they should be able to use it on their own during the activity.

Step 4. The class develops its own data-collection chart with the aid of the teacher. It is important that the children thoroughly understand the activity before the chart is constructed. The teacher should give a quick demonstration of what is to be done.

Step 5. Finally, the students should be able to develop their own data-collection charts, without the teacher's aid.

Sequencing the Use of Number Relations: Graphing.   Number relations as a process also includes a third aspect—**graphing.** Graphing, like all other aspects of science teaching, moves most appropriately from concrete to abstract forms.

Concrete Object Graphs.   In their most concrete form—the form most appropriate for children in kindergarten and first grade—**concrete object graphs** can be formed from real, concrete objects to show concepts like most, least, and none.

Preschoolers can even make people graphs—two or more lines of children showing traits of the children themselves. Hair color, clothing color or type, shoe style, favorite foods, or favorite television programs can be graphed by placing children in the various categories and having them form straight lines that can be compared. Discussion can then focus on questions like these:

1. Which line has the most children?
2. Which line has the least children?
3. Which food do most people call their favorite?
4. Which color are the fewest children wearing?

Similar to people graphs are graphs formed by placing actual toys, blocks, or other objects in columns. From this step, children can begin to make bar graphs.

Bar Graphs and Cartesian Coordinate Graphs.   Two kinds of **bar graphs** can be formed from object graphs. In the first case, children can cut strips of paper the length of each column of the object graph and paste them onto another sheet of paper to form a bar graph. In the second case, children can be given crayons and graph paper with large blocks. The child can then count the objects and color one block on the sheet of graph paper for each of the objects in the object graph.

The bar graph can then be divorced from concrete objects by having the children either count or measure objects and graph them directly as a bar graph.

Measurements such as height of plants over a number of days, temperature during the day, length of shadows, or the results of other activities can be graphed using the bar graph. Once the bar graph is understood, it can be extended into the histogram.

A **histogram** is a bar graph of a frequency distribution. The widths of the bars are proportional to the classes being shown, and the heights of the bars are proportional to the class frequencies.

Once they can use the bar graph with some ease, children can be introduced to the use of Cartesian coordinates in **Cartesian coordinate graphs**. The same sequence of steps as used with charts can be followed in introducing children to the use of coordinate graphing.

Interpreting Graphs.   In all cases, when teaching graphing, it is best to coordinate the development of graphs with the child's ability to read or interpret the information contained in the graph. Constructing a graph is fairly easy; interpreting a graph can be difficult. **Interpreting graphs** may involve the following:

1. reading data directly from a graph.
2. identifying trends in the data shown by the graph.
3. interpolating, that is, reading between the actual collected data in order to gain more information.
4. extrapolating, that is, going beyond the data to make predictions as to what could occur in the future or what occurred in the past before the start of the data collection.

Children will need help in all four of these graph interpretation skills, as well as in the construction of graphs from the data they collect. Coordination with the mathematics program in teaching graphing can be very helpful.

Activities 3.20 through 3.23 involve the use of space and number relations.

Space and Number Relations Activities

Activity 3.18

Purpose   To investigate the use of space and number relations in textbook activities.

Procedure
1. Obtain at least three science textbooks for three different grade levels (e.g., third , fifth, and seventh).
2. Locate two activities or experiments within each of the grade levels.
3. Read the description of the activity, and if necessary, carry out the activity.

4. How are the processes of space relations and number relations used within each of the activities?
5. How does the use of space relations and number relations vary from one grade level to another?
6. What could be done to extend the use of space relations and number relations as they are found in each of the activities?
7. Are the types of space relations and number relations appropriate to the grade levels? What could be done to make them more appropriate?

Activity 3.19

Purpose   To investigate the use of a chart for collecting data with children at the third through fifth grade levels.

Procedure
1. Develop a chart that allows individual children to collect the data from the following activity. Try the activity yourself and then make the chart, duplicating enough for each child to have one.
2. Collect the following materials so you have enough for a group of five children: a bucket of garden soil, magnifiers, paper towels, charts, tweezers, newspaper. Place the newspapers on the floor of a table and seat the children around them. Empty the bucket of soil on the newspaper.
3. Have the children use any appropriate senses as well as the magnifiers and the tweezers to determine what materials make up soil. Have the children use your chart to collect the data for this activity, that is, to record the materials they find in the soil. Have the students write on the back of their charts a definition for the word *soil* based on their activity. At the conclusion of the activity, collect the charts completed by the children.
4. Now try the same activity with a second group, but do not give the children a chart on which to collect the data. Have the children record their data however they wish to do so. Once again, have the students write a definition for the word *soil.*
5. Compare and contrast the two groups in terms of the data collected, the problems encountered, and the definitions written.

Activity 3.20

Purpose   To investigate the use of number relations with students in sixth through eighth grades.

Procedure
1. Obtain the following materials: Pyrex beaker (400 ml), alcohol burner and stand or hot plate, 200 ml of water, thermometer, timer, graph paper, pad, pot holder or tongs.
2. Place the 200ml of water into the beaker and determine the starting temperature by placing the thermometer in the water for about 2 minutes.

3. Place the beaker over the heat source and heat until the water boils. While it is heating, take and record the temperature of the water each minute. Be careful that the thermometer is not resting on the bottom of the beaker. If it does touch the bottom you will not get an accurate measurement. After the water boils, carefully remove the beaker from the heat and record the temperature every minute for the next 10 minutes. Assist the students in making a graph of each set of data, one for heating and one for cooling, using the Cartesian coordinate form.

4. Help the students calculate the rate at which the water heated to boiling point and the rate at which it cooled.

5. Using the appropriate graph of data, help the students determine the approximate temperature of the water after heating 2.5, 3.5, and 5.5 minutes. Using the appropriate graph of data, help the students determine the approximate number of minutes that would need to pass before the water returned to its starting temperature.

6. Try the activity with two different grade levels. Compare and contrast their use of graphing, calculation, and graph interpretation.

Summary

The process skills are an integral aspect of inquiry in science. At one time the use of processes and activity was seen as occurring after students had developed scientific concepts through reading and discussion. In a different approach, science process skills were seen as the content of the curriculum and again divorced from their use in inquiry. Finally, process skills were seen as an integral part of inquiry rather than as something that can be separated from either content or inquiry. The *National Science Education Standards* advocates the position that process skills cannot be separated from the act of inquiry.

The processes of observation, classification, communication, operational questions, space relations, and number relations can be used by children beginning at the preschool level and progressing to the sixth grade level and beyond.

The degree of difficulty changes depending on the age and ability of the children and is directly tied to the degree of abstractness of the process. Particularly in the case of space relations and number relations, the level needs to be carefully controlled so that it meets both the cognitive and skill-level abilities of the children. Both space relations and number relations can be highly abstract, involving numerical calculations and the interpretation of numerical data.

In most cases, the basic processes should be approached through the actual process of inquiry rather than divorced from inquiry and taught as separate entities. The exception to this procedure would be the processes of using space relations and using numbers in which the mathematical skills underlying the processes would need to be taught prior to their application to inquiry.

Chapter Vocabulary

The number following each term refers to the page on which the term is first introduced.

Applying the **CONCEPTS**

1. As you observe your fifth grade students at work, you notice that some of them are able to use hierarchical classification easily, some have no idea of how to use it, and two are able to classify hierarchically if given help. You decide to apply Vygotsky's zone of proximal development with the children who are beginning to use hierarchical classification. How would you go about doing this?

2. You have been asked by your principal to develop a curriculum guide to help children in your school learn to use the basic process skills. The principal has suggested having individual lessons on each of the process skills for each of the grade levels. You want to convince your principal that this is not the best strategy. How would you convince the principal? What suggestions would you make for a better way of teaching the basic process skills?

3. The basic processes of space relations and number relations overlap greatly with the area of mathematics. How could you use these two basic processes to combine science and mathematics in your classroom?

4. Modeling is a powerful means for teaching. It can be a highly effective way for helping students use the basic process skills in science activities. How could you, as a classroom teacher, use modeling to help your students use the basic processes effectively?

5. Using charts and interpreting graphs are skills that can be difficult for children to learn. How could you use Vygotsky's concept of scaffolding to help students develop their abilities in each of these areas?

References

Ausubel, D. P. 1960. The use of advance organizers in the learning and retention of meaningful verbal learning. *Journal of Educational Psychology* 51, 267–272.

Baust, J. A. 1981. Spatial relationships and young children. *Arithmetic Teacher* 29, 1.

Baust, J. A. 1982. Teaching spatial relationships using language arts and physical education. *School Science and Mathematics* 82, 7.

Brandwein, P. F., E. K. Cooper, P. E. Blackwood, M. Cottom-Winslow, J. A. Boeschen, M. G. Giddings, F. Romero, and A. A. Carin. 1980. *Concepts in science.* New York: Harcourt, Brace, Jovanovich.

Callison, P., R. Anschultz, and E. Wright. 1997. Gummy worm measurements. *Science and Children* 35(1), 38–41.

Field, J. 1997. Teaching science with broken pencils. *Science and Children* 34, 17–19.

Finley, F. N. 1983. Science processes. *Journal of Research in Science Teaching* 20, 1.

Fox, P. 1994. Creating a laboratory. *Science and Children* 31(4), 20–22.

Inhelder, B., and J. Piaget 1964. *Early growth of logic in the child.* New York: Harper & Row.

Karplus, R. (director). 1972. *Science curriculum improvement study teaching materials.* Chicago: Rand McNally.

Kepler, M. 1996. How to make hands-on science work for you. *Instructor* 105(6), 46–53.

Kuhn, D., E. Amsel, and M. O'Loughlin. 1988. *The development of scientific thinking skills.* San Diego: Academic Press.

Lee, K. S. 1982. Guiding young children to successful problem solving. *Arithmetic Teacher* 29, 5.

May, L. 1997. Developing logical reasoning. *Teaching Pre-K–8* 28(2), 22.

McAnarney, H. 1982. How much space does an object take up? *Science and Children* 19, 4.

National Research Council. 1996. *National science education standards.* Washington, D. C.: National Academy Press.

Padilla, M. J., and E. J. Frye. 1996. Observing and inferring promotes science learning. *Science and Children,* 33(8), 22–25.

Piaget, J. 1963. *The Psychology of Intelligence.* Totowa, N. J.: Littlefield.

Piaget, J. 1972a. *Judgment and reasoning in the child.* Totowa, N. J.: Littlefield.

Reif, R. J., and K. Rauch. 1994. Science in their own words. *Science and Children* 31(4), 31–33.

Ross, M. E. 1997. Scientists at play. *Science and Children* 35, 35–38.

Scarnati, J. T., and C. J. Weller. 1992. The write stuff: Science inquiry skills help students think positively about writing assignments. *Science and Children* 29, 28–29.

Schlichter, C. L. 1983. The answer is in the question. *Science and Children* 19, 3.

Shaw, J. M., and M. Cliatt. 1981. Searching and researching. *Science and Children* 19,3.

Sumrall, W. J., and J. Criglow. 1995. The "scoop" on science data. *Science and Children* 32, 6, 37–39, 44.

Tobin, K.G. and W. Capie. 1982. Lessons with an emphasis on process skills. *Science and Children* 19, 3.

White, E. P. 1982. Why self-directed learning? *Science and Children* 19, 5.

CHAPTER 4

THE CAUSAL PROCESSES OF SCIENCE

Chapter Objectives

Upon completion of this chapter, you should be able to:

1 discuss why children have greater difficulty in using the causal processes than in using the basic process;

2 sequence the causal processes for optimal teaching;

3 define each of the causal processes: interaction and systems, cause and effect, inference, prediction, and conclusion;

4 use each of the causal processes: interaction and system, cause and effect, inference, prediction, and conclusion.

Introduction

With only the basic processes of science, children can become fully involved in purposeful science activities. They can observe the characteristics of plants and communicate those characteristics to others by drawing, speaking, or writing. They can collect numerical data and transfer those measurements into charts and graphs, showing the information clearly and concisely. Children gain descriptive information through the basic processes. They get information about the physical characteristics of objects or phenomena. What they do not get is information about the relationships between those objects and phenomena. For example, first graders can observe the parts of plants without knowing how those parts work together in a plant, and sixth graders can see the light bulb in a complete circuit without considering what makes a good conductor or nonconductor. Eighth graders can observe the effect of moving a light source on the intensity of the light, but the basic processes do not generally ask them to look at the relationship between distance and intensity. By themselves the basic processes are just not enough to allow students to consider the cause-and-effect relationships that may exist among and between objects and phenomena. As soon as children begin to look at the cause-and-effect relationships within an activity or an experiment, they begin to use the causal processes. The causal processes allow children to take the descriptive information of the basic processes and make inferences, draw conclusions, and test predictions.

For children to use the causal processes effectively, they must first have some understanding of cause and effect. Children's ability to use cause and effect develops from precausal reasoning in preschool to logical use of cause and effect during the middle school years. Science textbooks and programs often show the use of inference, prediction, and conclusion in science activities, but just as often give the child little assistance in using these process skills effectively. And science programs and texts generally do not show how inference, prediction, and conclusion relate to two other process skills necessary if the child is to use these processes logically. The process skills that underlie prediction, inference, and conclusion are (1) the ability to determine cause and effect, and (2) the ability to recognize a system and its interactions.

Although cause and effect and interaction and systems are sometimes omitted from lists of process skills, each of them does fit the criteria for a process:

1. a process is a specific intellectual skill used by all scientists and applicable to the understanding of any phenomenon.
2. a process is an identifiable behavior of scientists and can be learned by any student.
3. processes are generalizable across content domains and contribute to rational thinking in everyday affairs. (Finley, 1983, p. 48)

For teachers, one of the most important concepts about the causal processes is that children at different ages use those processes in different ways.

The Development of Cause and Effect in Children

Through his research into how children explain common occurrences, Piaget (1972b, 1975) discovered children do not see cause-and-effect relationships in the same ways as adults see them. In fact, very young children find it difficult, if not impossible, to separate from the idea of human beings as the cause of all things or the idea that all things are living from real causes in the natural world. Until the child reaches 10 years of age, or more, his or her explanations of the "whys" of the world may not be logical, at least not according to adults.

Very young children, up to about 4 years of age, often use magical kinds of explanations. These children are certain that their words and gestures influence events occurring around them: Wishing, they think, can make something happen. Piaget refers to this type of explanation of causality as psychological.

The child interpreting the world in terms of **psychological causality** may, if faced with the prospect of broccoli for dinner, try wishing very hard for it to turn to ice cream. Although this may sound to us like a child's typical fantasy approach to life, the child who uses psychological causality really believes that wishing will cause a change. A preschool child's world is truly magical. But gradually, the magical approach to cause and effect disappears. Primary grade children are beginning to try to explain the world logically and so have different kinds of explanations from preschoolers.

Causal Explanations by Primary Grade Children

Primary grade children, up to about 7 years of age, use a variety of different kinds of causal explanations. Table 4.1 outlines the several types of precausal explanations used by primary grade children. Three of these are discussed here because they tend to be more frequently used than the others: phenomenism, artificialism, and animism. All of these explanations are called precausal by Piaget (1972b, 1975); that is, they do not show a logical approach to cause-and-effect relationships.

Phenomenism.   A causal explanation that relies on **phenomenism** makes it very difficult for the early primary grade child to draw conclusions from the data he or she collects during an activity. Water boils because it is in a pot. A boat floats because it is white. A seed grows because it has wrinkles.

The kind of explanations given by a child using phenomenism shows a child may attribute causation to anything that he or she perceives as important. Such explanations make it difficult for the child to consider the information collected during an activity with any sort of logic.

Artificialism.   A second possible precausal explanation used by primary grade children is **artificialism.** For the child who relies on artificialism, people are seen as the cause of all things or everything is made for people. How did Earth originate? People made it. How did a mountain form? People built it. What causes waves in

Table 4.1

Types of Precausal Explanations

Type	Definition	Example
Motivation	Causality is the result of a divine plan.	God causes clouds to move, boats to float, and so on.
Finalism	Causality is a simple fact without origin or consequence.	A magnet picks up tacks because it just does.
Phenomenism	Anything can cause anything.	Water runs downhill because there are fish in the stream.
Participation	Two things can act on one another over a distance because of some invisible emanation.	The Sun moves because the child walks down the street.
Morality	Phenomena are a result of moral necessity.	Boats must float because people would drown if they did not.
Artificialism	Events and phenomena are the result of human activity.	People made Earth.
Animism	All events and phenomena are seen as alive and conscious.	A car moves because it is alive.
Dynamism	Forces and life are confused.	Water runs downhill because the mountain pushes it.

the ocean? People swimming. Such explanations can be frustrating to the teacher, particularly during units of study dealing with the planets, stars, or Earth.

Animism.   The final type of precausal explanation considered here is **animism,** the most common of the three types. Children using animism see all things as alive and conscious. Children at this level of causal development tend to see the characteristic of movement as the major criterion for determining whether or not an object or phenomenon is alive. A second criterion is the usefulness of the object or phenomenon to human beings. A car is alive because its wheels move. A cloud is alive because it moves across the sky. A desk is alive because a person can write on it. These types of explanations may last until the child reaches 8 years of age. A full understanding of living and nonliving may not be reached until a child is in the sixth grade.

Causal Explanations of Intermediate Grade Children

As children move into the intermediate grades, they begin to recognize natural relationships and attempt to make logical explanations. The six types of causal thinking used by children between 7 and 10 years of age (Piaget 1972b, 1975) are found in Table 4.2.

Table 4.2

Transitional Forms of Causality

Type	Definition	Example
Reaction of Surrounding	The first genuinely physical explanation. The need for contact as a cause is seen so the surrounding medium is used.	Clouds move because, after some mysterious start, the cloud continues the motion.
Mechanical	Contact and transference of movement are used as explanations.	The motion of a bicycle is caused by the pedals. No chain is needed.
Generation	An extension of animism with the added idea that matter can be changed from one form to another.	Clouds form from smoke, which grows, like a living thing, into a cloud.
Substantial	Like causality by generation but without the ability to grow.	The Sun is a ball of clouds rolled together, but there had to be enough clouds at the start because clouds cannot grow.
Condensation and Rarefaction	Matter that makes up objects is more or less condensed depending on its type.	A stone is condensed and wood is rarefied so stones sink and wood floats.
Atomistic	Objects are made of tiny particles tightly or loosely packed together.	Water can be poured because it is made of tiny pieces.

Both maturity and experience are necessary if children are to develop the ability to use logical forms of causality. Finally, sometime after 10 years of age, children develop the ability to make logical explanations about cause and effect. They can finally make logical deductions from the observations made during an activity or experiment.

Causal Explanations of Upper Grade Children

Students at the upper middle school grades, 7 and 8, have generally developed a concept of cause and effect (Inhelder and Piaget, 1958). Those who have made the transition from concrete operational thought to formal operational thought processes have a concept of cause and effect similar to that of adults. For students at the seventh and eighth grade who are making the transition into formal operational thought, the concept of cause and effect may not be fully developed. Returning to Vygotsky's concept of the zone of proximal development, this transition can be assisted by having students who have made the transition and who have an understanding of cause and effect work with students who have not yet fully developed formal thought.

The ability to draw logical cause-and-effect relationships develops over the years of elementary and middle school until children are finally able to determine the actual cause-and-effect relationships in an activity or an experiment. The child's ability to determine causality helps him or her understand the processes of interaction and systems, cause and effect, inference, prediction, and conclusion.

Difficulties in Learning Causal Processes

The causal processes are more difficult for children to use effectively than are the basic processes. The first reason for this, the slow development of logical causality, was discussed earlier. The second reason for the difficulty experienced by children lies in the kinds of phenomena being considered.

Although some causal relationships are concrete and can be demonstrated easily, many are not and so must be inferred from the actions of objects or from the actions of inferred phenomena. The more concrete an experience, the more likely the causality demonstrated will be understood by the students involved. Equally important in understanding causality, however, are the immediacy of the action and its effect and the cause of the action. Cause-and-effect relationships that are immediate in space and time and the result of the child's activity are understood even by very young children. For example, in an early childhood center where the children were 3, 4, and 5 years of age, some of the children discovered that a board placed over a large cardboard cylinder made a seesaw. They also discovered that putting a sponge on the lower end and then jumping on the raised end would cause the sponge to fly up in the air. After investigating the seesaw and sponge for some time, the children were able to make the sponge reach nearly to the ceiling. When a teacher in the center asked the children how they got the sponge to go so high, they informed her that it went up high if you jumped hard or if someone big jumped on the end. After considering the size of the teacher, they decided she would make it go really, really high if she jumped on the end. She did. The sponge bounced off the ceiling! These children understood the cause and effect within this activity because it met the criteria of immediacy in space and time and causation as a result of the child's action. Even preschool children can understand cause and effect when the cause and the effect are immediate and caused by the actions of the children.

Finally, the causal processes tend to be more difficult because we give little attention to developing the child's ability to recognize those parts of a system that are important to the results and those that are not. Most children need assistance in determining which parts of a system are important to what occurs and which parts of a system are extraneous to a particular effect.

By sequencing the causal processes appropriately, we can help children develop the ability to look logically at the results of an activity. Here is a suggested sequence for using the causal processes in discussing the results of an activity:

1. interaction and systems

2. cause and effect

3. inference

4. prediction

5. conclusion.

This sequence (1) provides a foundation by considering interaction and systems and cause and effect as prerequisite skills, and (2) moves children from a relatively concrete foundation through a series of steps to the more abstract causal process of conclusion. As a teacher, this does not mean you should teach separate lessons on each of these processes, but rather that your questioning skills following up on an activity should help your students consider the system involved, the interactions that take place, and finally the cause-and-effect relationships.

Each of the causal processes is discussed in the rest of this chapter, including the sequence in which the various types of systems and predictions should be part of activities in the science classroom.

Interaction and Systems

Definition

A **system** is a group of objects and phenomena that act together. The relationships between and among the various parts of the system are known as **interactions.** A very simple system, for example, is a paper fan being used to move air to cool your face. The parts of the system are the paper fan, your hand and arm, the air, and your face. Within this system three major interactions take place: Your hand and the arm interact with the fan; the fan interacts with the air; the air interacts with your face.

Introducing the Process of Interaction and Systems

The process of interaction and systems is automatically used within activities, but students may not be aware they are using it. As students decide what they need for an activity or experiment, as they try to reason what they would need to do to cause a change, as they try to understand what is working together within a particular setting, students are automatically using the concept of interaction and system. As you begin to discuss the results of activities and experiments with your students, you need to help those students see and understand the use of interaction and systems within the activity or experiment.

In particular, the process of interaction and systems can be used when you discuss the results of an activity with your students. In this way, interaction and systems can help students draw logical conclusions from their activity results, identify the system, choose the parts acting together to cause the phenomenon, and then relate the objects to the phenomenon through inferences and conclusion.

For example, imagine a group of sixth or seventh graders investigating the concept of action and reaction using balloons, string, straws, test tubes, corks, baking soda, and vinegar. The students work in small groups to complete three activities. In the first activity, the students blow up a balloon, let it go, and watch it as it flies through the air. The students then record their observations of the balloon. In the second activity, they make a rocket by threading a string through the straw, attaching a balloon to the straw, then stretching out the string and blowing up the balloon. They watch what happens when the balloon is released, and record any observations. Finally, the students put vinegar into the test tube along with baking soda in a piece of tissue. The cork is put firmly into the opening of the test tube, the test tube and contents are given one shake, and then the test tube is quickly placed on the floor. The students observe what happens and write down their results.

In order to assist these students in drawing a common conclusion for all of these activities, you, as the teacher, can begin by using interaction and systems. For each of the three activities, ask the students what materials were needed, that is, the parts of the system. List the materials on the board in chart form. Once the students know the parts of the system, have them look for the ways in which those parts interacted and list those as well. Then have your students decide which of the interactions identified was the most important in causing the reaction. Finally, help your students look at the cause-and-effect relationships occurring because of those interactions. And, lastly, have your students draw a conclusion about all of the activities. Table 4.3 shows the resulting chart developed by the students and teacher.

Types of Systems

Within the process of interaction and systems are three types of systems, classified according to their concreteness and implying a sequence for their use in activities. Each of these types is discussed here.

Concrete Systems.   **Concrete systems** are those in which the components are all easily visible or easily sensed concrete objects. Examples of this type of system would be the pendulum, the lever, a pinwheel, a paper airplane, and a bouncing ball. Concrete systems are particularly important for children in the primary grades. At this level, children must have real objects and be able to directly manipulate those objects to see the effect of their own actions.

Partially Concrete Systems.   Systems in which the components are both concrete objects and inferred phenomena are **partially concrete systems** and should be considered second. Some examples would be magnets, gravity, bulbs and batteries, and tuning forks. In each of these cases, the system includes not only objects but also a form of energy. Because the energy form is not visible and must be inferred from its action on objects, these systems are more abstract than the concrete systems considered first. Students at the intermediate grades who have had experience with concrete systems will be able to work with partially concrete sys-

Table 4.3

Using Interaction and Systems in an Activity Discussion

Activity 1	Activity 2	Activity 3
System		
balloon, air, mouth, hands, lungs	balloon, tape, straw, string, lungs, hands	test tube, tissue, cork, baking soda, vinegar, floor
Interactions		
balloon–air	balloon–straw	cork–test tube
hand–balloon	balloon–hands	baking soda–vinegar
air–lungs	straw–string	tissue–baking soda
mouth–ballon	string–hands	test–tube–floor
Drawing		

Conclusion: When air is released or a gas is released, the gas or air goes one way the object goes the other.

tems. The more familiar the system to the students, the more likely they will be able to infer the nonconcrete phenomena.

Nonconcrete Systems.   **Nonconcrete systems** are those in which the major components are phenomena. This type of system should be considered last. It is not possible to divorce such phenomena from concrete objects, but the major effects are due to something unseen. Examples might be the effect of a current-carrying wire on a magnetic compass or the effect of light on a radiometer.

Nonconcrete systems are most appropriate for students at sixth, seventh, and eighth grade levels where a concept of cause and effect is more likely to have developed. However, keep in mind that students have to have had experience with concrete and partially concrete systems first. Even at the eighth grade level, students cannot be expected to immediately understand nonconcrete systems if they have had no prior practice with systems and interactions.

Children who have had experience in using interaction and systems as a part of the discussion of activity results are much more likely to be able to use the second of the cause-and-effect processes effectively: cause and effect.

Activities 4.1 and 4.2 are designed to develop your understanding of the process of interaction and systems.

Interaction and Systems Activities

Activity 4.1

Purpose   To develop your own ability to recognize the parts of a system and the interactions occurring in that system.

Procedure
1. Research any two of the following topics.
   a. How does an automobile engine work?
   b. How does a television set work?
   c. How does a CD player work?
   d. What cause a thunderstorm?
   e. What causes a hurricane?
   f. What causes a rainbow?
   g. How does a human being hear sounds?
   h. How does a human being digest food?
   i. How does a video camera work?
   j. What keeps an airplane in the air?
   k. What cause a volcano to erupt?
   l. What causes an earthquake?
2. After completing your research, answer each of the following questions:
   a. What are the parts of the system?
   b. What are the interactions?
   c. Which of the interactions are most important in causing the phenomenon you researched?

Activity 4.2

Purpose   To investigate the use of interaction and systems in textbook activities.

Procedure
1. Select three science textbooks representing three different grade levels.
2. Select three activities dealing with three different topics from each of the textbooks.
3. Analyze the use of interaction and systems in the activities.
   a. What systems are used in each activity?
   b. What interactions are shown in each activity?
   c. How would you classify the kinds of systems used in the activities: concrete, partially concrete, or nonconcrete?
   d. Is the type of system appropriate to the grade level? Why or why not?
   e. What could be done to make the types of systems more appropriate to the grade level?
   f. How could the use of interaction and systems be enhanced in each of the activities?

Cause and Effect

Definition

Cause and effect is the ability to determine which of two or more factors came first in a sequence and to correctly attribute some result to this factor. If a child can say that the string and the bob of the pendulum interact as a part of a system, it is a fairly easy step to see that lengthening the string causes the number of swings of the pendulum to decrease. The child can rule out the table as a cause (a phenomenalistic explanation) because the table is not a part of the system and because the table and the pendulum do not interact.

Inferring cause-and-effect relationships requires three steps. First, the system and its parts are identified. Second, the interactions in the system are determined. Finally, the effects of the interactions are determined. Assigning cause and effect is the ability to correctly attribute a certain effect to a certain occurrence or cause.

Introducing the Process of Cause and Effect

As with interaction and systems, cause and effect, as a process, should follow a sequence of development from concrete to abstract. The interaction that occurs when a block is hit by a marble and moved is easy to see. Children can quickly state that the marble caused the block to move. This is cause and effect at the concrete level. The kinds of cause-and-effect relationships considered at this stage would meet the criteria of immediacy in time and space as well as of causation by the child. At the next level, white light may be passed through a prism so the child can see the colors of the spectrum. This stage uses a form of energy and a concrete object. The interaction needs to be inferred, although the effect of that interaction can be easily seen. Finally, on an abstract level, students may be asked to determine the cause of a rise of temperatures as the result of a chemical reaction. Temperature is a measurement, not a concrete object. The result of a chemical reaction may be seen, but not the reaction itself. This level of cause-and-effect determination tends to be highly abstract.

The ability to say that one thing causes another is the beginning of the ability to make inferences.

The Development of Observation, Inference, and Conclusion in Children

Observation, inference, and conclusion are key scientific processes because they form the basis for the gathering and interpretation of data during an activity or experiment. These process skills develop in children as they move through the developmental stages. As a result of the use of observation, inference, and conclusion, children develop mental models. At times, the observations are based on physical models.

Observation, Inference, and Conclusion

Children in kindergarten through second grade, find the collection and interpretation of data difficult. These preoperational children are likely to have their observations colored by immediate perceptions rather than by actual occurrences of the activity. As these children interpret the data from an activity, their interpretations are likely to be egocentric and anthropomorphic in nature. In addition, preoperational children are unlikely to see possible contradictions between their perceptions and the actual data. In addition, the information they collect is difficult for them to order. What occurs first, second, third, and so on, is hard for the child to determine after the activity is ended.

Concrete operational children, generally third through fifth or sixth grade, have advanced over preoperational children in their ability to determine the sequence of data and observations. Now children are able to determine what occurred first, second, and so on. In interpreting the data from an activity, concrete operational children tend to look at a single characteristic during the early part of the developmental stage, but by the end of the stage, they are able to take several aspects of a system into account, although looking at each aspect separately, and interpret the effect of each of those aspects. In a situation that is written rather than concrete, concrete operational children stay within the confines of the description and merely redescribe the situation as given in the written description (Good, 1977).

Formal operational students, most likely to be in seventh or eighth grade, are fully capable of making objective observations and considering a variety of factors during those observations. In addition, formal operational students are able to take a written description of an activity and account for all of the relevant features of the activity. The formal operational student is also able to go beyond a written description to make inferences, using not only the data given in the description but also relevant past experience.

Models

Using **models** as part of a science class aids in the gathering and using of data much in the same way as using activities and experiments. **Mental models** allow children to develop a conceptualization that can then be tested and applied. An example of a mental model would be the idea that sound travels in waves. **Physical models** are often used to generate information that could be difficult for children to see in its real form. Examples of physical models are models of a heart, airplane, cell, eye, or human skeleton. As with observation, inference, and conclusion, the ability to use models develops along with the developmental stages.

Because preoperational children tend to be tied to transductive reasoning and so to consideration of specifics rather than generalizations, preoperational children tend to be unable to build a mental model by using specific facts. When it comes to physical models, preoperational children tend to consider the model as the real thing. Children in kindergarten through about second grade, on viewing a plastic model of a skeleton, may develop the idea that bones are made from plastic and glued together (Piaget, 1972a).

Concrete operational children, especially those at the second and third grades and in the early phases of this developmental stage, are able to develop mental models of scientific content, but only when those models are developed around the ideas of seriation, classification, and simple one-to-one correspondence. During this early stage, children also find it difficult to use models of objects because they tend to think of the model as the real thing (Piaget, 1972a). Consequently, using a balloon to represent a human lung may be interpreted by the early concrete child to mean that the lung is a balloon.

In the late concrete operational stage, usually fifth and sixth grades, children are able to use mental models as well as physical models, provided the mental models are founded in concrete experiences and the physical models correspond exactly to reality. Late concrete operational children no longer consider the model the real thing, but the child is not able to make a correspondence between reality and something that does not look like the real object (Piaget, 1972a).

By the formal operational stage, children are able to use mental models of reality. In the early phase of formal operations, about seventh and eighth grades, children are likely to have difficulty comparing two models, such as the wave theory and the particle theory of light, which account for the same phenomena. Because early formal operational students consider each model as representative of reality, they may become confused if they try to consider both models simultaneously. By the late formal stage, however, children are able to go beyond known explanations to search for explanatory models, to extend models, and to compare alternative models of reality in order to account for the data obtained during an experiment or an activity. When using physical models, the late formal operational child is able to consider and use models in which the parts bear little or no resemblance to actuality. For the most part, the children we teach in the elementary and middle school are not in the later stage of formal operations (Inhelder and Piaget, 1958).

With this as background in the development of the ability to observe, infer, predict, and model, consider the final three causal processes: inference, prediction, and conclusion.

Inference

Definition

An **inference** is an interpretation of the observations made during an activity or experiment. An inference may also be thought of as a statement showing a relationship among the parts of a system and frequently detailing a cause-and-effect relationship. As such, inferences are sometimes referred to as **explanatory inferences.** Usually, an explanatory inference is a highly tenuous interpretation subject to change and modification as more and more data are collected. It is also likely that multiple inferences can be made from the same set of data.

Multiple Inferences

The idea of **multiple inferences** is illustrated by the example of a group of seventh grade students shown the "collapsing can" demonstration. A gallon metal can containing a little water was heated until the water boiled and steam emerged from the opening at the top. Then the cap was screwed on tightly and the sealed can removed from the heat. As the can cooled, it collapsed, crumpling almost magically. A little cool water poured over the can caused it to crumple even more. After seeing this demonstration, these seventh graders inferred these possible causes for the collapse:

1. The heat made the metal soft and it melted.

2. The metal absorbed the water and it got soft.

3. The water was heavy and when you poured it over the can it smashed the can.

4. The water turned into steam and chased out some of the air. The outside air pushed on the can and collapsed it.

5. The water turned to steam and left the can kind of empty. The metal was too heavy for the air inside and it squashed.

6. You switched cans!

Faced with so many inferences, the teacher and the class were put into the position of having ideas to test: some through reading, one through careful observation of the teacher, and some through further activity. Testing these inferences allowed the children to work like scientists, but in a less formal way than using a true experimental procedure. Testing these inferences also allowed the children to use all of the primary processes, particularly asking and investigating operational questions. Testing these inferences also led to the cause-and-effect process of prediction.

Prediction

Definition

A **prediction** is a special form of inference that attempts to determine, on the basis of data collected, what will happen in the future. A prediction is not a guess. A guess is strictly that: It has no basis in data; it can be pulled out of a hat. A prediction, however, must have a sound foundation in data that was previously collected or in background experience. Thus a student may predict with confidence that 4 inches of water will evaporate from a particular container in eight days because the rate of evaporation has been shown to be, for that container, 0.5 inch per day. Because a prediction does have a sound basis in data just as inferences have a sound basis in data, predictions are sometimes referred to as **predictive inferences.**

The Two Types of Prediction

Predictions, or predictive inferences, can be divided into two categories depending on the basis for those predictions.

Concrete Predictions. Children make **concrete predictions** when they base their predictions on direct experiences with concrete materials. These predictions are generally made as a part of a science activity. In general they are making their predictions directly from the data they have collected. With concrete predictions there is no need for children to read supplementary material for background information or for additional information on which to base their predictions.

When working with young, preoperational children, always remember that children center on one characteristic at a time. Consequently, using prediction with children in kindergarten through second grade should allow them to consider only one trait in their predictions rather than having to look at a variety of characteristics at the same time. For example, children at the first grade level who are trying to make predictions about which objects will sink and which will float can first predict on the basis of the weight of the object, then on the size of the object, then on the shape of the object. For first graders, trying to make predictions that use both weight and size simultaneously or weight and shape simultaneously is impossible.

Theoretical Predictions. **Theoretical predictions** are based either (1) on a combination of data drawn from concrete experiences and reading matter, or (2) on reading matter alone. In the first case, children are using the written material to supplement what they have gained through concrete experience. For example, seventh graders could work with levers, then go to the textbook to find more information before they try to predict what could occur if the location of the fulcrum is changed. In the second case, students make predictions on the basis of theoretical material they acquire from reading or other verbal sources. For example, eighth grade students can read about the requirements for good nutrition in mice and predict what type of diet will cause mice to gain the greatest amount of weight over a period of time. Theoretical predictions are most appropriate for sixth, seventh, and eighth grade students.

Whether predictions are concrete or theoretical, students should have the opportunity to discuss with others what their predictions will be. The use of small groups in which students talk about what they think will happen, come to a consensus as to their prediction, and then must present and defend their prediction to the rest of the class is a good way of getting children not only to predict, but to confront their ideas and present their reasons. When their predictions are not supported by the results of testing those predictions, students should return to their groups to try to reconcile what occurred with what they thought would happen.

Testing Multiple Inferences Through Prediction

Multiple inferences can be made from most sets of observations. When there are multiple inferences, those inferences should be investigated to determine which of them is best supported by the data already collected and by new data that can be collected through testing predictions based on the inferences. For example, one of the multiple inferences made by the students watching the collapsing can demonstration was that the water poured over the can was heavy and so smashed the can. When asked how they could determine whether that inference was supported or not, the students decided on some factors they would want to test:

1. less water
2. more water
3. different kinds of liquids
4. no water.

From each of these factors listed, the students made predictions based on each of them:

1. If not as much water is used, the can won't collapse as much.
2. If more water is used, the can will smash flat.
3. If you use cooking oil instead of water, the can will smash more because oil is heavier.
4. If no water is poured over the can, the can won't smash.

Predictions 1, 2, and 4 were each tested separately. After discussion, the class decided it might be too dangerous to test the oil because oil could catch on fire. Although this teacher chose to have students test each of the inferences separately, a more productive way of testing predictions, and one which would have engaged students in problem solving and the development of their own activities, would have been through writing and testing operational questions. In this case, the first two items on the list could be turned into operational questions: "What would happen to the can if the amount of water used is changed?" This would allow students to test both an increase in the amount of water used and a decrease in the amount of water used. Although the third item listed could be rewritten as "What effect does the kind of liquid used have on the way the can collapses?" safety factors would still preclude testing the prediction. When testing predictions, using operational questions allows for a more interesting activity in which a variety of changes could be made and also allows students to engage their problem-solving skills as they develop a means for answering their operational questions.

Predictions, then, are made on the basis of data. But, once made, predictions should be tested to determine their validity. At times, students' predictions will need to be tested through reading. More often, however, student predictions can be tested through the use of concrete materials. Once the predictions have been tested, students can change or modify inferences on the basis of the new data and, finally, when all of the evidence is in, they can draw conclusions.

Conclusion

Definition

A **conclusion,** like a prediction, is a special form of inference. Many inferences can be drawn from the evidence of a single activity. As each inference is tested by means of predictions and activities, a particular inference may be revised or eliminated. Inferences have that property; they can be changed. But finally, after predictions have been tested and various inferences discarded or revised, a single inference should still be left that fits all of the data and to which all of the predictions point. The end product of the prediction and the testing phases is a conclusion.

Because conclusions are based on a greater amount of evidence than are inferences, conclusions are less likely than inferences to change. However, in the face of new, solid evidence even a conclusion may need revision.

Abstraction and the Causal Processes

The causal processes tend to be more difficult for children to use than the basic processes previously discussed. Although the causal processes are developed through the use of concrete objects, they still require a further cognitive step. The objects are visible, touchable, "smellable" entities, but the relationships among those objects must be inferred from the results of the interactions taking place. These inferences are not concrete in nature; they are the beginnings of abstraction.

A child can measure the length of a string as 20 cm and can count 60 swings of a pendulum in a minute. That same child can increase the length to 60 cm and can count 30 swings in a minute. The child directly measures length and number of swings. However, the child must infer from those measurements the relationship of string length to number of swings. An inference is not a concrete object but the result of a cognitive process. As such, it is an abstraction. But determination of cause and effect, although unlike the other processes in that it is a cognitive skill, is necessary for development of the child's ability to use the experimental processes, which require a determination of cause and effect prior to the writing of a hypothesis.

Because of the abstract nature of the cause-and-effect processes, children find their use difficult not only in the early grades but in the sixth, seventh, and eighth grades as well. The key is to move from the most concrete cases to the most abstract cases, allowing time for children to develop their abilities at each of the levels of concreteness.

Content and Teaching the Causal Processes

The use of the causal processes forms the heart of the scientific enterprise. It is through inference, prediction, and the determination of cause and effect that scientific knowledge is gained.

Children should use these processes for the same purpose they are used in the scientific enterprise: to gain knowledge. Rather than reading which animals are classified as mammals, students could do the following:

1. observe the overt characteristics of real, small mammals
2. infer the major characteristics of mammals
3. read to find the characteristics of mammals not observed directly
4. predict which of the animals from a list would be classified as mammals
5. test their predictions by classifying the animals and then researching the correct classification in textbooks, trade books, and films
6. draw conclusions detailing the characteristics used to classify mammals
7. test their conclusions by classifying other animals and testing their classifications.

Or, in studying magnetism, students could:

1. observe the interaction that occurs between a magnet and various metallic and nonmetallic objects
2. identify the parts of the system that interact
3. predict what will happen if layers of cardboard are placed between the magnet and the objects
4. test their predictions through concrete materials
5. draw inferences dealing with the interaction through cardboard of magnets with metallic objects
6. read to determine if the inferences are valid
7. draw a conclusion about the effect of magnets through cardboard and test that conclusion to be certain of its validity.

Students using the causal processes to learn content should be involved directly with concrete materials, so they develop a conceptual basis. They should move to written materials in order to develop a more thorough understanding of the content information. Moreover, the child's development of an understanding of cause and effect will permit his or her development of a more thorough understanding of the true experiment and its role in science.

The use of the causal processes to teach content allows students to structure their knowledge in a way that will be personally meaningful. In this way, the information will be consistent with their previous knowledge and developmental level.

Activities 4.3 through 4.6 are designed to allow you to investigate the use of inference, prediction, and conclusion in science teaching.

Inference, Prediction, and Conclusion Activities

Activity 4.3

Purpose   To investigate the use of inference, prediction, and conclusion in science textbook activities.

Procedure
1. Select three science textbooks representing three different grade levels.
2. Select three activities dealing with three different topics from each of the textbooks.
3. Analyze the use of inference, prediction, and conclusion in the activities.
   a. Which of these processes are used in each activity?
   b. How are these processes used in each activity?
   c. Are the predictions used concrete or theoretical? Is the type of prediction used appropriate to the grade level?
   d. Is there opportunity for the development and testing of predictions in the activity? If there is no opportunity, how could it be included?
   e. Is there opportunity for the development of multiple inferences? If not, how could multiple inferences be included?
   f. Is the use of inference, prediction, and conclusion appropriate to the grade level? Why or why not? If inappropriate, how could the use be made more appropriate?
   g. How could the use of inference, prediction, and conclusion be enhanced in the activities?

Activity 4.4

Purpose   To investigate the use of inferences with children.

Procedure
1. Arrange to work with two groups of students from any two of the following grade levels: fourth, fifth, sixth, seventh, eighth.
2. Collect the following materials: one Pyrex beaker (400 ml), one-half cup of granulated sugar, hot plate, potholder or tongs, wire hot pad or second potholder.
3. Without telling the group what the white material is:
   a. Have the students observe the material without tasting it.
   b. Pour the sugar into the beaker and place the beaker on the hot plate until the sugar has carbonized (turned black) and begins to rise to the top of the beaker.
   c. Remove the beaker from the heat using the tongs or potholder and have the group again make observations.
4. Have the group make inferences about what they have seen. Questions like the following will help them to infer:
   a. What could the white "stuff" have been?

      b. What do you think happened that made the white material turn black and seem to get larger?

      c. What could the black "stuff" in the beaker be?

5. Analyze the inferences made by the two groups. What similarities and differences did you notice in the ability of the two groups to make inferences?

Activity 4.5

Purpose To investigate the use of the process of prediction with students at various grade levels.

Procedure

1. Select two groups of students to work with from two of the following grade levels: fourth, fifth, sixth, seventh, eighth.
2. Try any of the following situations using the same situation with both groups. The first question or statements are to recall the students' background or previous experiences. Record the predictions made by the students.
3. Situations:
    a. What is it like when the Sun is behind a lot of clouds? What is it like at night? The planet Pluto is very far away from the Sun and so gets little light. What do you think it is like on the planet Pluto?
    b. In order to keep insects from eating food crops like corn, wheat, rye, and various vegetables, farmers spray pesticides that kill the insects. But scientists are now finding that some insects are becoming resistant to the poisons being used. The insects are no longer killed by the pesticides. What could happen if all of the insects that eat food crops are no longer killed by the pesticides?
4. Compare and contrast the two groups on their ability to make predictions based on the information given and the scenarios. To what do you attribute any differences in ability to predict?

Activity 4.6

Purpose To use the processes of interaction and systems, cause and effect, inference, and conclusion in teaching a science lesson to children at a selected grade level.

Procedure

1. Arrange to work with a small group of students at any grade level from fourth through sixth grade. The group should have no less than six students.
2. Using the science textbook or program in use by the class, select a science activity to teach the group.
3. Using the strategy described under "Introducing the Process of Interaction and Systems" on pages 00–00 as well as the type of chart shown in Table 4.3, prepare to teach the small group.

4. After you have taught your lesson, consider the following questions:
    a. How would you assess the success of your lesson in teaching the concept shown by the activity?
    b. What problems did you encounter in using the strategy for the use of interaction and systems, inference, and conclusion?
    c. What could you do to overcome these problems? What would you do differently?

Summary

The causal processes are the first of the scientific processes with which we move the child from the use of concrete objects to the use of abstractions. Because of this use of abstraction, the child needs to have attained a certain level of maturity in thinking. Piaget has placed the beginning of this level of maturity at approximately 10 years of age. Prior to that age level, children may supply precausal relations; that is, they may think of all things as being alive, made by humans, or magical. Later, once they discard the tendency to use precausal relations, children may have difficulty seeing that objects must directly interact for an effect to occur. Exposure to the causal processes should help children develop their ability to use more logical thought processes when it comes to the identification of causal relations in science activities.

As with most of science teaching and learning, presentation of the causal processes should move from the concrete to the abstract, so that the child has objects with which to work at first and thoughts or phenomena with which to work at the end.

The teacher can then couple causal processes with the basic processes in order to teach content material through the use of activity. Development of their ability to use the causal processes should also permit children more fully to use and understand the experiment as a means for learning science.

Chapter Vocabulary

The number following each term refers to the page on which the term is first introduced.

Animism, 108
Artificialism, 107
Cause and effect, 115
Conclusion, 121
Concrete predictions, 119
Concrete system, 112

Explanatory inference, 117
Inference, 117
Interaction, 111
Mental models, 116
Models, 116
Multiple inferences, 118

Applying the **CONCEPTS**

1. According to your textbook, children in second grade should learn the cause of day and night, why some kinds of animals are becoming extinct, and that things melt because heat energy causes the molecules to move faster. As you teach your children, you discover they have no understanding. Using what you know about cause and effect in young children, why are your students having difficulty with these topics?

2. Children in this first grade class are investigating simple machines. They investigate inclined planes by setting up ramps and rolling cars down them. When the teacher gathers the children together, she is amazed at their level of understanding. Most of the class can tell her that the higher the ramp the farther the cars will travel and the lower the ramp the less far they go. This seems very sophisticated cause and effect for young children. Are these children especially good at science, or is there some other reason for their level of understanding?

3. In a fourth grade class, the children complete an activity on electric circuits and write their own conclusions. The teacher collects the papers from the students, certain they will all have the correct conclusion. As he reads the papers, however, he finds that many of the students drew a conclusion that was incorrect. What would you suggest this teacher do to help his students understand the activity and draw more accurate conclusions?

References

Bellamy, M. L. 1983. What is your theory? *Science Teacher* 50, 2.

Finley, F. N. 1983. Science processes. *Journal of Research in Science Teaching* 20, 1.

Fox, P. 1994. Creating a laboratory. *Science and Children* 31, 4, 20–22.

Good, R. G. 1977. *How children learn science: Conceptual development and implications for teaching.* New York: Macmillan.

Inhelder, B., and J. Piaget. 1958. *The growth of logical thinking from childhood to adolescence.* New York:Basic Books.

Inhelder, B., and J. Piaget. 1964. *Early growth of logic in the child.* New York: Harper & Row.

Kuhn, D., E. Amsel, and M. O'Loughlin. 1988. *The development of scientific thinking skills.* San Diego: Academic Press.

Lee, K. S. 1982. Guiding young children to successful problem solving. *Arithmetic Teacher* 29, 5.

McAnarney, H. 1982. How much space does an object take up? *Science and Children* 19, 4.

Miller, K. W., S. F. Steiner, and C. D. Larson. 1996. Strategies for science learning. *Science and Children* 33(6), 22–25.

National Research Council. 1996. *National science education standards.* Washington, D.C.: National Academy Press.

Padilla, M. J., and E. J. Frye. 1996. Observing and inferring promotes science learning. *Science and Children* 33(8), 22–25.

Piaget, J. 1963. *The psychology of intelligence.* Totowa, N.J.: Littlefield.

Piaget, J. 1972a. *Judgment and reasoning in the child.* Totowa, N.J.: Littlefield.

Piaget, J. 1972b. *The child's conception of physical causality.* Totowa, N.J.: Littlefield.

Piaget, J. 1975a. *The child's conception of the world.* London: Routledge and Kegan Paul.

Reif, R. J., and K. Rauch. 1994. Science in their own words. *Science and Children,* 31, 4, 31–33.

Ross, M. E. 1997. Scientists at play. *Science and Children,* 35, 35–38.

Scarnati, J. T., and C. J. Weller. 1992. The write stuff: Science inquiry skills help students think positively about writing assignments. *Science and Children,* 29, 28–29.

Schlichter, C. L. 1983. The answer is in the question. *Science and Children,* 19, 3.

Shaw, J. M., and M. Cliatt. 1981. Searching and researching. *Science and Children,* 19, 3.

Sumrall, W. J., and J. Criglow. 1995. The "scoop" on science data. *Science and Children,* 32, 6, 37–39, 44.

Tobin, K. G., and W. Capie. 1982. Lessons with an emphasis on process skills. *Science and Children,* 19, 3.

White, E. P. (1982). Why self-directed learning? *Science and Children,* 19, 5.

CHAPTER 5

THE EXPERIMENTAL PROCESSES OF SCIENCE

Chapter Objectives

Upon completion of this chapter, you should be able to:

1 distinguish between an experiment and an investigation.
2 distinguish between quantitative research and qualitative research.
3 distinguish theory, hypothesis, and law.
4 describe the development of experimental abilities as identified by Piaget.
5 define each of the experimental processes: controlling variables, formulating hypotheses, interpreting data, defining operationally, and experimenting.
6 use each of the experimental processes: controlling variables, formulating hypotheses, interpreting data, defining operationally, and experimenting.

Introduction

Activity in science teaching and learning is vital for children in the preoperational and concrete operational stages of development for it is through direct activity that children develop concepts. However, simply doing an activity for the sake of doing an activity is not enough. For hands-on science teaching to be successful in helping students develop science concepts, those activities should (1) be purposeful, (2) be developmentally appropriate, and (3) develop an understanding of the role of activity in scientific research.

Purposeful activities are, first of all, those used as the primary learning experience rather than activities that simply illustrate something children have already encountered through reading or listening. A purposeful activity dealing with levers would be one in which students make a lever out of a ruler and a triangular block and then try balancing objects of differing weights, collecting data about the positioning of the objects, and finally determining that if a heavy and a light object are to be balanced on a lever, the heavier object should be closer to the fulcrum. This activity would be less than purposeful if students first read the concept of the heavier object being closer to the fulcrum and then showed this to be true by placing a heavy object close to the fulcrum and a light object further away so they can see the objects balance. Another example of an activity that does not have purpose is found in some elementary science textbooks where children are studying about rocks. In this case, after students are shown a few examples of rocks, including granite, they are given plaster, cups, water, and eventually paint. The activity is to make a fake rock out of plaster and then to paint it so it looks like a piece of granite. How much more purposeful it would be to have an activity in which students observe a variety of rock samples noting their characteristics, classify those rocks into categories on the basis of the characteristics, and then finally determine through the use of rock and mineral identification materials what types of rocks they have. Purposeful activities are those which children use to gain information for themselves. They are not, however, experiments. Rather, this type of hands-on activity should probably be called an investigation. The distinction between the two types of hands-on activities is an important one.

Investigations and Experiments

Investigations

Purposeful or not purposeful, these kinds of hands-on experiences are most accurately called investigations rather than experiments. As a consequence, if the investigations are purposeful, children from kindergarten through sixth grade can be engaged in activity that will help them develop science concepts.

Investigations have children using the basic and causal processes. Investigations result, most frequently, in descriptive rather than numerical data. Investigations are usually designed to find out how something works or to test a simple prediction. For example, an investigation with magnets would have children touch the magnet to a variety of objects around the classroom and make a list of those objects the magnet attracted and those the magnet did not attract. The children find that magnets attract some metal objects and do not attract any nonmetallic objects. The children then predict which objects in the hallway will be attracted and test those predictions. In this activity, the children are collecting data, drawing conclusions from that data, and gaining a concept of magnetism. What they are not doing is conducting an experiment.

Experiments

The **experiment** is a powerful tool of science. It is used by scientists to gain the evidence to support or refute a given hypothesis and through hypothesis testing to support or refute a given theory. In understanding the nature of an experiment, it is first necessary to understand the terms *theory, hypothesis, and law.*

Theory.   In the popular view, a theory is a kind of speculation often without any real foundation to support the speculation. Unfortunately, this popular view of a theory also pervades the public's view of scientific theories. In science, a theory is not idle speculation without support. In the natural world, events do not simply happen. Those events are related to other things in regular and systematic ways. Scientific theories attempt to capture those systematic relations and to use them to make predictions that can then be tested through observational consequences.

Observational consequences are statements whose accuracy can be determined by observation. For example, the molecular theory predicts that molecules in a substance with a high temperature are moving faster than those in a substance with a lower temperature. From this it is possible to predict that a drop of dye placed in hot water will spread through the water more quickly than a drop of dye placed in cold water. In order to test this prediction, drops of water are placed in containers of water and observed. When the observational consequences are true, a theory is supported. When observational consequences are false, the theory is damaged and in need of revision or, perhaps, replacement.

Thus a **theory** is a bundle of statements that can be used to explain events and can be supported or weakened by the observations made in testing predictions. Some examples of theories in science are the molecular theory, gravitational theory, continental drift, quantum theory, the Big Bang, and biological evolution.

Hypothesis.   Hypotheses are based on theories and are often used to test predictions made by those theories. In fact, the main function of a hypothesis is to suggest new experiments or new observations. Hypotheses may be stated in such a way that the hypothesis makes a positive prediction: If the amount of fat in the human diet is decreased, then the incidence of heart disease will also decrease. This hypothesis predicts a connection between fat consumption and heart disease and therefore can be tested through rigorously controlled experimentation. In other cases, the hypothesis is stated in the **null** form. That is, a prediction of no change is made. This is often used in educational research and is in this form: There will be no significant difference in science achievement between students engaging in a hands-on science program and students engaging in a textbook-only program. Of course, the researcher hopes to find a difference and so show the hypothesis to be invalid.

These two types of hypotheses give two slightly different definitions for what a hypothesis is. In the first case a **hypothesis** may be defined as an if . . . then statement showing a prediction. In the second case, a hypothesis may be considered as a statement to be proven wrong. Whichever type of hypothesis is used, it is still a statement to be tested through observation.

Law.   A **law** is an identification of a regularity applying to a broad class of phenomena (Parker, 1989). Newton's laws of motion, for example, describe how matter behaves under conditions of force, mass, and acceleration. The term *law* sometimes causes difficulty when that term is related to the daily use of the word. In daily use, a law is a statement telling one what is or is not appropriate in terms of behavior. It is against the law to take merchandise from a store without paying for them. And so, in common use, a law governs behavior. In terms of a scientific law, the law does not dictate how matter should behave but rather it describes how matter does behave under certain conditions. For example, the ideal gas law describes the behavior of gases under differing conditions of pressure, volume, and temperature.

Theories, hypotheses, and laws all attempt to give rational explanations or descriptions for the operation of the natural world. In order for theories to be accepted, the hypotheses derived from those theories must be tested through experimentation. In order for laws to be determined, they must have their foundation in data determined through experimentation. The experiment is based on the experimental processes.

The Experimental Processes

The experimental processes are welded into a single powerful tool for research in science. The experiment is the powerful tool used by scientists to gain the evidence to support or refute a given hypothesis. The experiment is also the means by which a scientist gains the information that will support or refute a scientific theory. Because the experiment is the basis for the factual knowledge of science, its structure and conditions are rigidly prescribed. Only by adherence to the rigorous conditions of the experimental method can scientists be certain that the results obtained are due to one particular factor and not to something else, which the scientist may not have considered important.

Once scientists have obtained the results of an experiment, they are ready for a second vital step in the scientific process. One set of results is not enough to convince the scientific community that a hypothesis is correct. Rather, the results of an experiment must be replicated in order to provide further certainty that the conditions of experimental rigor have been maintained. Normally, the results of an experiment are published or circulate, so that others in the scientific community can read the results and attempt to provide the necessary replication. At times the results are replicated, and the new ideas developed through the experiment become a part of the accepted knowledge which is science. At other times, the results cannot be duplicated and the results are discarded or modified. Another scientist frequently discovers some variable or some condition that was not considered in the original experiment and which affected the outcome.

The Experiment as a Research Tool

The experiment is the ultimate means for the development of scientific knowledge. Although the experiment is the ultimate research tool, that does not mean the experiment is something carried out only in a laboratory setting under rigidly controlled conditions. In many cases, qualitative research is utilized to develop the observations necessary to confirm or refute a particular hypothesis. The work done by Jane Goodall with chimpanzees, by Dian Fosse with gorillas, and by numerous other field researchers is generally **qualitative research** in which observations are made over a lengthy period of time, the observations are then interpreted, and conclusions are drawn. In other cases, the research is **quantitative research,** that is, based on a specified and highly controlled experimental design and with numerical data as the most frequent type of observations. To ensure that a cause is correctly attributed to a particular effect within the quantitative experiment, the experimental procedure must rigidly control variables. Although the research scientist and the elementary school science fair enthusiast all use or want to use quantitative experiments, they are not appropriate for all grade levels.

The Development of Quantitative Experimenting in Children

The processes involved in experimenting are the last of the scientific processes considered in detail by Piaget. These process skills develop during the formal operational stage of development, but their development is preceded by acquisition of certain skills on the part of the preoperational and concrete operational child. The experimental processes develop according to a general sequence of events tied to developmental stage and described here.

The Preoperational Child.   Preoperational children have not yet developed the ability to construct, carry out, or understand a true experiment. Although these children are not able to conduct true experiments, they can identify and test particular factors in the content of a hands-on activity. This ability is a prerequisite to the development of an ability to isolate and control variables.

The Concrete Operational Child.   Although children in the early concrete operational stage do not have a particular strategy for controlling variables during an activity, children at this stage of development are able to reject activities where a factor is uncontrolled when that factor is actually or intuitively obvious. In other words, children at this level realize that the effect of the surface on the height to which a ball will bounce cannot be tested if a Ping-Pong ball is used in one trial and a basketball is used in another.

By the late concrete operational stage, children attempt to carry out an experiment but vary more than one factor at a time or may vary one factor while saying they are varying a different factor. For example, children working with a pendulum may say they are going to vary the weight of the pendulum bob but actually vary the length of the pendulum. Or those same children may say they are going to vary the length of the pendulum and change both the length and the weight. Although the late concrete operational child is able to order the data gained through an experiment, he or she finds it difficult, if not impossible, to exclude the effect of interfering variables in interpreting that data.

Although late concrete operational children frequently arrive at the correct effect of a particular variable, that conclusion is often based on intuition and on faulty reasoning rather than on interpretation of the data actually collected during the experiment.

The Formal Operational Child.   Children in early formal operations stage, beginning at about sixth grade level and continuing into seventh grade, are able to control the variables in an experiment but may have difficulty isolating those variables that are not obvious. At this point children understand the necessity for making a hypothesis, planning controlled experiments, and collecting data but are likely to need help in organizing the data so that relevant information can be isolated and irrelevant data disregarded. A second characteristic of the early formal operational stage is that the student, after performing an experiment, is able to determine cause-and-effect relationships. The same student is unable to do the same thing when he or she is shown an experiment done by another individual.

By the later phases of the formal operational stage, eighth grade and above, students are able to control the variables in an experiment and base experiments and interpretations of data on a particular experimental model. The ability to understand experiments not done personally and to choose those that show a particular factor's effect is also a characteristic of late formal operational thinking.

Variables

Definition

Variables are all of the factors within a quantitative experiment that may be changed by the experimenter, that may change because of a change made by the experimenter, or that are kept the same because the experimenter wishes to rule them out as the cause of a change. Three types of variables are identifiable within a quantitative experimental procedure.

Types of Variables

The variable purposely changed by the experimenter in order to determine its effect on the rest of the system is called the **independent variable.** The experimenter expects a change in the independent variable to cause a change in some other part of the system. The changed variable, resulting from the manipulation of the independent variable, is termed the **dependent variable;** that is, it depends on the independent variable in order to change. A change in the independent variable usually results in a change in the dependent variable. If this change is to be correctly attributed to the change in the independent variable, all other aspects of the system must remain the same. The factors kept the same are referred to as **constants.**

As an illustration of these three types of variables, consider an activity in which a student tries to determine whether a magnet will act through cardboard as strongly as it does through air. The student is given a bar magnet, a box of steel pins, and five sheets of cardboard cut from a shoe box. First, the student sticks the magnet into the pile of pins, pulls it out, and counts the number of pins stuck to the magnet. All of the pins are then taken off the magnet and returned to the pile. Now the student decides to see what happens if the thickness of the cardboard is increased. First, a single layer of cardboard is placed on top of the pins and the magnet touched to the cardboard. The magnet and the cardboard are carefully raised together, and the number of pins attracted are counted. The student then adds additional pieces of cardboard one at a time and repeats the procedure with each new thickness.

In this activity, the child uses the same magnet, the same pins, the same pile for the pins, and the same type of cardboard cut to the same size for each of the trials. These are the parts of the system being held constant. The five sheets of cardboard are used to find out what will happen to the strength of the magnet as measured by the number of pins picked up. The amount of cardboard placed between the magnet and the pins is purposely changed by the child. Therefore, the thickness of cardboard is the independent variable. And, finally, a part of the system changes because of the change in the thickness of the cardboard: The number of pins attracted continuously decreases. The number of pins, then, is the dependent variable. The number of pins held by the magnet depends on the thickness of the cardboard.

Activity 5.1 is designed to involve you in identifying variables within a hypothesis.

Experimental Process Activity

Activity 5.1

Purpose   To develop your ability to recognize the three types of variables.

Procedure
1. For each of the following hypotheses, identify the independent variable, the dependent variable, and three factors that would have to be held constant when testing the hypothesis.

a. If the number of coils of wire around the core of an electromagnet is increased, then the strength of the electromagnet will increase.
b. If the area of a parachute is increased, then an object suspended from that parachute will fall more slowly.
c. If the stretch on a rubber band is increased, then the pitch of the sound produced when the rubber band is plucked will be higher.
d. If a marble is dropped into a basin of water, then the distance the water splashes will depend on the height of the drop.
e. If the surface area of a container is increased, then the water will evaporate more quickly.
f. If the strength of fertilizer is increased, then the rate of growth of a plant will increase.
g. If a heavy object is dropped from a height, then it will fall faster than a light object dropped from the same height.

The Control Group

Although control of variables is an attempt to be certain the results of an experiment can be attributed to the independent variable, a second safeguard is employed by scientists in order to be even more certain of the results. The second safeguard is the use of a control group.

A **control group** is a comparison group that receives no experimental manipulation but otherwise has the same characteristics as the experimental group. For example, if research is being done into the optimum amount of fertilizer to use to produce the greatest number of tomatoes per acre of land, the researcher plants a number of identical fields. Each field has the same amount of seed, the same type of soil, receives the same amount of water, and is planted using the same type of fertilizer, that is, whatever the farmer normally uses. Each of the other fields are treated with varying amounts of fertilizer. After the harvest, the yield of the experimental fields is compared with one another as well as with the typically fertilized field. In this case, the typically fertilized field acts as a control, so that other factors which might have increased yield can be ruled out. This control field gives additional assurances that the amount of fertilizer designated for optimum production was the actual cause of that production.

Children and Control of Variables

Control of variables is a process that only becomes possible when an individual has reached the level of formal operational thought, the final stage of development hypothesized by Piaget. It may also be the one stage of development identified by Piaget that is not reached by all normal human beings. Chiapetta (1976) showed that as many as 85 percent of adolescents and young adults do not reach the stage of formal operations.

In general the ability to use formal operational thought does not begin until the child reaches abut 11 or 12 years of age. The experimental processes are, therefore, best left until the sixth, seventh, and eighth grade levels. When children reach these upper middle school grades, they should begin with the process of controlling variables.

Stages in the Process of Controlling Variables.   According to Inhelder and Piaget (1958), the ability to control variables develops in four stages. During the first stage, the individual is unable to differentiate between the action of the variables and his or her own actions. The student at this stage may, when working with the pendulum, be unable to determine that how hard he or she pushes the pendulum has no bearing on the number of swings the pendulum makes in a minute. In the second stage, the learner is able to rule out himself or herself as the cause of a change but has difficulty distinguishing between relevant and irrelevant variables. In this case, the learner may discover that the length of the pendulum affects the number of swings but will remain unconvinced that other factors do not cause changes. In stage 3, the student is able to isolate one variable and keep others constant. The learner may, however, state that one variable is going to be manipulated, and then actually manipulate another. Consequently, the student may state that he or she is going to test for the effect of weight on the pendulum and actually test for the effect of string length. The child does this without realization. Finally, in stage 4, the individual becomes able correctly to manipulate and control variables, the same as the scientist does.

Relationship of the Stages in Controlling Variables to Teaching.   Children at stage 1 are not yet ready cognitively to work with the control of variables except in a situation that is highly structured by the teacher. Even then, it is unlikely children will be able to learn meaningfully. Rather than force stage 1 children to carry out a meaningless experiment, go back to the cause-and-effect processes and help the children develop the ability to identify the relevant parts of a system and attribute correctly cause and effect in simple investigations. Once children are able to identify relevant factors and to rule out their own participation, you can move to stage 2.

Stage 2 children are able to rule out themselves as a cause but may not be able to rule out all variables other than the relevant one. In this case, encourage children to identify all the factors they consider possible causes of an effect, develop experiments in which each of the factors tested in turn, and produce a chart that indicates which variables are direct causes of a phenomenon and which are not. Time will probably not permit each child to test each factor, or even each small group of children to test each factor. However, each small group could be assigned one factor to test and the results pooled to provide the total picture. Final conclusions can then be drawn on the basis of the testing of all identified possibilities rather than only one.

In stage 3, when children are able to identify factors independently and to rule out some, the problem is to be certain that the identified factor is actually being tested. This stage is easy for the teacher, who needs only check experimental procedure against intention to see if there is a correct match.

The last stage should be one of independent work, so that children who have developed the ability to use the experiment appropriately are able to do so. At this point the child is able to gain content information and to generate ideas that can be tested through experimentation or through the use of other sources of information.

The Other Experimental Processes

Control of variables is a vital aspect of experimentation, but it is not the only part of an experiment. Scientists cannot know which variables to control or manipulate without the guidance of a hypothesis. Without an interpretation of the data collected as the variables are manipulated, the scientist actually has learned nothing. And without the use of operational definitions the phenomenon under consideration may not be correctly identified by others who are replicating the experimental procedure. These other experimental processes are considered next.

Formulating Hypotheses

Definition. A hypothesis brings order to an experiment by determining what is being tested and what is expected as a result. **Formulating hypotheses** simply means developing a testable hypothesis.

As discussed earlier, the term *hypothesis* can be defined in a variety of ways. It is sometimes called an educated guess. This particular definition of a hypothesis has little real value in teaching children to learn to write and test hypotheses through quantitative experimentation. An educated guess could be something as simple as "It will rain tomorrow" or "There will be no mammoths in the zoo." In neither of these cases is there an actual hypothesis to test through control of variables. In other cases the hypothesis is called an "if . . . then" statement. This definition for a hypothesis provides the student with a format for writing a hypothesis and with a means for identifying the dependent and independent variables being tested in the resulting experiment. And, finally, a hypothesis may be defined as a "statement to be proven wrong." This is the form of the null hypothesis in which the researcher states, "There will be no difference in growth rate between plants that are given fertilizer and plants that are not given fertilizer." The experimenter then tests the hypothesis seeking to show that it is incorrect and that fertilizer does indeed cause a change in growth rate. This definition also is important to the teacher in terms of evaluating experiments conducted because it points to the idea that an experiment can, and frequently does, show the hypothesis to be incorrect. Keep in mind that students do not know what is going to happen, indeed should not know what is going to happen, and so may develop a hypothesis which is not validated by the experimental procedure. This should never be taken to mean a failure in experimentation as the student has, indeed, learned what happens and now can correct an erroneous or naive idea. In essence, the best way of looking at a hypothesis when teaching children to experiment is as a prediction of cause and effect in which the independent and dependent variables are clearly stated. For the previously described experiment with the cardboard, pins, and magnet, this statement could be an appropriate hypothesis:

> If the thickness of the cardboard is increased, then the number of pins picked up by the magnet will decrease.

From this statement, the experimenter can tell that the thickness of the cardboard is to be purposely changed. It is the independent variable. From this change in the thickness of the cardboard, the experimenter expects a change in the number of pins. The number of pins depends on the thickness and is the dependent variable. The hypothesis imposes order on the experiment.

Purpose of the Hypothesis.   A hypothesis focuses an experiment so the data collected by the experimenter are useful and organized. The hypothesis also gives an indication of the experimental procedure to be used in doing the experiment. The hypothesis is the starting point for the development of the procedure. Finally, the hypothesis indicates the kind of relationship that should be considered when interpreting the data collected.

Interpreting Data

Definition.   **Interpreting data** is the ability to perceive patterns in the information collected from an experiment and to express those patterns as a conclusion that either supports or refutes the hypothesis of the experiment. In interpreting data two basic processes are combined: using numbers and drawing conclusions.

In the experiment with the magnets and the pins, the following data were collected:

Pieces of Cardboard	Number of Pins
0	22
1	20
2	15
3	10
4	8
5	5
6	2

It is easy to see from this set of data that the number of pins decreases with the number of pieces—the thickness—of the cardboard. Returning to the hypothesis that an increase in the thickness of the cardboard will result in a decrease in the number of pins, the data indicate that the hypothesis is supported. However, if one were to draw the general conclusion that the thickness of any material determines the number of pins that will be picked up by a magnet, a great deal of additional testing would need to be done. The only information collected deals with cardboard.

To conclude that all materials will act in the same manner would be to draw a conclusion not warranted by the data.

Supported and Nonsupported Hypotheses.   At times, the interpretation of data will indicate that the hypothesis proposed by the experimenter was not supported. In this case, it is important to realize that the processes of hypothesizing and data interpretation were not incorrect nor did they fail. The fact that the data did not support the hypothesis does not make the hypothesis any less a hypothesis, nor does it invalidate the way in which the data were interpreted. In fact, the development and testing of nonsupported hypotheses are important to the practice of science. The amount of knowledge is increased by showing that a factor does not cause a change in a system. Experiments are successful even if the prediction made by the hypothesis is found to be not supported by the data. The child who is developing his or her ability to experiment cannot experience failure if he or she understands this feature of the experimental method.

Defining Operationally

Definition.   Defining operationally is the last aspect of experimenting. **Operational definitions** are those developed by the experimenter to satisfy a need experienced during the planning and carrying out of an experiment. For an experiment that is to be replicated by another individual, the operational definitions assure the second researcher will identify the same phenomena as representative of what the original researcher had considered.

An Example of Operational Definitions.   Once, doing a demonstration for a sixth grade class as a starting point for later experimentation by the children, I asked four different children to time how long it took for a candle placed under a gallon jar to go out. They all used the same clock, but the numbers the children gave for the time the candle took to go out were 63, 74, 97, and 128 seconds. Some variation is to be expected, but not 55 seconds. Why the difference? Each child had a difference, mental definition of "out."

63 seconds: It was out when I couldn't see the yellow flame.

74 seconds: It was out when I couldn't see any flame at all.

97 seconds: It was out when the little red spot on the flame was gone.

128 seconds: It was out when there was no more smoke coming
              from the wick.

In order to solve the problem of what was meant by the term *out*, I asked the students to come up with a definition of the word *out*. The operational definition developed by these students stated that the candle would be called out when there was no flame but a red spot or smoke could still be seen. This operational definition was appropriate for this class, at this time, and for this experiment. At another time or with another class, a different operational question might be needed. The children should create their own operational definitions rather than accepting definitions created for them by the teacher.

Teaching Children to Do Quantitative Experiments

Teaching children to experiment begins not with teaching children to write a hypothesis and control variables but rather with teaching children how to observe, how to classify, how to determine cause and effect, in fact how to use the basic and causal processes effectively. The experimental processes build on the ability to use the basic and causal processes.

The ability to develop a hypothesis is enhanced through the development of the processes of interaction and systems, cause and effect, and prediction. A hypothesis is, in fact, a prediction stated in terms of the cause-and-effect relationship that will be tested. If students have not had experience with these processes, writing a hypothesis will be virtually impossible. Controlling variables is based on the process of interaction and systems. Unless one can determine which materials and phenomena are important in terms of a particular system, it is difficult to determine what aspects of that system to select for testing. Experimenting is based on the processes of communication and operational questions. The use of communication enables the student to write an effective procedure, and the use of operational questions helps children learn how to set up an activity to find the answer to a question, how to set up an activity to solve a problem. Both of these processes contribute to the successful development of an experimental procedure. The experimental process of interpreting data requires that children have experience with observation, using numbers, using space/time relations, cause and effect, inference, and conclusion. The first three of these processes enable the student to collect data during the experiment, and the latter three enable them to draw a conclusion effectively from that data. And finally, the experimental process of operational definition is based on the basic processes of communication and the causal process of inference. One must first infer why there is a difficulty in interpreting a particular work and then must be able to accurately communicate a definition agreed upon by the entire group.

The use of the experimental processes requires that students already have developed their ability to use the basic and causal processes. Consequently, in working with students in the fifth and sixth grades who have had little or no experience with hands-on, activity-based science, it is inappropriate to start with developing true experiments. Instead, students should have the opportunity to work with the basic and causal processes, to develop expertise with those process skills before they attempt the development and use of true experiments.

Table 5.1 shows the relationship among the experimental processes, causal processes, and basic processes.

In working with the experimental processes, keep in mind that experimenting, which requires control of variables, is a particularly difficult task for children. It is

Table 5.1

Relationship Among the Experimental Processes, Causal Processes, and Basic

Processes

1. **Hypothesizing**
   a. Based on the basic processes of observation, communication, and operational questions.
   b. Based on the causal processes of cause and effect, interaction and systems, and prediction.

2. **Control of Variables**
   a. Based on the basic processes of observation and operational questions.
   b. Based on the causal processes of cause and effect, interaction and systems.

3. **Experimenting**
   a. Based on the basic processes of communication and operational questions.

4. **Interpreting Data**
   a. Based on the basic processes of observation, using numbers, using space/time relations, and classification.
   b. Based on the causal processes of cause and effect, interaction and systems, and concluding.

4. **Operational Definitions**
   a. Based on the basic processes of observation and communication.

the first of the science processes that requires the use of formal thought processes. Even the first step in an experiment, the development of a hypothesis, is difficult because it necessitates the use of logical cause-and-effect relationships.

As children in the intermediate grades begin to conduct experiments, they need a great deal of guidance. Children who have the opportunity to write and answer their own operational questions as well as to determine cause-and-effect relationships will probably have less difficulty in developing the ability to experiment than those children who have had little experience in these processes. The ability to experiment is the culmination of the ability to use the processes of science.

Timing the Teaching of the Quantitative Experiment

Teaching children to do true experiments can be effectively based on Vygotsky's concept of scaffolding, with the first attempts at conducting an experiment receiving extensive teacher support and later work with experimenting showing the gradual removal of that support until students are able to work independently.

Teacher-Structured Experiments

Because of their difficulty in using experimental processes, children's first exposure should be a **teacher-structured experiment,** with the teacher giving the hypothesis, the procedure, and the means for collecting the data. This structured step is designed to allow the children to see how an experiment is constructed with a hypothesis, procedure, and data collection. Naturally, you should conduct a discussion not only of the results of such experiments, but also of the procedures used in conducting the experiment. After the children are able to carry out the instructions of a preplanned experiment, they can be given a hypothesis and can develop as a group a procedure to test the hypothesis. At this time emphasize the variables under consideration and define, through use, each of the types of variables, while guiding children in their use and in their control.

Group-Structured Experiments

The second step in the development of the ability to experiment is the **group-structured experiment** in which individuals or small groups develop the procedure used to determine the validity of a predetermined hypothesis. At this stage, encourage children to find a variety of ways of testing a hypothesis, both to encourage creative approaches and to allow them to attempt a variety of conditions for testing. Children can be given the starting hypothesis through an interesting or challenging demonstration done by the teacher.

Student-Structured Experiments

Finally, children can be given background information and a problem to solve from which they can develop a **student-structured experiment.** In this stage children should be developing their own procedure and their own hypotheses rather than being provided with a ready-made problem and a ready-made hypothesis. Another possibility at this final stage is to have children develop experiments from operational questions. Because of the need for formal levels of thought, many children will be unable to carry out a true experiment without extensive teacher direction. For these children, make available the opportunity to investigate scientific phenomena through the use of operational questions and noncontrolled activities. The use of the process skills of science has been shown to be strongly correlated with the development of formal operational thought processes (Padilla, Okey, and Dellashaw, 1983)

But even those children who are unable to work individually with the experimental processes should be exposed to the processes of controlling variables, hypothesizing, and experimenting so that the concepts will not be entirely new to them when they make the transition to formal operations.

Activities 5.2 through 5.5 engage both you and students at the upper middle school levels in working with the experimental processes. In each case, carry out the experiment yourself and then work with a group of students to help them learn to carry out a true experiment. Keep in mind that students at the sixth grade level will need more assistance in experimenting than students at the eighth grade level. However, also keep in mind that students at the eighth grade level who have had no experience, or limited experience with designing and carrying out experiments, will need the same kind of guidance as sixth graders.

Experimental Process Activities

Activity 5.2

Purpose   (1) To develop you ability to carry out an experiment, and (2) to develop your ability to work with the experimental processes with students in the upper middle grades.

Procedure

1. Collect the following materials: ruler with a groove, small marble (1.5 cm), white paper, tape, book, 3 x 5 card, other materials as needed.
2. Make a 2.5 cm cube by marking 2.5 cm lines on the 3 x 5 card, forming a grid and then cutting out the following pattern.

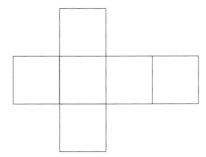

3. Fold along the dotted lines and tape the edges to form a cube with a top that can be opened and resealed.
4. Tape the white paper to a tabletop. Place one end of the ruler so it just touches the midpoint of one edge of the paper, and prop the other end up on a book so it is at approximately a 45-degree angle. Place the block at the base of the ruler.
5. Mark the position of the block by drawing a line around it and then finding the center point by drawing two diagonal lines.
6. Hold the marble at the top of the ruler. Release the marble. Mark the new position of the block by finding the center point. Measure the distance the block moved by measuring from center point to center point. Repeat three times and find the average distance traveled by the block.
7. List five or more variables that could affect the distance the block moves. Choose one of the five variables that you listed and write a hypothesis.
8. Develop and carry out an experiment to test your hypothesis. List your independent and dependent variables as well as those factors you held constant. Be certain to collect the appropriate data and to draw a conclusion as to the validity of your hypothesis.
9. Try the same experiment with a group of sixth, seventh, or eighth grade students. Using the information on the sequence for teaching students to experiment, prepare to teach the students to do a true experiment.

Activity 5.3

Purpose   (1) To develop your ability to carry out an experiment, and (2) to develop your ability to work with the experimental processes with students in the upper middle grades.

Procedure

1. Collect the following materials: room temperature water, table salt, Pyrex beaker, heat source, stirring rod, thermometer, graduated cylinder, balance, other materials as needed.
2. Determine the amount of salt that will dissolve in 25 ml of room temperature water.
3. After you have determined the amount of salt that will dissolve, list five factors that could affect the amount of salt dissolving.
4. Develop an experiment that could be used to test the effect of one of your factors. Include the following in your experiment: the hypothesis to be tested, identification of the independent and dependent variables as well as five constants, and the procedure you will follow.
   a. Carry out your experiment and draw a conclusion as to the validity of your hypothesis.
5. Try the same experiment with a group of sixth, seventh, or eighth grade students. Using the information on the sequence for teaching students to experiment, prepare to teach the students to do a true experiment.

Activity 5.4

Purpose   (1) To develop you ability to carry out an experiment, and (2) to develop your ability to work with the experimental processes with students in the upper middle grades.

Procedure

1. Collect the following materials: two metersticks, graph paper, tennis ball, masking tape, partner, other materials as needed.
2. Determine the height to which a tennis ball dropped from 100 cm will bounce.
3. After you have determined the height of the bounce, list five factors that could affect the height of the bounce.
4. Develop an experiment that could be used to test the effect of one of your factors. Include the following in your experiment: the hypothesis to be tested, identification of the independent and dependent variables as well as five constants, and the procedure you will follow.
   a. Carry out your experiment and draw a conclusion about the validity of your hypothesis.
5. Try the same experiment with a group of sixth, seventh, or eighth grade students. Using the information on the sequence for teaching students to experiment, prepare to teach the students to do a true experiment.

Activity 5.5

Purpose

(1) To develop you ability to carry out an experiment, and (2) to develop your ability to work with the experimental processes with students in the upper middle grades.

Procedure

1. Collect the following materials: gallon jar, candle, plasticine (for use as a candleholder), matches, container with sand (for used matches), stopwatch, partner, other materials as needed.
2. Light the candle, place the jar over the candle, and time how long it takes for the candle to go out.
3. After you have determined the time it takes for the candle to go out, list five factors that could affect length of time the candle burns.
4. Develop an experiment that could be used to test the effect of one of your factors. Include the following in your experiment: the hypothesis to be tested, identification of the independent and dependent variables as well as five constants, and the procedure you will follow.
   a. Carry out your experiment and draw a conclusion about the validity of your hypothesis.
5. Try the same experiment with a group of sixth, seventh, or eighth grade students. Using the information on the sequence for teaching students to experiment, prepare to teach the students to do a true experiment.

Content Teaching and the Experiment

The use of the experiment brings the child to a level of activity equal to that of the research scientist. Just as the scientist does not carry out an experiment solely for the purpose of experimenting, the child should not experiment just to learn the parts of an experiment or the general experimental processes.

The purpose of the experiment is also to gain content information. The key to using the experiment with children is to give them only enough background information to carry out the experiment and no more. In this way the child generates knowledge on his or her own rather than simply verifying what he or she has already been told.

In general, quantitative experiments can be most effectively used by children in the physical sciences. This is simply because the physical sciences have many topics that allow children to control variables easily. Children can experiment to find the effect of temperature on solubility of salt in water. They can experiment to find the effect of friction on motion. They can experiment to find the factors that affect the period of a pendulum. Qualitative experiments, however, are more appropriate for children in the biological sciences and in the earth sciences. Students can do qualitative research as they investigate a square meter environment, as they observe ducks at a pond, as they observe the behavior of ants in an ant farm. However, as students gain in the ability to use the experimental processes, and particularly in the ability to recognize and control variables, they can also begin to work more fully with experiments as a part of the biological and earth-space sciences. After the qualitative or quantitative research has been conducted, the child can use textbooks, trade books, magazines, computer programs, CD-ROM, the Internet, or other sources to determine the validity of the results or to add content information the children could not obtain experimentally. The experiment should begin to teach the content; the verbal material should extend the content. But because of the advanced nature of the thought processes required by the qualitative experiment, be certain that you make it possible for children who need to do so to use operational questions rather than hypotheses and to engage in noncontrolled activities rather than controlled experimental procedures. Although the controlled quantitative experiment is a vital tool of the researcher, it is more important to let the child learn in an effective manner than it is to push for the child to reach the level of process embodied in the quantitative experiment.

A good textbook abounds with activities that children can carry out to verify the content of that textbook. These activities generally not only provide the answers through pictures or through the written text but also do not ask the child to undertake either quantitative or qualitative experiments. The teacher can derive quantitative experiments from these activities by determining the content to be demonstrated through the activity, turning the content into a hypothesis, and having the students develop a procedure that will determine the validity of the hypothesis. This is best done prior to the students' review of the material in the text or the activity. To make the classroom more interesting, present more than one hypothesis for the textbook activity and have various groups determine which of the hypotheses has the greatest amount of supporting data. Activities can be turned into qualitative experiments by giving students a question and an area to observe in answering that question, time to collect data, and finally time to interpret that data in terms of the research question.

Both qualitative and quantitative experiments should be used with students as they gain in ability to use the experiment as a means to the collection of data.

Activities 5.6 and 5.7 are designed to engage you in analyzing the use of true experiments in textbooks for the sixth, seventh, or eighth grades and in turning an investigation into a true experiment.

Experimental Process Activities

Activity 5.6

Purpose   To investigate the use of true experiments in sixth, seventh, or eight grade science textbooks.

Procedure

1. Choose one textbook from each of the grade levels. Choose one chapter from each textbook dealing with the same or a similar topic.
2. Locate and read each of the hands-on activities included in the chapter of each textbook. Be certain to look at the teaching suggestions as well as at the text itself.
3. Analyze each of the activities in terms of the process skills used.
    a. Which activities rely on the basic and causal processes?
    b. Which activities engage students in the use of the experimental processes?
4. How many of the activities are investigations? How many of the activities are true experiments?
5. How does the use of investigation and experiment change from one grade level to another within the text series? How appropriate to the grade level is the use of investigation versus experiment?

Activity 5.7

Purpose To develop your ability to rewrite an investigation into the form of a true experiment.

Procedure

1. Choose any sixth, seventh, or eighth grade textbook. Find three investigations in the text that can be changed from an investigation to an experiment.
2. Write a procedure for each of the experiments that could be developed from the investigation.
    a. The experiment developed should have a procedure that could be followed by a student at the grade level of the textbook.
3. Working with a small group of students at the appropriate grade level, have the students use your procedure.
    a. What problems did the students encounter is working with the procedure?
    b. Rewrite your procedure to eliminate the problems encountered.

Summary

The experiment, which is composed of the individual experimental processes, constitutes the most powerful means that science has for gaining information. It is also the most difficult of the scientific processes for children to learn because it presupposes the ability to use formal thought processes.

Because the student must use formal operational thought processes, the experimental processes are best left until the upper intermediate grades, particularly the sixth grade. Even then, the child should be able to fall back on operational questions and noncontrolled activities when it is necessary for understanding.

In general, teaching the experimental processes moves from highly structured situations to situations the student structures alone. In this way the child gains more and more independence in the use of the experiment to enlarge his or her knowledge of the content of science.

Chapter Vocabulary

The number following each term refers to the page on which the term is first introduced.

Constants, 134
Control group, 135
Dependent variable , 134
Experiment, 130
Formulating hypotheses, 137
Group-structured experiments, 140
Hypothesis, 131
Independent variable, 134
Interpreting data, 138
Investigation, 129
Law, 131

Null, 130
Purposeful activity, 129
Observational consequences, 130
Operational definition, 139
Qualitative research, 132
Quantitative research, 132
Student-structured experiments, 142
Teacher-structured experiments, 141
Theory, 130
Variables, 133

Applying the CONCEPTS

1. Very often, when people talk about evolution or global warming, they make the statement, "it's only a theory." Are these individuals using the term *theory* in its scientific sense or in its common use sense? How would you respond to a person who says, "It's only a theory"?

2. Most science fairs require that all students entering, whether first graders or eighth graders, do a true experiment. How appropriate is this kind of project for students in the elementary and middle school years? When would you suggest science fairs begin requiring students to do true experiments?

3. Some of your seventh graders are ready to conduct true experiments and others are not. How would you use Vygotsky's zone of proximal development in this situation?

4. True experiments appeal to children who use logical and mathematical intelligence. How could you make the use of experiments more appropriate to children evidencing bodily, spatial, interpersonal, intrapersonal, or linguistic intelligences?

5. A sequence has been considered here for introducing students to developing true experiments. How does this sequence utilize Vygotsky's idea of scaffolding?

References

Aicken, F. 1991. *The nature of science.* Portsmouth, N. H.: Heineman.

Bellamy, M. L. 1983. What is your theory? *Science Teacher* 50, 2.

Beveridge, W. I. B. 1950. *The art of scientific investigation.* New York: Vintage Books.

Bogdan, R., and S. Biklen 1982. *Introduction to qualitative research in education.* New York: Aldine.

Chiapetta, E. L. 1976. A review of Piagetian studies relevant to science instruction at the secondary and college levels. *Science Education* 60, 124–136.

Finley, F. N. 1983. Science processes. *Journal of Research in Science Teaching* 20, 1.

Fox, P. (1994). Creating a laboratory. *Science and Children* 31, 4, 20–22.

Giere, R. N. 1984. *Understanding scientific reasoning* (2nd ed.) New York: Holt, Rinehart and Winston.

Glaser, B. G., and A. L. Strauss. 1967. *The discovery of grounded theory: Strategies for qualitative research.* New York: Aldine.

Good, R. G. 1977. *How children learn science: Conceptual development and implications for teaching.* New York: Macmillan.

Inhelder, B., and J. Piaget 1958. *The growth of logical thinking from childhood to adolescence.* New York: Basic Books.

Inhelder, B., and J. Piaget 1964. *Early growth of logic in the child.* New York: Harper & Row.

Kitcher, P. 1982. *Abusing science.* Cambridge, Mass.: MIT Press.

Kuhn, D., E. Amsel, and M. O'Loughlin 1988. *The development of scientific thinking skills.* San Diego: Academic Press.

Lawson, A. E. 1978. The development and validation of a classroom test of formal reasoning. *Journal of Research in Science Teaching* 15, 1.

Lawson, A. E. 1982. Formal reasoning, achievement, and intelligence: An issue of importance. *Science Education* 66, 1.

National Research Council 1996. *National science education standards.* Washington, D.C.: National Academy Press.

Padilla, M. J., J. R. Okey, and F. G. Dellashaw. 1983. The relationship between science process skill learning and formal thinking abilities. *Journal of Research in Science Teaching* 20, 3.

Pallrand, G. J. 1979. The transition to formal thought. *Journal of Research in Science Teaching* 16, 5.

Parker, S. P. (ed.). 1989. *McGraw-Hill dictionary of scientific and technical terms* (4th ed.). New York: McGraw-Hill

Piaget, J. 1963. *The psychology of intelligence.* Totowa, N. J.: Littlefield.

Piaget, J. 1972a. *Judgment and reasoning in the child.* Totowa, N. J.: Littlefield.

Shaw, J. M., and M. Cliatt. 1981. Searching and researching. *Science and Children* 19,3.

Tobin, K. G., and W. Capie. 1982. Lessons with an emphasis on process skills. *Science and Children* 19, 3.

Vygotsky, L. S. 1962. *Thought and language.* Cambridge, Mass.: MIT Press.

White, E. P. 1982. Why self-directed learning? *Science and Children* 19, 5.

PART THREE

CONSTRUCTING SCIENCE WITH ALL CHILDREN

CHAPTER SIX

SCIENTIFIC LITERACY AND SCIENTIFIC ATTITUDES

Chapter Objectives

Upon completion of this chapter, you should be able to:

1 discuss the role of scientific attitudes in the development of scientific literacy.
2 define each of the scientific attitudes.
3 discuss methods for developing each of the scientific attitudes in the classroom.
4 discuss the role of the teacher in developing scientific attitudes in the classroom.

Introduction

The goal of science education in the 1990s and beyond is the development of a scientifically literate population. Scientific literacy, however, does not simply mean individuals who can define scientific terms or who can recall factual information. According to *Project 2061: Science for All Americans,*

> Scientific literacy—which encompasses mathematics and technology as well as the natural and social sciences—has many facets. These include being familiar with the natural world and respecting its unity; being aware of some of the important ways in which mathematics, technology, and the sciences depend upon one another; understanding some of the key concepts and principles of science; having a capacity for scientific ways of thinking; knowing that science, mathematics, and technology are human enterprises, and knowing what that implies about their strengths and limitations; and being able to use scientific knowledge and ways of thinking for personal and social purposes (AAAS, 1989, p. 20).

This statement shows that both science content and scientific ways of thinking are a part of scientific literacy. Those ways of thinking are developed through the scientific attitudes.

Children beginning school are full of curiosity. They approach learning with interest and with enthusiasm. Interest, enthusiasm, and curiosity are vital to the development of scientific attitudes and scientific literacy in general. Unfortunately, many children leave middle school with a different attitude. During their elementary school and middle school years they acquire the idea that science is something for "smart people" or something so dull it could cure insomnia. Many children develop the idea that mathematics is tedious, dull, purposeless, and repetitive. And many children leave the middle school with the idea that science and mathematics are school subjects, subjects divorced from reality, and so not particularly useful in daily living.

This change in attitude from interest and enthusiasm to boredom and apathy is often the result of two things. First, the science curriculum often overemphasizes discrete facts, topics with no interest to students or with no relationship to the child's world. From this students learn that science is something you study in school, not something you use in the real world. Second, teachers often demonstrate attitudes that are inappropriate to the development of scientific literacy. They use only one source of information, accept only one possible answer, view the textbook as an authority for content, and single-mindedly adhere to a single teaching schedule and routine. From this, children learn that science is dull and routine. But, more importantly, as a result of this kind of teaching, children do not develop the scientific habits of mind, the scientific attitudes, that would allow them to become truly scientifically literate. *Science for All Americans* indicates that scientific habits of mind are useful to all people as they deal with problems involving evidence, logical arguments, uncertainty, and critical thinking. *Science for all Americans* then goes on to say that individuals who have not developed these habits of mind are "easy prey to dogmatists, flimflam artists, and purveyors of simple solutions to complex problems" (p. 13).

As teachers we can help our students develop scientific literacy and particularly develop of scientific habits of mind. The *National Science Education Standards* (National Research Council; 1996) encourage teachers to model the skills of curiosity, openness to new ideas, and skepticism that characterize science. *The Standards* also state that when teachers show enthusiasm and interest, they instill in their students those same attitudes. Teacher modeling, therefore, becomes vital developing of scientific habits of mind, that is, scientific attitudes. This modeling includes not simply govern how you act in the classroom, but also how you present and handle activities useful in developing the scientific attitudes. In the case of the scientific attitudes, what you do is far more important than what you say.

Developing Scientific Attitudes

In Chapter 1, we said scientists have a particular outlook or attitude toward the world that pervades their work. This outlook is a composite of a number of scientific attitudes, all of which should be considered part of the elementary school science program. When we help our students develop the scientist's habits of mind, the scientist's attitudes, we help them develop a true understanding of the nature of science, as well as an understanding of the methods of inquiry and the content derived from those methods. Here is a list of scientific attitudes we should model for children at the elementary and middle school grades:

1. curiosity
2. honesty
3. willingness to suspend judgment
4. open-mindedness
5. skepticism
6. objectivity
7. a positive approach to failure
8. respect for the environment
9. lack of superstition

Curiosity

The scientific attitude of curiosity is the basis for science itself. Stemming from the scientific value of longing to know and understand, **curiosity** is the spontaneous desire to explore the environment, to learn about and investigate its phenomena. It is the only one of the scientific attitudes teachers can expect to find naturally in children. The problem with the scientific attitude of curiosity is not in developing it but rather in maintaining it.

Maintaining Curiosity in Children.   In a fifth grade class where rocks had been the topic of study for nearly a month, one of the children arrived at school with a rock in the basket of her bicycle. It had taken both her and her brother to lift it into the basket. The rock was so large and heavy it had bent the basket out of shape. When the girl arrived at school she asked her classroom teacher to come and see what she had brought for science. Unfortunately, the teacher went out to see. The teacher immediately told the girl she had been irresponsible putting a rock that size into her bike basket. She should have taken better care of her belongings. Then, as a parting comment, the teacher added that the girl's parents were probably going to be angry about the basket. What a way to destroy curiosity!

If we want to maintain curiosity, we need to develop a classroom atmosphere where our students feel free to be curious. This kind of atmosphere occurs when we encourage questions from the children we teach and, more importantly, encourage children to investigate those questions to find the answers. Curiosity is not fostered when we ignore the questions children ask, belittle those who ask questions, or answer all questions from children in an authoritarian manner. Curiosity is fostered when children are able to investigate educationally valid tangents as well as the topics directly under consideration. For example, during a fourth grade science class dealing with birds in which the teacher had a professor from a local college bring in and discuss eggs from a variety of birds, one of the children asked about snake eggs. The question about snake eggs immediately led to frog eggs and insect eggs and even to whether sharks lay eggs. Although the classroom teacher was disconcerted by these questions occurring within a lesson on birds and with a guest speaker, the speaker, a biologist, discussed the various kinds of eggs with the class, drew diagrams of them on the chalkboard, and even added a few more types of animals that laid eggs to the list. She encouraged and responded to their curiosity.

Maintaining curiosity also means children have an opportunity to investigate things that are interesting at a particular time. As teachers we need to take advantage of what we call "teachable moments" and "spontaneous events" when they occur and not wait three months until the questions finally comes back as a part of the standard curriculum in science. A cocoon, a bunch of berries, a cement truck pouring concrete for a new sidewalk, all may generate a great deal of curiosity and often provide for a more effective lesson than the one planned for the day. Curiosity can also be maintained by a "wait, or ask, and see" attitude on the part of the teacher. Sometimes children get involved in tangent investigations which do not appear to be productive, at least not at the teacher's first glance. Most teachers react to these situations by telling the students to get back on task. However, if we want to maintain curiosity on the part of our students, as well as foster inquiry, we should first try to determine what students are doing and whether the investigation is productive. For example, while a class was investigating the materials making up soil, three third graders began a very different investigation. When the teacher looked back at the group's activity, they appeared to be smearing mud all over the table at which they were working. But rather than assume anything, the teacher asked the children what they were doing. They were attempting to determine how long it took for different thicknesses of mud to dry. They had thick mud at one end and plain water at the other end and a variety of thicknesses in between and were carefully timing how long each section took to dry. In this case, what looked like a mess was an interesting and productive investigation. Such investigations both promote and maintain curiosity. And, finally, because modeling of behavior is so powerful a tool for the development of scientific attitudes, you must demonstrate curiosity about the environment so the children see it as a desirable behavior.

Techniques for Maintaining Curiosity.   The classroom teacher with the rock in the bicycle basket had a perfect opportunity to encourage curiosity in her students. What could she have done? She could have done what the science specialist for the school did. First, she ignored the bicycle basket in favor of the rock. She helped carry the rock into the science room so the other students could see it. Then she had the students make observations of the rock and use those observations to try to identify the kind of rock. It was a huge lump of milky quartz. How huge was it? The students made predictions about how much the object weighed. They ended by placing it on a scale and finding it weighed 34 pounds! This teacher helped her students maintain their curiosity. In fact, teachers can maintain curiosity through a variety of techniques such as these:

1. Answer and investigate spontaneous questions from students. This is particularly effective when the class develops operational questions or experiments in order to find their own answers to the questions.

2. Use spontaneous events as a part of the curriculum rather than as an irritation. The noise from a cement truck should be an invitation to investigate rather than a reason to close all the windows and forge ahead with the unit on heat.

3. Use mystery boxes, probe boxes, or other puzzling objects to permit the child to investigate an unknown quantity.

4. Use **discrepant events,** that is, demonstrations or activities that have an unexpected result into the curriculum and so generate curiosity. Discrepant events provide a puzzle for which the class must find a solution.

5. Provide for open-ended, process-oriented activities, which the child may investigate in a no-fail setting and can lead to spontaneous investigations of other, related phenomena.

6. Maintain curiosity with discussion questions that children ask, pictures that are unusual, motion pictures and television programs with science content, and discussions of books with inaccurate or fantasized science content.

7. Provide books, magazines, and other sources of information on topics in which children have demonstrated some curiosity.

8. Remember that science has no taboo topics. All things are appropriate for investigation. All things are appropriate for discussion.

Curiosity helps children develop interest in a particular area of science. Once the child is interested in an area, there is little the teacher cannot accomplish with the child.

Honesty

Honesty in science is reporting the true outcome of an investigation or experiment, maintaining records which show all of the data collected not simply a sample of that data, and reporting what is observed rather than what one wishes to observe. Although honesty is not, of course, unique to the scientific community, it is essential to the scientific enterprise.

Developing Scientific Honesty in Children.   This scientific attitude requires a change in the way most teachers think about science content. Most of what teachers do in a classroom is geared toward right or wrong answers. A premium is put on getting the right answer. Wrong answers are given some form of sanction. Consequently, students often make their answers fit their predictions or hypotheses, say what they know the teacher wants to hear, or draw conclusions that are correct according to the textbook or prior knowledge but do not reflect the data they collected. All of these are scientifically dishonest. We need to help our students understand that reporting data accurately and honestly, and drawing conclusions which reflect the data, are far more important than getting a particular answer. In developing scientific honesty, you can do the following:

1. assist children in developing journals in which they maintain accurate records of their activities and investigations.
2. praise children for developing conclusions consistent with the data they collect but that may not reflect known scientific facts or principles.
3. discuss limitations that may exist within experiments or activities and may affect the accuracy of the results.
4. discuss with students how all of the data from an activity or experiment must be recorded and considered rather than only the data that reflect the desired outcome.
5. encourage students to present differing interpretations of data from experiments and activities and to discuss the merits of those interpretations in terms of the data which support them.

Willingness to Suspend Judgment

Willingness to suspend judgment requires that an individual wait until all of the facts are in before he or she makes a judgment or draws a conclusion. At times, it asks the individual to set aside a strongly held belief and to consider conflicting evidence. Children do not take up this scientific attitude spontaneously and so should see the teacher and others model this attitude.

Developing a Willingness to Suspend Judgment.   This scientific attitude is difficult to develop when the teacher uses only a single source of information in a science class. If our students are going to develop ability to withhold judgment, they need to use a number of sources of information, to determine the value and accuracy of sources, and only after much consideration to draw a conclusion that reflects the information. Students should have access to a wide variety of printed sources of information rather than just a single textbook. But willingness to suspend judgment does not only apply to written sources of information. It also applies to hands-on activities. If we are going to help our students learn to suspend judgment, we need to use more than one activity to teach a particular concept. One activity allows children to jump to conclusions, whereas a number of activities requires students to weigh and consider a variety of sources of evidence. Finally, if we are going to help our students develop a willingness to suspend judgment, we need to develop a classroom atmosphere in which children feel comfortable presenting evidence that conflicts with information presented by other students or by the teacher.

Techniques for Developing Willingness to Suspend Judgment.   In a classroom where willingness to suspend judgment is fostered, one would expect to see the following:

1. a variety of different sources of information including books, magazines, newspapers, films, filmstrips, and resource persons.
2. children learning which criteria can be used to judge the validity and/or bias of a source of information.
3. children discussing differing results for an activity or experiment and trying to determine the causes of those differences as well as the validity of the varying results.
4. students debating and discussing controversial issues in which all sides are considered no matter how popular or unpopular the view.
5. teachers presenting a variety of activities to show a particular concept.
6. displays of newspaper and/or magazine articles that show the development of a theory over time.
7. questions from teachers and students like these:
   a. What was your source of information?
   b. What evidence do you have to support that idea?
   c. Did you consider all of the information before you made a decision or drew a conclusion?
   d. How valid do you think your sources of information were?

Willingness to suspend judgment, as a scientific attitude, asks the learner to consider a variety of viewpoints and a variety of sources of information. It also asks teachers to model the attitude by using a variety of resources in teaching, by being familiar with a variety of viewpoints, and by not jumping to conclusions.

Skepticism

The scientific attitude of **skepticism** is one in which the individual maintains a doubting attitude. It is a trait that is important in most facets of life. For example, almost every time you turn on the television set, you are treated to a telephone number for a psychic network of one kind or another. Although a disclaimer is attached to all of these ads, "for entertainment purposes only," there is little doubt from the sales pitch that the psychics are supposed to be treated as real and authentic. But should they be? Are there such things as psychics? Can I get in touch with one on the telephone? Will a psychic really be able to tell me about my future? A skeptic is going to find the answers to questions like these before spending the money to call one of the numbers given. A skeptic is going to consult a variety of sources before making a decision. And a skeptic is going to continue to find information until all doubt is resolved. This kind of attitude is rare among both children and adults and so needs to be developed in the science classroom.

Developing Skepticism as a Scientific Attitude.   Skepticism cannot flourish in a situation where it is not considered proper to question the authority of the teacher or the textbook. Rather, we need to teach our students that it is not only all right to ask questions but desirable to do so, even when those questions challenge what is presented as fact. Errors do occur in textbooks, trade books, and newspaper or magazine articles. At times, new information is discovered after a text or book goes to press. Sometimes the source of the information is biased and the information presented inaccurate. When material is presented as fact without support, or when conclusions are drawn where additional evidence could cause a different conclusion, the information should be open to the skeptic's questioning.

Techniques for Developing Skepticism.   As teachers we can encourage the development of the scientific attitude of skepticism through the following:

1. consideration of sources of information by study of biased versus unbiased approaches.
2. presentation of a variety of differing sources of information during any unit of study.
3. consideration of a variety of activities in which a principle is clearly shown in the majority, but its opposite is indicated in some.
4. displays and reading of new advances in science, which may conflict with text or program material.
5. interviews in which the interviewer must probe for the resources of the interviewee.
6. comparison of fictional materials—books, comics, cartoons—with factual materials and a discussion of the differences in a "which is more accurate" framework.

7. viewing and discussing both print and televised advertisements and the claims they make in terms of the evidence presented.

8. using fake and real articles and having students decide how they could go about determining whether or not the articles are fake or real.

If you develop skepticism in your students, you may find yourself the object of their skepticism. As a consequence, you may hear questions like these:

What's the purpose for learning this?

Why can't I try it this way?

But I got the same answer. What's wrong with my method?

How do you know that's true?

Objectivity

To be objective is to look at many sides of an issue without prejudice. **Objectivity** asks us to start with a neutral position and attempt to determine what will happen in a particular situation or which position on a topic is most valid.

Problems in Working with the Scientific Attitude of Objectivity.   A major problem in working with the attitude of objectivity is that a wide variety of the topics tackled under the heading of science have emotional overtones. Interests, tastes, attitudes, values, and morality—a class will touch upon all of these at one time or another.

Consider the following topics. When we study insects in the elementary science program, the insects are usually butterflies, bees, and grasshoppers. Generally, these types of insects do not arouse highly negative feelings. But if the insects are roaches, mosquitoes, ants, or flies, we may have a hard time convincing our students these creatures have a place in the food web. The latter group tends to arouse feelings of disgust or, in locations where fire ants are common, fear. The affective component of any study may make it difficult for anyone to show objectivity.

However, objectivity also presents other problems. Objectivity asks us to approach any topic in a nonbiased way. But many topics, such as the study of certain types of insects, show that science is not necessarily devoid of attitudes, values, emotions, and previous learning. When the information presented in our science program is consistent with our value system it is easy to listen to, accept, and learn the information. Information that is not consistent with our values, beliefs, or previous learning may be shut out or negatively processed. In both students and teachers, the individual's value system affects his or her objectivity.

A third factor that influences the ability to be objective in the classroom is the child's developmental stage. Children in the preoperational stage of development tend to be highly egocentric. The egocentric child finds it difficult, if not impossible, to consider any viewpoint other than his or her own. Consequently, an egocentric child may reject, out of hand, anything that does not agree with his or her own viewpoint.

Finally, even teachers may find the attitude of objectivity difficult. In some cases, objectivity may be difficult for a teacher who is authoritarian. A teacher who has definite ideas about the information and attitudes students should develop will find it difficult to handle many sources of information and children who are drawing their own conclusions in various situations. Additionally, a teacher may find it difficult when a child draws conclusions that differ from his or her own belief system. The teacher cannot dictate beliefs to children, particularly in a society that is increasingly multicultural. In order for the children to learn to be objective, they must see objectivity on the part of the teacher.

Techniques for Developing Objectivity. Developing the child's ability to look objectively at the content of the science program means the teacher must change the customary pattern of teaching science in the elementary school.

Using a Textbook. Most textbook activities for teaching content are presented to illustrate the principle that has already been developed by the text. The student is told the purpose of the activity and so is told the outcome. Because the outcome is known prior to the activity, there can be no doubt in anyone's mind what will occur. The activity, therefore, illustrates rather than instructs. In many cases, even if the activity does not work as it is supposed to work, the children still see, or say they see, exactly what they were told the outcome would be.

Rather than illustrating what is already known, activities designed to develop objectivity should be presented in such a way that the students will not know the outcome. The activity should be presented so the learner is asked to determine the content rather than asked to illustrate the content. Foregone conclusions are closely allied to biases and have no place in the objective world of science. Teaching that uses activities in which the students are able to develop content from activity also helps those students develop conceptually.

Using Operational Questions. A second way to develop the scientific attitude of objectivity is to ask and investigate operational questions. Teachers should pose such questions in a neutral form so students must base their answers to the questions on the data collected rather than on the thrust of the question. Neutral questions are phrased like the following:

What is the effect of sunlight on plant growth?
What factors affect the amount of force needed to use a lever to lift an object?
How can the rate of evaporation of a liquid be increased?

Evaluation-Level Questions. A third possibility for the development of objectivity in children is for the teacher to propose evaluation-level questions, particularly when the student is asked to judge against a set of established criteria. Thus two theories can be compared using appropriate criteria developed either by the teacher or by the students in large or small group settings.

For example, a list of criteria for evaluation of one theory against another might include the fact to be considered by each theory followed by an unbiased outline of each theory, and a list of questions to be considered:

1. Which theory is best able to explain the facts? Why?
2. Which theory has the strongest scientific research to support it?
3. Which theory is best able to make predictions about what will be found or learned in the future?
4. Which theory has the best experimental and observational support?
5. What problems exist with each of the theories? How serious are these problems?
6. What data would be needed to strengthen each theory?
7. What facts might cause scientists to abandon each theory?

Discussing Controversial Topics.   As students reach the fifth through eighth grade levels and become more able to carry on discussions, controversial topics can be considered within the classroom. These discussions should take place in an atmosphere where all students feel free to voice or not voice opinions. Make no attempt to direct students toward a particular viewpoint, but rather model the behavior of listening to all sides of an issue and considering all sides before making a personal decision. When possible, consider the pros and cons of each differing viewpoint and help the students make charts showing the differing sides and their support.

Using Familiar Advertisements.   Advertising brings to students generally biased viewpoints. As students begin to consider advertising, they can also begin to consider what the advertisements actually say, or do not say. Students can begin to compare the actual specifications of two or more different kinds of cars, or toothpastes, or basketball shoes.

A Positive Approach to Failure

Although this attitude sounds as if students should be happy when they get a failing grade on a test, quiz, or project, it has nothing to do with grades. Having a **positive approach to failure** means that each testing of a hypothesis, whether supportive or nonsupportive, yields some new information that a scientist can incorporate into further experimentation. If the hypothesis is supported by the data, the experiment is viewed as a success. If the hypothesis is not supported by the data, the experiment is still successful. In the latter case, the scientist has still gained information, which he or she will use to construct new hypotheses for further experimentation. Consequently, even the experiment that fails to support a hypothesis provides new information.

A Positive Approach to Failure in the World of Science.   The failure to find supporting evidence for a hypothesis may be unusual in a school science program where the activities are specifically designed to illustrate particular hypotheses that have already been shown to be valid. In the actual world of science, however, so-called failure is much more common than success. Many years of cancer research are only now beginning to lead to cures for certain specific types of the disease. Thousands of failures have occurred in thousands of laboratories, yet although that elusive cure has not been discovered, each of the failures has increased knowledge of causes, cures, and possible paths for future research. The elimination one by one of possible causes means the search for a true cause is progressing.

The school science program that has a strictly content orientation does not allow students to develop the same attitude toward failure as is developed by a research scientist. A content-oriented program is generally directed toward a single, predetermined correct answer. This viewpoint is misleading in a number of ways. First of all, it shows science as an enterprise in which all things are known and in which all answers can be memorized because they do not change. Second, the content-only orientation gives the impression that a scientist always knows precisely what he or she will find as a result of an experiment or other form of research. And third, the content-only orientation tends to treat theory and fact as equivalent rather than dealing with the tentative nature of a theory. Showing that scientists do fail to confirm their hypotheses, that they do not know everything, and that what they can learn from their failures is important, brings to children a more realistic view of science.

The attitude of positive approach to failure also has the side benefit of reducing anxiety in those children who have become anxious about the work they do in school. Extreme anxiety can cause a decrease in the quality of a student's work. A particularly clear example of anxiety's effect on students is test anxiety in which a student's test grade is lower than anticipated as a result of fear.

When we help children learn from their unsupported hypotheses and incorrect predictions of operational questions, we also help those children who have constantly experienced failure experience success. We also help them see that they can learn from failure as well as from success.

Techniques for Developing a Positive Approach to Failure.   In general, the best technique for developing a positive approach toward failure is to institute a science program in which the content of the program is developed through the use of the processes of science, a program in which the procedures used for developing the content are considered equally important to the content that is derived and in which students learn from doing rather than from hearing or reading. We can also model the scientific attitude of honesty as we look at activities and their results. Within this general orientation toward the science program, certain techniques are particularly appropriate:

1. In the lower elementary grades, develop operational questions which the children respond to by making predictions of the outcome and testing their predictions.
2. In the upper elementary grades and in the middle school grades, use experiments in which students develop hypotheses that predict the outcome of the experiment.

3. Discuss the data collected from both operational questions and experiments in which incorrect predictions were made, trying to show what has been learned from that data.

4. Encourage children to make multiple inferences from their data and to develop ways of testing to determine the validity of those inferences.

5. Display magazine and newspaper articles in which research is discussed that did not produce the expected results. These are fairly common in topics dealing with medical research and with research in space.

6. Accept answers that are based on evidence, even when scientifically incorrect, and have the child develop a means for retesting a hypothesis.

7. Rewrite textbook activities and experiments so the outcome is not known. Have the children do the activities and experiments before they read the information in the textbook.

8. Model the scientific attitude of honesty in data collection and interpretation.

Respect for the Environment

Respect for the environment goes beyond ideas of recycling and keeping the environment clean to the idea that all aspects of the environment are interrelated, that the plants and other animals inhabiting our environment are worthy of our concern and respect. This should come through in our science classrooms in how we treat other organisms we study. Harvesting leaves for a collection that will allow students to learn to identify different kinds of trees and other plants is fine. But respect for the environment would mean taking only two leaves from a particular type of plant: one to show the upper surface and one to show the lower surface. Respect for the environment also means studying animals in their natural habitat while alive rather than making collections of dead insects or of organisms preserved in alcohol or formalin. Far more can be learned about an insect through observation of the insect in its habitat than through observation of an insect stuck on a pin. Additionally, respect for the environment can mean collecting frog eggs, placing them in a suitable environment, making observations of the development of the eggs into tadpoles and then frogs, followed by returning the frogs to the natural environment; observing the spider that crawls across the floor and allowing it to build a web rather than stepping on it; or capturing a harmless snake and releasing it in a more appropriate location rather than killing it. Respect for the environment is the beginning of the scientific values of consideration of consequences and consideration of premises.

Techniques for Developing Respect for the Environment.   The techniques for developing respect for the environment are simple:

1. Model the desired behavior. Modeling is the most powerful of all techniques for developing the scientific attitude of respect for the environment. Children who see the teacher capture a spider and take it outside to an appropriate location are likely to follow the same kind of procedure.

2. Develop activities that demonstrate the desired behavior. Constructing an insect zoo in which live insects can be observed and identified and then returning them to the environment is an appropriate activity for developing respect for the environment.

3. Discuss scenarios in which students decide the best course of action for a particular situation. For example; You are hiking through the woods when you come across a black snake right in your path. What would you do?

4. Study the role played in the environment by animals and plants not generally considered "good." For example, students could look at poisonous snakes, sharks, bats, spiders, poison ivy, or poison sumac.

5. Use CD-ROM and other programs to simulate dissections rather than dissecting preserved organisms killed for the purpose of dissection.

6. Limit activities and experiments utilizing living organisms to those that cause no harm to the organism.

Lack of Superstition

The last of the scientific attitudes to be discussed here is **lack of superstition.** The scientist generally looks for logical, physical causes for phenomena rather than for explanations based on paranormal or unproven phenomena. This is a part of the scientific value of respect for logic. Children should be encouraged to do the same, particularly when they are confronted by television programs, supermarket tabloids, and television advertisements all with some type of paranormal basis.

Techniques for Developing Lack of Superstition.   Developing a student's ability to look at the world logically and to seek out explanations based on scientific reasoning and laws can be difficult because some of the superstitions may be integrally related to a child's religious beliefs. Consequently, the teacher must tread lightly in working in this area. Modeling the attitude of objectivity is a necessity in this area. However, some techniques are appropriate for developing the attitude of lack of superstition:

1. Test old clichés to determine their validity. For example, "a watched pot never boils" can be tested to find out if water actually does boil when it is watched.

2. Check the validity of psychic predictions found in newspapers and on television.

3. Discuss alternative explanations for television programs dealing with ghosts, UFOs, and other phenomena.

4. Have older students consider the history of science and how explanations for various phenomena changed as better data was collected.

5. Compare science fact, science fantasy, and science fiction using books, films, and tapes.

Activities 6.1 through 6.3 are designed to allow you to explore the scientific attitudes in the classroom and in textbooks and to allow you to develop a file of materials useful in working with the scientific attitudes.

Activities for Working with Scientific Attitudes

Activity 6.1

Purpose   To investigate scientific attitudes within the science classroom.

Procedure
1. Arrange to observe a teacher working with the area of science. Arrange to observe this teacher at least three times.
2. Observe the science teaching done by the teacher. Ask the teacher for permission to tape-record or to make notes during the lesson.
3. As you are observing consider the following questions:
   a. How does the teacher encourage the development of scientific attitudes on the part of the class?
   b. What opportunities arose for the development of scientific attitudes that were utilized by the teacher? How were they used?
   c. What opportunities arose for the development of scientific attitudes that were not utilized by the teacher? How could those opportunities have been utilized?
   d. Did the teacher discourage or encourage scientific attitudes on the part of the students? How? What would you have done differently?

Activity 6.2

Purpose   To investigate science textbooks for the inclusion and development of scientific attitudes.

Procedure
1. Obtain the teacher's editions of science textbooks for at least two different grade levels from first through eighth.
2. Consider the following areas as you analyze those two textbooks:
   a. Does the introductory material discuss the development of scientific attitudes as a part of the program? How does the introductory material say scientific attitudes are to be included in the program?
   b. Read the teaching suggestions for at least two of the chapters in each textbook, and then consider the following two questions:
      (1) Do the teaching techniques advocated include attention to the scientific attitudes? If they are included, how are they included?
      (2) What could you, as the teacher using the textbook, do to increase attention to the scientific attitudes in each of the chapters?

Activity 6.3

Purpose   To develop a file of materials that could be used to develop the scientific attitudes in the science classroom.

Procedure
1. Consider the teaching suggestions outlined in this chapter for developing the scientific attitudes of objectivity, skepticism, willingness to suspend judgment, respect for the environment, and lack of superstition.
2. Develop a file of activities that could be used within the science classroom to develop these attitudes among the children you will teach.
3. Organize your file so that a specific suggestion will be easy to locate.

Affect and Learning

Scientific attitudes provide an important link between the content learned in the science program and the behavior of the child. Teachers can, for example, train anyone to write a hypothesis, control variables, carry out an experiment, and draw a conclusion from the data that he or she collects. But unless that individual also comes to value the experiment itself, as a powerful means for gaining knowledge, it is unlikely that the experiment or even the objectivity inherent in the experiment will be effective. Unless affective learning takes place, the content that teachers so carefully teach in the science program may never be used by the children.

Affect, then, should permeate all we do in the classroom. It is both an aid to internalization and an aid to the processing of information into memory. A pleasant learning environment with a knowledgeable teacher who embodies models of appropriate behavior works positively to develop both content and attitude. Research (Anderson, 1970; Fraser, 1978; Haladung, Olsen, and Shaughnessy, 1982) indicates that the affective aspects of the curriculum are most strongly influenced by the following:

1. the attitude of the teacher
2. the enthusiasm shown by the teacher
3. the personality of the teacher
4. interrelationships between the teacher and the students
5. the teacher's knowledge of the subject matter
6. the participation of students in active learning
7. a classroom low in anxiety

From this listing, you can see that the teacher is probably the most important classroom influence on the development of attitudes in children. This influence comes out most strongly in the fact that the teacher is a model for the behaviors he or she wants to see evidenced by the students. Modeling is, in fact, one of the most powerful teaching techniques available. It is teaching through example, through demonstration of a desired behavior or techniques in a natural manner. Apprenticeships are based on modeled behaviors: A master artisan shows an apprentice how to do a particular task. Scientific attitudes are best transmitted to children through the modeling of behavior by the teacher rather than through lecture, discussion, or other direct teaching technique. But because modeling is so powerful a technique, the teacher must be careful to maintain a neutral position in the classroom in the face of controversy and to be a model of the scientific attitudes that he or she wants to develop in the students.

Summary

The development of scientific literacy includes not only the development of scientific content but also the development of scientific habits of mind. Scientific habits of mind include the development of scientific attitudes. The scientific attitudes include curiosity, honesty, willingness to suspend judgment, open-mindedness, skepticism, objectivity, a positive approach to failure, respect for the environment, and lack of superstition. A variety of techniques can be used to develop each of these attitudes within the science program. However, the strongest techniques for developing scientific attitudes in children is modeling on the part of the teacher.

Chapter Vocabulary

The number following each term refers to the page on which the term is first introduced.

Curiosity, 152
Discrepant events, 154
Honesty, 155
Lack of superstition, 163
Objectivity, 158

Positive approach to failure, 160
Respect for the environment, 162
Skepticism, 157
Willingness to suspend judgment, 155

Applying the **CONCEPTS**

1. Some of your fifth grade students come to you with a bunch of interesting berries they found on the school's playground. They want to know what the berries are. What would you so in this situation to help your students maintain the curiosity they are showing about the berries?

2. As a science teacher you know that the scientific attitudes of objectivity and willingness to suspend judgment are important. However, when you begin a unit on Earth with your students, the parents of two of your students arrive in your classroom. They object to the information you are presenting to your students on the age of Earth. How would you handle this situation?

3. You have asked a city official to come to the school to talk with your eight graders about development occurring in your community. The official presents the viewpoint that all economic development is good for the community. After the official is finished with his presentation, your students begin to ask questions, showing they are skeptical about some of the comments. How would you handle this situation?

4. The principal of your school comes to observe your fourth grade science class. Your students are finishing an activity dealing with pendulums. You collect the data on the board and draw conclusions from the data. The students have found that not only the length of the pendulum but also the weight and the angle from which the pendulum is started make a difference in how many times it will swing. Even though the last two are incorrect, you praise your students and end the lesson. The principal is very upset that you taught the children incorrect science content. How would you respond to your principal?

5. You are about to begin a unit on the human body that includes information on drugs, alcohol, and tobacco. Your curriculum guide states that you should teach children to totally avoid drugs, alcohol, and tobacco. You have two problems. First, many of the children have parents who smoke or drink. Second, some research is showing moderate use of alcohol can actually be beneficial. How could you use the scientific attitudes to help you out of this rather difficult situation?

References

American Association for the Advancement of Science. 1989. *Science for all Americans: A project 2061 report on literacy goals in science, mathematics, and technology.* Washington, D.C.: Author.

American Association for the Advancement of Science. 1993. *Benchmarks for science literacy.* New York: Oxford University Press.

Anderson, G. J. 1970. Effects of classroom social climate on individual learning. *American Educational Research Journal* 7, 135–152.

Aspy, D. N., and F. N. Roebuck. 1982. Affective education: Sound investment. *Educational Leadership* 39, 7.

Beane, J. A. 1982. Self-concept and self-esteem as curriculum issues. *Educational Leadership* 39, 7.

Coble, C. R., and D. R. Rice. 1982. Rekindling scientific curiosity. *Science Teacher* 50, 2.

Dunfee, J. 1991. Investigating children's science learning. *The Education Digest* 36, 5.

Farley, J. R. 1982. Raising student achievement through the affective domain. *Educational Leadership* 39,7.

Fraser, B. J. 1978. Environmental factors affecting attitude toward different sources of scientific information. *Journal of Research in Science Teaching* 15, 491–497.

Fraser, B. J. 1987. Classroom learning environment and effective schooling. *Professional School Psychology* 2, 25–41.

Fraser, B. J., R. Nash, and D. L. Fisher. 1983. Anxiety in science classrooms: Its measurement and relationship to classroom environment. *Research in Science and Technological Education* 1, 201–208.

Fraser, B. J., and P. O'Brien. 1985. Student and teacher perceptions of the environment of elementary-school classrooms. *Elementary School Journal* 85, 567–580.

Gauld, G. 1982. The scientific attitude and science education: A critical reappraisal. *Science Education* 66, 1.

Haladuna, T., R. Olsen, and J. Shaughnessy. 1982. Relations of student, teacher and learning environment variables to attitudes toward science. *Science Education* 66, 671–688.

Kelly, T. E. 1989. October. Leading class discussion of controversial issues. *Social Education,* 368–370.

Lawrenz, F. 1975. The relationship between science teacher characteristics and student achievement and attitude. *Journal of Research in Science Teaching* 12, 10.

Moore, R. W. 1982. Open-mindedness and proof. *School Science and Mathematics* 82, 6.

National Research Council. 1996. *National science education standards.* Washington, D.C.: National Academy Press

Vanderhoof, B., E. Miller, L. B. Clegg, and H. J. Patterson. 1992, March. Real or fake? The phony document as a teaching strategy. *Social Education* 169–170.

CHAPTER SEVEN

DEVELOPING QUESTIONING SKILLS

Introduction

"Let's think about the film we just saw," this fourth grade teacher began and then started asking questions.

What was the film about?

What is a rain forest?

Where was the rain forest in the film located?

Where is Brazil on the map?

What kinds of animals were in the film?

Who can name some of the birds?

Who can name some of the fish?

Who can name some of the mammals?

What kinds of plants did the film show?

What was the name of the biggest tree in the forest?

What kinds of flowers did you see in the film?

What animal was carrying pieces of leaves?

What kinds of houses did the people live in?

What kinds of foods did the people eat?

How did the people dress?

What kinds of games did the children play?

What river did the film show?

Is the Amazon a big river?

The questions continued and continued and continued. At first, many of the children in the class were answering, but as the questions continued, fewer and fewer of the children put up their hands. As the final questions were reached, the teacher and a single child who was very interested in rain forests were having a dialogue about the film. The teacher felt the lesson had gone very well. The children were glad to move on to mathematics.

An observer sitting in the back of this teacher's classroom would probably notice something this teacher did not even notice: The teacher asked one question after another, each one asking for recall of specific facts found in the film. And the quick, factual questions had an effect on the children in the class. The more questions asked, the fewer students who responded.

In fact, this classroom would not be unusual. Questions make up the bulk of many lessons teachers teach. The questions teachers ask generally elicit short answers in which students recall information. And the most common pattern for questions within a lesson is for the teacher to ask the question and the student to quickly answer the question, a process repeated again and again.

Because so much time is spent in asking and answering questions and because questions can make or break a science lesson, we need to be especially careful with the kinds of questions we ask and the way in which we ask them. We also need to be aware of how we respond to the answers given by the students in our classes. And finally, we need to be aware of the kinds of questions that cause children to apply, analyze, and evaluate information rather than simply recall facts.

The questions we ask during science classes should allow children to think critically, to go beyond the simple regurgitation of words they have read or heard. The responses we get to questions should also help us know where children stand in ability to recall science facts, apply science concepts, and evaluate the results of their experimental activities. Questions should also allow children to use information creatively.

How, then, do we assure that our questions will accomplish everything we want them to accomplish? Planning. Only when we plan our questioning strategies can we be certain our questions will be appropriate to a particular science lesson. Our planning needs to take into account the kind of result desired. Questions that ask students to recall the information in their science textbooks are phrased differently and are asked in a different manner than questions that ask students to infer the cause-and-effect relationships they have observed in an experiment.

In order to develop your ability to ask questions during a science lesson, you will be considering three aspects of questioning in this chapter:

1. ways of classifying questions
2. ways of asking and responding to questions
3. the use of wait time in asking questions.

The Two General Categories of Questions

In the simplest classification, we find two kinds of questions in the science classroom. Based on the latitude allowed the student in answering the questions, this classification divides questions into either convergent or divergent.

Convergent Questions

Definition.   A **convergent question** is one in which a single answer is the correct answer to the question. This should not, however, be taken to mean that a convergent question always has a single word as an answer. For example, "What are the four seasons?" is a convergent questions with a four-part answer. And even though there is a single answer, that answer may be phrased in many ways depending on the child's ability to respond and on the child's background experiences. In generally, a question is convergent because it has an answer that may be judged as correct or incorrect immediately.

Examples of Convergent Questions.   Each of the following questions represents the kind of content found in the elementary school science program and is a convergent question.

1. How many legs does and insect have?
2. What is your textbook's definition of the word environment?
3. Of what three minerals is the rock granite composed?
4. If a Celsius thermometer reads 100 degrees, what would the temperature be in Fahrenheit?
5. Measured in centimeters, how long is the chalkboard in this room?

Using Convergent Questions.   Each of these questions has a single, rather specific answer that a teacher can immediately judge as correct or incorrect. In many cases, the answer can simply be memorized by the child or can be found using a simple measuring device. The important point, however, is that convergent questions focus on a single, correct answer; that is, they converge on the answer. Because of these characteristics, the teacher can use convergent questions in the elementary science class to accomplish the following:

1. review previously learned information in order to increase retention through use.
2. review observations made during an activity or an experiment in order to permit more accurate inferences and conclusions.
3. recall needed background information prior to an activity, demonstration, or experiment.
4. define vocabulary that will be encountered in reading material or that was previously defined through the use of materials.
5. recall background information in preparation for higher order questions.

Divergent Questions

Definition.   A **divergent question** is one in which the student is asked to use background material as well as personal experiences to answer a question that may have many equally valid answers. Divergent questions promote divergent thought and promote the creative use of information in science.

Examples of Divergent Questions.   The following questions are all divergent. As you read through these examples, compare them with the examples of convergent questions you were previously given. Once again, the content of the questions is typical of the content of the elementary school science textbook.

1. A box of bricks is too heavy for a single person to move from one place to another. What methods could be used to move the box?

2. Your favorite beach has been eroding away each winter until only a strip of sand 3 feet wide is left. What could be done to keep the rest of the sand from disappearing as well?

3. Nuclear energy, wind energy, solar energy, and energy from Earth have all been suggested as ways of supplying energy that do not use up our petroleum supplies. Which of these do you think would be best for our community?

4. You are one of the first colonists on the planet Mars. What it is like there?

5. What are some possible alternatives to a zoo for keeping rare animals like the giant panda, the California condor, and the whooping crane?

Each of these divergent questions has a number of possible answers. Because of the variety of possible answers, students can think more creatively and can apply material already known to new problems or situations. In the case of question 4, students can put their imaginations to work to create something new. For the most part, divergent questions do not have answers that can be memorized. They diverge from one question to many appropriate answers.

Using Divergent Questions.   Divergent questions, unlike convergent questions, can be used during problem-solving situations or during process activities in order to encourage thinking. Operational questions are divergent because they do not focus on a single specific answer. Questions that allow children to use their imaginations—say, to describe life on another planet or life in a period of time long past—are also divergent. Questions that make children create their own experiments to solve a particular problem are also divergent. A general key to the use of divergent questions is that they are used whenever children are to be involved in problem-solving situations or in situations where they are able to use their knowledge in new ways.

Activities 7.1 through 7.3 will allow you to practice recognizing and writing convergent and divergent questions.

Questioning Technique Activities

Activity 7.1

Purpose   To investigate the kinds of questions asked by a teacher during a typical science lesson.

Procedure
1. Observe a teacher during two 30- to 45-minute periods as he or she teaches a science lesson. During the first period, make a tally of the number of divergent and convergent questions the teacher asks.

2. Answer the following questions on the basis of the information collected:
   a. How many convergent questions were asked?
   b. How many divergent questions were asked?
   c. What is the ratio of convergent questions to divergent questions?
   d. What opportunities did you observe for the teacher to ask divergent questions rather than convergent questions?
3. During the second 30- to 45-minute time period, observe the students while the questions are asked. Then answer the following questions:
   a. What pattern of question and response emerges as you watch?
   b. How did the students react to the questions? Consider both verbal responses and body language.
   c. How many of the students are involved in answering the questions?
   d. How does the type of question being asked affect the students?

Activity 7.2

Purpose   To develop your ability to recognize convergent and divergent questions as found in a typical elementary or middle school science textbook.

Procedure
1. Select one textbook from a science series for third, fourth, fifth, sixth, seventh, or eighth grade. From that textbook select one chapter.
2. Read through the chapter including the teaching suggestions. List all of the questions you find in the chapter.
3. Classify the questions found in the chapter as either convergent or divergent.
4. How many questions did you classify as convergent? How many as divergent?
5. What does the type of questions asked tell you about the content emphasis of the textbook chapter?

Activity 7.3

Purpose   To provide practice in rewriting convergent questions into divergent form.

Procedure
1. Consider each of the following convergent questions. Rewrite each of them to allow for divergent thought.
   a. How many legs does and insect have?
   b. What three minerals are found in granite?
   c. Find the examples of energy being used in each of the pictures on page 34 of your textbook.
   d. According to your textbook, why are some animals in danger of becoming extinct?
   e. What does NASA list as three conditions for becoming an astronaut?
   f. Classify each of the following animals according to whether they are fish, amphibians, birds, reptiles, or mammals.

g. Measured in astronomical units, how far is it from the Sun to the planet Pluto?
h. What example of inertia did you see in class yesterday?
i. Use the glossary of your book to find the definitions of the following words: *corpuscle, vein, artery, capillary, plasma, platelet.*
j. What definition did the film you saw give for plate tectonics?
k. What are the four most common elements in living things?
l. Which of the following are observations and which are inferences?
m. What is the boiling point of water on the Celsius scale?

Classification of questions as either convergent or divergent is simplistic. Convergent questions come in many kinds. Divergent questions come in many varieties. In order to ask effective questions in the classroom, questions that elicit a variety of information and require a variety of kinds of thinking skills, we must look at questioning in another, complementary way.

The Cognitive Domain

The different and complementary way of looking at questions involves looking at the kinds of thinking skills required of the students, in particular the kinds of thinking skills required when students consider the content of science. This falls into the cognitive domain.

Benjamin Bloom and colleagues (1958) designated the **cognitive domain** as including such activities as remembering and recalling knowledge, thinking, applying material, solving problems, creating new ideas, and evaluating information. With all of these activities, the student can operate on the content material of the elementary science program. The range of these activities, moreover, suggests that much more can be done with the content of science than the simple recall of factual information on a test or quiz.

In classifying questions asked in the science class, we may use Bloom's six categories of the cognitive domain:

1. knowledge
2. comprehension
3. application
4. analysis
5. synthesis
6. evaluation

This listing moves from the simplest use of content information to its most complex use. We must keep in mind that this classification system is hierarchical, so that the student can attain the evaluation level only if he or she has factual knowledge, understanding of that knowledge, and the ability to apply, analyze, and synthesize that knowledge. One cannot be expected to apply science content that one does not comprehend. One cannot be expected to evaluate science content or to make science-related decisions without a knowledge of relevant facts or the ability to analyze a situation and determine its component parts. The arrangement of the levels of this taxonomy is not only from the simple to the complex but also from the concrete to the abstract. Moreover, questions on one level of the hierarchy make use of or build on the content elicited by questions on the previous levels.

With this information as background, let us consider each of the categories of the cognitive taxonomy in terms of questions for the elementary science classroom.

Levels of the Cognitive Taxonomy

Knowledge Level.   The **knowledge level** of the taxonomy includes behaviors that emphasize the student's recall or recognition of factual information. The student stores certain science content in his or her memory and later recalls that information as it is needed. The knowledge level consists of three major subdivisions: knowledge of specifics, knowledge of ways and means of dealing with specifics, and knowledge of the universals in a field.

Knowledge of Specifics.   **Knowledge of specifics** deals with the recall of specific bits of information such as terms, dates, persons, places, events, or sources of information. This can be called the hard core of facts or information that make up the content of science. Without mastery of this level of knowledge, the student may be unable to think about or to discuss many of the phenomena of science. Although the content at this level is in the form of words or symbols, they all have concrete referents.

Knowledge of Ways and Means of Dealing with Specifics.   **Knowledge of ways and means of dealing with specifics** consists of knowledge of how information is organized, studied, judged, and criticized. Although it is somewhat more abstract than the previous level, it still depends on recall. This level includes knowledge of trends, sequences, classifications, criteria, and methods. Although this level requires knowledge of each of these items, we do not expect the student to be able to use them; the student is still working with the recall of information.

Knowledge of Universals and Abstractions in a Field.   **Knowledge of universals and abstractions in a field** deals with the principles, generalizations, and theories used to organize the content of science. These are the broad concepts that dominate science and are generally used in studying phenomena or in solving problems. Once again, students are only expected to recall memorized information and not to use that information in any way.

Examples of Knowledge-Level Questions. The following questions represent knowledge-level questions. Each uses the kind of content found in elementary science textbooks.

1. Who was the first person into space?
2. What is the name of the largest planet in our solar system?
3. What is the system of measurement most commonly used in science?
4. What names are usually given to the poles of a magnet?
5. What is the order of stages in the development of a butterfly?
6. What are the three major groups of rocks found on Earth?
7. What example of a chemical change is found in your textbook?

Questions at the knowledge level are useful when the teacher wishes to recall information that the student has previously read or heard. At this level we do not expect the students to comprehend that information in any way. The understanding of information arises at the second level of the taxonomy.

Comprehension Level. The **comprehension level** includes those questions asked during a science lesson that determine whether or not the student understands information. The three sublevels of comprehension are translation, interpretation, and extrapolation.

Translation. The **translation level** is a sublevel that provides a transition between the behaviors classified as knowledge level and the higher cognitive levels of the taxonomy. Working at the translation level, the student must be able to tell what a word, definition, or concept means in his or her own words. This can also mean a translation of symbols into a written statement that gives the meaning of the symbols.

Interpretation. The **interpretation level** is a sublevel that asks the student not only to translate each of the major parts of a particular segment of content into his or her own words but also to go beyond those parts and give a total view of the essential meaning of the content.

Extrapolation. **Extrapolation** requires that the student go beyond the limits set by the information and apply some of the ideas to situations or problems not actually included in the original material. Extrapolations are actually inferences made from the information. Drawing conclusions from various written or concrete materials comes under the category of extrapolation.

Examples of Comprehension-Level Questions. The following questions illustrate the comprehension level of the taxonomy. As you read through them, compare them with the previous knowledge-level questions. Once again, the questions are representative of the typical textbook.

1. What is meant by the term *food web?*
2. Rewrite the following symbol in words: H_2O.
3. Look at the graph showing the rate at which various plants grow. Which of the conclusions following the graph are not supported?
4. Compare animals from the Age of Dinosaurs to the animals of today.
5. Which of the following terms does not belong to this sequence: *lever, pulley, screw, truck, inclined plane, wedge?*
6. From the three experiments with magnets and electricity, what conclusion can you draw about the relationship between electricity and magnetism?

When they attain comprehension, students are showing more than the ability to memorize. They are demonstrating the beginnings of an understanding of the science content they have been studying. On the next level, students begin to work with the information in settings that require more than memorization or simple understanding.

Application Level.   At the **application level** the student needs to use science content correctly in a situation where no method of solution for the problem is given. This differs from comprehension because at the comprehension level the student can use information only when specifically asked to use it. At the application level, however, the student does not need to be told what material to use. Because much of what is learned in elementary science should have applicability to real-life situations, the application level is of particular importance. Possession of knowledge and application of knowledge cannot be considered synonymous. It is possible to know something, yet not be able to use it in a problem-solving situation.

Examples of Application-Level Questions.   The application level of the taxonomy is shown in each of the following questions. Although the content may be found in the elementary science program, the activity these questions should elicit from the students is not necessarily found in the pages of the text. At the application level students must go beyond the bounds of the textbook and use information in new settings.

1. Classify the 12 rocks on the table using the most appropriate method.
2. If a bean plant grows at the rate of 2 cm per day, how tall will the plant be after 15 days?
3. Compare the conditions on the planet Mars to those found on Mercury.
4. Study the pictures of the Grand Canyon. What could have caused the features that you see in the pictures?
5. Using what you know abut simple machines, design a machine that could be used to move a giant Sequoia tree from California to Pennsylvania.

Application-level questions use the knowledge of science content as well as the comprehension of that content in new situations. The key term at the application level is the use of information. At the fourth level of the taxonomy, analysis, the individual begins to consider material in a more critical manner than previously.

Analysis Level. The **analysis level** emphasizes separation of material into its constituent parts and detection of the relationships between those parts. The analysis level can aid in a fuller comprehension of science content and can lead in to the evaluation level.

The analysis level is of particular importance to the elementary science curriculum. Through analysis students learn to distinguish between inference and observation, between facts and hypotheses, and between conclusions and supporting statements. At this level, students also learn to distinguish between relevant and extraneous material. Each of these skills is important in science as students gather data, draw conclusions from that data, and determine cause-and-effect relationships.

Analysis of elements, analysis of relationships, and analysis of organizational principles are the three sublevels of analysis.

Analysis of Elements. At the **analysis of elements** sublevel the student should be able to identify both the clearly stated facts of a written piece and the underlying assumptions of the author. Analysis of elements may include recognizing the assumptions on which a theory is based, distinguishing between fact and theory, and differentiating between conclusions and supporting statements.

Analysis of Relationships. Once the various parts of a piece of writing have been identified, the student must still determine the relationships among those parts. **Analysis of relationships** can include determining the relationships between a hypothesis and the evidence gathered during an experiment, seeing the relationships within the data collected, as well as determining cause-and-effect relationships.

Analysis of Organizational Principles. The **analysis of organizational principles** sublevel is the most complex level of analysis because it includes the task of analyzing the organization of a piece of written material. Students are asked to read in order to determine the author's purpose, point of view, or attitude.

Examples of Analysis-Level Questions. At the analysis level, questions like the following could be asked during the science class. Once again, although the content is considered in the elementary science program, the answers to questions like these can only come when the children use that content and their problem-solving skills.

1. Look at the following table. Which of the conclusions listed below it are supported by the data in the table?
2. Read the following paragraph. What is the writer's hypothesis? What evidence is given to support that hypothesis?

3. From studying the three experimental procedures used in class, the data collected, and the conclusions drawn, list the cause-and-effect relationships that were illustrated.

4. Listen to the tape recording of television commercials. What inferences do you think people are supposed to make about the product advertised? What observations can actually be made from the information given?

5. Read a newspaper article on using solar energy to produce electricity. Do you think the writer is for or against using solar energy? What evidence do you have for your decision?

As you can see from these five questions, at the analysis level students must use a higher level of reasoning than at any of the previous levels. Once again, however, the student cannot attain the analysis level unless he or she has the ability to recall and comprehend factual information pertinent to the question as well as to use that information in various situations. This need for higher reasoning abilities is also apparent at the next level—synthesis.

Synthesis Level.   The **synthesis level** requires an even higher level of reasoning ability than the analysis level and involves the putting together of parts to form a whole. Generally the parts are both previously learned science content and newly encountered material. At the synthesis level, the student is for the first time involved in the creative use of information. This is not the completely free creativity experienced by the author writing a novel or the artist treating a painting, but creativity in which the student must act within the limits established by a particular problem or a certain set of materials.

Performing a synthesis, the student must draw on material from many sources and put that material together in a product that did not obviously exist before.

The synthesis level provides the science teacher with an opportunity not present on the other levels of the taxonomy. At the synthesis level, the student can use information and skills from a variety of subject areas to aid in the solution of a science oriented problem. Art, music, language, math, and social science can all be brought into play at the synthesis level. It provides the teacher with an appropriate arena for developing relationships among subject areas and allows the student to use skills gained in varying subjects. The synthesis level also allows for problem solving in real situations.

The synthesis level consists of three sublevels: production of a unique communication, production of a plan, and derivation of a set of abstract relations.

Production of a Unique Communication.   **Production of a unique communication** has as its primary emphasis communication: getting ideas, feelings, or experiences across to others. Although the communication is unique, that does not mean pure creativity is required of the student. Rather, the student is constrained by limitations placed by the teacher, by the medium used, and by the experiential content from which the student is able to draw. Very different types of communications are produced if the child is writing a creative story rather than a report of an experiment or activity. The content of the final product is selected by the student rather than by the teacher, but it must fall within minimum standards set by the teacher.

Production of a Plan.   **Production of a plan** is a sublevel that has the primary emphasis on development of a particular plan of operation such as an experimental procedure or a procedure used to answer an operational question. The child's product at this level must satisfy the requirements established by the science teacher, but there is a great deal of room for creative variation within those requirements. Even devising an experiment or activity to test a specific hypothesis gives the student the leeway to approach that hypothesis from his or her own perspective and background.

Derivation of a Set of Abstract Relations.   In **derivation of a set of abstract relations** the student has to derive from either concrete data or phenomena some type of statement to explain or classify that data. This particular type of synthesis is of great importance to science, because it is through such a synthesis that students interpret the data they collect and draw conclusions from that data.

Examples of Synthesis-Level Questions.   At the synthesis level the teacher can ask the following kinds of questions to permit the student to use science content in a more creative manner:

1. Develop your own experiment to determine what effect talking to a plant has on its growth.
2. Pretend you are the first person to land on the planet Venus. You meet a Venusian. What is he or she like? What kind of life does he or she live on Venus?
3. Draw a mural showing what it would be like to live for one day in a cave.
4. Suppose you caught the Loch Ness Monster or Big Foot. What would you do with it?
5. Design a place that could be used to house the last pair of bald eagles in the world.
6. You live in a place where there is no way to keep track of time. What system could you invent that could be used by your fellow citizens?

The Importance of the Synthesis Level to Science Teaching.   The synthesis level is an important one for science teaching for a variety of reasons. For the first time, the student is able to work creatively with the content material he or she has acquired through reading and activity. For the first time the student is engaged in problem-solving processes that bring diverse subjects together: The child sees that science is related to other subject areas and to everyday life. At the synthesis level, the elementary school child has the opportunity to emulate the scientist as he or she attempts to solve a real problem.

Second, at the synthesis level the child has for the first time the opportunity to put his or her own ideas, feelings, and experiences into a response. Such affective involvement can allow the child to be fully engaged in the learning process.

Third, the synthesis level permits the child who has talents and abilities outside of science to apply those talents or abilities to the solution of a science-oriented problem. Consequently, the synthesis level provides the child with an opportunity to succeed in a subject area that may not fall high on his or her list of success-oriented situations. The artistic child can create a painting or sculpture, and the child who writes well can create a story.

Last, at the synthesis level the teacher finally leaves the control of the situation to the child and can watch how the students respond to the various situations presented. The child finally has the opportunity to show what he or she can really do in science.

Once the synthesis level has been attained, only one further level remains. At the evaluation level, the student is faced with one final cognitive task: making a judgment.

Evaluation Level. At the **evaluation level,** the student is asked to make judgments according to some established criteria about the value of ideas, solutions, methods, or materials. The criteria may be determined by the student or may be provided by the teacher.

Evaluation is placed at the highest level of the taxonomy because it involves a combination of all of the other behaviors: knowledge, comprehension, application, analysis, and synthesis. The evaluation level also provides a link between the cognitive and affective areas of behavior because values, likes and dislikes, and enjoyment are all involved in the process of evaluation.

The evaluation level, however, presents a difficulty not found at the other levels of the taxonomy: Evaluation involves a judgment. This is difficult because individuals tend to make judgments in relation to themselves. Adults tend to make judgments in terms of personal usefulness; useful ideas are rated highly, whereas those not perceived as useful are rated low. Children have an additional difficulty in making judgments.

Some children may find the use of objective criteria for evaluation close to impossible because of the egocentricity characteristic of the child during the preoperational stage of development. However, one of the goals of the elementary science program should be to develop in children the ability to evaluate on an objective basis rather than a subjective basis.

Although performance at the evaluation level is difficult for both children and adults, children can learn to evaluate material. The teacher should ensure that questions at the evaluation level, however, are suited to the child's background, level or ability, age, and level of knowledge.

The evaluation level has two sublevels: judgment in terms of internal evidence and judgment in terms of external evidence.

Judgment in Terms of Internal Evidence. In **judgement in terms of internal evidence,** students have to analyze data or conclusions from the standpoint of logical accuracy or consistency or some other criteria inherent in the material. For the most part, at this sublevel evaluation involves determining the accuracy of particular statements.

Judgment in Terms of External Evidence. In **judgment in terms of external evidence** students must evaluate material with reference to certain selected or recalled criteria. Usually this is accomplished by comparing a set of materials to a set of standards designed for the evaluation of such materials.

Examples of Evaluation-Level Questions.   Evaluation-level questions require that students use high levels of thinking and have the prerequisite knowledge implied by the question. Do not pose such questions unless the students have sufficient contact with the topic to be able to comprehend the questions and to recall the material necessary to answer. And always remember that it is not enough to simply ask an evaluation-level question. Probe so the student is providing his or her reasoning and not simply giving a quick response. For example, in question 4 below, a student may answer that it is very important. This is only a start. Probe by asking follow-up questions such as "Why do you think it is important?" "On what basis are you making you decision on importance?" and other similar questions.

The following are examples of evaluation-level questions:

1. You have done three experiments showing the effect of water on the growth of green plants. Which of these experiments do you think yielded the most accurate results? On what are you basing your answer?
2. Think about the cartoon *The Flintstones* and about what you have learned about prehistoric peoples. Which do you think presents the most accurate picture of life in prehistoric times? What reasons do you have for selecting one over the other?
3. We have four ideas about what to do with the Loch Ness monster if it is found. Which of these ideas do you think would be best and why?
4. How important do you think it is for scientists to explore planets like Venus, Mars, Saturn, and Jupiter?
5. Each of you has received a copy of a classification system made by a group of fifth grade students. Using the criteria for a good classification system that you learned in science, would you rank this as an excellent, good, fair, or poor system for classification?

The teacher attempting to work with evaluation level has to keep in mind that students must have the necessary prerequisite information as well as the fact that young children are egocentric. In addition, we need to probe students who answer evaluation-level questions with a simple yes or no answer or with an answer that has no supporting information. Students working on the evaluation level need to support their answers and discuss their reasoning. And finally, because the evaluation level can include an individual's values and feelings, we must be careful to show a respect for those values and feelings different from our own. The evaluation level should permit such differences to come through, but it may not be an appropriate time to evaluate those differences on the basis of which is purportedly best. Ours is a multicultural society, and the word best has little meaning in this area; we agree, however, that all must be respected.

Activities 7.4 through 7.6 are designed to assist you in recognizing and writing questions at a variety of different cognitive levels.

Questioning Activities

Activity 7.4

Purpose   To develop your ability to recognize the various levels of questions within the cognitive taxonomy.

Procedure

1. Read each of the following questions and then classify them in two ways: first as either convergent or divergent, second according to the level of the cognitive taxonomy represented by the question.

   a. Looking at the graph (presented to the student), what was the temperature of the liquid after three minutes of heating?

   b. (After reading information on the use of nuclear energy for electrical production), what assumptions are being used to defend the safety of this method of energy production?

   c. What was the name of the first space shuttle launched by the United States?

   d. Two methods have been used in this class for determining the number of stars visible on any given night. Which is the better method? Why?

   e. What are the three types of variables in an experiment?

   f. Knowing how the three varieties of rocks are formed, in which type of rock would it be best to search for fossils?

   g. Devise a plan that you feel would keep the giant panda from becoming extinct.

   h. How many categories of rock are generally used by geologists?

   i. Using the definition you have of a simple machine, classify the following as simple or nonsimple machines: tweezers, wheelbarrow, bicycle, staircase, truck, can opener, seesaw.

   j. What were some of the experiments leading to our present understanding of the atom?

   k. Using the ten criteria for a true hierarchical classification system, determine which of these classification systems is best.

   l. What do geologists mean by the term *fault?*

   m. A penny is placed on a stiff card and balanced over a glass; when the card is suddenly flicked away the penny will fall into the glass. What principle is illustrated in this example?

   n. In your opinion, how applicable is the study of science to everyday life?

   o. Write a story in which you describe the first encounter with a creature from another planet.

   p. Develop an experiment to test the effect of sunlight on the growth of a green plant.

   q. If each degree on the Celsius thermometer is three-fifths of a degree on the Fahrenheit thermometer, what would the boiling point of alcohol be in degrees Celsius if it is 179 degrees Fahrenheit?

  r. What is Earth's average distance from the Sun?

  s. In your own words, what is meant by the term *Pyramid of numbers?*

  t. What could happen to Earth if an asteroid were to collide with the planet?

Activity 7.5

Purpose To analyze the cognitive levels of the questions found in a typical science textbook.

Procedure

1. Return to the questions you recorded from a single science textbook (Activity 7.2).
2. Classify the questions according to the cognitive level shown by the question.
3. What levels of questions are shown most frequently? What levels of questions are shown least frequently. What does the frequency of questions tell you about the content focus of the textbook?
4. How could you change some of the knowledge- and comprehension-level questions found in the textbook to higher level questions, particularly to analysis, synthesis, and evaluation-level questions?

Activity 7.6

Purpose To provide practice in writing questions from each of the levels of the cognitive taxonomy.

Procedure

1. Read a section or chapter from a fourth, fifth, sixth, seventh, or eighth grade science textbook. For the section or chapter, write the following types of questions:
  a. five knowledge-level questions,
  b. three comprehension-level questions,
  c. three application-level questions,
  d. two analysis-level questions,
  e. two synthesis-level questions.
  f. two evaluation-level questions.

Using Questions Effectively

Factors in Effective Questioning

It is not enough to know there are various types of questions we, as teachers, can ask in order to enhance content learning in science. Such knowledge does not ensure that those questions will be asked appropriately.

To ask questions appropriately, we must take three factors into consideration. First, the question should be on a level that will elicit the kind of information desired. Second, the questions should be asked in an appropriate sequence. And, third, the questions should be asked in an appropriate manner, so that the student knows what is being asked and has the time to consider a response. We have already considered the level of question along with the kinds of information that can be elicited at each of the levels. The second step in appropriately asking questions requires sequencing.

Sequencing Questions

Suppose that the ultimate question for a particular lesson is at the application level: How could we move a box that weighs 700 pounds from the floor to the top of a table without using more than one person to do it?

In order to prepare the students for this application-level questions, it may be a good idea to prime their thoughts with some knowledge-level questions:

1. Name the six kinds of simple machines.
2. Draw a diagram of at least one of the kinds of simple machines.
3. What does your textbook say is the advantage of using a simple machine rather than only muscle power?

Similarly, the final question of a particular lesson might ask students to work on the synthesis level: Design an experiment to test the hypothesis that if the temperature of water increases then the amount of a solid which can be dissolved in that water will increase.

Students can be primed with questions from lower levels of the taxonomy such as these:

1. What is the purpose of an experiment?
2. What parts are generally included in an experiment?
3. What is a hypothesis?
4. What should be done in the procedure of an experiment to be certain the results are actually caused by the change introduced into the experiment?

Such sequences of questions prime the student for success by reviewing the prerequisites, then calling for the use of information. In this way, students move from simple to complex behaviors and have more possibility for success.

Asking Questions Appropriately

Finally, we should consider the manner in which questions are put to the students. Nearly every student has been subjected to rapid-fire questions, to unclear questions, to so-called psychic questions where students have to read the teacher's mind to determine the exact answer expected; none of these give the student a chance to arrive at the correct answer. Certain principles, however, do help teachers ask questions in a way that will allow students to answer correctly.

1. *Ask only one question at a time.* Asking, "what are three characteristics of green plants?" is more appropriate than asking, "What are the characteristics of green plants? Do you think all plants have these same characteristics? If all plants don't have the same characteristics, what do they have?" Asking three questions at once only confuses the student by permitting him or her no time to think, and because there are three questions requiring different responses, the student has no idea which question to answer.

2. *Phrase questions as questions, rather than starting with a statement and finishing with a question.* Rather than, "Dinosaurs ruled Earth for millions of years during what eras?"ask, "During what eras did dinosaurs rule Earth?" By beginning with a statement and ending with a question, you cause students to have to switch gears mid-sentence because different listening skills are used for statements and questions.

3. *Ask a question before designating who is to answer the question.* "John, what instrument is used to measure mass?" immediately tells the other students in the class that there is no need to listen further. John is going to answer so no one else must be concerned. A better form is, "What instrument is used to measure mass? John?"

4. *Ask questions suited to all of the students in the class.* Some questions should be easy and some difficult so all children have a chance to respond correctly.

5. *Ask questions that students can answer.* Questions that students cannot be expected to answer because they lack experience are frustrating to the teacher and simply unfair to the students. Children who are just beginning a unit of work dealing with matter cannot be expected to answer a question like this: "What is the difference between an element and a compound?" The teacher who asks this as a lead-in to a lesson on elements and compounds can be successful only in giving the students a message that they are stupid—they do not know the answer to a question the teacher seems to think they should know.

6. *Ask questions that elicit a variety of responses.* Such questions can be used even when a certain answer is desired because it is always possible to go back to the desired response. When many answers are given to a question, it is helpful to use the chalkboard or an overhead projector to make a record of the answers. Then, even if the first child to reply had the desired answer, it will be there to review.

7. *Always treat divergent questions as divergent questions.* When divergent questions are used, there is frequently a response that is desired by the teacher. Sometimes this response comes first. When this is true, the teacher should continue to get responses. If the first response is accepted and no others are received, the teacher has taken a divergent question and made it convergent.

8. *Ask questions that have been carefully planned to lead to the objectives of the lesson.* Planning questions in advance not only permits the teacher to be certain they will be appropriate to the lesson and will address a variety of levels, but also provides a jog for the teacher's memory during a lesson.

Listening to Children's Responses

Asking questions requires certain strategies of sequencing and of presentation. But once the question is asked your role in questioning does not end. As children respond, practice good listening skills:

1. *Listen to the answers the children give.* A nod, a smile, or just standing near the responding individual all help that child know you are listening and interested in what he or she is saying. Never call on a child to respond and then begin leafing through the teacher's edition of the text, looking for other materials, or taking care of a disruption by another student. If disruptions occur, ask the responding child to stop, take care of the problem, and then return to the responding child.

2. *Ask for clarification from the child when the answer is not clear.* Rather than trying yourself to tell the child what he or she said, have the child tell you more about the answer and try to clarify the material. Only then should you try to clarify. An opening statement like, "I think this is what you are saying. Tell me if I'm right," is a good way of indicating that you value the child's answer but are not quite certain of it's meaning. This also allows the child to know that he or she can correct what you are saying if it is not an accurate portrayal of the child's response.

3. *Provide equipment, materials, or drawings, that are referred to in the question.* Some children find it much easier to talk about materials if they have those materials in their hands.

4. *Reward student answers with discretion.* Every answer does not need to be rewarded. When you give a reward be certain the student understands what is being rewarded. Is that word *good* expressed for effort, creativity, a correct answer, or for being the first to respond?

5. *Try to find the cause of incorrect answers.* Ask the student how he or she came to a certain answer. Only by determining the reason for an incorrect response can you provide an explanation that will allow the student to change it to a correct one.

6. *Try not to reject an answer out of hand.* Some of the answers children give may not seem to have any bearing on the questions, but they may have bearing in the mind of the child. Rather than reject an answer or admonish the child to listen more carefully and not be silly, ask the child for further information. The child may see a direct connection between the answer you find absurd and the question.

Questions from Children

On the other side of the firing line, you will be asked questions by the children in your class. When those questions lend themselves to concrete investigation with materials, encourage the children to use those materials to find their own answers. When you can guide students to sources of information where they can find information for themselves, give them that guidance, even when you know the exact answer to a question. Teaching is not telling. Teaching is helping children learn for themselves.

But, there are bound to be many questions you cannot answer. When this occurs, a simple "I really don't know," followed by "How could we find out?" usually works very well. This strategy also provides the teacher with a real situation in which to have the students apply problem-solving skills.

Questioning, then, involves not only knowing the most appropriate way to ask and reply to a question but also knowing how to get children to reply at their maximum level. This last skill, getting children to reply at a high level, deserves a great deal of attention from you. A particularly powerful strategy for eliciting high-level responses is called "wait time."

Wait Time

Definition

Children need time to think, time to ponder the answers they will give to the questions asked during a lesson in science. During a recently observed science lesson, the teacher sat on a stool in the front of the class and asked 64 questions during a 15-minute period. At a rate of more than four questions per minute, the questions came so quickly that the children began to look glassy-eyed. The first 4 minutes of the lesson proceeded according to the following script:

TEACHER:	How many body parts does an insect have?
STUDENT:	Three.
TEACHER:	How many legs does an insect have?
STUDENT:	Six.
TEACHER:	What are the names of the three body parts?
STUDENT:	Head, thorax, and abdomen.
TEACHER:	What name is given to the outer skeleton of an insect?
STUDENT:	Exoskeleton.
TEACHER:	What is the exoskeleton made from?
STUDENT:	Chitin.
TEACHER:	What are three helpful insects?
STUDENT:	Bee, praying mantis, ladybug.
TEACHER:	What are three harmful insects?
STUDENT:	Locusts, mosquitoes, and termites.

TEACHER: What can be used in a garden to kill harmful insects?
STUDENT: A pesticide.
TEACHER: What harm can a pesticide do?
STUDENT: It can get into the food chain.
TEACHER: What is a food chain?
STUDENT: It shows which animals eat plants and which eat other animals.
TEACHER: Name one insect that eats other insects.
STUDENT: Praying mantis.
TEACHER: Name one insect that eats plants.
STUDENT: Aphid.

This question-and-answer period continued for another 11 minutes. Only once did the teacher depart from the knowledge-level questions illustrated here. She asked one application question, but when the answer did not come immediately, the teacher supplied the answer herself.

The pattern of this questioning is all too typical in the elementary school classroom:

Teacher ──────────▶ Student A
Teacher ──────────▶ Student B
Teacher ──────────▶ Student C

Other students do not have the opportunity to comment or to ask questions. In most cases, the answers given to the teacher consist of only one or two words, not even sentence fragments. The questions asked are at the knowledge level. Higher level questions cannot be asked when the setup requires four or more questions and their answers every minute.

A much better way of asking questions gives students time to think, provides time for answering, and even provides time for other students to comment. This time provided for students to think and for students to respond to one another is called "wait time" (Rowe, 1974). Generally we describe **wait time** as five seconds between when a question is asked and when a child is called on to respond. In addition, wait time includes a few seconds after the child answers, so you can be certain the child is finished talking and can allow other children to comment.

Lead-ins That Provide Wait Time.   Wait time should follow a question asked by the teacher. Because most children are not used to being given time to think, lead-ins to questions are helpful. These lead-ins alert students to the fact that they will actually have time to consider their answers. Some possible lead-ins include the following:

1. I want each of you to think about what you are going to answer, so I'm not going to call on anyone right away.
2. Think about this question. When you have an idea raise your hand. As soon as I see you, put your hand down until others have some ideas as well.
3. Think about what you have just seen happen and decide on one reason you think it happened. I'll give you some time to think before you answer.

4. Johnny said _____. Think about that for a few minutes. Do you agree or disagree with his idea? Why?

5. Think about this question, and as you are thinking, write down some ideas that come to mind. Be ready to share your ideas with others.

Once children realize they will actually have time to think, they tend to use that time effectively. Keep in mind, that the first child to put up a hand should not always be called on to respond. Rewards should go to the children who really think about their answers as well as to the child who is fast about getting a hand raised.

Results of Using Wait Time

The Changing Pattern of Response. A period of wait time following a question can change the sequence of response from:

to

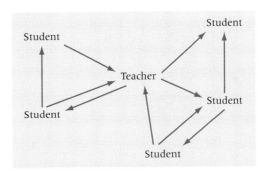

Rather than a question-answer session, the lesson becomes a discussion. Students comment on answers given by other students, ask each other questions, turn to the teacher for a response (not a question), then continue from there.

The use of wait time is a powerful technique; one teacher developed her techniques to the extent that she changed her class of 25 students only one of whom gave a desultory answer to a single question to a class where all of the students commented eagerly.

Benefits of Wait Time to Children. A number of benefits result from the use of a period of wait time both after a question is asked and after a student responds:

1. Teacher-centered questioning periods decrease, and child-to-child interaction increases.

2. Children show more indications of listening to one another rather than listening for the next question.

3. Fewer questions remain unanswered or receive an "I don't know" answer.

4. Students give longer responses to questions and use phrases and sentences rather than single words.

5. More students give evidence to support their responses or make inferences from data that they collect.

6. Rather than simply replying with memorized, factual information, students engage in speculative thinking.

7. More students contribute unsolicited, but appropriate, responses. The lesson, therefore, becomes more student oriented.

8. The number of questions the children ask increases, and the number of investigations the children propose increases as well.

9. The number of students who respond to questions increases. Rather than eliciting answers from a few facile thinkers, wait time allows the class ponderers and the so-called slow children time to think and develop answers.

10. Confidence in expressing ideas increases. Use of vocal inflection that asks "is this right" decreases.

11. Children become more frequent inquirers into science rather than readers of science. (Rowe, 1974)

Benefits of Wait Time to Teachers. The effect of wait time on children is impressive, but wait time also has effects on the teacher. First, the teacher tends to respond to students with a more flexible attitude and is more flexible in the range of acceptable answers; rather than a single correct answer, a variety of answers is permissible.

Second, the number and kinds of questions change. The number of questions decreases. It is simply impossible for the teacher to ask the same number of questions when he or she allows time for thought and student responses become more complex. Also, the kind of question changes as the teacher asks more high-level cognitive questions rather than simple knowledge-level questions. High-level questions such as those on the analysis and synthesis levels require more time for thought and response.

Finally, the teacher's expectations of students change. Children who were thought to be slow or nonverbal are seen as capable. Not only do more children become bright and verbal in the eyes of their peers, but those who appeared to be average and perhaps unable to handle high-level thinking become more capable. Children come to be viewed as learners rather than as memorizers.

Using Rewards with Wait Time. The benefits of wait time can be negated by inappropriate and constant application of rewards. Rewards are those encouragements you give to students as the result of some behavior. Words like *good, super, what a great idea,* and so on, are all rewards.

Although some rewards are good, the too frequent application of rewards can negate the good effects of wait time. Wait time is designed to allow many children to answer, to encourage speculative thinking, and to enhance inquiry behaviors. If you reward children early in the answering sequence, other children may decide not to respond because they fear their answers could not be as good as the first response give. Consider the following:

TEACHER: What are some of the ways of telling what kind of weather is headed our way?

STUDENTS: (A dozen children raise their hands.)

TEACHER: Tommy?

TOMMY: The kinds of clouds and the way the wind is blowing.

TEACHER: Excellent answer! That's exactly right!

STUDENTS: (Eleven hands go down.)

TEACHER: What could be some other ways?

STUDENTS: (No one responds. No hands go up.)

Although these students had a number of answers, they no longer had the inclination to answer. After all, Tommy's response was so good they could not possibly compete. And if Tommy's answer was "exactly right," it was quite possible that their answers were "exactly wrong." Rather than rewarding Tommy so profusely, the teacher should have rewarded all of the children, then returned to Tommy's answer as the best way to get into the lesson.

Wait time is also designed to allow children to exercise their inquiry skills. The idea of inquiry carries with it the connotation that all ideas are of equal value until evidence to the contrary is gathered. Such evidence enables the individual to differentiate between those ideas with supporting evidence and those without such evidence. A reward immediately designates one idea as correct and implies that another is incorrect. Therefore, says the child, if a particular idea is correct these is no need for further inquiry.

The key to the use of wait time and the acquisition of all of its benefits is to use rewards sparingly. Reward all answers at the same time, and then return to the answer that will best help children to understand the concepts being considered in the science lesson (Rowe, 1974).

Activities 7.7 and 7.8 ask you to put into practice the information found in this chapter on asking questions appropriately.

Questioning Activities

Activity 7.7

Purpose To investigate questioning strategies found in a science classroom.

Procedure

1. Arrange to observe an elementary or middle school science teacher for two 30- to 45-minute time periods.

2. Ask permission to take notes or to record the teacher during the lesson.
3. Observe the teacher's questioning strategies in terms of the techniques for asking and responding to questions in this chapter.

   a. What were the teacher's strengths in asking questions?

   b. What were the teacher's weaknesses?

   c. What was the effect of the teachers questioning strategies on the students in the class?

   d. What suggestions might you make to this teacher to improve his or her questioning strategies?

Activity 7.8

Purpose   To further develop your ability to analyze questioning strategies used in a classroom situation.

Procedure
1. Read each of the following questioning scripts. Using the information in this chapter, analyze each of the scripts for the questioning techniques used. What suggestions for improvement would you offer to each of the teachers in the scripts?
2. *Questioning Script 1* (time period is 2 minutes):

TEACHER:	Adam, what word is used for all of the air around Earth?
ADAM:	Atmosphere.
TEACHER:	Carol, what happens to the atmosphere as you get higher up?
CAROL:	It gets thinner.
TEACHER:	Ed, is the atmosphere a mixture or a solution?
ED:	A mixture.
TEACHER:	Gina, what holds the air to Earth's surface?
GINA:	Gravity.
TEACHER:	Inez, what is the most abundant gas in Earth's atmosphere?
INEZ:	Nitrogen.
TEACHER:	Ken, what percentage of the atmosphere is nitrogen?
KEN:	About 78 percent.
TEACHER:	Mark, do we breathe nitrogen?
MARK:	No.
TEACHER:	Oscar, what gas do we breathe?
OSCAR:	Oxygen.
TEACHER:	Patsy, what percentage of the atmosphere is oxygen?
PATSY:	About 21 percent.
TEACHER:	Ricky, what is the next most important gas in the atmosphere?
RICKY:	Carbon dioxide.

3. *Questioning Script 2:*

TEACHER:	What is the most important characteristic of a mammal? Tom?
TOM:	It has fur.
TEACHER:	No. I want the most important characteristic. Maria?
MARIA:	It has live babies?
TEACHER:	Let's not guess! What is the most important characteristic? Todd?
TODD:	It has warm blood?
TEACHER:	So do birds, Todd. What is the most important characteristic? Janice?
JANICE:	They feed milk to their babies.
TEACHER:	Good. I'm glad to see someone read the homework assignment.

4. *Questioning Script 3:*

TEACHER:	In this demonstration, the amount of matter in the container before the steel wool rusted should be the same as the amount of matter in the container after the steel wool rusted. But our container weighed more before the steel wool rusted than it did after. What could be some of the reasons why ours weighed more before rusting than it did after rusting? Betsy?
BETSY:	There could be a leak around the edge of the plastic wrap on the top of the jar so some of the water evaporated.
TEACHER:	What an excellent answer! That really shows you were observing and thinking! Now, what could be some other reasons?

(All hands went down and no one else responded.)

5. *Questioning Script 4:*

TEACHER:	Your book talks about some things that plants have. Who can name some? Susan?
SUSAN:	Flowers.
TEACHER:	Good. Plants have flowers. Flowers are used by plants to . . . what? What do flowers do for plants? Are flowers important to plants? John?
JOHN:	Flowers are used to make seeds.
TEACHER:	Listen to the question. Are flowers important? Now, John?
JOHN:	Yes.
TEACHER:	Flowers are important because they make seeds, and they also do what else? Terrie?
TERRIE:	They make the garden pretty.
TEACHER:	Yes, they do make a garden look pretty. What other things do flowers have? Think about that. What are some of the other parts of a plant? Is the whole plant made up of the flower? What other parts are there? Ray?
RAY:	Roots, leaves, stems, flowers . . .

TEACHER: (Interrupting). That's enough. Leave some for others. Ray said there are roots, leaves, stems, flowers. We already know there are leaves, roots, stems, and flowers. What else? Elsie?

ELSIE: Aren't there *two* more parts? Seeds and fruit?

TEACHER: Yes, Elsie, you're absolutely right. There were two more parts rather than just one more part. Now, how many parts does a plant have all together? Terrie?

TERRIE: Six.

6. *Questioning Script 5:*

TEACHER: In this demonstration, the egg was supposed to go into the bottle. Ours didn't do that. What happened instead? (Pause). Joey?

JOEY: The egg split in half and a little of the white fell into the bottle and got burned. The rest just stayed on top.

TEACHER: That's exactly what happened. What could be some of the reasons why the entire egg didn't go into the bottle the way it was supposed to? (Pause). Jean?

JEAN: Maybe the egg was too big.

TEACHER: Carlos?

CARLOS: Maybe the fire in the bottom of the bottle went out too fast so you didn't get a vacuum.

TEACHER: We've got two possibilities. What else? (Pause). Lee?

LEE: Maybe the bottle got too hot and made the egg hot and the egg got bigger than the top of the bottle and so it wouldn't fit through.

TOM: But the bottle would get hot, too, and expand so the egg should fall in. Maybe the egg was . . . or the jar . . . was sticky.

CATHY: Maybe the air pressure outside isn't high enough today to push the egg into the bottle.

MARIA: Maybe the egg needs to have the shell left on.

JACK: Maybe you shouldn't burn the paper in the bottle. Just put the egg on top.

TEACHER: Let's get one last answer. Tamika?

TAMIKA: Maybe you need a bottle with a different shape.

TEACHER: All of you have fine ideas. Now, I'm going to ask you to get into your groups and decide how we could go about testing these ideas to find out which of them is correct . . . if any.

7. *Questioning Script 6:*

TEACHER: According to the film that we just saw, what characteristics most distinguish birds from other animals? Jason?

JASON: They have feathers.

TEACHER: What were the three functions of feathers mentioned in the film? Marte?

MARTE:	For warmth, for flying, and . . .
TEACHER:	The third one is to shed water. What did the film mean when it used the word camouflage? (Pause). Tony?
TONY:	I think it meant that some kinds of birds hide.
TEACHER:	OK. What else does it mean?
WILL:	They hide without really hiding. It's like you can't see them, but they're really there.
TEACHER:	Good, but please remember to raise your hand. Jose?
JOSE:	I know what it means. It's like they blend into the ground or the grass.
TEACHER:	Sandra?
SANDRA:	Like a white . . . uh . . . I don't remember the bird's name . . . but that white . . .
PAUL:	Ptarmigan.
TEACHER:	Good. Go on, Sandra.
SANDRA:	I forgot.
TEACHER:	Jason?
JASON:	Camouflage means something can hide because it has coloring like the place where it lives. It blends into the background so you can't see it.
TEACHER:	Very good, Jason. I know I can always count on you to have the right answer. What were some of the other birds in the film that used camouflage? Let's get someone other than Jason.

Summary

Asking good questions in a science lesson involves more than simply phrasing a question clearly. First, you need to determine the purpose of the question. Is the question to determine whether the child holds certain information in his or her memory or is the question to determine whether the child can use that knowledge in some way? Second, you need to ask questions that will elicit a variety of cognitive behaviors, ranging from knowledge-level recall, to the creativity of synthesis, to the judgmental behaviors of evaluation. Third, you need to allow time for thought processes as well as for a student to finish a response. Remember, it can take two seconds or more for a student to do a hierarchical search through his or her memory. The child needs time to recall information and to shape that information into a response. Finally, you need to know how to respond effectively to questions, both to stimulate discussion and to reward ideas. Two keys here are to listen carefully and to reward sparingly.

Chapter Vocabulary

The number following each term refers to the page on which the term is first introduced.

Analysis level, 179
Analysis of elements, 179
Analysis of organizational principles, 179
Analysis of relationships, 179
Application level, 178
Cognitive domain, 175
Comprehension level, 177
Convergent question, 171
Derivation of a set of abstract relations, 181
Divergent question, 172
Evaluation level, 182
Extrapolation, 177
Interpretation level, 177
Judgment in terms of external evidence, 182

Judgment in terms of internal evidence, 182
Knowledge level, 176
Knowledge of specifics, 176
Knowledge of universals and abstractions in the field, 176
Knowledge of ways and means of dealing with specifics, 176
Production of a plan, 181
Production of a unique communication, 180
Synthesis level, 180
Translation level, 177
Wait time, 190

Applying the **CONCEPTS**

1. One of the problems often associated with education is the claim that students cannot think. That is, they can recall information but they have difficulty using that information. How could you use questioning skills in the classroom to help alleviate this problem of children being unable to think?

2. As a new teacher in an elementary school, an experienced teacher comes to you with a suggestion to make your teaching easier: Give your students lots of worksheets in which all they need to do is fill in the blanks or circle the proper term. That way, you will be able to grade papers quickly and easily. How would you respond to this teacher's suggestion?

3. A teacher tells you, "I never have discussions in my class. The students get too excited and too many different ideas are brought out. And sometimes the kids even come up say things I don't agree with. It's just easier to stick to the facts." How would you respond to this teacher's comment?

4. You are observing a seventh grade teacher who begins a lesson on vision problems by asking, "How would you feel if you had to get glasses?" Every one of the responding students states that he or she would feel terrible and not wear the glasses. The teacher then

spends 20 minutes telling the children they are wrong to feel that way and that should say they would feel good because they would be able to see better. What would you say to this teacher after the lesson?

References

Andre, T. 1979. Does answering high-level questions while reading facilitate productive learning? *Review of Educational Research* 49, 280–318.

Arnold, D. S. 1975. An investigation of relationships among question level, response level, and lapse time. *School Science and Mathematics* 73, 591–594.

Blank, M., and S. J. White. 1986. Questions: A powerful but misused form of classroom exchange. *Topics in Language Disorders* 6, 1–11.

Bloom, B. S. 1956. *Taxonomy of educational objectives: The classification of educational goals. Handbook I: The cognitive domain.* New York: McCay.

Blosser, P. E. 1975. How to ask the right questions. Washington, D.C.: National Science Teacher's Association.

Burns, M. 1985. *The role of questioning. Arithmetic Teacher* 32, 14–16.

Cliatt, M. J. P., and J. M. Shaw. 1985. *Open questions, open answers. Science and Children* 23, 14–16.

Dillon, J. T. 1982. The effect of questions in education and other enterprises. *Journal of Curriculum Studies* 14, 127–152.

Holliday, W. G., H. G. Wittaker, and K. D. Loose. 1984. Differential effects of verbal aptitude and study questions on comprehension of science concepts. *Journal of Research in Science Teaching* 21, 143–150.

Hunkins, F. P. 1972. *Questioning strategies and techniques.* Boston: Allyn & Bacon.

Rowe, M. B. 1974. Pausing phenomena: Influence on the quality of instruction. *Journal of Psycholinguistic Research* 3, 3.

Rowe, M. B. 1974a. Wait-time and rewards as instructional variables, their influence on language, logic, and fate control: *Part one, wait-time. Journal of Research in Science Teaching* 11, 81–94.

Rowe, M. B. 1974b. Relation of wait-time and rewards to the development of language, logic, and fate control: Part two, rewards. *Journal of Research in Science Teaching* 11, 291–308.

Sanders, N. M. 1966. *Classroom questions: What kinds?* New York: Harper.

Tisher, R. R. 1971. Verbal interaction in science classes. *Journal of Research in Science Teaching* 8, 1.

Chapter Eight

Constructing Science: Multiple Methods for Teaching Science

Chapter Objectives

Upon completion of Section 1 of this chapter, you should be able to:

1 develop a unit for science teaching.
2 discuss means for assessing by children.
3 assess prior knowledge held by children.

Upon completion of Section 2 of this chapter, you should be able to:

1 differentiate between inductive and deductive discovery teaching strategies.
2 describe the Learning Cycle and conceptual change model teaching strategies.
3 plan for the use of discovery strategies in the classroom.
4 determine the teaching strategy best used in a particular situation.

Upon completion of Section 3 of this chapter, you should be able to:

1 describe verbal teaching strategies: expository teaching and discussions.
2 plan for the use of verbally oriented teaching strategies in the classroom: expository teaching and discussions.
3 describe ordinary and discovery demonstrations.
4 plan for the use of demonstrations in the classroom.

Introduction

What does it mean to teach science to children? Ask six teachers and you will probably get six different answers. Some teachers see science teaching as vocabulary teaching. As long as the children in their classes can define vocabulary terms like *molecule, gravity, or force,* they feel they have taught science. Other teachers see science teaching as an extension of reading. Children in these classes read from science textbooks, trade books, and magazines, discuss what they have read, and keep journals detailing their reactions to what was read. Some teachers see science teaching as a combination of textbook and activity in which the textbook is used to teach the children the content and the activities are an addition to the textbook. The children learn by reading and discussing and then have fun doing the activities if there is time for them. And, finally, some teachers view science as continuous activity. Some of these teachers use activities for the sake of doing activities. The students are actively involved, but the purpose for the activities may not be clearly defined. In other cases, teachers use activities in a purposeful manner to help their students discover concepts for themselves.

Which set of teachers is "right" in how science should be taught? None of them, and all of them. Scientists involved in the pursuit of science do all of the things these teachers have their classes doing.

Science does involve vocabulary. In fact, scientists sometimes seem to speak in a foreign language. They use terms like *molecule, photosynthesis, gravity, spectrum, metabolism,* and *magma,* words not generally encountered unless one is reading or discussing information based in science. Each of these terms conveys a specific concept and so it is important that children learn correct vocabulary. This does not mean that children should learn lists of words and definitions, but rather that they should learn proper terminology in context and as an aid to conceptualization and communication.

Scientists do a great deal of reading about their chosen field of study. In planning an experiment, scientists read to determine what has already been done, what is already known, what pitfalls others have encountered in investigating a particular phenomenon. Scientists also read to find out about new instruments, new techniques in their fields, and new discoveries that may have bearing on their own work. Scientists frequently find differing opinions on the areas they are researching, and those differing opinions lead to new and different experiments. And reading is just as much a part of the scientific enterprise as quantitative and qualitative experiments are.

Scientists engage in laboratory and fieldwork. They design and test hypotheses through experimentation. Those experiments, however, are designed to test new theories or hypotheses based on previously developed theories. Scientists do not simply walk unprepared into the laboratory or into the field and begin working. Scientists have a purpose for their work. Just as scientists have purpose for their work, so should children have purposeful activities as a part of their work in science classes. In our science classes, our students should be actively engaged in the pursuit of new information and actively engaged in the replication of experiments to determine their validity. They should not be actively engaged simply for the sake of doing something hands-on.

And, finally, scientists communicate with other scientists as well as with non-scientists. Most scientists write for scientific journals within their field or for broad-based scientific journals. Some scientists also write for popular magazines and so communicate their work to the general public as well as to active scientists. In addition to writing, scientists present information at conferences, speak to local and national groups, and so present their knowledge to a wide audience. This dissemination of knowledge is a vital part of the scientific pursuit, for this is how new ideas are brought before the scientific community, how new ideas are tested to determine their validity, and how erroneous ideas are finally removed from the scientific record.

How then should science be taught? Science should be taught through a multiplicity of methods designed to incorporate reading, laboratory experiences, and communication into a coherent whole. If we are going to have a coherent science program, we need to take into account these three factors:

1. how the program can be successfully organized in order to provide coherence.
2. how the program can be sequenced so that information is presented in a meaningful manner.
3. how the information in the program can be presented so all aspects of science are included.

In the three sections of this chapter we first consider long-range planning through the use of a discipline-centered unit plan. Then we consider the various types of teaching strategies involving hands-on activities. And, finally, we consider verbal teaching strategies. In each teaching strategy we look at where the strategy is used, how it is planned, the problems that can be encountered, and how those problems can be overcome.

SECTION ONE: DEVELOPING A UNIT PLAN

The Unit Plan as an Organizational Pattern

A **unit plan** is a particularly effective means for organizing teaching over an extended period of time. Unit plans may be subject matter specific, interdisciplinary, or integrated. No matter what the type of unit, generally these six steps are used in planning and developing the unit plan:

1. Selecting a unit topic
2. Selecting unit concepts

3. Determining appropriate objectives
4. Selecting teaching strategies
5. Selecting teaching materials
6. Determining evaluation strategies.

The following is a discussion of the development of a discipline-centered unit plan. A **discipline-centered unit plan** uses as its basis a topic from the biological, physical, or earth-space sciences. A unit on volcanoes would be a discipline-centered unit plan. Interdisciplinary and integrated units are considered in Chapter 12.

Step 1: Selecting a Unit Topic

Selecting the unit topic may be the easiest aspect of unit planning. It is the easiest because most school systems have either a course of study (locally or state developed) that outlines the topics to be taught at each grade level or a textbook series that determines the topics for each grade level. If, however, neither a course of study nor a textbook is available for use, a new teacher can determine a unit topic in one of a variety of ways. The first way is to talk with other teachers at the grade level and determine what has been traditionally taught. The second way is to observe the children in the class, listening to their comments and discussions, and attempt to select a topic that will be of interest and educational value on the basis of those discussions. A third technique, especially useful with older children, is to ask them to make a list of things they are interested in or wonder about. Excellent topics are often found in this way, but there should be a caution as well. Sixth graders may want to study planets because they were involved in a very interesting unit on planets in fifth grade, fourth graders may want to learn about dinosaurs because the latest blockbuster movie is about dinosaurs, and first graders may want to learn all about volcanoes because they heard their older siblings talking about them. Be certain to probe children about their reasons for a topic before beginning the unit planning process. And be certain to talk with teachers from the previous grade to be certain a topic will not be repetitious.

Step 2: Selecting Unit Concepts

Selecting appropriate concepts for a unit depends on four basic factors. The first factor is the cognitive level of the students. Research shows that the majority of first graders are preoperational in their processes. Attempting to teach first graders engaged in a unit entitled "Matter and Energy" about the atomic structure of matter, the concept that temperature is a measure of the movement of atoms or molecules, or that matter is conserved in physical or chemical reactions would come under the category of lost causes. Preoperational children are not ready cognitively for such concepts. More appropriate concepts for preoperational children studying a unit on matter and energy would deal with defining matter as having weight and taking up space, with the effect of forces on matter, or with how matter behaves when it is heated, cooled, or mixed. All of these can be directly investigated by preoperational children in purposeful activities. The criteria discussed in Chapter 2 for appropriate science content at various grade levels can be applied here to the selection of unit concepts and topics.

The second factor when considering the concepts for a unit is the backgrounds of the students. In order for information to be meaningful to children, they must have some experience with which to relate the new information. Children in Nebraska have a difficult time comprehending what volcanoes are really like; children in Hawaii have no difficulty at all. Children in Florida or California are more likely to understand ecological concepts based in oceanography than are children in Kansas and Oklahoma. Children in cities have a greater concept of air and noise pollution than children in rural communities. And children in farming communities have more understanding of the interrelationships among plants, animals, and the nonliving aspects of the environment than children in inner-city areas. Suppose, for a moment, that the unit topic is "Forces That Change the Earth." Children on the New Jersey coast can look at beach erosion, children in the Midwest can look at floods and wind, and children in the inner city can look at this topic in relation to streets, buildings, and sidewalks. All will learn how natural forces change the environment, but it will be far more meaningful if they investigate their own environments than if they all consider the same environment. As concepts develop, children can then become involved in environments outside of their own areas. In one area children in a third grade class in Alabama investigated winter weather in terms of their own locale and then communicated via the Internet with children living in northern Maine. Through the children in Maine they also had the opportunity to communicate with children in Australia. By the time they learned it was summertime in Australia, they were well on the way to understanding the concept that "Weather in the winter varies from one place to another." They were able to understand this concept because they had first developed an understanding of their own winter weather.

A third factor to consider in writing concepts is the importance of the concepts for developing a child's understanding of the world at that time in the life of the child. Once the unit concepts are written, review them for their importance to the developing child. The central question at this point should be "Why am I teaching this?" Consider two concepts. The first is "Machines make work easier." The second concept is "Galaxies can be classified into three categories."

Machines make work easier. Why am I teaching that particular concept? One of the main reasons would be that children are continually seeing machines in their environment and considering this concept would help them understand why. It would also help children understand how machines have changed how people live today as compared to 25 or 50 years ago.

Galaxies can be classified into three categories. Why am I teaching this concept to children? The usual reasons given for this particular topic are these: (1) this may be the only time children encounter this unless they take a course in astronomy in college, and (2) it's in the textbook. Neither of these reasons particularly contribute to a child's understanding of the universe. It is not one of those topics that will be of use to most people other than professional or amateur astronomers who will no doubt discover it in other situations. There seems to be no immediate purpose for this particular concept and so it could easily be eliminated from a unit dealing with astronomy without detriment to a child's developing understanding of the universe.

The fourth and final consideration in selecting concepts is how the concepts are related to those of other units. If a science program is to be truly coherent, the units should be related to one another through their concepts. A unit on matter may develop concepts dealing with elements, compounds, mixtures, solutions, suspensions, and dispersions as well as with changes in matter, both physical and chemical. These concepts should then be used as children begin to study a unit dealing with living things so children develop the idea that living organisms are composed of elements and compounds, that solutions are vital to survival, that chemical changes take place within living things as they perform life processes such as metabolism. Concepts dealing with living things and their needs as well as with matter can then be applied to a unit dealing with pollution and the effect of various types of pollution on the environment.

The concepts selected for inclusion in the unit should provide a developmentally appropriate and content appropriate program in science rather than a series of disjointed experiences that have little relationship to the child's developing concept of the world. And because the concepts provide the coherence desired by the program, the concepts should be sequenced appropriately so each successive concept builds on the previous concept. See Table 8.1 for an example of concepts and concept sequencing appropriate to the unit topic "Plants Are Adapted to Their Environments" at the fourth grade level. Activity 8.1 deals with developing a unit topic and concepts.

Unit Planning Activities

Activity 8.1

Purpose   To apply the information contained in the preceding sections to the selection of an appropriate topic for a unit plan and to develop a list of concepts and subconcepts appropriate to that topic.

Procedure
1. Select a particular grade level from kindergarten through eighth grade. Review textbooks, courses of study, and curriculum guides for the selected grade level.
   a. Choose one topic to use in writing a unit plan.
   b. After selecting your topic, discuss why the topic is developmentally appropriate to the grade level selected. Refer to the information in Chapter 2 as you discuss your topic.
2. Using Table 8.1 as a model, list the concepts you would teach at the grade level selected. Be certain the concepts selected are developmentally appropriate.

Table 8.1

Unit Topic and Concepts

Unit Topic:

Plants Are Adapted to Their Environments

Grade Level:

Fourth

Concepts:

1. Many kinds of plants are found in the environment.

2. Plants have certain needs wherever they are found.

3. The kind of plant found in an area is determined by conditions in that area.

4. Plants show adaptations to the locations where they are found.

5. When conditions in a particular area change, the kinds of plants may also change.

Step 3: Determining Appropriate Objectives

The **objectives** of a unit detail what a child will be learning in the context of both the concepts and the outcomes of the learning process. In essence, objectives give detail to the concepts and to the total learning process. Although the objectives detail the learning outcomes, they should not be so narrow as to preclude a variety of means for the child to demonstrate that the objective has been accomplished but not so broad as to be meaningless.

For example, one of the concepts in the unit Plants Are Adapted to Their Environment is this: "Plants have certain needs wherever they are found." An objective that is too narrow would state; "Each child will be able to list in writing the four needs of plants: water, carbon dioxide, minerals, and sunlight."

This objective is so narrow that a student has only one way of showing that he or she has accomplished the objective: Write the four factors on a piece of paper. The child who is artistically inclined does not have the opportunity to create a poster to show the conditions, and the child who is mathematically inclined could not use a chart or table to show the same knowledge. In contrast, a too broad objective would state; "Each child will know the factors necessary for plant growth."

The word *know* is so broad as to show no means for demonstrating the knowledge gained by the child. How is the teacher to determine whether or not the child "knows," and how is the child to show that he or she knows? The word *know* is so broad as to be useless to both teacher and child.

An objective that would be narrow enough to allow the teacher to determine if the child has developed the concept would be; "Each child will be able to identify the factors necessary for plant growth."

The verb *identify* gives a demonstrable means for showing knowledge but does not limit the learner to a single means of identification. Learners who wish to present a written document can do so, and those who can present a poster, diagram, chart, graph, or other documentation of having reached the objective can also do so. The outcome may be uniform, but the means for presenting the outcome is not necessarily uniform.

Table 8.2 shows objectives dealing with each of the concepts that would be appropriate for an urban environment, and Table 8.3 shows objectives dealing with each of the concepts that would be appropriate for a rural environment.

Although the objectives shown in Tables 8.2 and 8.3 do not differ greatly, the local environment does play an important role in the locales that children investigate. In this way, the backgrounds of the learners are taken into account and the information becomes relevant to the backgrounds of the learners.

Children at the fourth grade level are generally concrete operational in their thought processes, and the more concrete and more personal the experiences used in learning the more likely they are to comprehend and retain the information as a part of their cognitive structures. By learning about plant adaptations within their own environments first, these children are more likely to comprehend material about the unknown environment: inner-city plants by rural children and woodlands by inner-city children, deserts by children of the northeastern United States and deciduous forests by children of the desert Southwest. Activity 8.2 provides you with the opportunity to develop objectives appropriate to your unit concepts.

Unit Planning Activities

Activity 8.2

Purpose   To apply the information contained in the preceding sections to the development of unit objectives.

Procedure
1. Using the concepts developed in Activity 8.1 and Tables 8.2 and 8.3 as models, develop the objectives you would use for your unit plan.
2. List the objectives in the sequence you would present them to a class at the grade level selected.
3. Discuss your reasons for the sequence selected.

Step 4: Selecting Teaching Strategies

Once the objectives have been determined, you can select the teaching strategies to be used in reaching those objectives. The objectives give you more than just a hint as to how instruction should take place. For example, objective 3a, "Each student will be able to describe the kinds of plants found in any three of the following areas: sidewalk cracks, building walls, window boxes, vacant lots, city parks, front yards" immediately shows the teacher, and the students, how the objective can be reached. Students need to directly observe the plants found in various areas so they can describe those plants. A field trip by the total class to a vacant lot or to a city park may be needed, but students could also make observations around the school

Table 8.2

Objectives for an Urban Environment

Concept 1:

Many kinds of plants are found in the environment.

Objective 1a: Each student will be able to describe ten or more plants found in the area around the school and home.

Objective 1b: Each student will be able to describe the commonalities among the plants found in their environment.

Concept 2:

Plants have certain needs wherever they are found.

Objective 2a: Each student will be able to conduct an investigation to determine the needs of grass plants for water or sunlight.

Objective 2b: Each student will be able to conduct an investigation to determine the best conditions under which to grow plants in a container.

Objective 2c: Students will work as a total group to develop and maintain a container flower and vegetable garden for the school.

Concept 3:

The kinds of plants found in an area are affected by conditions in that area.

Objective 3a: Each student will be able to describe the kinds of plants found in any three of the following areas: sidewalk cracks, building walls, window boxes, vacant lots, city parks, front lawns.

Objective 3b: Each student will be able to compare and contrast the kinds of plants found in any three of the following areas: sidewalk cracks, building walls, window boxes, vacant lots, city parks, front yards.

Objective 3c: Each student will be able to demonstrate the effect of the area in which a plant grows on its growth.

Concept 4:

Plants show adaptations to the locations where they are found.

Objective 4a: Each student will be able to describe the parts that all plants have in common.

Objective 4b: Each student will be able to describe how the parts of various plants are different depending on where they are found.

Objective 4c: Each student will be able to describe how plants in various locations are adapted to their environment.

Concept 5:

When conditions in a particular area change, the kinds of plants may also change.

Objective 5a: Each student will be able to keep records of changes in the local environment (e.g., a construction site), and how those changes affect plant life.

Objective 5b: Working in small groups, students will investigate the history of the area in which they live and present findings about how the area has changed during the past century.

Objective 5c: Working in small groups, students will be able to develop a plan for incorporating plants into the changed environment.

Table 8.3

Objectives for a Rural Environment

Concept 1:

Many kinds of plants are found in the environment.

Objective 1a: Each student will be able to describe ten or more plants found within the community.

Objective 1b: Each student will be able to describe the commonalities among the plants found in their environment.

Concept 2:

Plants have certain needs wherever they are found.

Objective 2a: Working in small groups, students will interview local farmers to determine the needs of their crops if they are to grow well.

Objective 2b: Each student will be able to conduct an investigation to determine the best conditions under which to grow plants in a small garden.

Objective 2c: Working in a large group, students will develop a plan for a school vegetable garden.

Concept 3:

The kinds of plants found in an area are determined by conditions in that area.

Objective 3a: Each student will be able to describe the kinds of plants found in any three of the following areas: sidewalk cracks, building walls, lawns, meadows, woodland, wetlands, or ponds.

Objective 3b: Each student will be able to compare and contrast the kinds of plants found in any three of the following areas: sidewalk cracks, building walls, lawns, meadows, woodland, wetlands, or ponds.

Objective 3c: Each student will be able to demonstrate the effect of the area in which a plant grows on its growth.

Concept 4:

Plants show adaptations to the locations where they are found.

Objective 4a: Each student will be able to describe the parts that all plants have in common.

Objective 4b: Each student will be able to describe how the parts of various plants are different depending on where they are found.

Objective 4c: Each student will be able to describe how plants in various locations are adapted to their environment.

Concept 5:

When conditions in a particular area change, the kinds of plants may also change.

Objective 5a: Working in small groups, students will investigate the history of the area in which they live and present findings about how the area has changed during the past century.

Objective 5b: Working in small groups, students will be able to develop a plan for incorporating plants into the changed environment.

building, on the way to or from school, or at home. In contrast, objective 5b, "Working in small groups, students will investigate the history of the area in which they live and present findings about how the area has changed during the past century" requires a teaching strategy different from that used with objective 3a. For this second objective, students could investigate the changes that have occurred by interviewing parents, grandparents, and great-grandparents, by consulting history books, by talking with local historians, or by reviewing old newspapers and magazines. The teaching strategy should match the objective.

Keep three things in mind when considering objectives and teaching strategies. First, the teaching strategy you select should match the objective. It may be easier for the teacher to show pictures of local plants, but the objective asks the student to make direct observations of a variety of locales. Showing and discussing pictures does not match the objective. Second, your teaching strategy should match the developmental level of the student. Children who are preoperational or concrete operational in their thought processes learn more effectively if they are involved in concrete experiences, in this case, direct observation of plants and their environments. In addition, this direct observation will be more effective if it comes before any use of written or oral materials. And, finally, in considering objectives and teaching strategies, always keep in mind the old adage "variety is the spice of life." A variety of different teaching strategies makes teaching more interesting for you as well as for the students. More important, however, is the need for a variety of teaching strategies to accommodate the different learning styles and intelligences of the students in the class.

Section 2 of this chapter details teaching strategies oriented around hands-on investigations, and Section 3 considers teaching strategies that are more verbal in nature.

Step 5: Selecting Teaching Materials

Just as the objectives are determined by the concepts and the teaching strategies are determined by the objectives, the materials are determined by the teaching strategies. Prior to beginning any unit of work the make certain that all materials and space can be obtained. It is fine to plan to develop a school vegetable garden, but if there is no space, no plants or seeds, the principal objects to using the school's water system to water the growing vegetables, and no one is willing to come with a rototiller to prepare the soil, that plan is useless.

The best strategy is for you to plan the objectives and strategies and then determine the materials needed. When a major project is planned, such as planting a garden or going on field trips, before incorporating those activities into the unit, you should be certain the school is willing to support the activities. Only after support is assured should you continue with that type of planning.

Once the major projects are accepted and the more classroom-oriented projects determined, look at the planned teaching strategies and begin a list of the needed materials. If students are going to investigate the needs of plants, they will need to have the materials available in adequate quantities. If students are going to plant a container garden, they should have the appropriate containers and other materials; if students are going to use magazines and newspapers to investigate changes in their environment, those materials should be available.

The first listing of materials should include those directly needed for the teaching strategies leading to the objectives. Once those materials have been determined, consider the peripheral materials: drawing paper, paints or crayons, scissors, glue, and other craft and art materials that may be needed as students present the results of their activities and investigations.

By this time you should know the materials you need to teach your unit, but you are still not finished. Once you decide on the required and peripheral materials, look beyond the exact concepts and objectives into other materials, written, visual, or aural, that are related to the concepts and might develop further interest in the students. Urban children may be investigating their local environment, but trade books dealing with other environments may spark additional interest. Children may be interested in various types of plants, in terrariums, in gardening, and in a variety of other plant-related topics. Films dealing with various plants and adaptations should also be available. Tapes of temperate forest, rain forest, savanna, and jungle sounds can add an additional dimension to the unit of study. And, of course, interesting and useful Web sites should be available for children to research.

A final piece of equipment may be added to the listing: a camera and film. As students get involved in their investigations and researches, you may want to take pictures in order to document your students' accomplishments. Using still pictures can result in a photographic montage for a bulletin board and class scrapbook. A video camera can provide a program for parents' night or for sharing with other teachers. A digital camera can add to a class Web page for dissemination to other classrooms in other areas of the community, nation, or world.

Step 6: Determining Evaluation Strategies

Chapter 9 deals with evaluation of science teaching and learning. At this point, it is necessary only to state that the evaluation techniques you select should match the objectives. If the objective asks that students describe similarities in plants, the form of evaluation should ask students to identify similarities in plants and not ask the students to name the parts of a plant found on a worksheet diagram.

The evaluation strategies should not only reflect the objectives for the lesson, they should also be authentic. **Authentic evaluation** is based on the activities and the work of the students as they interact with materials, with the teacher, and with one another. Authentic evaluation strategies can and should come directly from the activities and researches of the students. For example, as students design and set up activities to determine the conditions under which plants grow best, you can determine whether or not your students know how to design an activity appropriate to the question. You can also determine from the results of the activities whether your students are able to draw conclusions consistent with the activity results and whether or not they have identified the conditions under which a particular type of plant grows well. There is no need for a text or quiz to tell whether the students have accomplished objectives dealing with setting up an activity or drawing conclusions.

At this point we know what should be in a unit plan and you have the topic, concepts, and objectives for that plan. The next step, it seems, should be to consider the kinds of teaching strategies needed and how those strategies are developed. However, there is one last consideration before considering strategies. This final aspect has a great deal of impact on the final unit plan. At this point, you should assess the students and the background knowledge they will bring to the unit. When the background knowledge is known and the strengths and weaknesses in that knowledge determined, you can modify the objectives and concepts so they are more appropriate to the children in the class.

Determining What Children Already Know

Children, as we have seen, think in ways that are very different from those of adults. As children encounter the world they construct their own concepts and interpretations. For example, a kindergarten class was studying solids and liquids. They had, after many experiences with liquids, decided that wetness is one of the characteristics of liquids. The kindergarten teacher then asked the children to name some liquids. He collected a variety of examples: milk, water, orange juice, apple juice, coffee, root beer, and honey. At that point he asked children to tell him what made a liquid a liquid. The children told him that liquids are wet. He then asked the children to think about sand and whether it was a liquid or not. Only one child answered. It was a liquid. Why? Because she could pour it out of her sand bucket and it was wet.

"What do you mean, it's wet?" The teacher asked.

"When it's on the bottom of the ocean, it's wet," the little girl told him.

"What about when it's on the beach?"

"It isn't a liquid on the beach—just when it's under the ocean."

This child had constructed her concept of a liquid around the characteristic of wet, and no conversation would convince her that sand was not a liquid when it was wet but something else when it was dry. The teacher then knew he was going to have to continue with experiences with liquids if the child was going to construct a more scientific concept of a liquid.

Just as this kindergarten teacher needed to know the child's concept in order to provide more experiences and so change a misconception, so does a teacher of any grade level need to know what children think before beginning to develop the actual experiences in which the children will participate. What children think has a great influence on what they are going to learn.

In general, there are four basic ways to determine a child's and a class's current conceptions and misconceptions about a topic: (1) written pretests, (2) interviews, (3) class discussions, and (4) semantic mapping.

Written Pretests

A **pretest** is a short test of the information contained in a unit designed to determine how much of the information in a unit or textbook chapter the students already know. Written pretests are probably the most common way of determining what children already know about a particular topic. In constructing a pretest, look at the textbook, course or study, or established concepts and write questions for children to answer about the unit topic. For example, in the unit on plants adaptations, you might ask this question: "What do plants need in order to grow well?" Children who can answer this question are assumed to have the knowledge, and children who cannot answer this question are assumed not to possess that knowledge. Depending on the age of the children, such pretests may look only at simple questions involving filling in blanks, circling correct responses, or writing paragraphs.

Strengths in Using Pretests.   A pretest is a simple means of determining what children know about a particular topic. You can test all children in the class quickly and easily on the information in the unit. Consequently, pretests are time efficient.

Weaknesses in Using Pretests.   Although a pretest is quick and easy to use, the pretest also has some serious difficulties as a means of assessing background knowledge. First, the questions on a pretest tend to be very specific. Children may not know the answers to those particular questions, but they may have a great deal of knowledge about the area. For example, a child may not be able to list the nine planets in their proper order, but may know the names of the various space probes that have photographed the surfaces and what those photographs showed. A teacher asking for the names of the nine planets gets a false impression of this child's understanding of planets. Similarly, a child may be able to name all of the planets in order but think they are stars that revolve around Earth. Once again a false impression of the child's knowledge is obtained.

An essay format can help probe a child's comprehension of a topic, but may also yield a false impression. A child may have a great deal of knowledge about dinosaurs but may not be able to write well enough to communicate that knowledge.

Pretests can elicit some information from children, but the information may be misleading and, therefore, useless to the teacher attempting to plan a unit of work around the results. More probing is needed if you are going to gain accurate information about what your students already know about a topic.

Interviews

An **interview** assesses background information through a one-on-one conversation between teacher and student. You can use interview strategies to learn not only what children know about a particular topic but also what they think they know about a topic. An interview can help you find out both a child's concepts and a child's misconceptions. Using an interview strategy begins with the construction of the interview, or at least of the kinds of questions you want to ask. For example, an interview about dinosaurs at the fifth grade level might include the following questions:

1. What is a dinosaur?
2. What were dinosaurs like?
3. When dinosaurs were living, what was the world like?
4. How did dinosaurs live?
5. What happened to the dinosaurs?

As soon as the teacher begins to interview an individual child, however, the questions may change very quickly. The following is an interview with a fifth grader:

TEACHER: What is a dinosaur?

STUDENT: It's this really big animal that lived a long time ago.

TEACHER: What were dinosaurs like?

STUDENT: They were all really, really big. Like as big as a house. And they had fights all the time because they just ate meat and so they were always trying to eat each other.

TEACHER: Were there any dinosaurs that ate plants?

STUDENT: No. There were other kinds of animals that ate plants, but all the dinosaurs ate meat.

TEACHER: Tell me about these other animals.

STUDENT: A lot of them were like insects and worms and snakes and things. They would hide underground until the dinosaurs weren't around and then they'd come out and eat the plants and sometimes they ate dinosaur eggs. That's what made the dinosaurs stink.

TEACHER: Made the dinosaurs stink?

STUDENT: Right. Everybody says there aren't any dinosaurs because they stink. I guess the other animals made them go away or something. I never did get that.

This student had an interesting concept about dinosaurs, one that no teacher ever presented, but one he had constructed from a variety of misunderstandings.

Strengths in Using Interviews.   The strength of an individual interview is that you can probe the student's ideas and get an in-depth understanding of what a particular child thinks. From that information, you can develop lessons and experiences that will help the child construct a more scientific image of dinosaurs or of any topic.

Weaknesses in Using Interviews.   The use of an interview as a means of assessing what learners already understand or misunderstand is difficult for a variety of reasons. First, it is a time-consuming procedure. The amount of time needed to interview a particular child cannot be predetermined. A child who has a great deal of accurate information may need time to discuss that information with the teacher. The teacher who interviews a child with many misconceptions will need time to probe those misconceptions. Second, an entire class cannot be interviewed individually, so the teacher must select students representative of the class to interview. The accuracy of the information gained through the interview depends on the students selected for interview. The child in the interview about dinosaurs is not representative of most fifth graders and so a false impression could be gained by the teacher if this child's ideas are considered the norm. Interviewing the daughter of a vertebrate paleontologist can also provide a highly inaccurate picture of the class's level of knowledge. If you are using an interview as a way of preassessing students, select a representative sample of students to interview.

Cautions in Using Interviews.   First, and particularly with young children, the concepts held by the interviewee may be "cute" or "funny" according to adult standards. A teacher who has a child tell him or her that "clouds move because there are strings on them and people pull the strings," an actual response of a 6-year-old, cannot react to that response in any way other than to accept the answer as it is given and to probe a little further to see how the child sees that as working.

Second, the purpose of the interview is to determine what children know or think they know and particularly to determine the misconceptions held by the children. The purpose of teaching is to present accurate information and to change misconceptions. During an interview you cannot attempt to "teach" the child correct information. Instead, you simply accept what the child says without comment on the information.

Interviews give you a great deal more information about background information held by students than pretests do, but they may not give an accurate impression of the understandings of the children if the children interviewed are not, for some reason, representative of the class.

Class Discussions

A **class discussion** is a type of interview, beginning with a problem situation, in which the entire class is involved in the interview. Class discussions are conducted with the entire class working together. In general, such a discussion begins with the presentation of a problem related to the upcoming unit of work. For example, a group discussion prior to beginning a unit on simple machines with fourth grade children could begin like this:

> Two children want to play on a seesaw. Michael is a fifth grader and his sister Sarah is a second grader. When Michael sits on one end of the seesaw and Sarah sits on the other, Sarah is up in the air. No matter what she does she can't push hard enough to raise Michael from the ground. What are some things that could be done so that Sarah and Michael can use the seesaw together?

The question and situation embodied in the question are used as a springboard for discussion. It is your job, as the teacher, to initiate the discussion, to ask questions that will probe student answers in order to get further explanation, and to ask for additional possibilities. As the students discuss the question, note the ideas brought out by the students, most particularly their misconceptions and their areas of strength.

Like the use of pretests or interviews as ways of gaining information about students' understandings and misunderstandings, the use of group discussion for this purpose also has certain strengths and weaknesses.

Strengths in Using Class Discussions.   The real strength of this preassessment strategy lies in the amount of information gained. Most of the class participates in the discussion, so you are able to gain information from a broad range of students. In addition, as students attempt to explain their ideas to one another, they generally reveal more depth to their thinking than in interviews or pretests. You have the opportunity to ask questions that encourage students to give more information. And finally, the solutions students give to problems, whether workable or not, provide you with starting points for hands-on investigations.

Weaknesses in Using Class Discussions.   The first of the weaknesses is a problem for the teacher. Rapid-fire discussions may bring out more information than you are prepared to handle effectively. It is difficult to keep in mind the wide variety of ideas, of misconceptions or conceptions that surface. Taking unobtrusive notes can help, but taking notes during a discussion of this type can be disconcerting and so stifle discussion. The second weakness is summed up by this student's comment: "I still don't know the answer!"

The purpose of this type of discussion is to elicit ideas, not to come to a conclusion. Consequently, if students are used to discussions as a means for developing concepts or conclusions, the lack of conclusion can be difficult for them. Under no circumstances, however, should you use group discussion as a form of preassessment in an attempt to teach the correct answers to the question at this time. Instead, use answers as the basis for appropriate teaching strategies that will later allow students to solve the problem with understanding.

Cautions in Using Class Discussions.   Two cautions on the use of class discussions are needed. First, be careful of your reaction to statements made by students, particularly students in upper grades where students sometimes try to top one another with the absurdity of their responses. Such responses do not reflect the actual thought of the students and are often given to see the reaction of the teacher. In one eighth grade class, a discussion of why a battleship floats while a pin sinks led, in some unknown way, to a discussion of why a dead body floats to the surface of a river. After a few minutes of trying to "gross out" the teacher and receiving only a neutral response, attention returned to battleships and pins. The best response in these kinds of situations is to listen, remain neutral, and bring the discussion gently back to the topic. Second, the use of a discussion format is not fully appropriate for primary grade children where the child's use of language and ability to interact in a discussion format is not well developed. In one first grade class a discussion of a situation dealing with why a plant on a windowsill might have died ranged from plants, to grandmothers, to cats having kittens, to weeds in grass. The teacher really gained no information about her students' understanding of a plant's growth needs.

Semantic Mapping

A **semantic map** is a visual means for determining the conceptions and misconceptions of a group of students. It can be used with small groups or with the class as a whole. Semantic mapping in assessing background information involves six steps:

1. Place a word or short phrase on the chalkboard, overhead, or large sheet of paper.
2. Have students work individually to write down any words that come to mind on seeing and hearing the word or phrase. Allow a minute or two for this step, longer if needed.
3. Have students form groups of four or five. One student in each group should be appointed as the secretary. With the help of the group, the secretary makes a complete list of all the words listed. Groups can also add additional words to the list.
4. Develop categories that allow students to classify the listed words into groups.
   a. With younger children, the secretaries can read their lists and you can use questions to help the students develop appropriate categories.
   b. With older children, the students can identify categories in their small groups.
   c. Collect the categories and have the students decide as a class which categories to use in classifying the words.
5. Working as a total group, with you as the recorder, develop a semantic map showing the relationships of the terms listed to the classification categories selected.
6. Assess the strengths, weaknesses, and misconception of the class using the semantic map.

Figure 8.1 shows a semantic map developed for the word *energy* by a sixth grade class. In looking at the map in Figure 8.1, the teacher should first note that the class confuses the terms *energy* and *fuel* because under the category *kinds of energy* the class has generally listed fuels, not realizing the relationships among gasoline, natural gas, oil, and petroleum. A strength is shown in this class in the areas of magnets and simple machines as students show many related ideas including all categories of simple machines. An interesting concept is shown by the term *electric switch* in which the switch is seen as the source of light, heat, and sound. This would provide an interesting starting point for considering how one form of energy can be changed to another. The category *people* shows that students realize human beings use energy and that their source of energy is food. There are many other ideas shown in this map, ideas the teacher can use as a starting point for investigations. This analysis of the map constitutes the actual assessment aspect of the use of the map.

Strengths in Using Semantic Mapping.   Using a semantic map as a preassessment strategy has the advantage of including all children in the preassessment.

Figure 8.1

Semantic Map for Energy

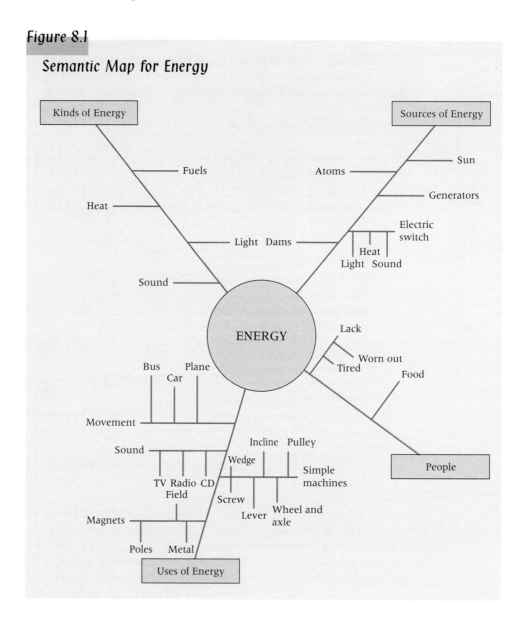

Each child participates through the development of the individual lists of terms, which are then categorized in the class map.

Weaknesses in Using Semantic Mapping.   The main weakness of using a semantic map is the amount of time need to develop the map. It is a time-consuming strategy, particularly in diagramming the terms, but the amount of information gained offsets this weakness. The second weakness is in the use of the map. The usefulness of the map depends on the skill of the teacher in interpreting

---

Box 8.1   *Summary of Preassessment Strategies*

Pretest	Interview	Class Discussion	Semantic Map
Tests what students already know about the material in the unit.	One-on-one conversation between teacher and student.	An interview involving the entire class.	A visual means for determining the background of the entire class.

Strengths

Pretest	Interview	Class Discussion	Semantic Map
All students. Simple to give. Efficient.	Can probe student answers. In-depth understanding of student's concepts.	Great deal of information is given.	Entire class is involved.

Weaknesses

Pretest	Interview	Class Discussion	Semantic Map
Highly specific. Tests knowledge of text content rather than student background.	Time consuming. Selection of students may determine the outcome. Teacher may try to teach rather than accepting incorrect responses.	May be too much information at one time for the teacher to handle easily. Students may think teacher is teaching and be confused by the discussion's lack of ending.	Time consuming. Teacher's ability to interpret the map determines the usefulness of the map.

---

the map. Teachers who lack background information on the topic under consideration or who have misconceptions of their own are not as effective in interpretation as are teachers with strong backgrounds in science content.

Box 8.1, shows a summary of the four strategies for preassessment, their strengths and their weaknesses.

Using Preassessment Information

The usefulness of any preassessment strategy is in how the teacher uses the information gained from the strategy. The preassessment information should guide the teacher's presentation of information in the unit.

This guidance should influence both the content of the unit and the teaching strategies selected for use during that unit. Preassessment affects the content by demonstrating the content areas within the unit which should be emphasized, deemphasized, or omitted. Areas showing weaknesses or misconceptions should receive greater emphasis in the unit. Areas that show some understanding, which show the topic has been studied previously, may receive somewhat less emphasis.

And, finally, areas that show high levels of knowledge and understanding may be omitted. In the unit on energy, students should probably spend some time considering the difference between fuels and energy, and more time looking at transformations of energy from one form to another, considering kinetic and potential energy, and studying uses of energy beyond uses of electricity. And children should probably not study simple machines or magnets again.

Preassessment should also assist you in selecting appropriate teaching strategies. For example, misconceptions should result in teaching strategies in which students confront those misconceptions through hands-on investigation whenever possible and so cause conceptual change to occur. However, as you select your teaching strategies, keep in mind, that just as scientists do not conduct their inquiries strictly in the laboratory but also use written and verbal sources of information, so should children use a variety of sources of information and the teacher use a variety of teaching strategies. Activities 8.3 and 8.4 apply the information dealing with preassessment strategies to your developing unit plan.

Preassessment Strategy Activities

Activity 8.3

Purpose   To have you develop examples of each of the four preassessment strategies discussed here. Each strategy should be appropriate to the unit plan under development.

Procedure
1. Using the concepts from your unit plan and the information on preassessment strategies considered in the proceeding sections, develop a sample preassessment strategy showing each of the four types.

Activity 8.4

Purpose   To utilize one of the preassessment strategies developed for your unit with an appropriately sized group of students.

Procedure
1. Arrange to work with a group of students of appropriate size. For example, if using an interview, arrange to interview about four students. The students should be at the grade level selected for your unit.
2. Administer your preassessment to the selected children.
3. Interpret the results of your assessment. How would the results affect the concepts and objectives already written for the unit?

Unit plans allow you to engage in long-range planning as you determine how an entire course of study will be conducted and what outcomes that course of study will have. Lesson planning constitutes short range-planning. In lesson planning you determine how a particular packet of information will be presented. Each lesson considers a particular teaching strategy.

Teaching Strategies: An Overview

According to the *Standards,* no one teaching strategy is appropriate for all situations, no one strategy can be best for all students in a particular situation. As teachers, we need to recognize the need for a variety of teaching strategies not simply because of the *Standards* but because good teaching in the science classroom requires a variety of strategies. First, we need a variety of strategies simply because of the differences in learning styles, intelligences, and backgrounds of the children we teach. A variety of teaching strategies is needed in order to provide all students with opportunities for learning. Second, we need a variety of teaching strategies because of the variety of content included within the area of science. It is easy to teach students about simple machines with hands-on strategies but not so easy to teach characteristics of the planets in this way. And, third, we need a variety of teaching strategies because of the variety of different circumstances under which we teach. An eighth grade teacher with a science laboratory may be able to do complex experiments with chemical reactions, an eighth grade teacher who has only a standard classroom without lab facilities may have to use a demonstration. A second grade teacher in a rural school can go out and observe various types of small mammals in a field, but an urban teacher surrounded by cement and asphalt may need to show a film or take a field trip to a zoo. Teachers need a variety of strategies to accommodate to students, content, and circumstances.

Teaching strategies can be divided into two basic categories: verbal strategies and materials strategies. Verbal strategies include those oriented toward reading, writing, or speaking. These strategies include the various forms of expository teaching as well as discussion. Materials-oriented strategies include both hands-on teaching strategies and demonstrations.

In sections 2 and 3 of this chapter, the following teaching strategies are considered with the hands-on strategies looked at first and the verbal strategies second:

1. Discovery teaching
2. Constructivist teaching
3. Ordinary demonstrations
4. Discovery demonstrations
5. Expository teaching
6. Discussions

As each strategy is considered, the appropriate uses, the method for planning, a sample lesson plan, and the problems that may be encountered are discussed. Figure 8.2 shows how the teaching strategies to be discussed relate to one another.

Figure 8.2

Teaching Strategies

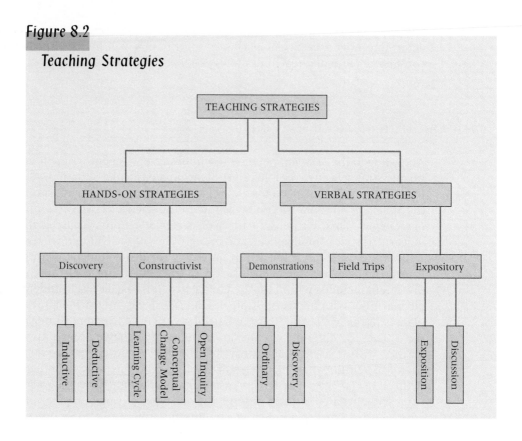

SECTION TWO: HANDS-ON
TEACHING STRATEGIES

1. *Discovery Teaching*
   a. *Inductive Teaching*
   b. *Deductive Teaching*

2. *Constructivist Teaching*
   a. *Learning Cycle*
   b. *Open Inquiry*
   c. *Conceptual Change Model*

   Hands-on strategies are the most appropriate for teaching science to children at the elementary school and middle school levels and should be used whenever possible. A variety of hands-on strategies exist including simple discovery teaching strategies, the more complex Learning Cycle strategy, and constructivist teaching strategies such as open inquiry and conceptual change models. In all cases, hands-on teaching should provide students with authentic learning experiences that develop the content of the science curriculum rather than illustrating information gained from expository teaching strategies or simply providing hands-on activity without purpose.

Types of Discovery Teaching Strategies

Discovery teaching strategies can be classified as inductive, deductive, or a combination of both known as Learning Cycle. No matter which variety of **discovery** strategy is being used, the purpose is still the same: to have children utilize materials in order to develop understanding of scientific content for themselves. This does not mean children will be reinventing the wheel or searching aimlessly for some unknown content, but rather that they will be engaging in carefully designed learning experiences.

Inductive discovery begins with the collection of a wide variety of information. From that information students then draw a conclusion suitable to the information. For example, students investigating magnets may make a list of the kinds of objects magnets do and do not pick up:

Picked Up		Not Picked Up	
staple	screw	soft drink can	cracker
pin	notebook ring	paper	pencil
paper clip	pen	shoelace	sweater
key	chain	penny	dime
earring	door hinge	globe	hair
nail	brick	carpet	

After considering the items on each of the list, the children, with guidance from the teacher, notice that the items on the "picked up" list are all made from metal and the items on the "not picked up" list are made from a variety of different kinds of materials. From this collection of data, the students draw the conclusion that "Magnets pick up some kinds of metals." They have used an inductive strategy in that they collected a wide variety of information and from that information, or data, they have drawn a conclusion suitable to the data. Induction moves from the collection of specific bits of data to the development of a generalization, or conclusion. Figure 8.3 gives a visual representation of this inductive discovery lesson.

Deductive Discovery.   **Deductive discovery** occurs when students begin with a generalization and then investigate that generalization in order to find specifics about it. This is not simply testing a statement to find out if it is true, but rather assuming that the statement is indeed true and trying to learn more about it. Younger children can investigate in the form of an activity, and older children can investigate through a controlled experiment. For example, students at the fourth grade level can investigate the characteristics of leaves. Because all students by this age know that plants have leaves, that is the generalization used as a starting point.

Figure 8.3

Inductive Discovery

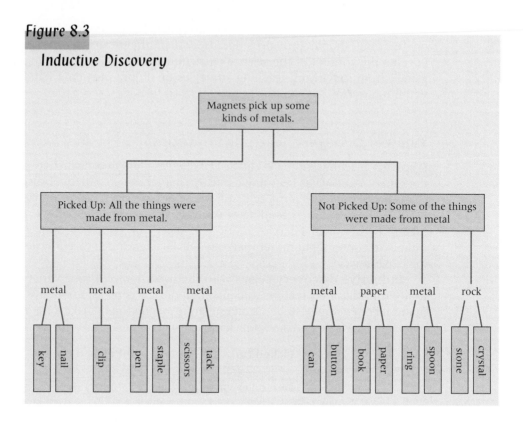

As students observe a collection of leaves, however, they begin to notice that the leaves have different edges, the veins in the leaves form different patterns, and the leaves are placed differently in the stems. From their observations, they learn that leaves can be classified by their edges as lobed, serrated, or smooth; by their veins as parallel, pinnate, or palmate; and by their placement on stems as opposite, alternate, or whorled. In this case the knowledge that plants have leaves is made more specific by considering how leaves can be classified by their specific characteristics. Figure 8.4 shows this deductive lesson in schematic form.

Learning Cycle.   The **learning cycle** is a combination of both inductive and deductive discovery teaching strategies in which a particular sequence of events is used to assist students in developing independent investigations. The Learning Cycle strategy generally begins inductively and ends deductively, although this is not a hard and fast sequence. In using Learning Cycle, students investigating ecosystems may begin by observing a terrarium. From their observations, they develop the generalization that "a terrarium must be balanced if it is to last." The teacher would then introduce help the students develop a definition of the term *balanced*. Students may then investigate the conditions that contribute to this balance, developing their own questions and investigating those questions for themselves.

Figure 8.4

Deductive Discovery Approach

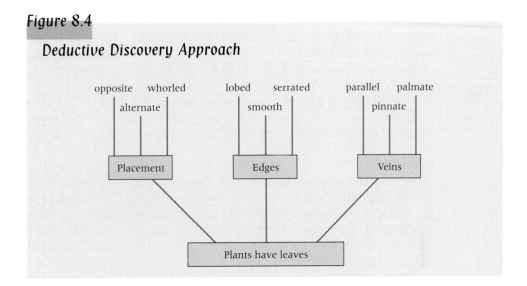

Uses of Inductive or Deductive Discovery

The teacher can use inductive or deductive discovery any time the content of the science program lends itself to exploration through the use of concrete materials. Inductive discovery is generally chosen as the teaching strategy when students have little or no experience with the content area. Through inductive discovery, children can use direct experiences to develop concepts in a new field of study. Deductive discovery, in contrast, is generally used when students have some background knowledge. Deductive discovery can then be used to add specifics to the general ideas already held by the students or to allow them to confront their misconceptions and assist them in developing more mature concepts. Inductive and deductive means of teaching should predominate in the elementary science classroom.

Discovery teaching should form the predominant method of teaching in the classroom because it is consistent with the developmental level of children in the elementary school. In addition, discovery teaching allows children direct investigation through which they are then able to construct their own concepts either through the integration of new information into the already existing cognitive structure or through confrontation of misconceptions.

Planning for Inductive or Deductive Discovery

Whether using inductive or deductive teaching strategies, the discovery-oriented lesson consists of three sections: problem, activity, and discussion.

Problem.   Any lesson presented to children should have a purpose. The discovery lesson begins with a challenge, or **problem,** that provides a purpose for the particular lesson. For example, in working with a deductive lesson dealing with the pendulum, Mr. Roth began by telling the students he had a problem. The problem was that he had a clock with a pendulum and even though it was supposed to keep perfect time, it didn't. In fact, it had to be reset every three days because it was slow. From that point, the teacher reminded the students that they knew a pendulum would swing a certain number of times in a minute, but could they think of anything that might make it swing more times or less times? The problem sets the stage for the activity that constitutes the major portion of the lesson.

Activity.   In inductive or deductive discovery, the teacher develops a laboratory experience designed to reach a particular endpoint. If the lesson is deductively oriented, the **activity** is designed to investigate the generalization. If the activity is inductive, the activity is designed to allow students to gather information that will allow them to develop a generalization. The activity should be structured enough that it will allow students to reach the desired endpoint, but not so structured there is not time within the lesson to investigate questions from the students. For example, as students investigated soil to determine what kinds of materials they would find in that soil, they began to ask if "every kind of dirt in the world" was made of the same kinds of materials. As they finished investigating the soil sample provided by the teacher, they were asked where they could get different soil samples. The children collected samples from around the school, home, and community to investigate. They observed each sample and discovered that soils did not always contain the same materials. In this case, an inductive lesson developed beyond the one the teacher had planned and into a more sophisticated investigation. The conclusions drawn from the data collected stated, first, that soil was made up of materials which had never been alive and materials that had once been alive and, second, that soil from different places had different kinds of materials.

Discussion.   Any discovery lesson should end with a discussion of the results found by the learners. The **discussion** is of particular importance with the inductive lesson because it is through the discussion that the children use their data to draw an appropriate conclusion. An appropriate conclusion to the previously described lesson on magnets would be that "magnets pick up some kinds of metals." This is all the lesson showed. It would be inappropriate to generalize from this experience that "magnets pick up iron, nickel, and cobalt." Although this is true, it is unlikely that students had a chance to investigate either nickel or cobalt. It is also unlikely that the second graders for whom this lesson would be appropriate would have any idea what kinds of metals they tested. This information can be developed through the use of expository teaching, particularly through the use of the textbook. In a deductive lesson, the discussion is designed to consider the factors tested, to weed out those that made no difference, and to emphasize those factors that are important. Once the discussion of results is finished, the teacher can, if it is appropriate to the lesson, introduce the new vocabulary connecting new terminology to the activity and the results. In both inductive and deductive strategies, the discussion is also the time when the teacher and the students return to the problem at the beginning of the lesson and attempt to solve the problem. For example, after investigating the pendulum and determining the length of the pendulum is the only factor in changing the number of swings in one minute, the teacher should then ask students what he should do about his clock. He should help the students develop the idea that if the clock is slow, the pendulum is too long, and it needs to be shortened a little. Figure 8.5 shows a lesson plan for an inductive lesson, and Figure 8.6 shows a lesson plan for a deductive lesson.

Problems in Using Inductive and Deductive Discovery

Discovery teaching, because of its orientation toward materials and children's use of materials, presents some problems that are not found in more teacher-directed and structured methods of teaching. These problems, however, can be overcome by good planning and classroom management skills.

Investigating Ability.   First, keep in mind that children are not inherently good investigators, nor do they automatically know how to work appropriately with materials. Establish rules on use, acquisition, and cleanup of materials early on. Even first and second grade children can learn to get, clean, and return materials to a central source. The more practice children have with using materials, the more competent they become in using those materials. Children need to learn how to make good observations, how to draw conclusions appropriate to their observations, how to establish cause-and-effect relationships, and how to design and carry out activities and experiments. You need to provide guidance in these areas as well as in the use of other process skills.

Time.   Because children are investigating independently, time is the greatest problem of discovery strategies. Children who are in the midst of activity do not want to stop even if the schedule does say it is time for reading. But although some do not want to end, others are quick to finish. Consequently, time is a dual problem. For those who are still actively involved when time is up, a place in the classroom should be provided where partly finished activities can be stored and worked at during free time. A windowsill, table, closet, or learning center works well for storage space. For those who finish early, a new question to investigate or new problem to solve may be all that is needed to renew investigation. However, when children have gone as far as their understanding will allow, there should be an alternative: other activities, books to read, a film or filmstrip to view, an Internet site to visit.

Differing and Incorrect Answers.   Because children are using materials and investigating on their own, you will frequently find scientifically incorrect answers or differing answers to the same activity. Because the goal of discovery teaching is to teach content, these differences must be resolved. When students obtain differing answers for the same questions, list all of the possible answers on the chalkboard and present the evidence for each of them. Children can then evaluate the various answers and try to determine which is the most probable. Once a choice is

Figure 8.5

Inductive Lesson Plan

Topic:

Soil

Objective:

1. As a result of the activity, each student will be able to identify five materials making up soil.
2. As a result of the activity, each student will be able to assist in the development of a definition of the word soil.

Materials:

Garden soil, newspaper, magnifiers, paper cups, paper and pencils, large sheet of paper, masking tape, felt-tipped marker.

Procedure:
Problem:

As I was preparing for today's science lesson, I thought I should use my dictionary to find out what soil is. When I opened my dictionary, I found something really strange. The word *soil* was there, but there was a blank space. The dictionary's writers had forgotten to put in the definition. So what we are going to be doing is investigating some soil and writing a definition we could send to the dictionary's writers so they'll have a definition.

Activity:

1. Have the students pick a partner to work with.
2. Give the following directions:
   a. Each partnership needs a sheet of newspaper, a cup of soil, a magnifier, and a pencil and paper.
   b. Put the newspaper on the desk to cover it and then dump the soil on the newspaper.
   c. Carefully look at the soil using the magnifier and write down everything you find in the soil.
   d. Ask the students to repeat the direction back to you, have one member of the partnership come up and get the materials, and then get to work.
3. While the students work, tape the sheet of paper to a wall or tack it to a bulletin board.

Discussion:

1. Collect the materials from the students.
2. Using the sheet of paper, collect the materials found by the students in the soil.
3. After all of the materials found have been listed, ask the students if there is any way to classify the materials.
   a. Guide them to the categories "materials from living things" and "materials from nonliving things."
   b. On the chalkboard or overhead, classify the materials found into the two categories.
4. Have the children look carefully at the categories and think about how they could use the information to write a definition of soil.
   a. Develop a definition based on the results of the activity and classification.

Evaluation:

1. Collect the lists of materials found in soil developed by each partnership.
2. Note those students who contributed to the definition of soil developed by the class.

---

made, use deductive discovery methods to determine the accuracy of the answer. When scientifically incorrect answers are obtained, children can use textbooks or other sources of materials to find out what "scientists think" and then brainstorm reasons for the differences between their findings and those of scientists. Students can then test their reasoning using materials.

Figure 8.6

Deductive Discovery Lesson Plan

Topic:

Solubility

Objectives:

1. As a result of this lesson students should be able to work in groups to develop a quantitative experiment to test one of the factors related to solubility of salt in water.
2. As a result of the activity and discussion, each student should be able to list three factors affecting solubility of salt in water.

Materials:

Salt, water, thermometer, stirring rods, plastic cups, beakers, hot plate, hot pad, tongs, hammer, plastic bags, balances, rock salt, kosher salt, table salt (different brands, iodized and not iodized), measuring cups or graduated cylinders, balances.

Procedure:
Problem:

1. Everybody knows that if you put salt in water, it will dissolve. But suppose I wanted to get the most salt possible to dissolve in water. What could I do? List the responses on the chalkboard.
2. Tell the class that they are going to be designing experiments to test the ideas listed on the board. Review with the class how to write a hypothesis, how to control variables, how to develop and carry out a quantitative experiment.

Activity:

1. Divide the class into groups of three or four. Have each group select one of the factors listed to test.

2. Each group should write a hypothesis and a procedure it will follow in testing the hypothesis. The procedure should be approved by the teacher before students begin working.
   a. Where problems exist in the procedure or hypothesis, discuss those problems with the group and help them find ways to remedy the problems.
3. Have each group carry out its experiment, collecting data and drawing a conclusion from the data collected.

Discussion:

1. Have each group describe its experiment and present its data and conclusion to the class. Record the conclusions on the chalkboard or overhead.
2. Make a list of the factors that could be changed in order to get more salt to dissolve in water.
3. Compare the results of the activities to the information found on solubility in the textbook or other sources of information.
   a. If differences occur, brainstorm reasons for those differences and test them using materials.

Evaluation:

1. Collect the hypotheses, procedures, collected data, and conclusions drawn by each group.
2. On a written quiz, have each student list three or more factors that affect how much salt will dissolve in water.

Tangents.   As children work with inductive or deductive discovery, they can be sidetracked from the task at hand by questions that come up as they investigate. These diversions into other activities are known as tangents. When a tangent occurs, first determine how relevant the tangent is to the problem under investigation. As noted earlier, those children coating the tabletop with mud may appear to be making a mess, but a question like "What are you trying to find out?" may reveal the mess is being used to determine how fast water evaporates from soil of varying thicknesses. Any tangent activity needs to be evaluated. If the direction of the tangent is valid and the activity contributes to the topic being studied, you should probably not interfere. In cases where the activity has become purposeless, the children will need to be drawn back into an appropriate path. Questions that help clarify the purpose of the activity or provide a problem for investigation are usually all that is needed to return the children to purposeful activity.

Chaos.   Discovery can be noisy, chaotic, and unmanageable. At least that is what many teachers fear will happen. True, discovery teaching is far more active, more noisy, and more messy than structured teaching strategies revolving around books and lectures. However, management of discovery teaching is not the problem many teachers expect. In fact, children who are involved tend to be less of a management problem than children who are not actively involved. However, if children tend to become too noisy or unruly, stop the children's work, review the ground rules, and have the children pick up where they left off. The one management strategy that you should not use is stopping work, taking away materials, and telling children they will not be permitted to use materials again until they learn how. How will children learn to use materials effectively if they are not able to use them?

Safety.   In using any hands-on teaching strategy, safety can always be a problem. Children should be made aware of safety precautions prior to starting any activity using hands-on teaching strategies. Here are some basic safety precautions:

1. Before doing any activity, review safety precautions with the students.

2. Always have students wear protective goggles during science activities.

3. Use plastic rather than glass whenever possible. If glass should break, clean up the glass fragments yourself rather than allowing students to do so.

4. Allow students to use heat sources only under your supervision. Hot plates or gas burners are probably best used with older students, but still with teacher supervision. For younger children, demonstrate when high heat is needed.

5. Have a fire extinguisher, sand, water, or a blanket handy to use in case of classroom fires. Keep a first aid kit handy.

6. Substitute household chemicals for more sophisticated chemicals whenever possible. For example, test vinegar in working with acids and bases rather than sulfuric acid. If strong chemicals are needed, demonstrate.

7. Check for allergies before using household chemicals or bringing live animals into the classroom. Some children are allergic to dish detergents.

Asthma may be triggered by strong odors. Many children are allergic to cats and other small mammals.

8. Caution children about tasting anything unless they are given directions to taste a material. When something is to be tasted, check for food allergies.

9. If investigating electricity, use dry cells rather than electrical outlets.

10. Warn children about mixing chemicals, even household chemicals, in ways not directed by the activity or experiment procedure. Mixing ammonia and bleach produces poisonous chlorine gas.

11. Store any hazardous materials according to safety guidelines and in a locked area.

12. Model safety procedures yourself. Students cannot be expected to follow safety guidelines if you do not follow them yourself.

Learning Cycle

Learning Cycle is a teaching strategy that utilizes both inductive and deductive discovery strategies in an extended science experience. In general, a complete Learning Cycle takes place over more than one day, often engaging children for a week or longer.

Learning Cycle was originally developed as a teaching strategy used by the *Science Curriculum Improvement Study (SCIS)*. In the *SCIS* program the student was a more active participant and the teacher was a more passive participant than in the traditional textbook-based program. The teacher functioned as a guide to the children, helping them organize their experiences into concepts that would be useful in further study. As an aid to this rather different role of the teacher and as an aid in getting children more actively involved in learning, the *SCIS* program developed the three stages of Learning Cycle: exploration, invention, and discovery.

Exploration Stage

During the **exploration** stage, the students freely explore the materials without the constraint of learning some particular concept. Rather than a particular outcome, the students have the opportunity to familiarize themselves with materials and identify problems to investigate in later lessons. Students use process skills such as observation, using numbers, making inferences, drawing conclusions, classifying, and communicating as they investigate the materials. For example, children might be taken outdoors to a field or vacant lot and be given time to freely observe the area, noting what they find as well as any questions that come to mind as they make their observations. There is no set of questions students need to answer, no particular observations they are asked to make. Instead, students are free to observe and investigate areas of interest to them. They are free to learn at their own rate and following their own interests Ebenezer and Connor (1998) refer to this stage as the concept exploration stage.

Invention Stage

In the **invention stage,** the children are introduced to new concepts. The teacher provides experiences and uses questioning strategies to help the children develop an understanding of the concept. The teacher and the students together develop a mutually agreeable definition for the concept with the aid of concrete materials, demonstrations, textual materials, and audiovisual materials. Also during the invention stage, the children have the opportunity to review and to discuss the validity of the applications of the concept being developed. At this stage, the concept is given a verbal label in order to help with communication and to ensure stability for the concept. In the invention stage, the students discussed their observations of the field or vacant lot, and with the assistance of the teacher as well as other sources of information developed a definition of an ecological community. Ebenezer and Connor (1998) refer to the invention stage as the concept explanation phase; Gega and Peters (1998) refer to this as the concept introduction phase.

Discovery Stage

In the **discovery stage,** the students have the opportunity to test the concept they learned during the invention stage through investigation, experimentation, and explanation. The purpose of the investigation or experimentation is to test the consequences of the concept in a variety of situations. During this stage, the students have keep the concept clearly in mind so it can be applied to many situations rather than to a single example. In the discovery stage, children might investigate the effect of changes on a particular community, might research communities other than that found in the lot or field, might set up terraria showing a variety of different communities and investigate how different factors affect the life and health of the community. In this stage, children have the opportunity to develop and investigate their own questions. Both Ebenezer and Connor (1998) and Gega and Peters (1998) refer to this as the concept application phase.

In general, the children control the learning cycle approach to learning because they determine the directions of the investigations and experiments in the exploration and discovery stages. As you can be see from Figure 8.7, which illustrates the planning for a Learning Cycle teaching strategy, the plan provides a framework for the teacher rather than a specific lesson plan leading to a specific outcome.

Problems Using a Learning Cycle Approach

The Learning Cycle approach is a difficult strategy for many teachers to use because it is very much student directed. Teachers often feel they do not have full control of the learning situation. As teachers begin to feel more confident with the approach and see the amount of learning that occurs as the result of the Learning Cycle approach, this feeling of unease usually decreases.

Figure 8.7

Learning Cycle Teaching Strategy

Topic:

Communities

Objectives:

1. Students will be able to explore a field and make records of their observations and questions.
2. Students will be able to give an example of a community and to describe what is meant by a community in their own words.
3. Students will be able to develop one or more activities to investigate questions about communities.
4. Students will be able to use more than one source of information as they investigate communities.
5. Students will be able to communicate their learning about communities to one another.

Materials:

Notebooks, pencils, aquaria, paper bags, plastic containers with lids, plastic bags, magnifiers, plastic gloves, trowels, books, magazines, audiovisual materials dealing with ecological topics, field guides, other materials as needed for student investigations.

Procedure:

Exploration Phase:

1. Tell the class that they are going to be visiting a field. They have the option of either working with another student or alone, but whatever they decide, their task is to investigate the field and to find out everything they can about it. They can use the trowels to dig into the soil, the plastic bags to collect specimens of soil or plants, the containers for insects or other small creatures, and the paper bags for any specimens of fungi. In their notebooks they should write down any observations they can of the field and any questions that come to mind as they are exploring.
2. Take the class to the field and provide ample time for exploration.
3. Before returning to the classroom, have the children share their observations with one another.

Invention:

1. In the classroom, use the field guides and other materials in identifying the plants and animals collected. Release any animals to the environment or place in an appropriate terrarium for continued observation.
2. Have the students continue with their discussion of the field environment.
3. Based on their observations and on the discussion, define the term *community*.
4. Make a list of the questions students have about the field community and have the class decide which questions can be investigated in a hands-on manner, which through the use of written or other sources of information.
5. Relate the concept of a community to other situations beyond that of the field.

Discovery:

1. Give the students the opportunity of working alone or in small groups to investigate the questions. Provide assistance in setting up activities and experiments, in locating materials, and in locating additional sources of information.
2. Remind students to keep records of their investigations and to decide how they will go about presenting their findings to others in the class.
3. When students are ready to present their findings, provide a forum for presentation and discussion.

Evaluation:

Students should be evaluated on their records and their presentations according to a checklist based on the listed objectives.

Note: The Learning Cycle strategy is designed for an extended period of time. The above plan would not be used in a single science class period.

A second problem with Learning Cycle can be the materials needed. Learning Cycle is a materials-intensive teaching strategy. The exploration stage has children investigating freely with materials or a situation, such at the field or lot, and so the materials are determined by the teacher. The discovery stage, however, allows the students to investigate questions and problems of their own devising and so the kinds of materials needed may not be easily predetermined by the teacher. In addition, the kinds of materials needed to support the investigations of the students may not be readily available in some schools. This problem can be overcome by a teacher who is willing to become a collector of materials, who can quickly make substitutions of materials, and who keeps a record of the kinds of investigations done by students from one year to another. Many times, the kinds of investigations and, therefore, the kinds of materials remain fairly consistent from year to year.

Materials also include, however, written sources of information as well as audiovisual materials. Begin to collect information prior to the beginning of any unit of information and then catalog the information, its source, and its location for use in successive years.

The third difficulty is in the time required for the more intensive investigations developed during the Learning Cycle approach to teaching. Using blocks of time for subject matter areas as well as integrating subject matter areas as appropriate can help with this problem.

The fourth difficulty with this strategy is often space. Investigations involving plants or animals require the space for cages, plants, terraria, and other relatively large items. Investigations into simple machines require fairly large flat surfaces. Investigations involving simple chemicals require areas where spills cannot cause damage to surfaces. In many cases simply using windowsills or working on the floor can provide a solution to the problems. When floor space is not sufficient, working in a hallway, in the cafeteria, or outdoors may provide the solution. Covering surfaces with inexpensive plastic tablecloths that can be hosed clean can solve the problem of spills for activities with a certain level of messiness.

Finally, the fifth problem is often the most daunting. In order to use Learning Cycle effectively, you must feel confident in your own ability to do and understand science. You need to be able to set up and carry out activities. You also need to have a depth of understanding of the content information that allows you to guide your students in developing their concepts and activities. The greater your depth of knowledge, the more confident you feel using this teaching strategy. Consequently, you may need to seek out sources of information so you can build up your own background knowledge about a particular topic.

The problems encountered in working with Learning Cycle are numerous, but they can be overcome. In fact, collecting materials, planning for student investigations, and learning information yourself can be as exciting for you as for the children. It is a dynamic and fun (for both you and your students) way to learn science.

Learning Cycle provides opportunities for students to learn on their own through their own investigations. As a consequence, Learning Cycle may be considered a **constructivist teaching strategy;** that is, students construct knowledge for themselves based on their own conceptualizations rather than being presented knowledge by the teacher. Two other teaching strategies are also considered constructivist in nature.

Open Inquiry

Open inquiry provides a degree of freedom not found in any other technique. In **open inquiry,** the teacher presents a starting point for investigation, provides the materials that could be used to investigate, and then allows the students to use any method they wish to actually investigate. This strategy is particularly appropriate for preschool, kindergarten, first, and second grade children who are preoperational in their thinking. It provides the opportunity for children to investigate particular phenomena in ways that are appropriate to their cognitive structures and to their level of background (Wolfinger, 1994).

Open inquiry, because it is so intensely child centered, cannot be used to teach specific content. It is too unstructured to assure that all children or even a majority of children will reach a certain end point or concept. Instead, use open inquiry as a way of developing background knowledge in children, of developing problem-solving skills, and of developing inquiry skills. Because of the emphasis on the child's activity and the child's development of background rather than on specific content information, open inquiry is a no-fail science teaching strategy. The child determines the outcome rather than the teacher, and so the child's satisfaction in learning is the determinant of success.

Planning an Open Inquiry Lesson

In planning for an open inquiry lesson, follow these four general steps:

1. Decide on a starting activity that you will use to initiate the children's investigations.
2. Decide on a method for getting the children started.
3. Collect any materials that the children might use in their activities.
4. Decide on follow-up questions to aid the children in discussing their findings.

The Starting Activity.   The starting activity for an open inquiry lesson is the initiation point for the investigations. The more active children can be in their investigations, and the more senses they can use in their investigations, the more changes they can make in the materials used or in their actions, the better. Listening to the questions children have or watching them at play can often provide a starting point for an opening inquiry activity. The following are good open inquiry activities for children:

1. investigating rolling objects
2. investigating mixing materials
3. investigating bubbles

4. investigating pinwheels
5. investigating objects in water
6. investigating shadows
7. investigating balancing
8. investigating mixing colors
9. investigating bouncing objects
10. investigating constructions

Beginning the Activity. The key to an open inquiry activity is the beginning. An open inquiry activity needs to have a starting point that will help children initiate activity, but not one which will direct children into only a single course of investigation. The following are appropriate methods for initiating an open inquiry activity:

1. Have the materials in a central location and ask the children what they could do with those materials. This is a good opening strategy for an activity where children investigate rolling objects.
2. Provide children with a challenge. In working with structures, the teacher might challenge the children to build the tallest structure they can build.
3. Interact with the materials yourself and then move away as the children begin to investigate for themselves. Sitting at a table mixing materials to find out what happens is a good way of initiating the activity dealing with investigating mixing.
4. Provide the materials and ask children what they can find out about a particular phenomenon. This is a particularly appropriate way to begin an activity with bubbles.
5. Use a child's question or comment as a means of initiating activity. A child's question about how to get a balance to "be straight" could be the beginning of an active investigation of balancing. (Wolfinger, 1994)

Collecting the Materials. This may be the hardest part of the development of an open inquiry activity. You can begin to collect materials on that basis of what you think the children will do with those materials. However, you can only predict what children will do and what they will need. Young children do not think like adults, do not have the background information of adults, and so they can rarely determine exactly what children will do or need. The best strategy is to simply collect everything possible and see what the children need or use. This does not mean, however, that you should put out every possible material. Instead, put out some materials and gradually add to those materials as the children begin to investigate. In particular, children who have had little experience in investigation can be overwhelmed by too many materials. However, the materials should not be so limited that the children can only investigate in one way, so that their initiative and creativity is limited.

Determining the Follow-Up Discussion.   The follow-up discussion should focus on what the children found as they investigated. Do not make any attempt to lead the class to a particular conclusion or end point but instead listen to what the children found and their ideas. Questions should focus on: (1) What did you try? (2) What did you find out? (3) What happened when you _____? (4) What kinds of materials did you use?

Do not attempt to have children explain "why" events happened. Remember, this teaching strategy is used with young children, children who have yet to develop a firm understanding of cause and effect. Asking children to explain cause and effect is developmentally inappropriate. However, children are increasing their background information and developing the cognitive structures that will allow them to develop a concept of cause and effect as they mature.

Planning for an open inquiry activity is very different from planning for any other type of lesson. Figure 8.8 shows this difference in planning.

Problems Using Open Inquiry

As with any teaching strategy, open inquiry can present problems in its use within the classroom. First, open inquiry tends to look, and sometimes can be, chaotic. It is quite possible during open inquiry for a class of 20 children to be carrying out 20 different activities. This can appear to be chaotic. Fortunately, the teacher can easily maintain control during an open inquiry lesson. Children who are actively involved tend to cause few problems. In order to prevent problems, however, be certain that children know the rules established for classroom behavior and that you have a technique for gaining the attention of all the children in the class, so behavior problems can be quickly corrected. Second, open inquiry can be very noisy as children discuss their findings and demonstrate their activities for one another. Children should be free to discuss their activities with one another. However, should the noise level become high enough to be disruptive to the learning process, ask for a reduction in noise level. Turn out the lights, ring a bell, play a chord on the piano, whistle or clap to get the children's attention. Silence the children, and then tell them they may continue more quietly. Third, as mentioned previously, anticipating and locating enough materials can be a major problem of open inquiry. Although it is impossible to anticipate everything children will need, select open inquiry activities that can be accomplished with easily obtainable materials: junk and common household or school materials. When an open inquiry lesson continues for more than one day, encourage children to bring in other kinds of materials they may require. Then keep a record of the kinds of materials the children actually use, so you may obtain them the next time you do the activity.

The fourth problem is that of any child-centered and materials-oriented teaching strategy. Because children can investigate up to their own limits, some will finish quickly and others will not want to stop at all. The problem of children finishing at different rates can be solved by having other activities for children to do as they finish or by asking questions that may initiate new investigations on the part of the children. The final problem is a philosophical one. For many teachers, the fact that

Figure 8.8

Open Inquiry Lesson Plan

Topic:

Investigating Bubbles

Objectives:

As a result of this lesson, each student will:
1. investigate bubbles.
2. contribute to a discussion of the activity.

Materials:

Bubble blowing liquid, straws, bubble blowers and pipes, fly swatters, cardboard tubes, colander, slotted spoons, whisks, plastic bowls and containers, paper and plastic foam cups, some with the bottom removed, food coloring, salt, sugar, water, plastic tablecloth, paper towels.

Procedure:

1. Begin the activity by putting the materials on the plastic tablecloth and then blowing bubbles yourself. Ask the children to find out what they can about bubbles using the materials available. Remind the children using straws to blow out, not suck in!
2. Allow ample time for the children to investigate.
3. Gather the children together and have them talk about what they discovered about bubbles using questions like these:
   a. What are some of the things you did?
   b. What are some of the things you found out?
   c. How can you make big bubbles? Little bubbles? Lots of bubbles?

Evaluation:

Use anecdotal records and a checklist to observe the students as they investigate and as they participate in the discussion of the activity.

there is no specific outcome, no particular piece of science knowledge to be learned is a problem. These teachers may want to use open inquiry as an introduction to a particular unit of work, as a device for developing background information that can then be used as a basis for developing more specific content information.

Conceptual Change Model

Conceptual change model is a true constructivist strategy based on the work of Joseph I. Stepans (Stepans, Saigo, and Ebert, 1995). In essence, the **conceptual change model** encourages students to confront their misconceptions and then change their conceptual framework to incorporate information gained from direct activity that conflicts with the misconception. The result is conceptual change in which misconceptions or naive concepts are transformed into more mature concepts.

The conceptual change model begins with assessing of the current concepts held by the learner using interviews or discussions and then proceeds to the development of teaching strategies that allow students to confront their misconceptions through activity. The lessons themselves then focus on particular ideas, use direct, hands-on activities, and require a minimum of scientific terminology. The major factor is that the students confront their ideas and utilize the information from the activities to generate more mature concepts.

In general, the conceptual change model utilizes these six steps (Stepans, Saigo, and Ebert, 1995):

1. *Commit to an outcome.* In this first step students are given a particular problem situation and are asked to make predictions about what will happen in that situation. Working in small groups, the children not only make a prediction about what will happen, but also develop a reason to support their prediction. As students discuss their predictions within their groups, they are also revealing their own beliefs about the particular situation.
2. *Expose beliefs.* In this second step, the students present their prediction and their reasons for making those predictions to the entire class.
3. *Confront beliefs.* In this step, the students are given the opportunity to test the outcome of the situation through the use of hands-on activity. In their small groups, they discuss the data collected and the results.
4. *Accommodate the concept.* In step 4, the students consider their predictions and the actual outcome of the activity in light of their predictions and, where there is conflict between prediction and outcome, they attempt to reconcile those conflicts.
5. *Extend the concept.* After the concept has been developed, students try to make connections between the concept learned in class and situations outside of the classroom, in other words, in real-life situations.
6. *Go beyond.* Finally, the students are encouraged to go beyond what they have investigated in class by investigating other questions that arise as they investigate the original activities.

Although this sequence seems to indicate that one activity, one situation to consider is all that is needed to provide for conceptual change, this is misleading. The conceptual change model requires a variety of activities so that students are confronted with their misconceptions in a variety of slightly different and slightly more sophisticated situations.

In one situation using a conceptual change model, the teacher discovered that students thought the north end of a magnet would be stronger because they lived in the Northern Hemisphere. The real problem here was not how to help students confront this misconception, but rather how to gather data that would help them confront the idea in its totality: the Southern Hemisphere. Using the Internet, the teacher established contact with a school in Australia and with a school in Sweden. Each of the teachers then presented their classes with this first situation:

A magnet is put into a box of paper clips, first the north pole and then the south pole. After each pole of the magnet has been in the box for ten seconds, it is taken out and the number of paper clips counted. Which is most likely to be true?

1. There will be many more paper clips on the north pole.
2. There will be many more paper clips on the south pole.
3. There will be approximately the same number of paper clips on each pole.

The students worked in groups of four to come to a decision and to develop an explanation about what would happen. The groups shared their explanations with their classmates. The majority of the groups were certain the north pole would hold more paper clips because they lived in the Northern Hemisphere. Each group then had the opportunity to try out the activity and to collect the data. When the results were collected, the groups determined that there were approximately the same number of paper clips on each pole, with some groups showing more on the north pole and some showing more on the south pole. As they considered the information, some of the groups decided that the hemisphere of Earth made no difference, and others decided they were not far enough north for the location to make a difference. At this point the teacher presented a second situation.

Children in Sweden are doing the same activity. They are much further north than we are. When they put the north and south poles into the paper clips, which of the following will occur?

1. The north pole will have many more paper clips.
2. The south pole will have many more paper clips.
3. Both poles will have about the same number of paper clips.

Once again the students worked in small groups to determine their predictions. Some of the groups predicted no difference, based on their previous experience. Other groups, more certain of the effect of location on Earth, predicted that because Sweden was farther north, the north pole of the magnet would have more paper clips. The teacher then asked the children in the Swedish school to conduct the activity and to send their raw data to the class. After considering the data, the students in the original school could find no difference between the north and south poles of the magnet. One more experience, however, was added to the lesson: the Australian school.

Again students were confronted with a situation:

Children in Australia are going to try the same activity. Australia is in the far Southern Hemisphere. The magnet is put into the box of paper clips. What will happen?

1. The north pole will have many more paper clips.
2. The south pole will have many more paper clips.
3. Both poles will have approximately the same number of paper clips.

The small group discussions yielded the same predictions: The poles would have the same number of paper clips because it had to do with the magnet itself and not with the location of the magnet on Earth.

When the data came through from the activity conducted in the Southern Hemisphere, the class cheered. There was no difference between the two poles even though Australia was far south.

The children then considered how this information was important in real life and decided that the most pertinent application was with a compass. If the location on Earth affected how a magnet worked, then compasses probably wouldn't work the way they were supposed to work. The class did, however, wonder if compasses did work any differently depending on where they were, and so the teacher assisted in developing activities that would help the students to further investigate compasses and their behavior.

This teacher was particularly fortunate to have access to the Internet and so to additional sources of information that would help in the solution of the problem of the magnet. In the vast majority of conceptual change lessons, the teacher does not need to go beyond the classroom and the information the students can collect directly. Figure 8.9 shows a lesson plan using the conceptual change model that reflects the described lesson.

Problems Using the Model

The problems of using the conceptual change model are the problems of using any discovery-oriented approach: time to interview and to work with activities, materials, room to work, and teacher background knowledge to assist students. An additional problem also crops up in this teaching strategy. The additional problem is in the development of activities that will allow students to confront their particular misconceptions. You may find a starting activity in a book of science activities, but to translate that activity into an experience that will allow for conceptual change, you must have a fairly sophisticated understanding of science content and of the misconceptions of the students in order to develop appropriate experiences.

SECTION THREE: VERBAL TEACHING STRATEGIES

1. *Demonstrations*
   a. *Ordinary Demonstrations*
   b. *Discovery Demonstrations*
2. *Expository Methods*
   a. *Expository Teaching*
   b. *Discussions*
3. *Field Trips*

The following teaching strategies are divided into two sections. The first section deals with demonstrations that form a bridge between hands-on strategies in which students work directly with materials and purely verbal teaching strategies in which

Figure 8.9

Conceptual Change Model

Topic:

Magnets

Objectives:

As a result of this lesson each student will be able to:
1. make predictions and develop reasons for those predictions.
2. carry out activities to test predictions.
3. utilize the results of activities to make additional predictions about outcomes.
4. develop a more mature understanding of the effect of hemisphere on magnets.

Materials:

Magnets, paper clips, computer with Internet capabilities, copies of each problem situation.

Procedure:

1. Present the first situation. Allow time for students to work in small groups to come to a consensus and to develop a reason for the prediction.

   Situation 1: A magnet is put into a box of paper clips, first the north pole and then the south pole. After each pole of the magnet has been in the box for ten seconds, it is taken out and the number of paper clips counted. Which is most likely to be true?
   a. Many more paper clips are on the north pole.
   b. Many more paper clips are on the south pole.
   c. Approximately the same number of paper clips are on each pole.
2. Have each group present its prediction and reason to the class as a whole.
3. Do the activity suggested by the situation. Collect the results of the activity and draw a conclusion. Give the students an opportunity to consider the results in terms of their original predictions.
4. Present situation 2 to the class and repeat steps 1 and 2.

   Situation 2: Children in Sweden are doing the same activity. They are much further

north than we. When they put the north and south poles into the paper clips which of the following will occur?
   a. The north pole will have many more paper clips.
   b. The south pole will have many more paper clips.
   c. Both poles will have about the same number of paper clips.
5. Using the Internet, have the students in the Swedish class carry out the activity and transmit the results to the class. Discuss the results and draw a conclusion. Give the students an opportunity to consider the results in terms of their original predictions.
6. Present situation 3 to the class and repeat steps 1 and 2.

   Situation 3: Children in Australia are doing the same activity. They are much further south than we. When they put the north and south poles into the paper clips which of the following will occur?
   a. The north pole will have many more paper clips.
   b. The south pole will have many more paper clips.
   c. Both poles will have about the same number of paper clips.
7. Using the Internet, have the students in the Australian class carry out the activity and transmit the results to the class. Discuss the results and draw a conclusion. Give the students an opportunity to consider the results in terms of their original predictions.
8. Discuss with the class how the information they gained today might be important in the world around them. If questions arise or suggestions for additional investigations, assist students in developing and carrying out their investigations.

Evaluation:

Evaluate the lesson on the basis of a checklist developed to reflect the stated objectives.

the teacher presents information and no concrete materials are placed in the hands of the students. The second section deals with those purely verbal strategies in which words are the primary means for communicating science information. Field trips that utilize both hands-on and expository strategies in combination are considered separately.

Demonstrations in the Science Classroom

Two kinds of demonstrations are frequently used in the elementary or middle school science classroom. The first type of demonstration, known as an **ordinary demonstration,** is the more common of the two types. The ordinary demonstration is used to teach science content information through the use of process skills. The second type of demonstration is known as a **discovery demonstration,** a method of teaching problem solving in which the teacher silently conducts the demonstration and the students attempt to determine the reason for the demonstration's outcome. In a discovery demonstration, the teacher is teaching problem solving rather than teaching content information as in the ordinary demonstration. In both types of demonstrations, the students are cognitively active in trying to determine what happened during the demonstration and why it happened.

Ordinary Demonstrations

The ordinary demonstration is the type of demonstration with which most people are familiar. In this case the teacher, or designated individual, stands before the class, shows something, and then helps the class understand what happened. The only person actually involved with materials is the person who shows and then explains what happened to the students. When done in this way, the ordinary demonstration is not cognitively engaging for the students. If an ordinary demonstration is to be done well, it should involve more than a simple show and tell procedure. The first step in making a demonstration cognitively engaging is to use the demonstration for an appropriate reason.

Reasons for Using Ordinary Demonstrations.   There are a number of reasons for doing a demonstration. Like the demonstrations themselves, these reasons range from poor to excellent. Possibly the worst reason for demonstrating was given by the teacher who said that she demonstrated "because it keeps the room neater than if you let children do activities for themselves." A neat room may be commendable, but it should not be a reason for preventing children from interacting with materials. Running a close second for worst reason to demonstrate this: "Give these kids materials and they'll tear the place apart." In reality, children who are not actively engaged are far more likely to cause problems than are those who are working with materials. If children do not work well with materials, it is often because they have had little or no opportunity for hands-on instruction. Taking materials away or never allowing children to use materials is not a way of helping children learn to do activities and experiments.

Those two reasons for demonstrating, although sometimes used, are always poor. So, why should we choose to do a demonstration? Here are five reasons for doing a demonstration that are highly appropriate:

1. The teacher should demonstrate when there is some danger involved. This includes the use of open flames, open coil heating units, and strong chemicals.

2. The teacher should demonstrate how to use a piece of equipment properly: microscope, thermometer, balance, graduated cylinder, and so on.

3. The teacher should demonstrate when there is some spectacular effect that can initiate or end a unit of study: a model volcano erupting, a dramatic chemical change, a model rocket launch.

4. The teacher should demonstrate when the action needs to be stopped periodically to show important changes or to point out specific points. In decomposing sugar, the teacher can stop the action periodically by removing the sugar from the heat, so the various changes can be shown.

5. The teacher should demonstrate when there is not enough equipment, substitutions cannot be made, and the activity is particularly appropriate for illustrating a concept. In some schools, this will be the most common reason for demonstrating.

If lack of equipment is the most common reason for demonstrating, then it is particularly important that ordinary demonstrations be done well. In this case, ordinary demonstrations are substituting for hands-on teaching strategies.

Planning and Conducting an Ordinary Demonstration. The purpose of an ordinary demonstration is to teach children content information through the use of such process skills as observing, predicting, concluding, inferring, cause and effect, and others appropriate to the demonstration. If you are going to do a demonstration effectively, you cannot treat that demonstration as "show and tell" in which you simply show the students something and then tell them the how and why behind the demonstration. The following procedure will help you get away from show and tell and into a more appropriate means for demonstrating.

Introducing the Demonstration. A good demonstration allows students to engage in problem solving. Consequently, the first part of the demonstration sets up a problem to be solved. For example, in doing a demonstration to decompose sugar, a sixth grade teacher began by telling the class that she was going to make some caramels and was heating the sugar when the phone rang. After talking on the phone for a while, she returned to finish making the caramels. After they were cool, she tried one of the pieces of candy and it tasted horrible. In fact, it tasked like a charcoal briquette. She then posed this question: "What happened to my candy?"

After getting a variety of possible answers to the questions, this teacher introduced the demonstration as a way of finding out what happened.

Doing the Demonstration.   Once the students have a problem to solve, do the demonstration. If equipment is being demonstrated so students can use it themselves in investigations or experiments, demonstrate exactly how that piece of equipment is used in the correct, step-by-step order. If the demonstration is of an activity, do the activity, stopping action as necessary and holding any comments to a minimum. Students should be able to focus fully on the demonstration, and the less you talk the more focused the students can become. Returning to the example of decomposing sugar, after presenting the problem, the teacher placed some sugar in a Pyrex container and asked the students to make observations of the sugar. As the students made their observations, she recorded them on the chalkboard under the category "before." After all the observations had been made, the teacher placed the container on a hot plate. As changes begin to occur, the teacher stopped the action so the students could see what was happening and make additional observations. These observations were listed under the category "during." The final results were classified under "after."

Following the Demonstration.   After the demonstration is concluded, use questions to help students determine what happened during the demonstration. Through careful questioning, our sixth grade teacher helped the students develop the idea that the sugar was no longer there, but had decomposed into carbon, carbon dioxide, and water vapor. Finally, the teacher returned to the starting problem, "What happened to the candy?" Through the demonstration, the students were able to answer the questions: The sugar was heated too long, the water vapor and carbon dioxide escaped, and the carbon was left behind. The candy tasted like a charcoal briquette because it was charcoal (carbon)!

In a good ordinary demonstration, tell as little as possible, adding information only when your students do not have the needed background and using questions as much as possible to help your students use the demonstration to develop the content for themselves.

Problems in Using an Ordinary Demonstration.   An ordinary demonstration, like any teaching strategy, can have problems in its use. In general, those problems are relatively easy to overcome.

The first of those problems is probably the one teachers fear most: The demonstration doesn't work. Even foolproof demonstrations have been known to fail: The egg that does not get forced into the bottle, the can that doesn't collapse, the balloon that does not get bigger as the bottle is heated. No matter how frequently you do a demonstration or how carefully you do it, there are times when that demonstration does not work. The first feeling one experiences is panic and a feeling of "now what do I do?" What you do is turn the failure into a success, and possibly, a better lesson.

Your best course of action when confronted with a demonstration that does not work is to try it again just in case the reason was something simple. If the demonstration does not work the second time, tell the students what usually happens and challenge them to try to determine why the demonstration did not work as expected. Be prepared to try their ideas, to have some of the children show their ideas, and finally to find out what caused the failure. Even if your demonstration never works as planned, the students will still have gained valuable experience in using problem-solving techniques, making inferences and observations, analyzing a system, and determining cause and effect.

A second problem with ordinary demonstrations can be with restlessness or inattentiveness. In most cases, this problem can be solved by presenting demonstrations that are exciting to watch. During the course of a demonstration, you can regain wandering attention by posing questions that ask your students to use the processes of observation, inference, interaction and systems, and cause and effect. In other words, get the children more involved.

A third problem with demonstrating is visibility. With large classes children may not be able to see the demonstration. Seating the children in a semicircle around the demonstration table can be a solution. If your class is too large for this approach, you may want to divide the class into two or more smaller groups and conduct the demonstration for each group. The final problem occurs when children are unable to solve the problem presented to them. This is generally due to a lack of background information. Sometimes, the inability to solve the problem provides impetus to further study of a topic. For example, presenting the decomposing sugar demonstration at the start of a unit on chemistry when students have little background can provide purpose for the study of chemical changes. Students may not be able to solve the problem at that time, but they will be able to solve it later in the unit. At other times, the teacher will probably want to select a demonstration and a problem that will allow the students to use already developed background information to solve the problem. It is helpful, just in case some information is not available to the students, to have reference materials available for use as students engage in problem solving. Figure 8.10 shows the lesson plan that would be used for the demonstration in decomposing sugar.

An ordinary demonstration, then, is a means of teaching science content through processes and using materials, but the teacher is the only person to handle those materials. The teacher closely plans the final result of the demonstration and guides students through questions to the final conclusion. The teacher also plans the second type of demonstration, but the end point is the development of problem-solving skills rather than a particular bit of content selected by the teacher.

Discovery Demonstrations

The discovery demonstration is used for a single purpose: to develop problem-solving skills. Children are presented with a problem in the form of a demonstration and are challenged to determine the cause of the phenomena. Because problem solving is the main purpose of the demonstration, it makes no difference whether the children accurately determine the cause of the occurrence or not. If the thinking is

Figure 8.10

Ordinary Demonstration Lesson Plan

Topic:

Chemical Changes

Objective:

After participating in the demonstration dealing with decomposition of sugar, each student will be able to write the definition of a chemical change.

Materials:

Sugar, Pyrex beaker, hot plate, tongs, hot pad or pot holder, goggles

Procedure:

1. *Introduction*
   a. Tell the class that you have a problem for them to solve. The problem is that you made caramels last night and they taste awful. You did it the same way as always, starting with heating the sugar, but while you were doing that the phone rang. You talked for a while and then went back to making the candy. Even though you did everything the same, when you tasted the caramels, they tasted like charcoal briquettes.
   b. Ask the class what they think happened. List their idea on the board.

2. *Demonstration*
   a. Place a quarter cup of sugar in the Pyrex beaker. Have the students make observations of the sugar and list the observations on the board.
   b. Turn on the hot plate and have students put on their goggles. Place the beaker on the hot plate.
   c. Have the students watch what happens. Remove the beaker from the hot plate at each of the following points so that the students can observe the changes:
      (1) just beginning to turn liquid.
      (2) as a brownish red liquid.
      (3) as it begins to turn black and bubble.
      (4) as the black material begins to climb the sides of the beaker.
      (5) after the beaker is filled with a black, foamy material, Stop.
   d. Remove the beaker from the hot plate and place it on the hot pad or pot holder. Turn off the hot plate.
      (1) make observations of the black material and list them on the chalkboard.

3. *Discussion*
   a. Use the following questions to help students determine what happened.
      (1) What differences do you see between the sugar we began with and the material now in the beaker?
      (2) What were some of the changes the sugar went through as it turned to this black stuff?
      (3) What is sugar made from?
      (4) What do you think the "smoke" that came off could have been? Why?
      (5) Considering what sugar is made from, what do you think could be left in the container? Why?
      (6) What do you think happened to the oxygen and the hydrogen that were part of the sugar if the carbon is left behind?
      (7) Do we still have sugar in the container?
   b. Return to the problem of the candy. Ask the class what they think happened that caused the candy to taste like charcoal.
   c. Review with the class the fact that they no longer have sugar in the beaker. Introduce the term *chemical change* to describe what occurred.

Evaluation:

Have each student describe in writing what is meant by the term *chemical change* as it relates to the demonstration.

logical and based on the information derived from the demonstration, the lesson is a success.

The Basis for a Discovery Demonstration.   The discovery demonstration is based on the inquiry training model of J. Richard Suchman (1962). The inquiry training program was designed around three broad objectives: (1) development of the skills of searching and of data processing, which would allow children to solve problems autonomously, (2) development of a means for learning that would allow children to develop concepts through analysis of concrete problems, and (3) development of intrinsic forms of motivation.

In order to attain these objectives of inquiry training, children were shown motion pictures depicting short demonstrations taken from physics. The title of each of the filmed demonstrations asked why the outcome of the demonstration occurred. The program developers used physics problems in the training because the number of variables would be limited.

The films were designed to present a problem. The teacher's role was to develop an environment where inquiry could take place. Rather than telling students about the phenomena they had seen, the teacher was to help the children to structure concepts and develop reasoning.

The inquiry training model focused on the process by which information was acquired rather than on the final information.

Inquiry training and discovery demonstrations differ in two ways. First, the episode to be considered is shown directly through materials used by the teacher rather than through films. Second, the students receive more guidance from the teacher than the students in inquiry training did. The purpose of the guidance is to help students learn how to engage in problem solving.

Planning a Discovery Demonstration.   The discovery demonstration has a specific six-step teaching sequence, which enables the children to solve the problem presented or to use problem-solving skills to attempt to solve the problem:

1. introduce the demonstration by telling the students you will be showing them something. Tell them that it is going to be their job to try to figure out why what they will see occurs.

2. silently show the demonstration and the materials used in the demonstration.

3. after the demonstration is over, collect on the board or overhead the answers to the following questions:
   a. *What materials did I use?* asks for the list of materials. If students are uncertain of the name of an item, ask what they would call it.
   b. *What did I do?* asks for the steps of the demonstration in their exact order.
   c. *What happened?* asks for the final occurrence, not the reason for the occurrence.

4. tell the class that they now have the opportunity to ask you any questions they would like to get more information, provided the questions can be answered with a yes or a no answer. Theory questions, that is, those questions that ask if the result occurred because . . . are considered "illegal" and cannot be asked.

5. divide the class into small groups of four or five students. Each group is charged with coming up with an explanation for what occurred. As the groups work, they are free to ask any additional yes-no questions to gain more information.

6. have the students present their explanations to the class, including any supporting evidence. Whenever possible, students should also develop a means for testing their solution using materials.

If a group or groups has come up with the actual reason behind the occurrence, congratulate the class. If no group comes up with the actual reason, congratulate the class on their thinking skills and leave the demonstration at that point. At a later time, students can be encouraged to investigate the occurrence more fully and to determine the actual reason for what happened. If you launch immediately into an explanation of what "really" happened, students are less likely to engage in problem solving at another time. The emphasis turns from a problem-solving experience to getting the "right answer."

Problems in Using Discovery Demonstration.   One of the main problems with using a discovery demonstration is locating a demonstration pertinent to the unit of study, difficult enough to challenge the students to think, yet not so difficult that students cannot possibly determine the solution to the problem. One way of finding appropriate demonstrations is to look for misconceptions held by students and then develop the demonstration around those misconceptions.

The remaining problems are more problems for the teacher than problems of the demonstration itself. First among these is the silent demonstration. Teachers tend to be verbal people for whom telling information is second nature. The teacher cannot tell information in this type of demonstration. For some teachers simply maintaining silence is very hard. Second, and perhaps harder than the keeping of silence, is that you must be able to answer any question students have about the demonstration. Consequently, you cannot be uncertain about any aspect of the demonstration. You must be able to answer the questions asked by the students, and the only way to be able to do that is to be absolutely certain about the demonstration, its materials, its causes, its interactions. Finally, the fact that the explanation for what happens does not occur immediately can be difficult for many teachers. Some feel they are leaving children with erroneous ideas if they do not immediately explain the "real" reason when children cannot determine it themselves. In this situation, keep in mind that if students have used the processes of science appropriately, have deployed problem-solving strategies appropriately, and have come to a logical conclusion, the lesson is a success. The purpose of the discovery demonstration is to teach problem solving, not content. The content can be approached at another time with a different teaching strategy.

The discovery demonstration is a way to promote problem-solving skills in a specific situation. The kinds of skills learned in the discovery demonstration can then be applied to more hands-on strategies in which children set up and carry out investigations for themselves.

The lesson plan, in Figure 8.11 shows the planning used for a discovery demonstration.

Figure 8.11

Discovery Demonstration Lesson Plan

Topic:

Problem Solving

Objective:

Each child will participate in the problem-solving session by doing one or more of the following:
1. providing one or more answers to the data collection questions.
2. asking one or more questions.
3. contributing to the small group's development of a solution to the problem.

Materials:

Empty ditto fluid can (well rinsed and aired), cap for the can, hot plate, tray, pot holder or tongs, water.

Procedure:

1. Tell the class that they are going to be watching a demonstration. Their job is going to be to try to explain why what they will see happened. In order to help them with the explanation, you are going to ask them three questions: what did I use, what did I do, and what happened. After those questions are asked, they will have the opportunity to ask you questions to get more information, but those questions must be answered with a yes or no. The only yes-no question you can't answer is one that asks if an explanation is correct. Finally, they will work in small groups to develop a reason for what happened.

2. Do the following demonstration:
   a. Turn the hot plate to high.
   b. Show that the can is empty.
   c. Pour a small amount of water into the can. Do not put the cap on the can.
   d. Place the can on the hot plate.
   e. When steam begins to escape from the can, place the lid on the can and quickly remove it from the heat, placing it on the tray.
   f. Wait for about a minute.
   g. Pour a little cold water over the can and watch it collapse.

3. Collect on the board the answers to the three questions: what did I use, what did I do, what happened.

4. Ask for questions from the children that can be answered with a yes or a no.

5. When no more questions are asked, have the class divide into small groups with each group developing a reason for the collapse of the can. Remind the students that they can ask additional yes-no questions as they develop their ideas.

6. Have each group present its explanation and the evidence they have for the reason.

Evaluation:

Using a check list, indicate which students accomplished the stated objective.

Verbal Teaching Strategies

Verbal teaching strategies include not only the teacher as a lecturer, but also reading, using films or filmstrips, guest speakers, or research involving written sources of material. In general, verbal teaching strategies are used in four ways:

1. to develop background information that children will need in order to understand, design, or carry out an experiment or hands-on activity.

2. to give directions for an activity, experiment, or other classroom procedure.

3. to wrap up an activity, experiment, or other classroom procedure.

4. to present information not available to students in any other way.

Providing Background Information

As stated early in this chapter, no scientists walks into a laboratory or field setting unprepared. Prior to conducting any experiment, the scientist has studied the area thoroughly. Consequently, children who are developing activities or experiments, preparing for a field trip, or beginning a new field of study should be engaged in the use of a variety of written and oral materials. The purpose of these materials is not to answer all the questions students might have about a particular topic, but rather to provide students with enough background information that they can ask pertinent questions, develop purposeful activities, or benefit from the observations made on a particular field trip. In using verbal strategies for this purpose, provide students with a wide variety of materials. Students should have the opportunity to read, view, and study the materials on their own or in small groups with similar interests, then come together to present their findings to the total group.

Giving Directions

When giving directions for an activity, the teacher always uses a verbal strategy. Certain *do not's* should be observed when giving directions as well as certain *do's*. First, do not give out materials before you give directions. The materials will be much more interesting than anything you can say. Second, do not expect children to follow written directions without your review of those directions. Third, do not expect children to understand directions without a myriad of questions, before they start the activity as well as during the activity. With all of the *do not's* in mind, do follow the following sequence for giving directions: It is effective when both written instructions and materials are to be used:

1. Read the instructions to the students or simply give them orally.

2. Review the instructions by asking various students what should be done first, second, third, and so on.

3. Give out the written instructions and have the children read them silently.

4. Ask for questions.

5. Have the students get their materials.

6. Tell them to get to work. But be prepared for questions once students start. Circulate around the room to be certain students are following the instructions.

This particular strategy for giving directions has certain advantages. First, children are forced to listen to the directions because they know they will be asked to review them orally. Second, students whose reading skills are not adequate to the use of written directions or students who learn best aurally have heard the directions orally and so can succeed in the activity. Third, students who learn better through written materials have the written instructions in front of them and so can use those effectively. And, finally, all students benefit from having received the directions not once, but three times: from the teacher, from fellow students, and from the written format.

As a Wrap-Up

Activities and experiments should be the main source of information for students in the elementary or middle school science class. However, not all information in textbooks or courses of study can be learned through hands-on experience. Consequently, verbal teaching strategies can be used after an activity or experiment to extend and clarify the information gained concretely. For example, through activities dealing with balloons students can develop the idea that if the air is expelled in one direction, the object travels in the opposite direction. They cannot, however, from these activities develop Newton's law of action and reaction. The textbook, teacher, or other verbal source of information can be used to extend the learner's understanding beyond the activity.

Presenting Information

Although the hands-on strategies in which children conduct activities and experiments and so gain their information in a first-hand manner should make up the bulk of the elementary science program, textbooks and courses of study often contain topics that cannot be approached through direct investigation. Planets, constellations, atoms and molecules, the internal structure of Earth, plate tectonics, and rain forests are found in many textbook series. Such topics do not lend themselves to direct investigation by students and so verbal teaching strategies are necessary. In many cases, the teacher is presenting this information to the students through lecture, film or filmstrip, direct text reading, or guest speaker. When verbal teaching is used in this format—known as **expository teaching**—you need to plan your teaching in the most effective manner.

Planning an Expository Lesson

For an expository lesson to be meaningful to the learner, David Ausubel (1963) suggested that new information be related to the knowledge already possessed by the learner. The learner, therefore, should have encountered the material previously in some form. To assure that this encounter has occurred, the teacher should use an advance organizer as the first step in preparing an expository lesson.

Advance Organizers. An **advance organizer** is a verbal device, first suggested by Ausubel, that provides relevant introductory materials, so the learner has at least heard about the materials presented in the lesson. The organizer presents a broad survey of the information to be covered in more detail during the exposition to follow. Advance organizers may be either expository or comparative.

Expository Organizers. When presenting completely unfamiliar materials to your students, use an expository organizer at the start of the lesson. Basically, the **expository organizer** presents several broad generalizations to which detail will be added. The speaker, in essence, states that he or she will consider certain points and lists those points in the order of the subsequent presentation.

For example, students in a fifth grade class are about to begin a unit on chemistry. An advance organizer could take the following form: "Today we are going to begin a new unit. As you read the first few pages of your textbook, I want you to look for three things. First, look for what your textbook says chemistry is. Second, look for the kinds of things chemists study. And, finally, look for how chemistry applies to our daily lives."

With this brief bit of information as a starting point, students are alerted to the fact that the important information in the reading deals with the definition of chemistry, what chemists do, and how chemistry is important to daily life. Although this is related to reading a textbook, it could just as easily be information to be gained from a lecture, film, or guest speaker. An expository organizer gives students a hint as to the important facts to be gained from the expository presentation. An expository organizer is most effective with individuals who have no background in a particular topic.

Comparative Organizers. The expository organizer is useful when the information to come is new to the listener. Many times, however, the listener possesses some knowledge similar to the new material. In that case, the teacher can use a comparative organizer. A **comparative organizer** compares new material to that already known in a way that will highlight the similarities between the two and will indicate, as well, what information is to come. A teacher could use the following organizer with children who are about to classify rocks for the first time and who have experienced in classifying other objects:

"Last week we classified shells that we collected into a number of different groups. Some of the groups we used were based on color, shine, weight, and even how hard they were. Today we are going to be classifying rocks according to some of the characteristics used by geologists. Just like the shells, rocks can be classified by their color, their shine, their weight, and their hardness. There are some other characteristics that we can use as well, but first, we'll look at the same characteristics as we used with shells."

In this organizer, the students are reminded of something familiar: classifying shells. The shells' characteristics are reviewed. Then the lecturer introduces the idea that rocks can be classified in the same way as shells are classified. Students are told they will be using those same traits for rocks. This type of organizer is reassuring: The new material is not really new; it is just something familiar in a new guise.

Sequencing a Lesson.   Once he or she has presented an organizer, the teacher must follow the sequence in the expository or comparative organizer. Following the presentation of the new material, the teacher should complete the lecture by once more pointing out the important points.

In developing new information with students through the use of the expository method, remember the following advice:

1. use an advance organizer.

2. follow up with the information you intend to present to your listeners in the order shown by the organizer.

3. be brief—children do not give attention to verbal presentations for long periods of time.

4. use pictures, drawings, charts, and models to add another dimension to the presentation.

5. periodically through the presentation, ask questions to check student comprehension of the information presented.

Problems Using the Expository Method

The expository method of teaching has inherent in it a number of problems, all of which stem from its strictly verbal nature:

1. Verbal presentations are difficult for children in the elementary grades to follow. Elementary grade children are preoperational or concrete operational in their thought processes and both types of thought require concrete materials in order to understand concepts and ideas. As children reach seventh and eight grade they are more able to listen to and benefit from a verbal presentation.

2. Verbal presentations are limited by the student's attention span. Pictures, slides, and other visual aids help maintain a high level of attention, but the total time is still short.

3. Verbal learning tends to be passive learning. Only the teacher is active in the learning process, whereas the students should be active.

4. Any verbal presentation is organized according to the teacher's idea of a logical order. Because the adult's level of cognitive development is different from that of the students, the order may not be equally logical to those students.

5. What is said is not always what is heard. People interpret what they hear in terms of their own backgrounds. Consequently, the reception of something that seems to be clearly presented can be muddled by preconceptions, misconceptions, and previous experiences.

The lesson plan in Figure 8.12 shows an expository lesson designed for sixth grade students. The lesson would be presented to the students prior to a field trip to a local wooded area and shows a lesson that definitely would not work in a hands-on manner.

Discussions in the Science Classroom

All too frequently what passes for **discussion** is really a lecture with periodic breaks for students to ask questions. In a true discussion, however, the students should talk as much as and preferably more than the teacher. A discussion is an open forum in which students can express their opinions as well as review factual material. In addition, the discussion is a natural opportunity for students to exercise their command of the processes of communication, inference, and conclusion as well as to demonstrate the scientific attitudes of objectivity, willingness to suspend judgment, and curiosity. Two kinds of discussions are generally encountered in the classroom setting.

Open Discussions. Consider first the following discussion that took place in a fifth grade class. A picture alleged to be of the Loch Ness monster appeared in the daily newspaper. The dark, shadowy object in the picture could have been anything from a rock to a tree to an unknown creature from the depths of the loch. The children were, however, firmly convinced that it was the Loch Ness monster and wanted to talk about it. One part of the article that accompanied the picture mentioned the expedition that had taken the photograph hoped to capture the monster. A natural question evolved from that statement: What should be done with the Loch Ness monster if the team does capture it?

The first two responses were to be expected: Stuff it and put it in a museum or put it in a zoo. At first the rest of the group agreed, but as the children considered these two alternatives, they decided that neither alternative was satisfactory. In the first case, you might be killing the only Lock Ness monster in existence. In the second case, a zoo is like a cage and the animal would need a cage as big as a lake to be "happy." The idea of a cage the size of a lake presented obvious problems.

At that point, the teacher posed a second question: What else could be done? We don't want to kill Nessie and a cage in a zoo would be difficult. What other possibilities are there?

The children came up with a variety of ideas, from turning the entire loch into a cage to just leaving the animal alone. By the end of the 40-minute period, the

Figure 8.12

Expository Lesson Plan (Eighth Grade Level)

Topic:

The pyramid of life shows environmental interrelationships

Objectives:

1. As a result of this lesson, each student will be able to define the terms *pyramid of life, decomposer, carnivore, herbivore,* and *omnivore.*
2. As a result of this lesson, each student will be able to describe in writing the interrelationships within the natural world as shown in the pyramid of life.

Materials:

Pictures representing the natural resources of sunlight, water, air, and soil; pictures of green plants, pictures of animals showing carnivores, herbivores, omnivores, and humans; pictures of molds, mushrooms, and other decomposers.

Procedure:

1. *Advance Organizer:* In this lesson you are going to be listening to a presentation about how the parts of the environment are related to one another. During the presentation, particularly listen for:
   a. The categories into which the different parts of the environment can be classified.
   b. How the different parts of the environment are connected to one another.
   c. The name for the diagram used to show these interrelationships.
2. *Presentation:* Use the following procedure for each level of the pyramid.
   a. Draw the lowest level of the pyramid on the board making it large.
   b. Tell the class that this level represents the starting needs for our environment. Show pictures to illustrate soil, water, air, and sunlight. Display the pictures; then in the level drawn on the board, write the terms *soil, air, water, sunlight.* Refer to them as natural resources.
   c. Continue with this procedure until the full pyramid, including the decomposers, has developed according to the diagram here.
   d. Tell the class the diagram constructed on the board is known as a "pyramid of life." It is also called a "pyramid of numbers" and an "energy pyramid," but those other names and their meanings will be considered later.
3. *Questions:*
   a. Each time a question is asked about one of the levels, erase the name of the level and ask the following questions:
      (1) Suppose all of the herbivores were to suddenly die out? What would happen to the rest of the pyramid? Replace the word *herbivore.*
      (2) Suppose all of the plants died out. What would happen to the rest of the pyramid? Replace the word *plant.*
      (3) Suppose all of the carnivores died out. What would happen to the rest of the pyramid? Replace the word *carnivore.*
      (4) Suppose all of the resources were used or were polluted so they could no longer be used. What would happen to the rest of the pyramid? Replace the words *sunlight, water, air, soil.*
      (5) Suppose all of the omnivores died out. What would happen to the rest of the pyramid? Replace the word *omnivore.*
      (6) Suppose all of the decomposers died out. What would happen to the rest of the pyramid? Replace the word *decomposer.*
      (7) So far, what happens if a level of the pyramid is disturbed?
      (8) Now, suppose human beings became extinct on this planet. What would happen to the rest of the pyramid?

(9) As you look at the pyramid of life, which parts of the pyramid are most important to maintaining the environment? Which parts may be the least important?

4. *Summary*

   a. Summarize the presentation by once more defining each of the new vocabulary terms: *pyramid of life, resource, carnivore, herbivore, omnivore, decomposer.*

   b. Summarize the idea that the various parts of the environment are interrelated and that a change in one part will cause a change in other parts.

Evaluation:

1. Have students write definitions for the following terms in their own words: *pyramid of life, natural resource, carnivore, omnivore, herbivore, decomposer.*

2. On the same sheet of paper, have students describe in their own words how the parts of the environment are interrelated.

Diagram:

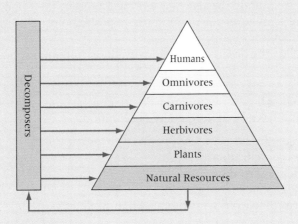

children had come to their own conclusion. The best thing, they decided, would be to capture the monster, keep it in a huge cage in the loch, study it, then let it go back to the loch and leave it alone.

From this description, we can see that an **open discussion** is one in which the children determine the topic and the role of the teacher is to ask those questions that will lead the children to consider various ideas. The teacher might also be responsible for defining unfamiliar terms and for taking the opposite point of view in order to show the other side of an issue. There can be no planning because the open discussion is spontaneous by definition. You do need to make a decision at the start of the discussion, however. You need to decide whether to pursue the topic or whether to redirect the attention of the students and whether the topic itself is appropriate or not. Films, newspaper articles, magazine articles, even television programs can provide appropriate or inappropriate topics for discussion. The dinosaurs of *Jurassic Park*, the latest article on cloning, or a television program on UFOs can provide an appropriate springboard for discussion. Once the topic has been deemed appropriate, it can be used to promote scientific processes and attitudes.

Planned Discussions. Not all discussions are or should be open. Most of the discussions that take place in the science classroom should be planned, and planning is one factor affecting the degree of success. In a **planned discussion,** the teacher determines the topic of the discussion, plans the questions, and guides the students toward some predetermined goal. A planned discussion is generally used when a topic is controversial, having a variety of different sides, and is used not simply to bring out the various sides of an issue but also to promote objectivity and critical thinking.

Preparing for a Planned Discussion. A discussion needs some starting point: A question is good, but an object or other device is better. Second, a discussion needs someone, frequently the teacher, who will present the opposite point of view. This is the devil's advocate role: taking the opposite point of view whether you believe that point of view or not.

The following discussion began with these statements, posted on the door of the classroom as the sixth grade arrived:

Be it known to all who enter this realm that the following statements are true and have been verified by observation:

Snakes are born from wet grass.
Flies come from rotten meat.
Witches turn milk sour.
Frogs are born out of mud.
Mice come from wheat wrapped in wet cloth.

These statements are held to be true. Anyone who does not believe will be punished by banishment from the realm.

—By Order of the Chief Scientist

Naturally, seeing something new the children stopped and read the sign. A few laughed. A few looked oddly at the teacher and said, "That's not true! Is it?" The teacher's reply was, "Of course it's true."

The children's challenge then became to convince the teacher that the assertions on the chart were not true. Verbal attempts to convince the teacher were all met with counter comments: Nothing was acceptable. Finally, a child left the room, went to the cafeteria, returned with a chunk of raw meat, put it in the teacher's hand and said, "Prove it." This, of course, was the outcome the teacher desired from this discussion: the idea that it is necessary to prove or disprove a theory through experimentation, rather than through discussion.

Although these children came to this conclusion on their own, such is not always the result. Discussions can fizzle unless the teacher is ready with questions that will lead the class to the desired outcome.

When you plan a discussion, then, first have a starting point: a picture, chart, or challenging question. Second, plan a series of questions that will lead to the end point or objective of the discussion. These questions will not be on the knowledge or comprehension levels. Rather, children should be working on the analysis, synthesis, and evaluation levels during the discussion. Keep one point in mind: A discussion is neither a lecture nor a question-and-answer session. You, as the teacher, should say less than the students—much, much less— and not attempt to impose your ideas or beliefs on the students.

Problems Using the Discussion Method. The problems of the discussion method are three: It is verbal, and it is controversial, and it can be dominated by one individual.

The major problem with the discussion method is that it is verbal. Children in the elementary school are cognitively more attuned to hands-on, concrete experiences than they are to verbal teaching. For children at the preoperational level, discussions are generally impossible. Children at this level, generally kindergarten, first, or second graders, are not yet able to present their ideas verbally, to maintain a consistent viewpoint, or to defend their ideas with verbal information. Discussions are generally more appropriate at the third through eighth grade levels.

Second, successful discussions present more than one point of view and whenever there is more than one point of view, controversy follows. The teacher must make certain that the students have enough information at hand so any discussion contains accurate information from all sides of the issue rather than hearsay or opinions biased toward one side or another. As the teacher you must make certain your students respect differing viewpoints and show the same respect yourself. This is particularly important where those viewpoints represent the teaching of the home or religious body. A discussion should never deteriorate into a verbal attack on one represented set of beliefs or values. If this seems to be happening, a good strategy is to suggest the students do some research into the differing viewpoints before continuing.

Finally, the last problem of the discussion lies in who does the talking. The most common pitfall is for the teacher to take over the discussion and begin to lecture students. This is most likely to occur when the students begin to challenge the teacher's own beliefs, and he or she feels compelled to set the students straight on a particular issue. Rather than taking over the discussion, try asking questions, presenting your point of view as a simple part of the discussion, and preparing yourself to be overruled once in a while.

But the teacher is not the only individual who can dominate a discussion. A child can try to dominate the discussion, either because he or she has superior knowledge or because of a dominant personality. The child with superior knowledge could be asked to play the role of moderator, and the dominant personality could be given the attention he or she needs by asking other children to decide what evidence could be used to support or refute what the dominant child has said.

There is also the child who does not overtly participate. In many cases, this child is listening to the discussion and may be participating nonverbally through eye contact, body posture, or facial expression. Respect the right of a child not to participate

Figure 8.13

Discussion Lesson Plan (Sixth Grade Level)

Topic:

Experimenting is a way of proving or disproving an idea.

Objectives:

1. As participants in the discussion students will be able to present and defend their ideas.
2. As a result of the discussion, students will be able to state that experiments can be used to prove or disprove ideas.

Materials:

Chart, glass, water, soil, three similar containers, jar lid, gauze, tape or rubber band.

Procedure:

1. Prominently display the chart found on page 00 where it can be seen by the class as they enter the room.
2. If no one questions the statements, ask:
   a. Do you think these statements are true?
   b. I think all of these things are true. How could you change my mind?

c. Be ready to contradict every verbal attempt, no matter how ridiculous the contradiction.

3. Additional questions, if necessary, to lead to the desired objectives:
   a. What could we do to prove the statements are wrong?
   b. What are some possibilities other than words and arguments to convince me these statements are wrong?
   c. How could we use these materials to prove the statements are wrong?

Evaluation:

1. Mentally note which children have participated in the discussion.
2. Have each child write one effective way to prove an idea right or wrong.

in a particular discussion. The child may be choosing not to participate because the ideas expressed conflict with his or her value system. The child may be silent because of a lack of knowledge in a particular area. To try to force a child who does not wish to participate to do so can lead to increasing discomfort for the child and a power struggle for the teacher. Respect the right of the child to be silent on occasion, just as you respect the right of an adult to be silent on occasion.

The lesson plan in Figure 8.13 shows a discussion based on the poster described on page 258.

Field Trips

Field trips are not necessarily verbally oriented any more than they are necessarily materials oriented. How a field trip is categorized depends on the field trip itself. For example, a trip to a museum in which children are guided through an exhibit of fossils by a museum guide will probably be verbal in its orientation. However, a trip to a pond in which children gather data about the water, plant and animal life, and environmental conditions, is definitely a hands-on teaching strategy. Consequently, field trips may be planned as inductive or deductive discovery lessons or as expository lessons.

Whichever type of lesson is used, planning for a field trip involves certain preliminary work:

1. Always visit the field trip location prior to taking a class to the site. Never rely solely on the recommendation of other teachers or friends. Such recommendations may give you possibilities, but only you can decide whether the site is appropriate for your class or not. If it is a guided site, talk with the guide to see what kinds of experiences are provided. If you have students in your class who are visually, auditorily, or orthopedically impaired, make certain the site will allow full participation by those children.

2. Once you have decided to go to a guided site, talk with the guide about what you want your students to get out of the field trip. Be certain the guide knows the age level of your students. A presentation designed for seventh graders is not going to be appropriate for first graders. Also discuss with the guide any time constraints you might have.

3. If the site is outdoors, arrange time for the students to explore on their own. Students need a chance to see what is there for themselves before they are expected to conduct more formal explorations. This time to explore freely will also give students a chance to build up background information that may be of use later in listening to a guide or conducting an activity.

4. Arrange for transportation to and from the site. Be certain, at the same time, to have permission slips for all of the students. Finally, check a day or two ahead of time to be certain all is ready.

5. Arrange for parents to accompany the students, or, if possible, combine your field trip with that of a high school class to the same area. Younger students benefit by having an individual guide, and older students have the benefit of helping the younger ones understand what they are seeing.

6. Prepare the students for the field trip with hands-on activities that will build up their background information. Students who are well prepared will gain more from the field trip than students who are simply going on the trip. If they will be on a guided trip, it may be helpful for the students to prepare questions for the guide.

7. Following the field trip, have a follow-up discussion of the trip and follow-up activities to engage the students with the information gained. If there was a specific guide for the trip, write a thank-you note. Young children enjoy writing and illustrating their own individual notes. Older students may want to create one note that all of them sign.

8. Be prepared. Find out which students experience motion sickness. Locate the bathrooms, the gift shop, and the snack or lunch area. Take along a first aid kit. On a field trip, expect anything.

Field trips can provide experiences that are not available within the classroom situation. The field trip can expand the students' horizons by relating the work done in the classroom to the real world.

Activity 8.5

Purpose To analyze unit plan concepts and subconcepts to determine the most appropriate teaching strategies.

Procedure
1. Return to the list of concept and subconcepts developed for your unit plan.
   a. Analyze each concept as to whether it can be taught through a hands-on strategy or a verbal strategy.
   b. Decide which of the teaching strategies presented in this chapter would most effectively teach the concepts. Provide a rationale for your strategy selection.
   c. Consider the kinds of strategies which can be used for your concepts and subconcepts. Do hands-on strategies predominate? If verbal strategies predominate, reconsider your topic concepts and subconcepts to allow for greater use of hands-on strategies.

Activity 8.6

Purpose To write hands-on strategy lesson plans appropriate to the teaching strategies selected for each concept and subconcept of the unit.

Procedure
1. Using the sample lesson plans provided in this chapter, prepare lesson plans for each of the concepts identified as appropriately taught through hands-on strategies.
2. Critique each of your plans for developmental appropriateness and make any changes which might be necessary.
3. Critique each of your plans in terms of the safety factors listed in this chapter. Make any change which might be necessary.

Activity 8.7

Purpose To write verbal strategy lesson plans appropriate to the teaching strategies selected for each concept and subconcept unit.

Procedure
1. Using the sample lesson plans provided in this chapter, prepare lesson plans for each of the concepts identified as appropriately taught through verbal strategies.

2. Critique each of your plans for developmental appropriateness and make any changes which might be necessary.
3. Critique each of your plans in terms of the safety factors listed in this chapter. Make any change which might be necessary.

Summary

A wide variety of teaching strategies exist for the teacher of science, generally divided into those techniques using predominantly verbal techniques and those using predominantly materials-oriented techniques. Verbal techniques are generally classified as either demonstration techniques or expository techniques such as exposition or discussion. The demonstrations provide a bridge between verbal-oriented strategies and materials-oriented strategies: They involve the use of materials by the teacher but much of the instruction remains verbal. In the case of materials-oriented strategies, discovery techniques and constructivist techniques are found. Strategies such as ordinary demonstrations, inductive discovery, and deductive discovery are teacher structured to lead students to particular content outcomes. Strategies such as Learning Cycle, open inquiry, and the conceptual change model are designed to help students construct knowledge for themselves and so are considered constructivist approaches to teaching.

Chapter Vocabulary

The number following each term refers to the page on which the term is first introduced.

Activity, 226
Advance organizer, 253
Authentic evaluation, 211
Class discussion, 215
Comparative organizers, 253
Conceptual change model, 238
Constructivist teaching strategy, 234
Deductive discovery, 233
Discipline-centered unit plan, 203
Discovery, 223
Discovery demonstration, 243
Discovery stage, 232
Discussion, 226, 255
Exploration stage, 231
Expository organizer, 253
Expository teaching, 252
Field trip, 260

Inductive discovery, 223
Interview, 213
Invention stage, 232
Learning cycle, 224
Objectives, 206
Open discussion, 256
Open inquiry, 235
Ordinary demonstration, 243
Planned discussion, 258
Pretest, 212
Problem, 225
Semantic mapping, 217
Unit plan, 202
Verbal teaching strategy, 251

Applying the
CONCEPTS

1. Children come to our classrooms from a variety of different backgrounds and demonstrating a variety of different intelligences and cognitive levels. Why does this make it important to have a variety of different teaching strategies?

2. A wide variety of teaching strategies exists. How would you go about determining which teaching strategy to use in a particular lesson?

3. "In this school, every day is lab day in science. I want to see children actively involved in hands-on science every day." This was the comment made by a principal to a new teacher. How would you respond to this particular principal?

References

Airasian, P. W., and M. E. Walsh. 1997. Constructivist cautions. *Phi Delta Kappan* 78(6), 444–449.

Anderson, O. R. 1992. Some interrelationships between constructivist models of learning and current neurobiological theory, with implications for science education. *Journal of Research in Science Teaching* 29(10) 1037–1058.

Anderson, C., and D. Butts. 1980. A comparison of individualized and group instruction in a sixth grade electricity unit. *Journal of Research in Science Teaching* 17,2.

Ausubel, D. P. 1963. *Psychology and meaningful verbal learning.* New York: Greene and Straton.

Barrow, L. H. 1979. The basics—communicating, thinking, and valuing. S*chool Science and Mathematics* 70, 8.

Blankenship, T. 1982. Is anyone listening? *Science Teacher* 49, 9.

Boulanger, F. D. 1980. Instruction and science learning: A quantitative synthesis. *Journal of Research in Science Teaching* 18, 4.

Bonnwell, C. C., and J. A. Eison. 1991. *Active learning: Creating excitement in the classroom.* Washington, D.C.: ASHE-ERIC Higher Education Report.

Brophy, J. 1992. Probing the subtleties of subject-matter teaching. *Educational Leadership* 49(7), 4–8.

Brown, A., and J. Campione. 1994. Guided discovery in a community of learners. In K. McGilly (Ed.), *Classroom lessons: Integrating cognitive theory and classroom practice* (pp. 229–270). Cambridge, Mass.: MIT Press.

Bruni, J. V. 1982. Problem solving for the primary grades. *Arithmetic Teacher* 29, 6.

Burns, M. 1982. How to teach problem solving. *Arithmetic Teacher* 29,6.

Champagne, A., R. F. Gunstone, and L. E. Klopfer. 1983. Naive knowledge and science learning. *Research in Science and Technological Education* 1(2), 173–183.

Dreyfus, A., E. Jungwirth, and R. Eliovitch. 1990. Applying the "cognitive conflict" strategy for conceptual change—some implications, difficulties, and problems. *Science Education* 74(5), 555–569.

Driver, R., H. Asoko, J. Leach, E. Mortimer, and P. Scott. 1994. Constructing scientific knowledge in the classroom. *Educational Researcher* 23(7), 5–12.

Driver, R., and B. Bell. 1985. Students' thinking and the learning of science: A constructivistic view. *School Science Review* 67(240), 443–456.

Driver, R., and G. Erickson. 1983. Theories in action: Some theoretical and empirical issues in the study of students' conceptual frameworks in science. *Studies in Science Education* 10, 37–60.

Ebenezer, J., and S.Connor. 1998. *Learning to teach science: A model for the 21st century.* Upper Saddle River, N.J.: Merrill.

Ebert, C., and E. Ebert. 1993. An instructionally oriented model for enabling conceptual development. In J. Novak (Ed.), *Proceedings of the third international seminar on misconceptions and educational strategies in science and mathematics.* Ithaca, N. Y.: Cornell University.

Gega, P. C., and J. M. Peters. 1998. *Science in Elementary Education* (8th ed). Upper Saddle River, N.J.: Merrill.

Gil-Perez, D., and J. Carrascosa. 1990. What to do about science "misconceptions." *Science Education* 74(5), 531–540.

Joyse, B., and E. Calhoun. 1998. *Learning to teach inductively.* Boston: Allyn & Bacon.

Kauchak, D. P., and P. D. Eggen. 1998. *Teaching and learning: Research based methods.* Boston: Allyn & Bacon

Orlich, D. C., R. J. Harder, R. C. Callahan, and H. W. Gibson. 1998. *Teaching strategies: A guide to better instruction.* New York: Houghton Mifflin.

Schneider, L., and J. W. Renner. 1980. Concrete and formal teaching. *Journal of Research in Science Teaching* 17, 6.

Smith, W. S. 1983. Engineering a classroom discussion. *Science and Children* 20,5.

Stahl, S. A., and C. H. Clark. 1987. The effects of participatory expectations in classroom discussion on the learning of science vocabulary. *American Educational Research Journal* 24, 542–556.

Stepans, J. I., B. W. Saigo, and C. Ebert. 1995. *Changing the classroom from within: Partnership, Collegiality, and constructivism.* Montgomery, Ala.: Saiwood.

Suchman, J. R. 1962. *The elementary school training program in scientific inquiry.* Champaign/Urbana: University of Illinois.

Suydam, M. 1982. Update on research on problem solving: Implications for classroom teaching. *Arithmetic Teacher* 29, 6.

van Ments, M. 1990. *Active talk: The effective use of discussion in learning.* New York: St. Martin's Press.

Victor, E. 1974. The inquiry approach to teaching and learning: A primer for the teacher. *Science and Children* 12, 2.

Watson, B., and R. Konicek. 1990, May. Teaching for conceptual change: Confronting children's experience. *Phi Delta Kappan* pp. 127–133.

Welch, W. W. 1981. *What research says to the science teacher* (Vol. 3). Washington, D.C.: National Science Teachers Association.

White, E. P. 1982. Why self-directed learning? *Science and Children* 19, 5.

Wolfinger, D. M. 1984. *Teaching science in the elementary school: Content, process and attitudes.* Boston: Little, Brown.

Wolfinger, D. M. 1994. *Science and mathematics in early childhood education.* New York: HarperCollins.

Chapter Nine

Evaluation in
Science Learning

Chapter Objectives

Upon completion of this chapter you should be able to:

1 discuss the purposes for evaluation in the science program.
2 discuss the differences between traditional and nontraditional forms of evaluation.
3 discuss a variety of strategies for evaluating students' achievement in science content, science process, and problem solving.
4 discuss the development of a portfolio.
5 discuss the use of the portfolio in the assessment of student progress in science.

Introduction

"I love using hands-on activities in my classroom. "The kids get excited about learning and they understand what they are learning. I'd do them everyday if I could but there's one problem. I have to give the kids a grade in science on their report cards. How can I do activities with the kids and then give them a grade for science? I have to have them read the book and answer the chapter questions. That's so I can give them a test on the material in the book. If I get behind, I just leave out the activities, since I can't grade them. If I don't use the book, then I can't give a grade and I have to give a grade."

This teacher echoes the feelings of many teachers in the science classroom. They see science activities as an important and successful way of teaching science, but they are not quite certain how to relate the active, hands-on activities to the grades that go in a report card. Consequently, some of these uncertain teachers use tests, quizzes, and worksheets as a means of grading in science with activities a fun aspect of science that has nothing really to do with grades or learning.

This teacher's evaluation of science learning focuses on only one aspect of the total science curriculum. She is seeing science as science content. Consequently, it is hard for her to understand how to evaluate the other aspects of science teaching and learning: process and attitudes.

What we need, then, in the science classroom are ways of evaluating the total science program, not just the content, not just the process skills, not just the attitudes, but the entire curriculum. This means we need to understand the purposes of evaluation in science teaching and then use a variety of kinds of evaluation to meet those purposes.

Purposes for Evaluation in Science

Why do we evaluate in science teaching? In essence, there are two major reasons for evaluating. The first, of course, is to determine the progress our students are making in learning science. In order to chart that progress, we first have to make certain we know what we want our students to learn. Consequently, the objectives we are trying to accomplish need to be stated clearly and concisely. It is the objectives that tell us the outcomes for our daily lessons and for our units of instruction. As we look at those objectives, we need to be certain they are reflecting the total science program. Some objectives should deal with content. The content of science is the basis for most units, most textbooks, most courses of study. And, most certainly, we do want our students to be literate in science content information. But science content is only one aspect of science, and so we do want some of our objectives to deal with process skills through the context of hands-on investigations and experiments. Process skills engage students in collecting information and in making sense of that information. In this way students gain an understanding of the method of science. And we want some of our objectives to deal with developing investigative skills in science, that is, with developing investigations and experiments which will answer the questions students ask for themselves. Through student-developed investigations we again help students understand the nature of science.

Most teachers think of evaluation only in terms of the students in a class and the report cards those students will get. But evaluation should not end with the students or with the grades sent home to parents. Evaluation should also include the teacher and the curriculum. As teachers we need to reflect continually on our teaching, on the success and failure of our lessons and units. Evaluation should assist us as teachers in determining whether or not the teaching strategies we selected were appropriate to the class and whether or not we were successful in teaching the various aspects of science.

Evaluation should also help us look at our total science curriculum and whether or not that curriculum is leading the students toward the goal of scientific literacy. As teachers we can consider this aspect of evaluation by looking back at the entire school year and assessing our teaching. We want to look at our successes and build on those successes. We also want to look at our failures and, in keeping with the scientific attitude of positive approach to failure, determine what we have learned from those failures.

In the following sections we consider methods for evaluating content, process, and investigation in both traditional and nontraditional manners.

Evaluating Science Learning

Introduction

Traditional evaluation is based on the concept that students should learn certain things by a certain point in time. Because we can identify those things through our objectives we can also determine whether or not the students have learned them (Dorr-Bremme, 1983; Ebel and Frisbie, 1986). For example, if we decide first graders should be able to name the four seasons in their correct order, then we can ask children in first grade to tell us the names of the seasons. If we decide eighth graders should be able to explain the origin of earthquakes as a result of plate tectonics, we should be able to ask students at the eighth grade level to write a paragraph explaining the origin of earthquakes.

In much of its use, traditional evaluation is divorced from the learning experience. The best example of this idea of divorcing evaluation from learning is the Friday test day many of us are familiar with from our own school days. Traditionally, Friday has been reserved for the final spelling test, the math test, the science test, and the social studies test. No lesson: just a test. When we say evaluation is divorced from learning, we mean the evaluation is separated from the experiences used by children as they learn.

Nontraditional evaluation is based on the idea that all students should learn certain things, but those students may learn those things at different rates, often in different ways, and may even demonstrate their learning in a variety of ways. Nontraditional forms of evaluation are also an integral part of the learning experience rather than separated from the experience. In a nontraditional assessment format, students learning how to carry out an experiment demonstrate their understanding of experimental procedures not by answering multiple choice questions on a test but by carrying out an experiment and using the procedure, results, and conclusions as evidence of their learning (Hart, D. 1994)).

Science learning can be evaluated in a variety of ways (Hein and Price, 1994; Haney and Madus, 1989). In the paragraphs that follow, we consider some of the traditional and nontraditional ways of evaluating science learning in students. The following types of evaluation are discussed:

1. Anecdotal records
2. Teacher observation
3. Checklists
4. Interviews
5. Rubrics
6. Activity results
7. Journals
8. Tests and quizzes

Anecdotal Records. An **anecdotal record** is a way of informally observing students at work in order to determine their progress. Anecdotal records can be used to assess content development, use of process skills, or use of investigative skills. Anecdotal records are particularly appropriate to kindergarten and primary grade students, but can be used at any grade level. The main thing to keep in mind in using anecdotal records is to observe not infer. This distinction between an observation and an inference is an important one. Observations are descriptions of the child's behavior at a particular time. Inferences are interpretations of that behavior, often assumptions of the meaning of the child's behavior. For example, a valid observation of a first grade child would state the following:

> Joey worked in the science area for twenty minutes. He used the magnifier to observe the rocks in the center and then put the rocks into piles according to a characteristic of the rocks. He told Marcella that he had rocks that were shiny, rocks that were white, and rocks that were ugly. When he went outside to play he collected two more rocks to put in the center.

This statement indicates how much time Joey devoted to the science center and exactly what he did during that time period. It is an observation of the child's activities.

Or a teacher might make this statement:

> Joey enjoyed looking at the rocks in the center and learned a great deal by putting them into groups.

A child who passes 20 minutes in a particular center, shared his ideas with another, and added to the rock collection probably did enjoy it, but he could have stayed in the center that length of time because he saw nothing more interesting, because the other centers were in use, or even because he did not feel well and the quiet center was a refuge for him. As for learning "a great deal" about the rocks, this is a subjective statement. If the teacher wanted to indicate that learning was indeed taking place, then he or she might make this observation:

> Joey drew a picture of the rocks he had seen in the center. He dictated a story telling how the rocks were the same and how they were different to go along with the picture. In the story he talked about the color, weight, and luster of the rocks.

Although anecdotal records are most appropriate for young children (Correro, 1988), this does not mean you cannot use them with students at the middle school level. An appropriate anecdotal record for sixth grade level might state:

> Greta collected the materials she would need for her investigation of inclined planes and set up the incline. She rolled the car down the incline three times and measured how far the car traveled each time. She then wrote a hypothesis to test and began her experiment. After changing the angle of the incline four times, Greta put away the materials and began to work on a graph of the results.

This anecdotal record of a student at sixth grade level working with an inclined plane gives an indication of her ability to design and carry out an experiment, to collect results, and to develop a graph. It gives a great deal of information about the development of the experimental processes.

Simply because anecdotal records are often connected to young children does not mean they cannot and should not be used with older students. The trick in using anecdotal records at any level is to make a number of observations of a student over a time period so that development of a particular skill can be assessed.

Teacher Observation.   Teacher observation is an informal means of assessment in which the teacher simply watches the interactions occurring among and between students as they work on a particular task or activity. Unlike anecdotal records, teacher observations focus on the total group rather than on individual students within the group and are designed to assess the activity the students are conducting and its effect on those students. From this type of evaluation the teacher can determine whether or not the activity is appropriate to the children, the curriculum aspect of evaluation, and whether or not the children are engaged and learning from the activity. In essence, the teacher is not evaluating the content of the lesson but rather the effectiveness of the teaching strategies in engaging the children in the learning process.

As you observe the students at work, look for any problems that may be occurring in following directions, in using equipment, or in carrying out a specified proce-

or investigation. Unlike other forms of evaluation that indicate specifics and ask that each specific be evaluated separately, a rubric looks at the total product and assesses that product holistically.

A scoring rubric is based on the stated objectives and is specific to a context. It allows the teacher to look systematically at the product of learning, at the context specified in step 2, and to determine the success the students have had in reaching the objectives. As they assess holistically, most rubrics have three to five levels of achievement, each of the levels having specific criteria. Meeting the criteria for a particular level means one receives the score for that level. Figure 9.4 shows two rubrics. The first is used for evaluating a mural showing the solar system. The second is used for evaluating an experiment.

Rubrics can also be combined with other forms of evaluation to provide a more comprehensive evaluation. For example, a checklist and a rubric or an essay and a rubric could be combined in assessing an activity. Figure 9.5 shows this combination of rubric with another assessment device.

Activity Results. The results of science experiments and investigations should be evaluated through the experiments and investigations themselves. Teacher observation can help you determine how well your students follow directions, use materials, or work together in a group as they carry out those investigations. **Activity results,** the papers they use to record the results of those investigations and experiments, can be used to evaluate their success in working in a hands-on manner.

Activity results sheets are not work sheets, at least not the mindless fill-in-the-blanks-type work sheets so prevalent in many schools. The degree of specificity found on an activity sheet is related to the level at which students are working. An activity sheet for students just learning to do experiments might have complete instructions for the experiment and then include a chart for data collection and a space for a conclusion. An activity sheet for students who have experience in designing and carrying out experiments may simply have sections designated hypotheses, procedure, data, conclusion. The activity sheet should be suited to the both the grade level of the students and the level at which they are working.

In evaluating activity results, keep in mind that you are evaluating not one but two areas: content and process or investigation. The evaluation of process skills using activity results is relatively easy. Look to see if the hypothesis is written properly or if the operational question is clearly stated. Look to see if the procedure actually tests the hypothesis or provides a way of finding an answer to the question. Look to see if the procedure was followed and the data collected suited the procedure. Look to see if the observations are really observations, the measurements are accurate, the parts of a system correctly identified. Look to see if the conclusion is drawn from the data. Developing a checklist of the process skills or investigative actions you want to evaluate can make this procedure more effective. Using a rubric is also a way of systematizing attention to scientific investigation skills.

Evaluating the content aspect of an investigation or experiment is a little trickier than evaluating the process aspect. It sounds as if it should be easy: See if the students got the right answer. Keep in mind, however, that students can perform an investigation or carry out an experiment perfectly and, because of equipment or

Figure 9.4

Rubrics

EVALUATING A MURAL

Level Four: Superior

Mural is scientifically accurate including attention to size and distance relationships. There is high artistic quality with a variety of media used in developing the mural.

Level Three: Very Good

The mural is scientifically accurate including attention to size and distance relationships. The artistic quality is good but the variety of media is limited.

Level Two: Good

The mural is scientifically accurate in terms of planetary characteristics. Either distance or size relationships have been included but not both. The artistic quality is good but only one medium has been used.

Level One: Adequate

The mural shows some problems with scientific accuracy in terms of planetary characteristics, size or distance relationships. Artistic quality is lacking and only one medium was used.

Level Zero: Inadequate

Extensive problems with scientific accuracy exist. Planetary characteristics, size and distance relationships are incorrect or outdated. Artistic quality is poor. No use of color or other artistic attributes.

EVALUATING AN EXPERIMENT

Level Three: Scientist

The experiment shows a clearly worded hypothesis, control of variables, and a set procedure. The data is accurately recorded and clearly displayed. The conclusion accurately reflects the data.

Level Two: Lab Assistant

The experiment shows a clearly worded hypothesis, and a set procedure. There is some difficulty with control of variables. The data is accurately recorded and clearly displayed. The conclusion accurately reflects the data.

Level One: Student

The hypothesis is stated as a question rather than a hypothesis. Some evidence of control of variables and set procedure. The data are not clearly displayed. The conclusion does fit the data.

Level Zero: Trainee

The hypothesis is written as a question. No control of variables is evident. The procedure only partially tests the hypothesis. The data are not recorded or are not clearly recorded. The conclusion does not fit the data.

human error, find a result that is not "right" in terms of the content developed. In assessing the content aspect of investigations and experiments, we need to look at three categories of content responses: scientifically correct, scientifically incorrect, scientifically dishonest.

Scientifically correct content conclusions are those that show exactly what scientists have found in the same situation. In other words, your students got the "right" answer. In this case, after doing an experiment on the effect of length on the number of swings of a pendulum, your students conclude that the longer the pen-

Figure 9.5

Example of Evaluation of Pendulum Experiment

**COMBINING A RUBRIC
WITH A CHECKLIST**

Checklist

- ☐ Obtained all needed materials from the supply area.
- ☐ Used all materials according to the activity directions.
- ☐ Used all measuring devices appropriately.
- ☐ Cleaned up materials when finished.
- ☐ Returned all materials to the supply area

Rubric

Level Three (5 points): Followed activity directions accurately, collected and recorded all data, graphed the data, and drew a conclusion appropriate to the data.

Level Two (3 points): Followed activity directions accurately, collected and recorded all data, drew a conclusion appropriate to the data. No graph of data was included.

Level One (1 point): Followed activity directions, collected and recorded data, drew a conclusion not appropriate to the data collected. No graph of data included.

Level Zero (0 points): Did not follow activity directions, no collection of data, no graph, no conclusion drawn.

**COMBINING A RUBRIC
WITH AN ESSAY**

Essay

Consider the experiment you carried out to test factors affecting the number of times a pendulum will swing in a minute and the class discussion of the results as you answer the following question: You have a grandfather clock with a pendulum. The clock tends to run fast. What could you do to adjust the pendulum in order to make the clock neither gain nor lose time during a week?

Rubric

Level One (5 points): wrote a hypothesis appropriate to the question, developed an experiment to test the hypothesis including control of variables, collected data, and drew a conclusion appropriate to the data.

Level Two (3 points): wrote a hypothesis appropriate to the question, developed an experiment to test the hypothesis, collected data, and drew a conclusion appropriate to the data. Some variables were not controlled.

Level Three (1 point): wrote a hypothesis appropriate to the questions, developed an experiment to test the hypothesis. Did not control variables. Conclusion was not appropriate to the data.

Level Four (0 points): investigated question without developing an experiment to test a hypothesis through control of variables.

dulum, the fewer the number of swings. Students drawing a scientifically correct conclusion obviously should be given full credit for the content aspect of the activity.

Scientifically incorrect content conclusions are those that fit the results obtained by your students as they do the experiment or investigation but the conclusion is not accurate in terms of known scientific content. In this case, your students collect data about the pendulum and from their results draw the conclusion that the heavier the pendulum bob the slower the pendulum will swing. If the conclusion fits the data, students should be given full credit for the content aspect of the activity. Give full credit for a wrong answer? Yes! These students have drawn the only conclusion they can from the results obtained. It is, according to their activity, correct. They have reported their results with scientific honesty. The key, of course, is to help the students determine why their conclusion differed from known scientific fact. By having students try to determine why their answers differed from scientific fact, you encourage problem solving and curiosity in your students.

Scientifically dishonest content conclusions are scientifically accurate but *do not reflect* the data collected. In this case students either knew what was supposed to happen and wrote that down in order to have the correct conclusion or looked up what was supposed to happen and wrote that down in order to be right. This type of procedure is in direct contradiction to the scientific attitude of honesty, and students should not be given credit for this type of response.

Journals.   A **journal** is a means of combining science with language arts in a way that enables students to present information that was learned in an open-ended manner. A journal can be used by students to do a number of things. First, a journal can be used to collect the data from an activity. This may be in the form of written statements of observation, inferences, and predictions or more formal data collection in the form of measurement, graphs, or charts. Second, the journal enables students to write about what they have learned from a particular activity conducted in the science class. It can show the conclusions the student drew from the activity, the explanations the child developed to explain what was seen or experienced, and the connections drawn between the activity results and previous learning. Third, a journal entry can include notations of information sources used by a student as he or she researched a particular topic. It may contain names of paper databases found in the library, persons consulted on the topic, and useful Internet addresses. Fourth, a journal can be used to ask questions. As students study a particular topic, they often develop additional questions. The questions can be recorded for comment by the teacher or for later research by the questioning student. And, finally, a journal can be a place for reflection on topics under consideration as the student comments on his or her perceptions of the worth of the topic, the interest generated, or simply records trains of thought experienced during the study of the topic.

Whatever use, or uses, the journal is put to, the teacher needs to be a frequent reader and commenter. Student questions need to be answered. Student reflections need to be acknowledged. And student misconceptions need to be confronted through additional activities and resources. The journal cannot be left to the end of a unit of study. A teacher needs to read and react to the journal continuously.

Tests and Quizzes.   In developing a pencil and paper test, consider the age of the students, the subject matter, and the teaching strategies used. For children at the kindergarten, first, and second grade levels, **tests and quizzes** are the least appropriate kinds of evaluations available to science teachers. In fact, the Southern Association on Children Under Six (1990) and the National Association for the

Education of Young Children (1988, 1989) came out strongly against the use of pencil and paper tests for young children. Tests and quizzes may be more appropriate for older students, but other forms of evaluation are far more appropriate to elementary and middle school learners. The subject matter should be considered so you evaluate the entire range of the information presented rather than simply the vocabulary or dates and places of events. And, finally, the teaching strategies should be reflected in terms of the kinds of questions. If the instruction has been geared toward the memorization of information, then test questions should reflect that focus. If instruction has been geared toward developing concepts and thinking skills, which hopefully they have, the evaluation should reflect that focus.

Probably the best starting point for the construction of a pencil and paper test is with a table of specifications that describes the form and the substance of the test which will be constructed. The information included in the table of specifications for the test should include the following:

1. The form of the test items to be used: multiple choice, fill in the blank, matching, true-false, essay, short answer.
2. The number of items of each form: based on the length of the test and the amount of time that will be allotted to the test.
3. The kinds of tasks the items will present: recall of knowledge, application, analysis, synthesis, evaluation, computation, and so on.
4. The number of tasks of each kind: based on the teaching strategies used and the time allotted to the testing procedure.
5. The areas of content to be sampled: the content topic included in the area of study form the foundation for this section.
6. The number of items in each of the content areas: based on the emphasis given to the content area during the teaching phase.

The table of specifications allows you to construct an effective test that will truly consider the information you have presented to the students. As such, the construction of a table of specifications helps you overcome some of the common problems with testing students. First, the table of specifications allows you to construct on objective measure of the information gained by the students and of their ability to use that information. The test constructed from the table of specifications allows you to use student responses rather than simple teacher observation. Second, the table of specifications requires you to think about the test that will be given prior to its construction. All too often, teachers leave the construction of a test to the last minute. This last minute preparation generally means the test reflects your memory of the content rather than the actual content of the unit of study. Third, the table of specifications allows you to construct a test that is sufficiently long to sample the content of the unit of study adequately. Tests that are too short may not allow students to show what they have learned. Tests that are too long are frustrating to students. If all of the students are able to at least provide an answer to all of the questions within the allotted time, the test is the correct length. Fourth, the use of a table of specifications allows you to overcome the general problem of testing only the factual, and sometimes, the trivial aspects of a unit. By giving attention not only to an overview of the content but also to the types of items to be given on the test, you are more likely to include questions that ask for understanding and application rather than questions simply asking for recall of knowledge. And, finally, the table of specifications allows you to develop a greater variety of item types from essay to multiple choice to true-false (Wesman, 1971; Wiggins, 1989; Wiggins, 1992). Some specific tips for the development of these types of questions are given here.

Developing Essay Questions.   Essay questions are generally used because of the emphasis placed on writing an answer over simply selecting an answer. The **essay question** therefore requires more thinking and reasoning on the part of a student as well as the ability to compose in written form effectively. Prior to the third grade level, essay tests are ineffective with children because their writing skills are not sufficiently developed to allow them to compose their thoughts, and their preoperational thought processes generally do not permit them to use language effectively. As children enter concrete operations and become more proficient in writing, they should be introduced to essay questions. In composing essay questions, the first consideration is in composing a question that will allow students to demonstrate their command of factual knowledge. The question should require the use of important information from the unit of study. Second, essay questions should be specific enough that one answer to the question will be clearly better than another answer to the question. In order to assist children in knowing the kinds of information to include in the essay, include a statement that indicates the kind of information you expected. For example, do not simply ask children this:

Describe vascular and nonvascular plants.

State the question so that students have a better idea of what they should include in their answers:

Describe vascular and nonvascular plants. In your answer include a definition of each term, examples of both nonvascular and vascular plants, and how those plants are similar to and different from one another.

Finally, be certain that children are given practice in answering essay-type questions during the unit. Unless students know how to approach an essay, unless they have been given some practice in composing answers, the use of an essay may be too daunting for children to even attempt. Also, if students are not used to essay-type questions on tests, do not expect them to be proficient in their first attempts. Students who have never been expected to answer an essay question need time to develop their ability to answer this type of question.

Developing True-False Items.   **True-false items** are often criticized as requiring only rote learning and recall of factual knowledge. This is not necessarily the case because true-false questions can be constructed that will allow for evaluation of understanding as well as recall. In developing true-false items for a test, first be certain the item asks for something important. Consider the following two true-false items:

1. Albert Einstein worked in a patent office.
2. Albert Einstein developed an equation showing the relationship existing between matter and energy.

Both of these items are true, but the second item is far more important than the first. Knowing one of Einstein's many important accomplishments is far more important than knowing he worked in a patent office.

Second, make sure the item tests understanding of terminology rather than simply recalling a particular phrase. Consider the following two items:

1. Plate tectonics and continental drift help explain the current location of the continents of the world.
2. A map of the continents as they appeared 250 million years ago would look very different from a map of the continents as they are today.

In the first item, the student will correctly respond to the item if he or she recognizes the formal terminology. In the second item the student must understand the formal statement, which includes the concepts of plate tectonics and continental drift, and recognize the truth or falsity of the item. Item 2 is more appropriate than item 1.

Third, a good true-false item is clearly and concisely stated but not so short that the full sense of the item is lost. Consider the following three items:

1. Animals are different in different places.
2. Animals living on different parts of Earth are sometimes different from animals living in other parts of Earth, but not always, because of the different kinds of habitats.
3. Animals found in the different biomes of Earth may differ from one another.

In the first item, the sentence is so short that it is difficult to determine the actual meaning or the response desired. It is easy to argue that it could be correct or incorrect. In the second item, the statement is so lengthy that the meaning can be easily lost while reading the statement. The third item is an appropriately stated true-false item.

Finally, in constructing true-false items, try to avoid trick questions, especially those in which a negative statement is used. The following examples show the use of trick questions:

1. Plants, like orchids, growing in high cold areas are often short and dense.
2. One of the evidences that Earth is rotating on its axis is day and night with the Sun appearing to rise in the west and set in the east.

In the first case, the trick is the identification of orchids as growing in high cold areas. In the second case all is well except for the Sun appearing to rise in the west. The only purpose for the inclusion of this type of information is to trick the reader into an incorrect response to the question.

In general, when constructing true-false items, pose the question clearly, concisely, and without tricks that are simply there to confuse the learner. The items should be such that those who know the information will see the truth or falsity of the item and those who do not will find the incorrect answer as plausible as the correct one.

Developing Multiple Choice Items.   Multiple choice tests are probably the most commonly used type of test. The questions tend to be straightforward and can be written so that anything from factual knowledge to the evaluation of knowledge can be evaluated (Killoran, 1992). **Multiple choice items** consist of a stem and a list of possible responses from which the student selects the single response that completes the statement begun in the stem or answers the question posed by the stem. In developing a multiple choice item, the first step is to develop a question or an incomplete sentence. This question or incomplete sentence forms the stem of the item. Once the stem has been written, state the answer to the question or complete the statement in as few words as needed to make the answer clear. Finally, develop a few good answers to the question or completions to the sentence. Good multiple choice items deal with important ideas and frequently with the use of those ideas, rather than with trivial facts or simple definitions of terms.

Probably the most difficult aspect of developing multiple choice items is the production of alternative responses. Those responses must be plausible so the student must discriminate among the answers in order to determine the best possible response. Consider each of the following multiple choice items:

1. Clocks with second hands were first used in:
   a. 1860.
   b. 1680.
   c. 1960.
   d. 1780.
2. In 1815 Humphrey Davy invented the safety lamp. This invention:
   a. earned him very little money.
   b. stopped house fires.
   c. stopped electrical shocks from lamps.
   d. made coal mining safer.
3. Which of the following probably caused the greatest changes in the length of life in the twentieth century?
   a. the availability of accurate information on nutrition.
   b. the development of antibiotics and vaccines.
   c. the use of more vitamins in the diet.
   d. the use of better preservation techniques for food.

Item 1 is a simple request for recall of a date. The item is poor, however, not simply because it asks for simple recall but also because it asks for the recall of trivial information. The mental answer to this particular question is likely to be "who cares." In item 2, the information is not trivial. The problem is that anyone with even a little knowledge of the safety lamp will be able to select the correct answer because the others are unlikely answers. Item 3 is an appropriately constructed multiple choice item. The information is of some importance and the responses are all plausible.

All of these kinds of assessments are used in schools. What we need to consider is how to organize that information so it can be used effectively in evaluating students for reporting purposes. Activity 9.1 looks at the kinds of assessment strategies found in science textbooks, while Activity 9.2 involves you in developing assessments appropriate to a unit plan.

Assessing Science Learning Activities

Activity 9.1

Purpose To investigate the kinds of evaluation strategies advocated by a science textbook.

Procedure
1. Obtain a science textbook for any grade from first through eighth. You will need the teacher's edition and any additional evaluation materials that may be a part of the series.
2. Read through the sections dealing with evaluating the learning taking place.
   a. What kinds of strategies are represented?
   b. What is the predominant evaluation strategy shown in the textbook?
   c. How appropriate are the strategies to the age of the students who would be using the textbook?
   d. Do the evaluation strategies represent the focus of the textbook as described in the introductory materials? Why or why not?
   e. Consider any tests or quizzes used in the book.
      (1) What kinds of questions are used?
      (2) According to the cognitive taxonomy, what levels are represented by the kinds of questions?
   f. How does the textbook use checklists, teacher observation, rubrics, or activity results in evaluation?
   g. What suggestions would you make for improving the evaluation used in the textbook?

Activity 9.2

Purpose   To design evaluation strategies appropriate to a unit plan or text-book.

Procedure
1. Using either the unit plan developed as a part of Chapter 8 or a textbook unit, develop an example of any of the following evaluation strategies that would be appropriate to the unit topic, activities, and grade level:
   a. anecdotal records
   b. teacher observation
   c. checklists
   d. interviews
   e. rubrics
   f. activity results
   g. journals
   h. test or quiz
2. Show where each would be appropriately used in the unit plan or text-book.

Organizing in Traditional Assessment

Traditional assessment generally involves determining which children have reached particular objectives at a particular time and which children have not reached those objectives. The results of these assessments are then used in assigning grades to students.

There is no standard way of grading students. School systems generally have their own practices and guidelines. In some settings, a standard scale is given to teachers: 92–100% is and A, 82–91% is a B, and so on. In other settings the teacher determines the level necessary for a student to "pass" a subject area. In some school systems, teachers are required to give a "daily grade," that is, to have an evaluation recorded for every subject area taught every day. In other school systems, the teachers decide how often they will evaluate their students. In nearly all cases, the teachers in a school keep a grade book, either paper or electronic, that shows each student's records in a subject matter area. As a new teacher, you need to learn the requirements of your school and school system.

No matter what the requirements of your school or school system, there are some points to keep in mind in working with a traditional evaluation system. First, be certain your objectives are clearly stated and your evaluations are determining whether or not students have met those objectives. As mentioned in Chapter 8, in lesson planning the objective and the evaluation of a lesson should sound redundant. Second, be certain the evaluation strategy selected is the best for evaluating the objective. A pencil and paper test is appropriate for determining whether or not your students can define terms. A rubric is appropriate for looking at a finished project. An interview is appropriate for evaluating understanding. Just because the evaluation is considered to be traditional does not mean only pencil and paper tests are used. Third, be certain your evaluation strategies evaluate all aspects of your science program. Evaluate process skills, investigative abilities, and content. Just because the evaluation is traditional does not mean that only science content should be evaluated. Fourth, use variety in your evaluation. Your students will come from a variety of different backgrounds. Your students will have a variety of different intelligences. Your students may be at different levels of cognitive development even though they are in the same grade level. Using a variety of different evaluation strategies allows students to demonstrate their accomplishments in ways appropriate to them. Fifth, use forms of evaluation that are cognitively appropriate to your students. Using written tests with young children is not appropriate. Using checklists and anecdotal records as well as interviews is appropriate. And, finally, not everything needs to be evaluated. In the case of evaluation, quality is far more important than quantity.

Assigning grades to students is one of the most difficult tasks of a teacher. In using traditional evaluation, assigning grades is based on attainment of objectives. Students who reach our objectives receive high grades. Students who do not reach our objectives receive lower grades. As a teacher you will not be doing yourself or your students any favors by allowing students who have not reached your objectives to pass a particular subject area.

If that sounds harsh, it is. But it also indicates one of the difficulties with traditional assessment. Traditional assessment is based on criteria external to the learners. Traditional assessment is based on the idea that all learners can and should reach those external criteria at the same time. Nontraditional assessments have evolved in response to this concept of all students reaching the same point at the same time.

Organizing in Nontraditional Assessment: Portfolios

A **portfolio** is a collection of a student's achievements over a period of time as shown by a variety of different examples of student work. The main purpose of the portfolio is to show an individual student's growth over a period of time. Consequently, the portfolio is not used to determine whether students have reached particular objectives at specified times, but rather how far students have progressed as they move toward objectives at their own pace.

The portfolio is particularly useful for students from diverse cultural backgrounds, students with learning problems, and gifted students (Tippins and Dana, 1992). Students from diverse backgrounds, particularly those with limited English language skills, are frequently unable to demonstrate their actual level of learning on pencil and paper forms of evaluation. Additionally, students from culturally diverse or disadvantaged backgrounds often face testing situations with greater dread than do students from the cultural mainstream or from advantaged backgrounds. This dread of tests often results in test scores that are lower than those of other students and so do not show the learner's true achievements. The portfolio allows the learner who is unable to perform well on a traditional form of evaluation to demonstrate growth in learning in other ways. For the student who is mentally retarded or learning disabled, the use of the portfolio can give a more realistic picture of the student's learning. For the learner who is mentally retarded, the portfolio can show learning based on the individual's starting point rather than on some criterion established for average learners. A student's progress toward the goals established for that individual can be easily demonstrated. Students with learning disabilities that make it difficult for them to demonstrate learning through written formats can show their achievement through drawings, audiotapes, videotapes, and projects. And, finally, the gifted student has the opportunity through the portfolio to show areas of outstanding achievement which go beyond that commonly shown by the students in a class or measured by a standard test situation. In particular, gifted learners with musical or bodily intelligence can be shown in performance rather than in a static pencil or pen mark on a piece of paper. The portfolio gives all students an opportunity to document their learning in science (Perrone, 1991; Rezba et al., 1995; Engle, 1990; Grace and Shores, 1992).

Portfolio Components

In order to be meaningful, a portfolio should show a wide variety of materials. Those materials can include all of the traditional forms of assessment described previously as well as the following items, which are generally not a part of traditional evaluation (Paulson et al., 1991; Danielson and Abrutyn, 1997).

Work Samples.   Samples of student work should form the bulk of the portfolio. **Work samples** include writing samples, both rough drafts and finished products; drawings; photographs of projects including students at work on those projects and the finished project, photographs of students working in heterogeneous, homogeneous, or cooperative groups; copies of reports, papers, or journal pages; and tape recordings or videotapes of students reading or presenting their work.

Rating Scales.   Rating scales can be included in the portfolio when a behavior has several different aspects or components. In a **rating scale** each behavior is rated on a continuum from the lowest to the highest level and is marked off at certain points along the scale. A rating scale can be used to observe a child's work with other children in interdisciplinary activities or can be used to show progress for an individual child. For example, a rating scale could be used in assessing the student's progress in writing a science research paper at the seventh grade level. In this case the rating scale could include such items as *uses only one source* to *uses a variety of sources; presents only one draft* to *revises first draft;* or *does not check for accuracy of spelling or punctuation* to *checks spelling or punctuation before turning in paper.* The rating scale is most effective if it is used with similar types of work over a period of time and is attached to the work sample so that the progress can be documented.

Peer Reviews.   As students progress through the grades, they should become more able to listen to and provide feedback to their peers. A **peer review** is an assessment of a student's work done by the other students in the class. As students engage in giving reports, peers can provide written reviews of the reports. As students work in heterogeneous, homogeneous, or cooperative groups, they can provide feedback to one another of individual work within the group as well as the work of the group as a whole.

Group Reports and Projects.   Students working in groups, whether cooperative or otherwise, often produce group reports or group projects. If the product of the group's work is a written document, copies of that document can be placed in the portfolio for each member of the group. The inclusion of a group report will be most helpful if it is accompanied by peer reviews that discuss the work of individual and group members while working on the report. If a project is the result of the group work, photographs or tapes of the project can be most effective in documenting the work of the students.

Computer Printouts.   For students who are involved in the use of computer technology in the classroom, examples of their work and of their work in progress as documented by computer printouts should be included in the portfolio.

Student Reflections.   The development of the portfolio is accomplished through joint participation of the student and the teacher. A **student reflection** is the student's own evaluation of the samples of work included in his or her portfolio. Student reflections develop the student's ability to self-assess. For a young child, this may simply be a comment that one picture is better than another or that one report of an investigation is better than another. Also effective for young children is an interview in which the child talks about his or her work and the record of that interview is included into the portfolio as the student reflection. For the older student, the self-assessment should ask the child to indicate why he or she views one piece of work as better than another. Additionally, the child should have the opportunity to comment on work that is not successful and to comment on why the work sample was unsuccessful.

Photographs.   Photographs of students at work can effectively document the course of an investigation or experiment. Photographs can also document the development of a project such as a mural of the solar system from the planning stages, to the drawing stages, to the completed mural. And, finally, photographs can also provide documentation of science fair projects or culminating projects for a unit. The best use of photographic evidence are photographs that show how the project or activity developed from planning to final stages.

Videotapes.   Videotapes can be particularly useful in documenting group work as they can not only show the physical activity of the students involved in the group but can also capture the discussion occurring as the group works. Videotapes can also be useful in documenting oral presentations, class discussions, and other activities that include both a verbal and physical component.

When used most effectively, the portfolio is an ongoing assessment of the student's progress that develops continuously over the child's school career. It is a record of the child's growth from topic to topic, project to project, year to year. It is the ultimate in cumulative records for the student's educational career.

Using the Portfolio in Evaluation

Evaluating the Curriculum.   The portfolio, unlike simple, traditional forms of evaluation, can be used not only to determine student achievement and communicate that to parents, but also to evaluate the effectiveness of teaching strategies and the total science curriculum program. In looking at teaching strategies, the portfolio gives you an opportunity to view the results of your teaching, to see if it was effective or ineffective, and to see if you present some areas of study more effectively than others. The portfolio is a longitudinal record that gives you an opportunity to assess the development of research skills, group work skills, and thinking skills in your students over time. It gives you an opportunity to assess the effectiveness of the activities and procedures you selected for teaching in terms of the effect of those procedures and activities on student learning. This ability to evaluate the success of your teaching strategies and activities will result in more reflective thinking on your part and in a greater likelihood that you will become aware of needed changes in your presentation of a unit of work (Kulm and Malcolm, 1992).

Teacher Evaluation of the Portfolio.   The portfolio is also used to evaluate the achievement of an individual learner. The most appropriate use you can make of the portfolio is in making comparisons between the student's current work and his or her earlier work. A portfolio is designed to compare a student's work at the start of the year to that same student's work as the year progresses. A portfolio is not designed to allow comparison of one student with another and, in fact, the portfolio should never be used to make such student-to-student comparisons.

In using a portfolio to assess the learning taking place over the course of a year, the first step is to establish the learning objectives for that year. Without a clear concept of where your students are going, it is impossible to determine whether or not progress is being made. Once you establish objectives, you can look at the progress of students in terms of those objectives.

In order to assess the child, look at the examples of work in the portfolio and note areas of strong progress and areas of little or no progress. When you find areas of weakness, you can use the checklists, anecdotal records, and work samples contained in the portfolio to determine whether the student is participating fully in activities that will allow him or her to strengthen areas of weakness. If your additional observations show the student is participating in classroom activities that address the areas of weakness, you might use greater observation of the student during those activities as well as interviews with the child to determine why there are difficulties. If the student is not participating in activities that will strengthen areas of weakness, you need to determine why the student is not participating and find ways to encourage greater participation. At times, you will discover areas of weakness on the part of a student that are not being addressed by the current grade-level program. For example, a student did not learn about vertebrate animals in the fifth grade and so when humans are presented as vertebrates in the sixth grade the student is at a loss. When this is the case, you may wish to develop some independent projects for the learner so he or she can develop in a particular area. When you find areas of weakness among students from diverse backgrounds, give attention to developing culturally appropriate materials and projects as well how to remediate areas of difficulty. And when you find weakness in an area among the majority of class members, go back and look at your own teaching strategies in that area in order to develop more appropriate and effective methods of teaching. Sometimes you will even find it necessary to reteach certain areas so that students can develop the needed skills. When evaluation shows a weakness, the third grade teacher cannot blame the second grade teacher for not having taught the material and the eighth grade teacher cannot blame the entire elementary school program for not having taught the material and then go on to something new. No matter what the grade level at which material *should* have been taught, it is the responsibility of the teacher who discovers the area of deficiency to reteach concepts or skills that are missing.

Discussing the Portfolio with Students and Parents. As the teacher you should not only evaluate the portfolio for your benefit, but also discuss the work in the portfolio with the student. Learners benefit from reviewing their work over a lengthy period of time. It gives them a chance to see how much they have learned, to receive praise for their accomplishments, and to develop an understanding of why certain areas are being emphasized in current work. Students, no matter what the grade level, need to know why they are being asked to perform certain tasks, particularly when those tasks are remedial in nature.

Discuss the portfolio with the parents as a means of demonstrating the child's learning over a period of time. The first task in working with portfolio assessment with parents is to be certain they understand its use. Most parents are not familiar with the idea of a portfolio. Their concept of assessment is likely to be grades, tests, and passing or failing. Parents need to be educated in the use of a portfolio. When discussing the portfolio with parents, begin by helping parents understand what the portfolio is designed to do, and then show the parents the objectives that are being evaluated through the portfolio. Use the objectives in conjunction with the work samples to demonstrate areas of strength, areas of weakness, and progress over time. Discuss the work samples so that parents understand the purpose of the activity within the program, the strengths and weaknesses shown in the work samples, and your reasons for indicating that growth in a particular area is showing strength or weakness. Always remember to show those work samples to the parents within the context of the goals and objectives of the total science program. For example, if an objective of the program is to develop in seventh grade students the ability to conduct a true experiment, discuss the goal with the parents to be certain they understand what is meant, show the parents some of the examples of work demonstrating the student's use of experiments, and discuss specific changes in the student's ability to do an experiment.

When you present the assessment portfolio to parents, make sure you do not use the contents of the portfolio to compare one child to another. The purpose of the portfolio is to demonstrate an individual child's growth within the program over time, not to demonstrate that one child is progressing faster or slower than another child within the program.

Portfolios as Permanent Records. There is one last area in which the contents of the portfolio can be useful to others besides you, as the current teacher, the student, and the student's parents. The contents of the portfolio should also be discussed with the teacher who will have the student at the next grade level. The student's portfolio can be used to demonstrate effectively the achievement and progress made at the current grade level and can assist the teacher at the next grade level in developing appropriate learning materials for the student. If used appropriately, the portfolio can add yet another dimension to the planning done from one grade level to another and can enhance the cohesiveness of the total school program. If the portfolio is used appropriately, then the portfolio should be added to continuously as the child progresses through school (Wolf, 1989).

Technology and the Portfolio. If the portfolio is used as a truly cumulative record of student progress, then it should be added to each year the child is in school. One consequence of this continual addition process is that the contents of the portfolio grow ever more extensive and so become bulky and difficult to store. A technological alternative to the paper portfolio is a **laser disk portfolio** in which the contents of the paper portfolio are transferred to a single laser disk. The laser disk can be used to record anything from scanned images of a student's written work to videotapes of the student reading aloud, working in a cooperative group to carry out an investigation, or creating a mural (Campbell, 1992). Large amounts of data can be added to or retrieved from a disk with great ease. The disk itself, however, is so small that it can be stored with far more efficiency than a paper portfolio. The use of computer technology can allow for the development of a truly cumulative record that is also easy to handle.

Summary

One of the most difficult tasks the teacher must face is evaluating student achievement. In traditional forms of evaluation, tests and quizzes are given priority. Such forms of evaluation give the teacher immediate information about achievement at a particular point in time.

The construction of tests and quizzes is not an easy task. The teacher frequently leaves that construction to the last minute and so the test or quiz produced may reflect what is easily recalled and easily tested. A more appropriate means of test construction is through a table of specifications that allows the teacher to analyze the content to be tested, determine the emphasis to be placed on each topic within the content, consider the kinds of questions to be asked, and decide on the number of questions of each type to be asked. In this way, the test is more likely to reflect the content of the unit or lesson being evaluated.

Two difficulties with pencil and paper forms of evaluation is that they do not assess all of the types of learning taking place within the interdisciplinary social studies curriculum, nor do they demonstrate the child's progress over time. In order to assess all facets of the program adequately and to show the child's progress over time, the portfolio is developed. A portfolio can include tests and quizzes but also includes a variety of other materials: observational checklists, anecdotes, videotapes, audiotapes, photographs, peer reviews, and self-reflections, among other items. The portfolio is then used to discuss the child's progress with the child as well as with the parents of the child and the teachers in succeeding grades.

In its most appropriate form, the portfolio is cumulative over the child's school career. Because a truly cumulative portfolio can become quite bulky, the laser disk can provide compact means for portfolio production, storage, and retrieval.

Chapter Vocabulary

The number following each term refers to the page on which the term was first introduced.

Activity results, 275
Anecdotal records, 269
Checklists, 271
Essay questions, 280
Interviews, 271
Journal, 278
Laser disk portfolio, 290
Multiple choice items, 282
Nontraditional evaluation, 268
Peer reviews, 286
Portfolio, 285

Rating scale, 286
Rubrics, 273
Scientifically correct, 276
Scientifically dishonest, 278
Scientifically incorrect, 277
Student reflections, 287
Teacher observation, 270
Tests and quizzes, 278
Traditional evaluation, 268
True-false items, 280
Work sample, 286

Applying the CONCEPTS

1. As a first grade teacher, you use teacher observation, checklists, anecdotal records, and interviews to evaluate your students rather than the more traditional worksheets and tests. During parents' night some of the parents question your kinds of evaluation, stating they want to see more tests because that's what they had when they were in school. How would you respond to these parents?

2. As an eighth grade science teacher, you see the advantages of portfolio evaluation but your school still requires you to give a grade every six weeks. What might you do to combine portfolio evaluation with the traditional giving of grades?

3. As you review the portfolios for the children in your fourth grade class, you notice a group of students having difficulty with graphing, another having difficulty with drawing conclusions from data, and a third group showing some misconceptions about sound energy. How could you use this information in planning for your next unit on energy and motion?

4. Your principal has made it very clear that you are to use the tests that come with your science textbook when you evaluate your students in science. As you review those tests you notice that they mainly deal with the vocabulary in the unit and that none of the tests deals

with the science process skills. What could you do that will allow you to follow the directions of your principal but also evaluate more effectively? What might you do to change the principal's mind about using the book's tests as the sole source of evaluation?

References

Campbell, J. 1992. Laser disk portfolios: Total child assessment. *Educational Leadership* 49, 69–70.

Correro, G. 1988. *Understanding assessment in young children. Developing instructional programs K–3.* Jackson, Mississippi Department of Education.

Danielson, C., and L. Abrutyn.1997. *An introduction to using portfolios in the classroom.* Alexandria, Va.: Association for Supervision and Curriculum Development.

Dorr-Bremme, D. W. 1983. Assessing students: Teachers' routine practices and reasoning. *Evaluation Comment* 6, UCLA Center for the Study of Evaluation.

Ebel, R. L., and D. A. Frisbie. 1986. *Essentials of educational measurement* (4th ed.). Englewood Cliffs, N.J.: Prentice Hall

Engle, B. 1990. An approach to assessment in early grades. In C. Kamii (ed.), *Achievement testing in the early grades: The games grown-ups play.* Washington, D.C.: National Association for the Education of Young Children.

Grace, C., and E. F. Shores. 1992. *The portfolio and its use: Developmentally appropriate assessment of young children.* Little Rock, Ark.: Southern Association of Children Under Six.

Haney, W., and G. Madus. 1989, May. Searching for alternatives to standardized tests. *Phi Delta Kappan* 684.

Hart, D. 1994. *Authentic assessment: A handbook for educators.* Menlo Park, Calif.: Addison-Wesley.

Hein, G. E., and S. Price. 1994. *Active assessment for active science.* Portsmouth, N.H: Heinemann.

Killoran, J. 1992, February. In defense of the multiple-choice question. *Social Education* 108.

Kubiszyn, T., and G. Borich. 1996. *Educational testing and measurement: Classroom application and practice* (5th ed.). New York: HarperCollins.

Kulm, G., and S. M. Malcom. 1992. *Science assessment in the service of reform.* Washington, D.C.: American Association for the Advancement of Science.

Maeroff, G. I. 1991, December. Assessing alternative assessment. *Phi Delta Kappan,* 278.

National Association for the Education of Young Children. 1988. *Statement on standardized testing of young children 3 through 8 years of age.* Washington, D.C.: Author.

National Association for the Education of Young Children and Early Childhood Specialists in Departments of Education. 1989. *Guidelines for appropriate curriculum content and assessment in programs serving children age 3 through 8.* Washington, D.C.: Author.

Paulson, F. L., P. R. Paulson, and C. A. Meyer. 1991. What makes a portfolio a portfolio. *Educational Leadership* 48, 802–806.

Perrone, V. (ed.). 1991. *Expanding student assessment.* Alexandria, Va.: Association for Supervision and Curriculum Development.

Rezba, R. J., C. Sprague, R. L. Fiel, and H. J. Funk. 1995. *Learning and assessing science process skills* (3rd. ed.). Dubuque, Iowa: Kendall-Hunt.

Southern Association on Children Under Six. 1990. *Developmentally appropriate assessment.* Little Rock, Ark.: Author.

Tippins, D. J., and N. F. Dana. 1992, March. Culturally relevant alternative assessment, *Science Scope* 51.

Wesman, A. G. 1971. Writing the test item. In R .L. Thorndike (ed.), *Educational measurement* (2nd ed.). Washington, D.C.: American Council on Education.

Wiggins, G. 1989, May. A true test: Toward more authentic and equitable assessment. *Phi Delta Kappan* 703–704.

Wiggins, G. 1992. Creating tests worth taking. *Educational Leadership* 49, 26.

Wolf, D. P. 1989, May. Portfolio assessment: Sampling student work. *Educational Leadership* 46, 36–38.

Chapter Ten

The Inclusive Classroom

Chapter Objectives

Upon completion of this chapter you should be able to:

1 describe the public laws that have resulted in the inclusion of disabled children in the regular classroom.

2 discuss the reasons for including science in the education of all children.

3 define and discuss the terms *inclusion* and *collaborative program*.

4 discuss the inclusion of culturally different and gifted children in the regular classroom.

5 describe the use of cooperative learning within the science classroom.

Introduction

"When I first started teaching, all the children in my class were pretty much the same. If there were children in the neighborhood who had problems, they either went to special private schools or they went to special classes in this school. I even remember a time when the "regular kids" came at 8:30 and the "special kids" came at 8:45. The 'special ed' classes were basically geared to children who were slow to learn. And I guess we assumed that any child with a handicap would be slow.

"Then I met Jerry. He had cerebral palsy affecting his right arm and leg and so was in the 'special ed' class. I didn't pay much attention until I realized Jerry was tutoring some of my 'average' kids in math. Something didn't fit. How could he be 'slow' and still be tutoring my kids?

"Now when I go into my classroom and look around, I see a lot of differences. My kids are not all the same. Joey has to use a walker to move from one place to another. Tamika has hearing aids and sits where she can see me and the board easily. Three of them have learning disabilities and Lisa is mentally impaired. The thing is, all of us are learning.

"Some of the other teachers are against including all children in classrooms, but I'm all for it. Whenever I have to make modifications to help my kids learn, I think back to Jerry. He's a doctor now."

Public Laws and the Inclusive Classroom

Mrs. Baker, the teacher just quoted began her teaching career in the late 1960s, a time of exclusion rather than inclusion. The changes in classrooms and in the way in which children with special learning needs are treated began in 1975 with **P.L. 94-142,** the Education for the Handicapped Act, which set federal guidelines for special education services. As a part of this act, the categories of disabilities were described, the services to which students might be entitled were clarified, and the concept of **least restrictive environment** was mandated. It was this latter concept, least restrictive environment, that began the changes from special classes for special students to educating special needs students in the regular public school classroom through the use of **individual education programs (IEP).**

In 1986, **P.L. 99-457** was passed. This law extend the provisions of P.L. 94-142 to very young children: birth to 5 years of age. Because of the ages of the children involved, and because the parents of these children are their main teachers, this law focused on the family. In fact, education plans written under this law were designated individual family service plans.

And, in 1990, P.L. 101-476 was passed to reauthorize P.L. 94-142 and to change the name of this 1975 law to the Individuals with Disabilities Act (IDEA). This reauthorization made some significant changes in P.L. 94-142 as well. The first was a change in terminology in which *disability* replaced the word *handicapped*. The other change was that autism and traumatic brain injury were added to the categories of disabilities (Ballard et al., 1987; U.S. Department of Education, 1993).

These three laws set the stage for great changes in the way in which we educate children. They also implied that all children should be receiving an education in all subject matter areas, an implication that is a basic premise of the *National Science Education Standards* of 1995.

Why do all of our children need the opportunity to learn science? The answer is simple. All children who are educated in our schools will reach adulthood in the same highly technological society. In terms of the kinds of societal issues and problems children will face as adults, it makes no difference whether a child is hearing or visually impaired, orthopedically impaired, or having difficulty maintaining attention; whether a child is gifted or slower to learn; whether a child is from the mainstream culture or culturally different. The same kind of information will be needed by all children who as adults are confronted with problems of pollution, global warming, medical ethics, genetic research, or a hundred other issues. And because all of the children who will be the adults of the future need to have a basic education in science, you, as a science teacher, need to know when and how to adapt the teaching strategies used in science teaching to the variety of children in the classroom.

In this chapter we first consider science teaching and disabled children.   In order to look at this important area of science teaching, we consider the following:

1. the categories of special needs children according to P.L. 94-142.
2. the meaning of the terms *inclusion* and *collaborative programs*.
3. the use of IEPs and collaborative programs to make adaptations for special needs children.

Categories of Children with Special Needs

Children with Learning Disabilities

Children who are learning disabled are often confusing to teachers because they are of average intelligence or higher, learn some subject matter areas easily, but have great difficulty with other areas. Rather than experiencing difficulty in learning because of intellectual or sensory deficits, students who are **learning disabled** experience difficulties due to problems in information processing. That is, they have difficulty with attention or with perception, memory, or expressive language. In addition, learning disabled students may use poor strategies for learning. For example, students may be passive rather than active learners who watch as others work with materials rather than getting involved themselves. Consequently, the learning disabled student may fall short of teacher or parental expectations or may experience high levels of success in one area while simultaneously failing in another. The achievement of a learning disabled student may also vary from day to day so that one day is filled with success after success and the next day is filled with failure after failure. And, at times, the information learned one day may not be recalled the next (Lerner, 1989).

Learning disabled students typically experience difficulty in one of the more basic of the school subjects: reading, language, or mathematics. In fact, reading is the major problem area for learning disabled elementary school children, with mathematics and handwriting as other areas of particular difficulty (Lerner, 1989).

In addition to difficulties with specific subject matter areas, some learning disabled students show high levels of activity in the classroom. These children seem to be constantly in motion and so may have difficulty sitting still, listening, or paying attention to school tasks. Others, although not overly active, may be impulsive or easily distracted by activities and children around them. Highly distractible children generally have difficulty focusing their attention on the task-oriented aspects of their learning environment, on the specific lessons and activities used to teach those lessons. As children move into the upper elementary grades, those with learning disabilities may be unable to work independently, often because their organizational skills are poor. This leads, then, to poor academic skills (Lerner, 1989).

Two recent additions to the terminology of learning disabilities are attention deficit disorder (ADD) and attention deficit hyperactivity disorder (ADHD). ADD is characterized by inattention, distractibility, impulsivity, and in attention deficit hyperactivity disorder (ADHD), hyperactivity. However, children who show these characteristics should not automatically be labeled as ADD or ADHD because these same traits may be indicative of environmental factors or of children resisting a particularly inappropriate learning experience. Children from backgrounds where they are not expected to sit quietly or where impulsiveness is not seen as a problem may not have gained the skills necessary to conform to school rules in these areas. Additionally, very young children who are expected to sit for long periods of time, attending to tasks involving written or verbal information, and without talking to one another may exhibit the same traits of restlessness, inattention, and distractibility sometimes used to identify learning disabled children.

Children with Mental Impairments

Children who are mildly impaired have learning problems that affect all academic areas. Children who are **mentally impaired** generally have problems both in learning and in social interactions. When it comes to social interaction, children who are mildly impaired may not meet the standards of personal independence or social responsibility found in other children from the age group and cultural group (Jones, 1992). It is not only the school environment that causes difficulties but the social environment as a whole. Because the total social environment is included in assessing a child's behavior, the child's cultural background must be taken into account. For example, European American children are expected to be active, to ask questions, and to participate in discussions with adults and Asian American children are expected to be quiet, obedient, and to listen to adults without asking questions or joining discussions. Quiet obedience would be an appropriate behavioral pattern for an academically challenged Asian American child, but it may be an inappropriate behavioral pattern for a European American child (Slavin, 1989; McCormick, 1990).

Mentally impaired children generally enter school behind their average peers in terms of academics and developmental level. Consequently, they are generally not ready at the kindergarten or first grade levels to begin standard academic instruction. This does not mean these children will not acquire basic school skills. They do. It simply means they may need to begin those skills at a later age level than average children and that they will take longer to master basic academic skills (Kitano, 1989). By the conclusion of their academic careers, most mentally impaired children have attained upper elementary level skills in reading and mathematics. Consequently, mentally impaired children are frequently mainstreamed into the regular classroom as their least restrictive learning environment but have additional assistance in academic work through resource teachers.

In some areas, the school experience is particularly challenging for mentally impaired children. These children may have particular difficulty in focusing attention, remembering information, and transferring skills and concepts learned in one situation to another. Tasks that involve abstract reasoning, problem solving, or creativity pose particular problems for academically challenged children. Abstract reasoning is an area of particular difficulty because academically challenged children do not reach the level of formal operational thought necessary for true logical thought.

Children with Sensory Impairments

The **sensory impaired** category includes children with hearing impairments, visual impairments, children with speech or language impairments, and deaf-blind children. Visually impaired children are generally classified as blind or low vision. Blind individuals are those who receive so little information through their sense of sight that they must learn through their other senses. Students with low vision, however, are able to use their residual vision to learn. In the regular classroom, students with vision problems may require assistance in learning to move about the classroom and the school. Such impaired children may also need encouragement in order to interact with their sighted peers.

Children with hearing impairments may be deaf or hard of hearing. Hard of hearing individuals hear well enough to understand speech, usually with the assistance of a hearing aid. But deaf students receive so little information through their sense of hearing that speech comprehension cannot occur through hearing. For the hearing impaired child, difficulty in speech and language development is the major educational problem. Consequently, children with hearing losses may be academically delayed in subjects related to language, such as reading, spelling, or written expression.

Children with Orthopedic Impairments

Although the orthopedically impaired is a small group, it is an exceptionally diverse group; physical and health disabilities encompass a wide variety of different conditions and disabilities ranging from invisible to obvious, from mild to severe. Children who are **orthpedically impaired** include those with functional limitations such as body control, hand use, or mobility as well as children with medical conditions that affect strength and stamina. Physically disabled students may also include children with missing limbs, spinal cord injuries causing paralysis, and muscular dystrophy. Two of the most common physical problems are cerebral palsy and epilepsy. In addition, health disorders such as diabetes, heart conditions, asthma, hemophilia, cancer, and AIDS may also cause children to be physically disabled.

A child who has an orthopedic disability is not necessarily a handicapped child. A disability results in impairment of function. A child who is in a wheelchair has a disability. When the disability interferes with the child's ability to function in a particular situation, it becomes a handicap. The disabled child in the wheelchair becomes handicapped when he or she cannot easily enter the school building or cannot reach the materials needed to complete a science project because they are on too high a shelf. A child with cerebral palsy becomes handicapped when he or she cannot reach needed research materials because they are behind a door the child cannot open due to lack of hand or arm strength.

In the regular classroom, students with physical or health disorders may encounter few if any academic problems. If special needs do arise, they are more likely to involve physical or social problems. Students who use wheelchairs, walkers, or canes may need to have the physical environment modified so there is space for them to maneuver easily and materials are easily accessible. If academic difficulties occur, they are generally due to missing school rather than to slow learning due to the disabling condition.

Children with Traumatic Brain Injury

Traumatic brain injury includes children who have experienced serious head injuries from sports, falls, automobile accidents, bicycling accidents, or other accidents. These children have a wide range of characteristics. Some may have limited strength or alertness. Some may be developmentally delayed. Some may have short-term memory problems. In other cases, children with traumatic brain injury may have temporary vision or hearing problems or may be subject to irritability and sudden mood swings. The kinds of problems these children experience depends on the specific injury experienced and so it is important that the child's physician be consulted. And, finally, the needs of these children may change across time.

Children with Autism

Autistic children usually show a lack of social responsiveness beginning at a very early age. Often autistic children avoid eye contact and physical contact. As they mature, they have difficulty being aware of the feelings of others and usually try to avoid contact with peers. In addition, autistic children may show repetitive body movements, use unusual language patterns like repetition of other people's speech or their own, or may even lack speech. Autistic children often have behaviors that are routinized: how they take out books, how they fill out a paper, how they arrange their belongings, or even how they get dressed. These routinized behaviors allow the autistic child to feel comfortable.

Children with Serious Emotional Disturbance

Children with **serious emotional disturbance** often have difficulty with interpersonal relationships; they respond inappropriately in emotional situations, perhaps using violence as a response to teasing. Consequently, these children may have difficulty in making and keeping friends. However, not all children in this category act out behaviors; some show no emotion. They may show little or no emotion when a classmate is ill or injured. Children with serious emotional disturbance show their behaviors over a long period of time, in a variety of different settings, and are very different from their peers in their responses.

Children with Other Health Impairments

Some of the students we teach may have an illness or disorder that has an impact on their ability to learn. Children with severe asthma, with arthritis, with multiple sclerosis, or with hearing problems that require a modification of the physical education program or require long absences from school can fall into the category of **other health impairments.** The kinds of effects on learning depend on the kind of health problems. Consequently, the child's physician should always be consulted in working with these children (Fauvre, 1988).

Children with Multiple Disabilities

Children with **multiple disabilities** may be children who have an orthopedic impairment as well as a health impairment, children who are visually impaired as well as hearing impaired, or children who are mentally impaired as well as having a physical disability. This category is generally used only when it is impossible to separate the disabilities and so designate one as primary and others as secondary or tertiary.

Inclusion and Collaborative Programs

Inclusion brings children of all types into the regular classroom. In the inclusive classroom children with learning disabilities work alongside and with children with orthopedic impairments, children who are gifted work with children who are mentally impaired, and children who are average work with children who have visual impairments. Students who are included, rather than placed into special classes or pulled out of their classroom for special assistance, benefit from having more appropriate instruction and a less fragmented educational program (Algozzine, Morsink, and Algozzine, 1998; Raynes, Snell, and Sailor, 1991; Smith, 1998). Unlike students who were separated from their peers and labeled with words to identify their disabilities, students who are included in the regular classroom do not know the stigma of being labeled as different (Lilly, 1992). Students who are included but who cannot benefit completely from the academic program of the regular classroom still learn. These students have the opportunity to learn important social skills by observing their peers (Vandercook and York, 1989). But children who are interacting with their disabled peers also have opportunities for learning. In particular, nondisabled students are learning to view their disabled peers as peers and so begin to learn tolerance and acceptance (Bilken, Corrigan, and Quick, 1989). And, from the point of view of science education, students who are included are more likely to have a good science education program. In the past, when disabled students were isolated into special classes or pulled out of the regular classroom for special help, science was considered expendable and students rarely had a science program, let alone a good science program (Simpson and Myles, 1990). In essence, inclusion has benefits for all students rather than simply for those students with disabilities.

But even though inclusion creates a positive learning climate for all children, there is still a problem. The problem lies in creating appropriate educational experiences for all of the students in the classroom. Simply including children with disabilities is not enough. They must also receive an appropriate education. One way of assuring that disabled children receive appropriate educational experiences comes through the use of collaborative programs.

Collaborative Programs

Collaborative programs bring together classroom teachers, special educators, parents, counselors, and paraprofessionals as a team. The purpose of the team is to determine how to provide the best possible education for all of the students present in the inclusive classroom. The collaborative team works to identify the needs of the students, to design educational experiences to meet those needs, to provide assistance in the classroom, and to share their expertise with others. The final outcome of the collaboration is an educational program for each disabled child that can be implemented by the classroom teacher (Bailey et al., 1992).

The starting point for developing this appropriate program is the individualized education program (IEP) for the included student. An IEP is a plan developed for an individual child which shows the goals, strategies and evaluative measures that will be used to help the child reach a particular learning or behavioral need. Usually, the IEP has an annual goal as well as short-term objectives that a student will accomplish as he or she works toward the annual goal. The IEP often suggests modifications to classroom instruction that will be needed in working with the student (Friend and Bursuck, 1996; Waldron, 1996).

Once the IEP is written and accepted by the collaborative team, it is the teacher's turn. It is up to the teacher to implement the modifications to learning suggested by the IEP. How extensive are these modifications? It depends on the needs of the students (Cohen, 1991).

In Mr. Wilson's class, four students with disabilities are included. One of the students is autistic and the others have learning disabilities. On Friday, he meets with the special education resource teacher to show her the lessons planned for the following week. On Tuesday, the students will be conducting a hands-on investigation in which data will be collected and a conclusion drawn. The modifications suggested are relatively easy to make and use. On Tuesday, when Mr. Wilson hands out the data collection sheets for the investigation, most of the class receives the usual sheet with spaces for them to write their answers. The learning disabled students, who have difficulty with written communication, have sheets in which a variety of responses are provided and they need only underline the one that best suits the occurrences during the activity. The autistic student who does not have responsive language skills receives a sheet in which the responses are there and the student need only underline the description of what is occurring during the investigation.

This is a simple modification. All of the students receive a similar data collection sheet. The only difference is the kind of response required of the students. In other cases the modifications may be more extensive. Whether modest or extensive, the kinds of modifications are based on the characteristics of the students. Some of the kinds of modifications you may be expected to make are discussed next.

Some Specific Strategies for Children with Disabilities

Students with Learning Disabilities

In general, three types of strategies are commonly used with learning disabled student: prompts, additional instruction, and extra time (Lewis and Doorlag, 1989).

Prompts.   Prompts are features added to learning tasks that help learning disabled students focus attention on relevant instructional tasks. Prompts can provide additional structure to a learning task and so can help the student know exactly what to do. Prompts can include bold print, color coding of work sheets, dashed lines indicating how many letters a particular word has, or boxed areas to indicate where an answer should be placed.

Additional Instruction.   Learning disabled students with poor recall can be helped through additional guided practice or direct instruction. When using additional guided practice or additional direct instruction, break the subject matter down into small steps so information can be presented as slowly as necessary. Present the information in a way that differs from the first presentation rather than simply repeating the same information, in the same way, but in smaller steps. Several practice opportunities should be available to the student so that repeated exposure is given. Monitor practice opportunities through peer tutors, adult volunteers, or self-correcting materials in order to be certain practice materials are used effectively and in order to provide immediate reinforcement to the learning disabled child. Computer-based programs, especially tutorial programs, can also be beneficial here.

Additional Time.   For some of your learning disabled students, difficulty with reading or language or with maintaining attention may mean that the most important adaptation to the program will be additional time to complete assignments, particularly assessments and hands-on activities. Learning disabled students may also need a quiet place to work that is free of distraction. In addition to the quiet work location, your learning disabled students may need extra time to complete work both inside and outside of class. And, finally, if you have students who have particular problems with language, try using spelling dictionaries, typewriters, or word processors. Taped or oral tests may make test taking more appropriate for a learning disabled student.

In addition to general strategies that may make it easier for the learning disabled child to succeed, there are some specific strategies for working with learning disabled children who have reading difficulties. For your students who have difficulty with reading comprehension, try using an advance organizer to provide an overview before the student reads a passage. You may also want to try a list of questions to guide reading, a graphic organizer, or a prereading organizer to help your students. The SQ3R method for reading (discussed in Chapter 11) is particularly appropriate for helping a learning disabled student improve reading comprehension.

The ADD or ADHD child may pose additional problems over those of other learning disabled students. Helping these children learn to maintain attention may mean using a verbal clue to alert students to important verbal information (Forster and Doyle, 1989). Simply saying "listen" or "everyone ready?" or "let's get started" can help with directing attention to the task at hand. Once you have the attention of the students, present lessons at a brisk pace using a wide variety of instructional strategies. Include different kinds of questions, vary your tone of voice, and make certain students know you may ask questions at any time. As students start to shift attention from a task, moving closer to the student is useful in regaining a student's attention.

The IEP is particularly important with children with learning disabilities, because this category covers a great many learning problems. With learning disabled students a blanket approach to changing instruction is not appropriate.

Children with Mental Impairments

Mentally impaired children are able to learn but their learning is at a slower pace than that of children of average ability. As a consequence, mentally impaired children often perform at a level expected of younger children. Because it is difficult for these students to learn, their instruction must focus on areas that will help them become more self-sufficient (Cartwright, et al.,1989). A science program that allows children to demonstrate the application of academic skills to the solution of problems rather than the isolation and memorization of specific skills is particularly appropriate to these children.

Certain techniques are useful in working with mentally impaired children. When it comes to applying the basic skills of reading, writing, and mathematics to science learning, a science program that includes reading, writing, and mathematics as a natural part of the program allows the student to develop these skills in context rather than in isolation. Mentally impaired children should be provided with a variety of opportunities for practice of a skill in context. Finally, break instructional tasks into small steps sequenced to allow for learning ease. This also includes developing alternative activities for children who are not yet able to complete the more standard age- or grade-appropriate tasks. For example, at the seventh grade level when other students are investigating through the use of an experiment, a mentally impaired child may be conducting an investigation of an operational question (Bauer and Shea, 1989; Lewis and Doorlag, 1991).

For the mentally impaired child, your most appropriate teaching strategies will be those that allow the child to work directly with concrete materials. If you must use verbal materials, be certain your content is well sequenced and presented in small steps with much repetition and practice. When you use verbal presentations, base them on the concrete experiences the child has already had. As you can see, hands-on science is appropriate for mentally impaired children. However, when you use hands-on activities with these children, be certain the activities are appropriate. Appropriateness can be accomplished, first, by making activities open ended so the mentally impaired student is able to carry the activity as far as he or she can while allowing other students to carry the activity further. Second, use familiar materials to illustrate new concepts. The mentally impaired child should not need to accommodate to new and different materials while at the same time attempting to learn new content information from those materials. Third, if an activity is lengthy, break it into small steps, each one easily completed and understood. And, finally, using small groups or cooperative learning groups with mentally impaired students is a good strategy. In this way the mentally impaired students have the assistance and support of other group members. The key is to select the group members carefully so all are fully included in the group work.

Children with Sensory Impairments

For the visually impaired child, teaching strategies that involve the student with concrete materials are vital. Through hands-on experiences, visually impaired children are able to construct a mental image through their tactile experiences. Once a concept is constructed through first-hand experience, you can introduce verbal materials. If you must use verbal instruction, be careful to explain concepts clearly and in detail, and be certain not to draw or write anything on the chalkboard or overhead projector without also giving a detailed verbal description (Ireland, Wrais, and Flexler, 1988). Additionally, giving a visually impaired student a model to handle during a verbal explanation is often helpful. Describe the structure of a flower while a student has a chance to touch a large model of a flower.

When you use hands-on activities in the science program, few adaptations will be needed. No evidence indicates the visually impaired child is more prone to accidents than the nonimpaired child, so there is no reason to limit interaction with materials. Instructions for activities can be tape-recorded, provided in large print, or in Braille depending on the child's ability. When you are using concrete materials, students with visual impairments may need to work with a partner or partners so the activity can be carried out as effectively as possible. Once again, small groups and cooperative learning groups are particularly effective. You may also want to provide materials especially developed for the visually impaired including maps and globes with strong relief, rulers and measuring devices with raised gradations, or plastic rather than metal or glass objects. You may also need to provide a substitute activity if the predominant sense used in the activity is sight. This adaptation may be as simple as providing a model with raised relief rather than topographic map or as extensive as developing an entirely different activity for the child.

Probably the greatest adaptation needed for visually impaired children is in printed materials. However, textbooks and trade books are available in Braille for the child who is able to read Braille, in large print, or on tape. Computer-aided devices can scan written materials to show enlarged print on a screen. In some cases you may need to provide audiotapes for a child. You may also want to provide a scribe or a tape recorder for visually impaired children to make records of their activities.

As with visually impaired children, concrete, hands-on techniques are highly appropriate for children with hearing impairments. Hands-on techniques provide the direct, visual experiences hearing impaired children need in order to construct concepts. In using verbal teaching strategies, constantly and consistently enhance your presentations with illustrations, pictures, drawings, models, charts, and graphs. When using films, screen the film prior to classroom use in order to determine whether the hearing impaired child will be able to gain the concepts from the visual portion of the film. If not, you may want to provide written materials before showing the film in order to make the film more comprehensible. When classroom discussions are held, encourage hearing impaired children to participate orally with the teacher repeating comments that may not be understood by others in the class. If you have a student who is unable to speak clearly, encourage him or her to write comments or questions that are read to the class by the teacher or another student. If an interpreter is in the classroom in order to assist the deaf child who uses manual communication (sign language), the interpreter should convey the child's comments orally to the class.

Children with Orthopedic Impairments

The orthopedically impaired child generally needs no adaptation of teaching strategies used in the classroom. Only in a case where you have a child with limited mobility of the head and neck might you need to make some adaptations of your teaching methods. The main change is to stay within the child's view rather than moving extensively around the classroom.

For the most part the orthopedically impaired children are able to participate in all of your classroom activities. Adaptations are needed when access to materials is limited by the child's use of a wheelchair, walker, or canes. In these situations, you may need to change the location of materials in order to provide easy access. Placing a plastic bag or bucket that can be placed on the lap of a child in a wheelchair or slung over the shoulder of a child using canes or walker will make carrying objects far easier. Accessibility, however, includes not only materials but also chalkboards, bookcases, storage areas, coat racks, bulletin boards, display cases, and activity centers. Children in wheelchairs may need special tables or lap boards on which to write. If a child has weak hand muscles or spasticity in the hands, you may want to assign a partner to assist with the manipulation of materials. As with the other groups discussed, small group learning or cooperative learning is beneficial to students with hearing impairments.

Field trip locales can be a challenge for the teacher of an orthopedically impaired child. Scout out field trip locales prior to the trip to be certain they are accessible to the orthopedically impaired child and to make certain the child can accompany the class to all locations.

The specific kinds of modifications you are asked to make depends on the kind of impairment, the IEP's short and long-term goals, and the methods you intend to use in presenting the materials. The purpose of collaboration with special educators, parents, counselors, and others on the collaborative team is to determine the kind of modification that will allow the disabled child to learn most effectively in the regular classroom. When extensive modifications are needed, the paraprofessional is available to directly assist in the classroom. Activities 10.1 through 10.3 will allow you to further develop your knowledge of special needs children in the classroom of collaboration.

Activities for Special Needs Children

Activity 10.1

Purpose   To develop an understanding of collaboration in the classroom.

Procedure
1. Arrange to interview the teacher who is working in a collaborative program.
2. Discuss with the teacher the collaborative team members and the contributions made by each of the team members.
3. Discuss with the teacher the kinds of modifications needed for children included in the class and how those modifications are implemented.

Activity 10.2

Purpose   To observe the interactions of special needs children in a regular classroom.

Procedure
1. Arrange with a first through eighth grade teacher to observe in his or her classroom a student who has been identified as having special learning needs.
2. Observe for at least three half-hour periods over one week. Try to observe at different times during the day.
3. As you observe, consider the following:
   a. How does the student interact with others in the class?
   b. What special attention does the student receive from the teacher?

    c. What adaptations of materials or content have been made for the student?
4. After you have had an opportunity to observe the child in the classroom setting, discuss with the teacher the kinds of adaptations needed by the child.

Note: Be as inconspicuous as possible in making your observations. If the student notices your observations and becomes uncomfortable, stop immediately.

Activity 10.3

Purpose   To investigate the kinds of suggestions made in textbooks for adapting science content and science teaching to the needs of special students.

Procedure
1. Obtain a science textbook, teacher's edition, for a first through eighth grade textbook.
2. Choose two chapters dealing with different topics within the text.
3. Read any material in the preface of the text dealing with teaching special needs students in the classroom. Then read the teaching suggestions given for working with special needs children in the two chapters.
4. How does the textbook adapt the content to special needs students?

Children with disabilities are not the only students with special needs you will have in your inclusive classroom. Although inclusion is generally interpreted to mean including children with disabilities, the inclusive classroom also includes children from culturally diverse backgrounds.

Children from Culturally Diverse Backgrounds

Today's classrooms are models of today's society. Just as the towns and cities of the United States are home to people from varying ethnic and cultural backgrounds so are classrooms home to children of a variety of backgrounds. Consequently, classrooms at the elementary and middle school levels have children who are a part of the mainstream culture, children whose home lives mirror their family's cultural background but not that of the mainstream cultural group, children who speak more than one language, and children who speak only one language, a language different from that found in the classroom in its entirety or in its dialect. Cultural diversity in the classroom means the teacher should have not only an understanding of how culture can affect learning but also a repertoire of skills for working with children from differing backgrounds (Lonner and Tyler, 1988; Golhick and Chinn, 1994).

Awareness of differences in the cultural and ethnic backgrounds of children should not, however, lead the teacher to develop stereotypes of children. It is inappropriate to lump children into a broad category as if the category automatically delineates that child's learning traits. Each culture of origin has differing customs, differing ways of viewing the world. And, additionally, simply having a Japanese, Italian, German, or Thai name does not make a child a member of a minority culture. A child may be a fourth-generation Italian American without any understanding of traditional Italian culture. The majority of children in the classroom will be English-speaking members of the dominant American culture.

Even though the majority of children in a classroom are from the mainstream culture, some children come to school with backgrounds and experiences far different from those of their peers. These cultural differences are most likely to be apparent in three areas that affect learning: learning style, communication style, and language (Manning and Baruth, 1996).

Learning style is the way individuals receive and process information. Some individuals learn better in a kinesthetic manner, that is, by getting actively involved in their learning. Still other children learn best from written or from oral material. At times, children from differing cultural backgrounds are unable to benefit fully from the instructional program because their learning and behavioral styles do not match the instructional styles used by their teachers.

Communication style refers to the way in which individuals from a particular culture interact with one another. Students whose culture, verbal or nonverbal, is unacknowledged or misunderstood in their classrooms are likely to feel alienated, unwelcome, or out of place (Walker, 1988).

Language refers, first, to the child's use of the dominant language of the classroom. Children may be fluent only in the language of their country of origin, may be bilingual first- or second-generation Americans, or may have no knowledge of the language of their ancestral land. The only way to determine if a student uses English in a nonstandard manner is to talk with the student and look at samples of written work. Language also refers to the use of language for communication within the culture.

Most cultures have certain rules that are followed when individuals within the culture communicate with one another. Some cultures follow strict rules of how subordinates communicate with those having more status or power, as in when children communicate with adults; other cultures are far more flexible in their communication styles. In general, Hispanic and Asian American groups tend to be more formal in their communication styles than African or European Americans (Ramirez, 1988).

In some cultures the right of the individual to express feeling is guarded and individuals learn to accept and deal with intense expressions of feelings. In other cultures, the outward expression of feelings is expected to be subdued. African Americans differ from European Americans in that the former tend to show greater emotional content in their interactions. Consequently, some African American students may express their differences of opinions with teachers vehemently and passionately and seem to go beyond the bounds of appropriate behavior.

Many Asian and Pacific ethnic groups find the frankness of European Americans disconcerting. Rather than the direct approach favored by individuals with a European background, these cultures prefer a more indirect approach, once which politely maintains interpersonal relationships. Consequently, with some children, a less direct approach to criticism of work and a less direct approach to topics is preferable. However, in some instances the value of an indirect approach is not fully comprehended. For example, children coming from impoverished backgrounds where they are used to being told exactly what to do may not perceive their teachers as serious when they use an indirect, polite manner in expressing their wishes (Villegas, 1991).

Just as the use of verbal communication can differ from one culture to another, the use of nonverbal communication can also differ. As simple a nonverbal signal as eye contact can have different meanings in different cultures. For example, among European Americans, anger is often displayed through silent glares while among African American children may express the same emotion by rolling their eyes. Additionally, African American and Hispanic American females often express this emotion not through eye contact but through stance. Hands on the hips is a sure sign of anger.

Eye contact can also indicate how the student is expressing respect for authority. For example, in European Americans one expresses respect for authority by looking the authority figure directly in the eyes, but in African America, Asian American, and Pacific American children respect for authority is often shown by not looking the person directly in the eyes. Activities 10.4 and 10.5 will allow you to explore the cultural diversity of local classrooms and to develop your knowledge of culturally appropriate activities.

Activities for Culturally Different Students

Activity 10.4

Purpose   To investigate the various cultures that may be found in classrooms in your area.

Procedure
1. Prepare to interview at least four teachers in a local school.
2. Discuss with the teachers the backgrounds of the students in the class. Focus on cultural backgrounds of the students in the class.
   a. What backgrounds are represented in the class?
   b. Are any students speaking English as a second language? Are any non-English-speaking students in the class?
   c. What kinds of adaptations are needed for children from different cultural backgrounds?

Activity 10.5

Purpose To investigate the kinds of suggestions made in textbooks for adapting science content and science teaching to the needs of culturally different students.

Procedure
1. Obtain a science textbook, teacher's edition, for a first through eighth grade textbook.
2. Choose two chapters dealing with different topics within the text.
3. Read any material in the preface of the text dealing with teaching culturally different students in the classroom. Then read the teaching suggestions given for working with culturally different students in the two chapters.
4. How does the textbook adapt the content to culturally different students?

Cultural differences may result in special learning or interaction considerations in the science classroom (Cegelka, 1988). The foremost idea in working with culturally different children in the classroom is to present the history of science as including contributions from various cultures. Europeans did indeed develop a great deal of the science we now study, but during the time when Europe was in the Dark Ages, scientists in the Arab world, in the Far East, and in Central and South American cultures were making contributions to an understanding of the world. Second, in looking at the nature of science be certain to present science today as being conducted by scientists from a variety of nations and a variety of cultures. Attention to cultural diversity as a part of the history and the current practice of science can result in a particular strength (Hauser, 1996). However, even though diversity is a source of strength for the classroom, there are still certain considerations for working with children from diverse backgrounds you should consider.

Hands-on teaching strategies are appropriate to children from a variety of different backgrounds. When verbal teaching strategies are used, you may need to base the verbal presentation on the experiences of the children. In some cases, the expectations of a teacher from the mainstream culture may differ from that of the child's culture. For example, you may expect your students to engage in discussions where ideas are debated and challenged, even those of the teacher. For children from a traditional Asian background, this kind of discussion is very difficult. In the traditional Asian culture, children are expected to be quiet and obedient and the teacher is not challenged. In other words, be aware of the viewpoint held by the child's dominant culture and be respectful of that child's ways (Tiedt and Tiedt, 1990).

When there are children in the classroom for whom English is a second language, illustrate verbal material with pictures and drawings in order to aid understanding. If children speak nonstandard English, do not correct the child's grammar or usage during discussions. Instead of correcting language, continually model the language to be used in the classroom situation and work on the development of the ability to use standard English at other times. Help children who speak nonstandard

English to understand when the need is for standard English and when the non-standard dialect is appropriate. If the child does not speak English at all, try to have activity instructions written in the child's first language. A parent, college professor, or high school teacher can help in translating directions to other languages (Ramirez, 1988).

Classroom activities involving hands-on strategies in cooperative groups are as appropriate for the culturally diverse students in the classroom as for the children from the mainstream culture. If materials being used in an activity are unfamiliar, allow time for exploration of those materials and do not assume that because you are familiar with the materials all students will be familiar with them. Activity 10.6 helps you to develop a file of teaching materials on scientists from diverse backgrounds.

Activities for Culturally Different Students

Activity 10.6

Purpose   To develop a file of biographies of scientists from diverse backgrounds.

Procedure
1. Using a variety of resources, develop a file of scientist biographies showing the following areas:
   a. Scientists of differing national origins
   b. Male and female scientists
2. As part of the biography, list:
   a. Name
   b. Field of study
   c. Contributions to the scientific world
   d. Country of origin
   e. Other information showing the diversity of the scientific world

A third group of children in the regular classroom may also need some special attention. The third group consists of gifted children (Gallagher, 1988).

Gifted Children in the Regular Classroom

Some forms of intelligence are easy to identify. The child of 8 who plays Chopin is musically gifted. The child of 12 who dances in the ballet is bodily gifted. The child of 9 who paints realistic landscapes in oil is spatially gifted. The child who begins learning algebra in second grade or who reads at the age of 3 is mathematically or linguistically gifted. But for many children, the opportunity to manifest a particular intelligence is not readily available. Rather than show a particular, specific intelligence, these children may show some of the general characteristics of the gifted (Miller, 1993; Gardner, 1985; Gardner and Walters, 1985). These characteristics may be divided into three general areas: behavioral characteristics, learning characteristics, and creative characteristics (Baska, 1989).

Behavioral Characteristics

Many gifted children learn to read earlier and with greater comprehension than other children. They read widely, quickly, and intensely and have, as a result, large vocabularies. These children are often able to pick up and interpret nonverbal cues and can draw inferences that other children miss. Because gifted children can concentrate and attend for longer periods of time they are often able to work independently at an earlier age and for longer periods than other children. Because of their wide interests, quickness to learn basic skills, and intrinsic interest in learning, their behavior is sometimes coupled with high levels of energy. As a consequence, gifted children are sometimes labeled as hyperactive or undisciplined, characteristics that may be the result of boredom (Parke 1989; Ziv and Gadish, 1990).

In terms of problem solving, the behavior of gifted children is well organized, goal directed, and efficient. Gifted children may also exhibit forms of problem solving uncharacteristic of their age level or unique. There is a tendency among gifted children to want to do everything for themselves, which can cause friction with other children and frustration in teachers or parents who know it would be quicker to perform a task for the child.

Learning Characteristics

Gifted children learn basic skills quickly and with less practice than other children. More important, however, they take great pleasure in learning. Their abilities at abstraction, conceptualization, and synthesis are generally better developed than those of average children. Additionally, they are often skeptical, critical, or evaluative. They tend to spot inconsistencies in content information and behavior quickly. Children may challenge what they have read in a textbook because they read conflicting information elsewhere. And because they read widely, gifted children have a large storehouse of information regarding a variety of topics that can be quickly recalled. Some gifted children attempt to dominate discussions in order to show their store of knowledge; others share their information in small packets at varying times. Be aware that the store of knowledge of a gifted child may be disconcerting. A gifted child may know more about the rain forest than you do, or may even correct content errors. Finally, gifted children often have rapid insight into cause-and-effect relationships. They show a ready grasp of underlying principles and can often make valid generalizations about events, people, and objects. Keep in mind that even if the gifted child grasps the concept you should not assume that all children understand the concept (Kitano and Kirby, 1986; Baska, 1989; Klein, 1989).

Creative Characteristics

Gifted children tend to be fluent and flexible thinkers, two attributes of creative thinking. They are able to produce a large variety of inferences from a set of data, to identify the consequences of a particular course of action, or to identify related ideas and utilize those relationships in developing new concepts. Gifted children are able to use many different alternatives and approaches to problem solving. Gifted children are often original thinkers, looking for new, unusual, or unconventional associations or combinations among items of information. They often have the ability to see relationships among seemingly unrelated objects, ideas, or facts. They are also elaborative thinkers, producing new steps, ideas, responses, or other embellishments to a basic idea, situation, or problem. These characteristics are true whether the child is thinking in terms of mathematical problems, dance steps, musical forms, or artistic products.

Gifted children also have a high level of curiosity about ideas, events, objects, and situations. They are less intellectually inhibited than other children and so may challenge, debate, or present different opinions. This tendency can be difficult for a teacher who is certain there is only one way to do a task, only one outcome for problem solving, or only one technique for showing the results of research. Finally, the gifted child often displays intellectual playfulness, fantasizes, and imagines readily. The presence of a gifted child in the classroom can help the teacher to think in new and different ways and become more flexible in teaching strategies and reactions to ideas and discussion.

Strategies for Working with Gifted Children

As with other groups of children with special learning needs, gifted children may also need some adaptations if they are to learn to their potential. Probably the most appropriate means of adapting the science program for gifted students is **enrichment.** In its most general form, enrichment allows the gifted child to pursue additional studies in the stronger areas of intelligence (Parke, 1989; Wheatley, 1989). Some specific techniques within the general strategy of enrichment are considered here.

Independent Study and Independent Projects.   Both of these means of enrichment involve the selection of a topic by the student followed by the development of an independent project that allows for in-depth study. Possibilities include library research projects culminating in written or oral reports, experimental research, construction of models, or development of creative writing projects, art work, or musical projects.

Learning Centers.   Learning centers designed and organized by the classroom teacher are a way of enriching the science program. In general, a learning center has a variety of activities from which the child selects those activities of most interest. Activities should provide variety in the use of multiple intelligences and be open ended so the gifted child can determine the direction of the activity and decide when closure should occur. The learning center is designed around the current topic of study but permits the child to work independently in areas of greatest interest.

Mentorships. Mentorships involve children working with experts in a particular field of study so they can work together to develop an extensive, idiosyncratic project. A mentor could be a high school student, a parent, a college or university professor, or anyone else willing to take time to share his or her expertise with children.

Computer Simulations and Programs. A variety of programs can be used as enrichment for gifted students. Simulations and interactive videos are particularly appropriate for the gifted child and can be used independently. In addition, computer networks allow students to interact electronically with other children having similar interests and abilities in other cities, states, and nations. Chapter 13 discusses the use of computer-based technology more fully.

Problem Solving. Problem solving involves students in divergent thinking through creative problem solving. Although individuals can work with problem-solving activities, this is more appropriately done in small groups. Small groups allow for brainstorming and the generation of more extensive ideas than individuals may generate working alone. Here are some types of problem solving situations:

1. *What would happen if . . .* or *What would have happened if . . .* questions. For example, "What do you think would happen if all of the rain forests were cut down so the land could be used for farming?"

2. *Thinking of product or situation improvements.* For example, "How could we improve our technique for determining the number of bacteria in a culture plate?"

3. *Finding a variety of ways of interpreting information.* For example, students could be given the information collected from a paleontological site and asked to come up with interpretations of the site.

4. *Determining a solution.* In this form of problem solving, students are given a problem and asked to present solutions. For example, students can be presented with the problem of saving a particular species endangered because of increasing farming in an area that was previously a forest.

5. *Answering a challenge.* In this technique, students are challenged to find a way of solving a particular problem. For example, students could be asked to develop a way of constructing a bridge across a mountain gorge (Feldhusen, 1989)

Activities 10.7 and 10.8 allow you to explore the inclusion of gifted children in the classroom and to look at how text materials are adapted for gifted students.

Activities for Gifted Children

Activity 10.7

Purpose   To interview teachers who have a gifted child or children in the regular classroom.

Procedure
1. Prepare to interview at least four teachers in a local school.
2. Discuss with the teachers the inclusion of gifted children in the regular classroom. In particular, focus on:
   a. the behavioral characteristics of gifted children in the regular classroom.
   b. the learning characteristics of gifted children in the regular classroom.
   c. adaptations needed for gifted children in the regular classroom.

Activity 10.8

Purpose   To investigate the kinds of suggestions made in textbooks for adapting science content and science teaching to the needs of gifted students.

Procedure
1. Obtain a science textbook, teacher's edition, for a first through eighth grade textbook.
2. Choose two chapters dealing with different topics within the text.
3. Read any material in the preface of the text dealing with teaching gifted students in the classroom. Then read the teaching suggestions given for working with gifted students in the two chapters.
4. How does the textbook adapt the content to gifted students?

Teaching Strategies for the Inclusive Classroom

In Chapter 8 a wide variety of teaching strategies were considered for use at the elementary and middle school levels. Each of these strategies is appropriate for the inclusive classroom provided the collaborative team and the IEP make appropriate modifications. However, one additional strategy needs to be considered and is considered here because of its power in creating positive interactions among all children in the classroom (Sharan, 1980; Slavin, 1994) a vital factor in the success of inclusion in the classroom. This strategy is cooperative learning.

Small Group Learning in the Science Classroom

In many cases, the difficulties associated with having children with various disabling conditions or cultural differences may be solved in a relatively easy manner. Students with various kinds of disabilities may need to work with partners so that equipment can be used successfully. Students who are at risk or who come from differing cultural backgrounds may lack information that other students have. Grouping students can help develop the background needed. Gifted students may have a wealth of information and ideas they can easily share with others. Working in small groups and cooperative groups is a good strategy for allowing a highly knowledgeable student to share information. Because science is often conducted in groups in laboratory settings, working in small groups and cooperative groups is a good way of showing another aspect of the nature of science (Webb and Farivar, 1989; Johnson and Johnson, 1994; Putnam, 1997).

Cooperative Learning in Science

Cooperative learning and small group learning are not the same thing. In small group learning, students are generally divided into groups, asked to decide how they will work in that group, and then generally left to sort things out for themselves. The dominant child usually dominates. The more passive student is often left on the sidelines. Although the groups may function well in completing a particular task, there is little assurance that all of the children in the group will have an equal opportunity to participate. Cooperative learning, in contrast, is a structured approach to group work that provides an opportunity for all students to participate on an equal basis. In the following sections, two approaches to cooperative learning are considered: (1) cooperative groups in conducting hands-on activities, and (2) cooperative learning in working with research materials, particularly verbal materials.

Cooperative Learning and Hands-On Activities.   In working with hands-on activities, cooperative groups allow all students to participate in the activity on a relatively equal basis. In beginning to work with cooperative learning in this manner, the teacher first determines who will be in the group, decides on the job each member of the group will accomplish, provides an opportunity for the students to work, and then provides for presentation and discussion of the results (Hassard, 1990).

Developing the Groups.   In developing the cooperative learning groups, first consider the proposed activity, which will help determine how many students need to be in the group. In general, cooperative learning groups for activities have between three and five students. Once the size of the group has been determined, consider the composition of the group. The groups should be as diverse as possible so that students can bring both their strengths and their weaknesses to a particular group. The same group should not be kept for all activities. Instead, the groups should change on a regular basis, although not with every activity. This gives students an opportunity to work with a variety of others in a cooperative manner.

Assigning the Jobs.   In cooperative learning groups, each member of the group has a particular task to complete. In working with a hands-on activity, here are the most common jobs:

1. *Materials director:* obtains all of the materials needed for an activity, cleans the materials as needed, and returns the materials to their original location when the activity is completed.

2. *Experimenter:* reads and interprets the directions and then performs the actual manipulations of the materials.
3. *Observer:* collects and records the data for the activity.
4. *Presenter:* organizes the group's report and presents the findings to the rest of the class during the general discussion.

Although these jobs are assigned to the students, this does not mean that only the observer watches what is happening or only the presenter draws the conclusions. All of the members of the group observe in order to be certain the observations for the activity are as complete and accurate as possible. All of the members contribute to the final report and to drawing an appropriate conclusion. The observer makes certain all of the data from the group is recorded and the presenter makes certain the final report is well organized and representative of group thought.

Providing Work Time.   Naturally students need time to work on the hands-on activity. Your role during this work time is not to present additional information to the students but rather to observe the groups at work, provide assistance when necessary, and generally make certain everything goes smoothly. Provide assistance during the work time only when assistance is requested by the groups or when you observe something that could be dangerous. Do not interfere simply because a group is obtaining results that differ from the expected.

Presentation and Discussion of Results.   Once the activity has been finished, provide time for the presenters to present the results of the activity. Discussion of the results should follow the presentation of the various conclusions in order to be certain all students comprehend the content information being shown by the activity. In addition, when differences in conclusions occur, this is the time for problem solving. Cooperative groups work to determine possible reasons for differences and then develop ways of determining whether the reason is correct or not (Hassard, 1990).

In working with cooperative groups in hands-on activities, the cooperative groups may be working with inductive or deductive discovery, with inquiry, or with a conceptual change model. The cooperative group is a means for organizing the students within the particular teaching strategy. In the next use of cooperative learning groups, the group strategy is a variation of expository teaching.

Cooperative Learning: Jigsaw

Jigsaw is a cooperative learning strategy designed to help students learn concepts and facts through research involving mainly written materials. In its essence, jigsaw involves students working in groups, but each member of the group becomes an expert in a particular body of information. The expert then teaches the rest of the group that information. The total group is then expected to be knowledgeable about all of the information covered. In the end, all of the pieces of information studied by the experts in the groups fit together like the pieces of a jigsaw puzzle to make a whole. For jigsaw to work effectively, three stages are necessary: planning, implementing, and evaluating.

Planning.   Planning for jigsaw is a particularly important aspect of this cooperative learning strategy and requires five basic steps. In step 1, the teacher identifies a body of science information that can be broken into a variety of subtopics. For example, the topic "Environments" can be divided into a variety of areas. In step 2, the teacher divides a large body of content into three or four subtopics. After the division into subtopics is made, make certain the amount of information within each subtopic is approximately equal. In working with the topic "Environments," the topic could be divided into (1) steppe, (2) temperate forest, (3) savannah, (4) tropical rain forest, and (5) marine. These subtopics will be researched by each of the experts. Step 3 involves the teacher in locating a variety of resources that can be used to research the topics. As cooperative learning strategies can be used as a means of integrating students with learning problems into the regular classroom, those resources should show a variety of reading levels as well as a variety of presentation types: books, films, filmstrips, CD-ROM databases, audiotapes, and so on. In step 4, the teacher develops expert sheets or charts to ensure that students learn essential information. Figure 10.1 shows an expert sheet that could be used in studying the topic "Environments." And finally, in step 5, the teacher divides the class into groups, making certain the groups are heterogeneous in their form.

Figure 10.1

Expert Group Sheet

TEMPERATE FOREST

LOCATION:

CLIMATE CHARACTERISTICS:

PLANT LIFE:

ANIMAL LIFE:

ENVIRONMENTAL PROBLEMS:

Implementation.   The final phase in planning jigsaw in the classroom is that of implementation. The first phase of implementation is given to explaining the procedures and the expert sheets to the students. Basically, as the teacher you would tell the students the groups in which they will be working and that each member of the group will be responsible for a particular area of study. You then show the expert sheets so the students are aware of the kind of information they will be attempting to find and the resources you have made available for use. Finally, you set a time for when the experts must be ready to present their information to the other members of the group. If there are students in a group who have difficulty in reading or locating information, then a buddy system can be implemented in which two students work together to locate the material. At this point, the students in the group decide among themselves who will research each area of study. In the case of studying environments, one student would be responsible for arctic, one for temperate, one for tropical, and one for aquatic environments.

Once the students begin to work, you have three jobs. First, you monitor the work of the groups, assisting when help is needed. Second, you periodically bring together the expert groups, all of the students responsible for a particular area, to discuss what they have found and to compare information or share resources. And, finally, you monitor the teaching as the experts present their information to others in the group.

Evaluation.   The final stage in working with jigsaw is to evaluate the learning that has taken place. Two forms of evaluation are often given. First, a group test on the information studied is taken. On this test, all members of the group can work together to decide on the answers to the questions. Second, approximately a week after the group test, an individual test is given. Students have similar questions to the group test but are required to work alone in responding to the questions.

Jigsaw, one of a variety of cooperative learning strategies, is a highly appropriate means for working with facts and concepts within the science classroom, particularly a diverse classroom. Activities 10.9 and 10.10 focus on the use of cooperative learning in the science classroom.

Activities for Special Needs Students

Activity 10.9

Purpose   To apply the information contained in this chapter to the developed unit plan.

Procedure
1. Assume you will be working with a classroom in which students with special needs, including a gifted child, are in the classroom.
2. Return to your unit plan as developed in Chapter 8. Show how might you need to adapt your lessons to special needs students.

Activity 10.10

Purpose   To incorporate cooperative learning strategies into science teaching.

Procedure
1. Return to the unit plan developed in Chapter 8 and select two activities.
2. Show how you would incorporate cooperative learning techniques in working with the two hands-on activities.
3. Show how would you would use jigsaw in working with the content of the unit.

Summary

P.L. 94-142, passed in 1975, developed the concept of least restrictive environment, thus placing children with varying disabilities into the regular classroom setting. From this start, the concept of inclusion and collaborative programs has developed. Inclusion brings children with varying disabilities into the elementary and middle school classroom, and so the teacher is likely to have children who are slower to learn than the average child as well as children with learning, visual, hearing, orthopedic, or other disabilities within the classroom. In order to assist the teacher, collaborative programs have developed in which the regular teacher works with a team of professionals to determine the best possible learning experiences for the students in a class.

Whether the child is considered disabled, culturally different, or gifted, he or she has the right to experience success within the classroom. Consequently, adaptations of the science program, based on the collaborative meetings and the IEPs developed, are needed.

Children who are mentally impaired may need learning materials written to a lower grade level. Those who are hearing or visually impaired may need assistance from an individual who is able to sign or to take notes for the student. Children from different cultural backgrounds need to understand science as a human endeavor involving men and women from a variety of different ethnic and cultural backgrounds. The consequence of this viewpoint is greater depth and richness to the science program. Finally, students who are at risk for academic failure may need special consideration in developing background experiences or missing skills before they are able to participate effectively in the total science program.

Just as the selection of content for the general science program should be based on the characteristics of the children who will experience the program, the adaptation of content for the child who is disabled, culturally different, or gifted should be based on the needs of the child. The purpose of modification is not to weaken or dilute the science program but rather to provide a program that maintains its integrity while providing experiences appropriate to all children.

One type of teaching strategy is uniquely attuned to the needs of the diverse classroom. Cooperative learning allows students with differing abilities and disabilities to work together and pool their strengths as they learn. Cooperative learning when doing hands-on activities allows all students to participate in a hands-on activity. Jigsaw, a strategy for learning content information, allows heterogeneously grouped students to contribute to one another's learning.

Chapter Vocabulary

The number following each term refers to the page on which the term is first introduced.

Autistic, 298
Collaborative program, 300
Communication style, 307
Enrichment, 312
Inclusion, 299
Individual education programs (IEP), 294
Jigsaw, 316
Language, 307
Learning disabled, 295
Learning style, 307

Least restrictive environment, 295
Mentally impaired, 296
Multiple disabilities, 299
Orthopedically impaired, 297
Other health impairments, 299
Public law 94-142, 294
Public law 99-457, 294
Sensory impaired, 297
Serious emotional disturbance, 299
Traumatic brain injury, 298

Applying the **CONCEPTS**

1. You have just been told that your expertise as a teacher is going to be rewarded by making your classroom an "inclusion class." Before your students arrive for the first day of school, what information would you want to gather? How would you use this information in developing your science program?

2. As you review your science textbook, you discover that one of the topics studied under the human body unit deals with health and nutrition. You think this will make an excellent unit in which to incorporate information from various cultures. How might you go about doing that? What information would you collect first? How would you use that information?

3. As a third grade teacher you have a student who is reading Stephen Jay Gould's book *Wonderful Life*. When you ask her what it is about, she informs you that it deals with the possible identification and reidentification of Cambrian fauna discovered in the Burgess Shale. How would you handle this situation in the classroom?

References

Algozzine, B., C. V. Morsink, and K. M. Algozzine. 1988. What's happening in self-contained special education classrooms? *Exceptional Children* 55, 259–265.

Bailey, D. B., V. Buysse, R. Edmonson, and T. M. Smith. 1992. Creating family-centered services in early intervention: Perceptions of professionals in four states. *Exceptional Children* 58, 298–309.

Ballard, J., B. Ramirez, and K. Zantal-Weiner. 1987. *Public Law 94-142, Section 504 and Public Law 99-457: Understanding what they are and are not.* Reston, Va.: Council for Exceptional Children.

Baska, L. K. 1989. Characteristics and needs of the gifted. In J. Feldhusen, J. Van Tassel-Baska, and K. Seeley (eds.). *Excellence in educating the gifted.* Denver: Love.

Bauer, A. M., and T. M. Shea. 1989. *Teaching exceptional students in your classroom.* Boston: Allyn & Bacon.

Bilken, D., C. Corrigan, and D. Quick. 1989. Beyond obligations: Student's relations with each other in integrated classes. In D. K. Lipsky and A. Gartner (eds). *Beyond separate education: Quality education for all* (pp. 207–221). Baltimore: Brookes.

Cartwright, G. P., C. A. Cartwright, and M. E. Ward. 1989. *Educating special learners* (3rd ed.). Belmont, Ca.: Wadsworth.

Cegelka, P. T. 1988. Multicultural considerations. In. W. Lynch and R. B. V. Lewis (eds.). *Exceptional children and adults* (pp. 545–587). Glenview, Ill.: Scott, Foresman.

Cohen, E. 1991. Strategies for creating a multiability classroom. *Cooperative Learning* 12(1), 4–7.

Fauvre, M. 1988. Including young children with "new" chronic illnesses in an early childhood education setting. *Young Children* 43, 71–77.

Feldhusen, J. F. 1989. Thinking skills for the gifted. In J. F. Feldhusen, J. Van Tassel-Baskra, and K. Seeley (eds.). *Excellence in education for the gifted.* Denver: Love.

Forster, P., and B. A. Doyle. 1989. Teaching listening skills to students with attention deficit disorders. *Teaching Exceptional Children* 21(2), 20–22.

Friend, M., and W. Bursuck. 1996. *Including students with special needs: A practical guide for classroom teachers.* Boston: Allyn & Bacon

Gallagher, J. J. 1988. National agenda for educating gifted students: Statement of priorities. *Exceptional Children* 55, 107–114.

Gardner, H. 1985. *Frames of mind: The theory of multiple intelligences.* New York: Basic Books.

Gardner, H., and J. M. Walters. 1985. The development and education of intelligences. In *Essays on the intellect.* Alexandria, Va.: Association for Supervision and Curriculum Development.

Gollnick, D., and P. Chinn. 1994. *Multicultural education in a pluralistic society* (4th ed.). New York: Merrill/Macmillan.

Hassard, J. 1990. Science experiences: *Cooperative learning and the teaching of science.* Menlo Park, Calif.: Addison-Wesley.

Hauser, W. 1996. Multicultural education for the dominant culture. *Urban Education* 31 (2), 125–148.

Ireland, J. C., D. Wray, and C. Flexer. 1988. Hearing for success in the classroom. *Teaching Exceptional Children* 20(2), 15–7.

Johnson, D., and R. Johnson. 1994. *Learning together and alone: Cooperation, competition, and individualization* (4th ed.). Needham Heights, Mass.: Allyn & Bacon.

Jones, C. J. 1992. *Social and emotional development of exceptional students: Handicapped and gifted.* Springfield, Ill.: Charles C. Thomas.

Kitano, M. K. 1989. The K–3 teacher's role in recognizing and supporting young gifted children. *Young Children* 44(3), 57–63.

Kitano, M. K., and D. E. Kirby. 1986. *Gifted education: A comprehensive view.* Boston: Little, Brown.

Klein, E. 1989. Gifted and talented. In G. P. Cartwright, C. A. Cartwright, and M. E. Ward (eds.). *Educating special learners* (3rd ed.). Belmont, Calif.: Wadsworth.

Lerner, J. W. 1989. *Learning disabilities* (5th ed.). Boston: Houghton Mifflin.

Lewis, R. B., and D. H. Doorlag. 1991. *Teaching special students in the mainstream.* New York: Merrill.

Lilly, M. S. 1992. Labeling, a tired, overworked, yet unresolved issue in special education. In W. Stainback and S. Stainback (eds.). *Controversial issues confronting special education: Divergent perspectives* (pp. 85–95). Boston: Allyn & Bacon.

Lonner, W. J., and V. O. Tyler. 1988. *Cultural and ethnic factors in learning and motivation.* Bellingham, Wash.: Western Washington University Press.

Manning, M. L. and L. G. Baruth 1996. *Multicultural education of children and adolescents.* Boston: Allyn &Bacon

McCormick, L. 1990. Cultural diversity and exceptionality. In N. G. Haring and L. McCormick (eds.), *Exceptional children and youth* (5th ed.). Columbus, Ohio: Merrill.

Miller, L. 1993. *What we call smart: A new narrative for intelligence and learning.* San Diego, Calif.: Singular.

Parke, B. N. 1989. *Gifted students in regular classrooms.* Boston: Allyn & Bacon.

Putnam, J. 1997. *Cooperative learning in diverse classrooms.* Upper Saddle River, N. J.: Merrill/Prentice Hall.

Ramirez, B. A. 1988. Culturally and linguistically diverse children. *Teaching Exceptional Children* 20(4), 45–46.

Raynes, M., M. Snell, and W. Sailor. 1991. A fresh look at categorical programs for children with special needs. *Phi Delta Kappa* 73, 326–331.

Sharan, S. 1980. Cooperative learning in small groups: Recent methods and effects on achievement, attitudes, and ethnic relations. *Review of Educational Research* 50, 241–271.

Simpson, R. L., and B. S. Myles. 1990. The general education collaboration: A model for successful mainstreaming. *Focus on Exceptional Children* 23 (4), 1–10.

Slavin, R. E. 1989. Students at risk of school failure: The problem and its dimensions. In R. E. Slavin, N. L. Karweit, and N. A. Madden (eds.), *Effective programs for students at risk.* Boston: Allyn & Bacon.

Slavin, R. E. 1994. *Cooperative learning* (2nd ed.). Needham Heights, Mass.: Allyn & Bacon.

Smith, J. D. 1998. *Inclusion: Schools for all students.* Belmont, Calif.: Wadsworth.

Tiedt, P. L., and I. M. Tiedt. 1990. Multicultural teaching: *A handbook of activities, information, and resources* (3rd. ed.). Boston: Allyn & Bacon.

U.S. Department of Education. 1993. *Fifteenth annual report to Congress on the implementation of the Individuals with Disabilities Education Act.* Washington, D.C.: U.S. Department of Education.

Vandercook, T., and J. York. 1989. A team approach to program development and support. In J. York, T. Vandercook, C. MacDonald, and S. Wolff (eds.). *Strategies for full inclusion* (pp. 21–43). Minneapolis, Minn.: University of Minnesota, Institute on Community Integration.

Villegas, A. 1991. *Culturally responsive pedagogy for the 1990's and beyond.* Princeton, N.J.: Educational Testing Service.

Waldron, K. A. 1996. *Introduction to special education: The inclusive classroom.* Albany, N. Y.: Delmar.

Walker, J. L. 1988. Young American Indian children. *Teaching Exceptional Children* 20(4), 50–51.

Webb, N., and S. Farivar. 1994. Promoting helping behavior in cooperative small groups in middle school mathematics. *American Educational Research Journal* 31(2), 369–395.

Wheatley, G. 1989. Instructional methods for the gifted. In J. Feldhusen, J. Van Tassel-Baska, and K. Seeley (eds.). *Excellence in educating the gifted.* Denver: Love.

Ziv, A., and O. Gadish. 1990. Humor and giftedness. *Journal for Education of the Gifted* 13(4), 332–345.

CHAPTER ELEVEN

SENSITIVE ISSUES IN THE SCIENCE CLASSROOM

Chapter Objectives

Upon completion of this chapter you should be able to:

1 discuss how to handle sensitive issues in the science classroom through use of the scientific attitudes.

2 discuss the use of critical thinking skills as a means for approaching some sensitive topics in the science classroom.

3 discuss some of the fallacies of thinking that lead to acceptance of nonscientific ideas.

Introduction

My sixth grade students were studying the human body. We had studied the respiratory, circulatory, digestive, and muscloskeletal systems without difficulty. In spite of a great deal of giggling from the students, we had even studied the excretory system. With the nervous system and the reproductive system still to go, I decided to have the students study the nervous system first. Even though the parents wanted their children to learn about human reproduction, the nervous system still seemed less troublesome to handle than human reproduction. We began with nerves and worked our way up to the brain and to learning. During one of the class discussions on the brain, the subject of emotions came up. Naturally. In sixth grade children are bundle of emotions, many of which they do not yet understand. The discussion was lively and at the end the children left the science lab to return to their classroom.

The next morning I received a phone call from an extremely irate father demanding to know why I was psychoanalyzing the children in school when I was not qualified to do so! This father, a psychiatrist, had listened to his daughter discussing what had happened in school that day, and had immediately taken a conceptual leap so far beyond reality as to be absurd. We talked for less than ten minutes about what had occurred in class that previous day, and the incident ended with both of us laughing over the event. At that point, we both decided to heed the advice of a kindergarten teacher of long experience who once told parents: "If you'll believe only half of what your children tell you about what goes on in school; I'll believe only half of what your children tell me about what goes on at home."

Although this incident ended amicably, many times teachers are confronted by parents concerned about the contents of their children's education. Certain topics such as the human body, animal rights, evolution, and environmentalism can be especially difficult to handle in the classroom. These kinds of topics are considered sensitive issues.

Why Are Some Issues Sensitive?

A **sensitive issue** is any topic in the science curriculum that is controversial and so can cause parents to become concerned about what their children are learning. In school contexts, almost any issue can become a sensitive issue depending on the children in the school and the background from which those children come. Parents can object to reading books because they contain stories which do not have happy endings or to Halloween stories that contain witches or ghosts. Mathematics books can be objected to because story problems do not carry names showing ethnic categories. Social studies textbooks may show too much or too little of the contributions of minority groups, may show alternative family systems, or may show too much or too little of the religious heritage of a nation. And science textbooks frequently include content information that is objectionable to one or more factions within a school setting. Particularly controversial in the science curriculum are the human body, use of animals in science activities, animal classification, environmental issues, and, as the champion of all controversial topics—evolution.

Why are some topics within the science curriculum controversial? In general, controversy is the result of three factors: family values, economic factors, or religious beliefs. Family values, outside of religious factors, can easily come into play when children are confronted with topics the family considers inappropriate for discussion. The human body and environmental issues seem to cause more conflicts with family values than other topics. Of course, when it comes to the human body, sex education is the area causing most difficulty. Some parents want their children to learn about the reproductive system and human reproduction, and others prefer that their children know nothing about that particular aspect of human development until they are told at home. Environmental issues can become controversial if family values focus on animal rights or environmental activism in general. In this case, the use of animals in science activities, even activities that cause no harm to the animals, or presentation of information showing the many sides of environmental issues can conflict with the values parents are attempting to instill in their children.

The second factor causing a particular topic to be sensitive in nature is an economic one. Ecological topics most frequently become controversial for this reason. Protecting endangered forest animals is noncontroversial unless one's family or community are engaged in the lumber industry. Protecting wetlands is laudable unless one's family owns areas that cannot be used as desired because they are wetlands. Limiting insecticides and chemical fertilizers is commendable unless one is a farmer attempting to grow crops on nearly depleted land or in the face of insect attack. Considering the adverse effects of hunting is a worthy pursuit unless a family's situation makes hunting a necessity. And looking at the damage done to land by strip mining is difficult in a mining-dependent community.

Finally, probably the most common cause for controversy in the classroom is conflict with religious beliefs. Study of the human body with attention given to human sexuality is highly controversial in terms of study of human reproduction or alternative lifestyles. Consideration of the classification of animals when human beings are placed into that classification can offend religious beliefs which place *homo sapiens* in a category of its own and above "animals." And, of course, the most difficult topic of all when it comes to controversy based on religious beliefs is that of biological evolution. It is there that religion and the science curriculum most frequently clash.

How then can you handle the inevitable controversy arising in the classroom? Some of these issues can be handled simply by informing parents of topics and how they will be handled prior to study, other topics provide an opportunity for you to model and use the scientific attitudes, and many allow you to develop logical thinking in children. Activity 11.1 provides an opportunity for you to explore sensitive issues in your own community while activity 11.2 focuses on developing a file of materials for teaching sensitive issues.

Learning Activities for Sensitive Issues

Activity 11.1

Purpose To investigate topics in science that could be sensitive in the community where you plan to teach or are teaching.

Procedure
1. Prepare a list of the topics commonly taught in elementary or middle school science classes.
2. Arrange to interview at least one classroom teacher, one principal, one parent, and one community leader about the topics.
3. Discuss with those persons the topics they may find sensitive. Use questions to determine why the topic is considered a sensitive one in the classroom and to determine what the person being interviewed would want to see done about the topic.
4. Using the information obtained, describe how you would handle those issues deemed sensitive in your classroom.

Activity 11.2

Purpose To develop a file of magazine and newspaper articles dealing with controversial topics in science.

Procedure
1. Using newspapers, news magazines, and other sources, develop a file of articles dealing with controversial topics related to science. Topics may include:
   a. Environmentalism
   b. Genetic research
   c. Medical ethics
   d. Paleontological discoveries
   e. Astronomy/Astrology
   f. Pseudoscientific areas: UFOs, unknown animals, psychic predictions, and so on.

Informing Parents

Many classroom problems with sensitive issues such as study of the human body, evolution, use of animals in science activities, and classification of animals including human beings in that classification can be resolved by notifying parents what you will be doing prior to beginning study of the topic and then keeping parents notified of what is being taught through periodic newsletters.

Newsletters

A **newsletter** is a brief written report prepared for a special group, in this case for parents. When using newsletters to inform parents of science topics, send the first newsletter before you begin studying the topic. If parents receive a newsletter prior to the start of the study, they can ask questions about how a particular topic will be handled in the classroom. In addition, parents are forewarned about the topic, and can, if they wish to do so, ask to have their children removed from the classroom during that time. In the newsletter informing parents of a topic that will be studied in the future, give an overview of the topic, describing clearly and concisely the kind of information to be included. You may even want to include the concepts considered in the unit of study or the objectives to be accomplished. You may also wish, if a textbook is being used, to include the title of the chapter and the page numbers so parents can review the information for themselves. If a text is not being used, you might include a list of trade books or other sources of information. If the possible reason for controversy is the use of animals in the classroom, you might want to include a description of some of the activities and a list of the precautions which will be taken to assure that neither the animals used in the activities nor the children using those animals will be harmed. It is also helpful to include a telephone number or an e-mail address for parents who have questions about the topic.

While the topic is under consideration, you might want to send home additional newsletters to inform parents about the activities their children are doing in school. Including samples of children's work, with their permission, is also a good idea for follow-up newsletters. Many difficulties can be stopped before they begin simply by informing parents directly. If they hear secondhand reports of classroom activities or infer from the title of a unit of work the content, parents can develop an erroneous concept of the curriculum. Informing parents directly stops erroneous speculation.

Once the newsletter is written and prior to sending it out to parents, be certain to have the principal read the newsletter and react to it. Your principal may have suggestions on how to improve your newsletter. But whether or not the principal makes suggestions, you want to secure his or her approval before sending out the newsletter to parents.

Classroom Visits

In addition to newsletters, parents can also be invited to the classroom to observe what is happening and to participate in the activities if possible. In inviting parents to the classroom, follow school policies. If it is policy for parents to inform teachers when they will be coming to the classroom, then they should do so in the case of sensitive issues as well. If school policy is to allow parents to drop in at any time during the school day then it should be the same for parents interested in seeing how particular topics are being handled in the classroom.

Parent-Teacher Discussions

At times, it will be necessary to talk directly with concerned parents. When parents ask to talk with you directly, set up a mutually convenient time to do so. Know why you are including a particular topic in the science curriculum. Listen carefully and with empathy to parental concerns, but be able to defend your educational choices in a clear, concise, logical, and professional manner. Be able to tell parents the reasons you have for including a particular topic. Be certain you can show parents how that topic fits within the total viewpoint of science the curriculum is designed to develop. Be prepared to discuss with concerned parents the reasons for sensitive topics within the curriculum. Be prepared to present your viewpoint factually and professionally.

Informing parents about sensitive topics to be considered in the science classroom can result in a lessening of concern over sensitive topics and an increase in support for the educational program, but it is only one strategy. Once you begin to teach that particular topic, then you need to be concerned with how you approach the topic in the classroom. Activities 11.3 and 11.4 focus on parents and teaching sensitive issues in the classroom.

Learning Activities for Sensitive Issues

Activity 11.3

Purpose   To develop a newsletter that could be used to inform parents about a particular topic to be studied in the science classroom.

Procedure
1. Select a topic from your unit or from your interview in Activity 11.1.
2. Develop a newsletter that could be sent to parents to inform them about the topic which will be studied. Use the information contained in the previous section to help you develop the newsletter.

Activity 11.4

Purpose   To role-play an encounter with parents who are concerned about a sensitive issue within the science classroom.

Procedure
1. Select one of the sensitive issues in number 4. Assign two persons to play the role of parents and one to play the role of the teacher.
2. Research the topic so you are aware of the kinds of concerns parents may have and the reasons for including the topic in the science curriculum.
3. Present a parent-teacher conference dealing with the topic.
4. Topics:
   a. evolution
   b. reproductive system
   c. animal rights
   d. pseudoscience: crystals, astrology, ESP, psychic predictions, and so on
   e. biological classification
   f. age of Earth
   g. other

Scientific Attitudes and Sensitive Issues

There is probably no better place within the science curriculum to model the scientific attitudes than in the context of sensitive issues in the classroom. They provide the perfect opportunity to model objectivity, skepticism, honesty, willingness to suspend judgment, and respect for the environment (Gauld, 1982).

Objectivity

Many issues are sensitive because they are controversial and any topic that is controversial has more than one side, frequently many sides. Hunting is one of those topics. To the avid deer hunter, hunting season is an important recreational period during the year. To the conservationist, hunting season may be viewed as an opportunity for culling a herd so that it does not become too large for a parcel of land to support it. But to the animal rights activist, hunting may be viewed as an unconscionable activity. And to the poor, rural family, hunting may be viewed as a necessity if there is to be food on the table. By considering hunting from all sides of the issue, the teacher models objectivity for the students and the students have the opportunity to draw conclusions based not only on the factual information presented in the classroom but also incorporating family and religious values.

When considering the variety of viewpoints on a sensitive issue in the classroom, be certain you really model objectivity for the children. It is not sufficient to present all sides of an issue if one side receives an hour's worth of attention and the other sides get a combined total of five minutes. If you have strong feelings about a particular issue or have little knowledge of a particular issue, invite guest speakers to come to the classroom to present the other viewpoints. In selecting guest speakers, carefully screen the individuals to be certain they will present their viewpoints logically, factually, and with respect for other viewpoints.

Skepticism

"My dad said the government is going to come in and take away our house and our land. After it rains my backyard gets real wet and it takes a long time for it to dry up. So my dad said the government passed a law that said it could do that because we have wet land." The child who said this was terribly upset about the prospect of losing his home to "the government." It was the perfect opportunity for this teacher to exercise the scientific attitude of skepticism. The teacher suggested the class do some research into wetlands and legislation dealing with them. After researching legislation dealing with wetlands, the student understood that a badly drained backyard did not really count as a wetland area. When your students make statements about sensitive issues that do not have a basis in fact or about which you are uncertain, an opportunity is provided for you to model a skeptical attitude. Encourage your students to research their statements in order to determine whether they are factual or not. In addition, encourage other children to challenge their classmates to support their ideas or to cite their sources of information (Kelly, 1989).

When using skepticism within the context of sensitive issues, however, you must model a high level of sensitivity. A student may be exposing a long-held belief, a parent's statement, or an idea that was misinterpreted. Whatever it is, you cannot treat student comments as amusing, silly, annoying, or absurd. Instead, suggest that information be checked and then assist the student in finding ways to check it (Vanderhoof, et al., 1992).

Honesty

In terms of scientific attitudes, honesty generally refers to being certain to report all data from an experiment accurately. The attitude of scientific honesty also means that a scientist looks not only at the data which support his or her hypothesis but also at the data that do not support it and report that data accurately as well.

This same kind of consideration should be used when exploring sensitive issues in the classroom. Neither you nor your students should be selective in reporting the results of activities or researches. Information found may conflict with cherished beliefs, but that information cannot be hidden away because of that conflict. You can model this idea when information conflicts with your own beliefs and ideas. You may even go one step beyond the simple reporting of information to showing children that your ideas have changed because of that new information. Scientific honesty not only means being honest in the reporting of data but also means being honest in sharing one's views and changes in views.

Willingness to Suspend Judgment

Willingness to suspend judgment is akin to honesty and objectivity when using scientific attitudes to consider sensitive issues. Willingness to suspend judgment means modeling the behavior of having all of the possible information and considering all of the possible information before coming to a decision. In considering classification of human beings as animals, willingness to suspend judgment would mean looking at the characteristics of living things in general: sensitivity, respiration, homeostasis, reproduction, cellular nature, nutritional requirements. These characteristics would then be applied to human beings to determine if they fit the minimal requirements for living things. Then the five kingdoms in the standard classification system could be considered with their characteristics: monera, protista, fungi, plants, animals. From the characteristics of these kingdoms, students could determine to which human beings are most closely related. Finally, students should look at the characteristics of the various phyla, classes, and orders of animals and compare their characteristics to those of human beings. It is difficult not to include *homo sapiens* within the animal kingdom when all of the information is considered.

The teacher should model this scientific attitude when controversy arises. Concepts are developed and changed when all of the information is in, when all of the information is considered, and not when the teacher tells children they are wrong and simply corrects them. Once again, however, sensitivity on the part of the teacher is needed.

Respect for the Environment

The last of the scientific attitudes to be considered here is respect for the environment. This one has the greatest impact on the use of living things, particularly animals in classroom activities.

To model respect for the environment in the context of animal use in the classroom, make certain that live animals are treated with care so they are not harmed in any way by activities or handling by the children in the class. When live animals are collected for a terrarium, modeling respect for the environment means the activity ends with students returning those animals unharmed to the environment. To head off difficulties with students who are animal rights activists, try to avoid insect collections and animals preserved through taxidermy as part of classroom decor. Live animals are always far more interesting and educational than insects stuck on pins or bobcats mounted and stuffed.

In addition to care of animals in the classroom, respect for the environment also includes the use of animal dissection in the classroom. Rather than dissect animals, there are computer programs that simulate dissection and are as effective for elementary age children as actually dissecting a frog or other animal.

The final consideration under the use of animals in the classroom may not be exactly a sensitive issues problem, but it can be a problem of animals in the classroom. Some people simply do not care to handle some kinds of animals. As a teacher do not force children to handle animals to which they have an aversion. You can provide opportunities for the child to handle an animal if he or she wishes, and some of those showing an aversion may decide it really is safe, but others may never wish to pick up a snake, iguana, or mouse. Or, you may be the one with the aversion. In this case, your best strategy is honesty. Telling students that you do not care to hold the boa constrictor and then designating one of the children as the snake handler for the day is perfectly all right in the classroom. Refusing to permit a child to bring in a snake because you dislike snakes is not all right. As a teacher you do not want to communicate your aversions to the class in a way which may cause some of the children to model that behavior.

Logical Thinking

Although many topics can be handled simply through the use of newsletters or modeling of scientific attitudes, other kinds of issues require a more concerted effort on the part of a teacher. Although evolution is not a sensitive topic among scientists and the only controversy is in the mechanisms rather than in the reality of whether biological evolution occurred, it is a highly sensitive, a highly controversial issue for biblical literalists. In addition, students may express ideas that are unusual to say the least: crystals as sources of healing powers, astrology as a way of telling the future, the existence of ghosts and apparitions, visits by extraterrestrials in the present or past, and even curses and spells by witches as causes of illness. These are often called **pseudoscience,** that is, false science. Pseudosciences are those areas that claim to have scientific backing, but which in reality do not. Pseudoscientific ideas are often encountered by teachers. As science teachers we need to handle pseudoscientific information in the classroom, but handle it in a way which is sensitive to student needs as well as accurate in scientific content. One appropriate way of handling both evolution and pseudoscientific ideas in the classroom is through attention to logical thinking. This attention includes not only strategies for logical thought but also awareness of how errors in thinking are made.

Errors in Thinking

When it comes to explaining the world, its happenings and its contents, human beings often look for answers and explanations that suit their beliefs rather than making decisions based in fact and logic. Adults often make errors in thinking and children are just as prone if not more so to such errors. The kinds of errors in thinking that occur can be classified into three basic categories: problems with scientific thinking, problems with pseudoscientific thinking, and problems with logical thinking.

Problems with Scientific Thinking (Giere, 1984). Three basic kinds of problems in scientific thinking can be described. The first is the idea that an idea held by an individual influences the observations made by that individual. In a simple example of this idea, consider an opportunity to make observations. The object of observation is a white mug from which dangles a tea bag tag and string. If asked to smell the contents of the mug without being able to look at the contents, most individuals will smell tea even though the tag and string are attached to a paper clip submerged in plain tap water. The expectations held by the individual will so color the observations that supporting information will be collected even if it isn't there. The same kind of thing can happen with predictions based on astrology. Believers tend to remember when the predictions were accurate rather than when they were not, tend to see the predictions as closer to reality than they might be. In cases where children are demonstrating this problem with thinking, it will be helpful for you to assist them in collecting accurate information over a period of time and then to help them draw conclusions from that data.

A second problem in scientific thinking occurs because there is an observer. People, and other animals, change their behavior when they are being observed. When behavior is changed by the observer, erroneous conclusions can be developed. With children, the effect of the observer may be even greater than simple changes in behavior due to direct observation. Children sometimes alter what occurs in an activity purposely in order to get particular results. As an example, one group of children investigating rolling objects predicted that a steeper incline would cause a toy car to roll farther than a slight incline. They made certain their results came out as desired by giving the car a little harder push at the top of the steep incline. In order to combat this error in thinking, you can do one of two things. If changes in animal behavior because of observation occur, you can work with children to provide an indirect means of observation. One teacher who wanted students to observe behavior of gerbils set up a mirror that could be observed easily and allowed the children to be unobserved as they watched the animals. In the second case, when children are making changes themselves, you might want to reemphasize the scientific attitude of honesty and discuss how to develop better and more accurate records. In addition, you might remind students of the scientific attitude of positive approach to failure so they realize it makes no difference whether a hypothesis is supported or not so long as the data are accurate and the conclusion appropriate to the data.

Finally, the kind of equipment used can influence the results of an investigation or experiment. Students who are attempting to use magnifiers on pond water may decide the water is free of unicellular life. The water may be teeming with paramecia, amoebas, and other creatures, but the magnifiers are not strong enough to give the necessary information. A microscope shows what a magnifier cannot. Erroneous conclusions may be drawn simply because the instruments in use cannot show the needed data.

Some of the errors in scientific thinking that result in odd or erroneous ideas on the part of students may be due to the students themselves and to the equipment they use. As a teacher, you need to take into account these kinds of problems in working with science activities and with ideas that may be strongly held by students.

Problems with Pseudoscientific Thinking (Kirchner, 1983; Giere, 1984). Problems that result in acceptance of pseudoscientific claims such as those of astrology, crystal healing, or visits by extraterrestrials often begin with acceptance of evidence which should probably not be considered. Very often such claims are based on anecdotal information rather than on hard data. **Anecdotal information** is information collected outside of experimental procedures and may include memories, stories, and personal experiences that have neither been verified nor replicated. There are many reports of a creature of some size living in Loch Ness, but not one piece of hard evidence has been obtained: a footprint, a piece of skin or flesh, a recording of a noise, a sonogram showing the confirmed presence of an animal. Anecdotes from those living along the loch are fun, but cannot be considered as scientific proof. Similarly, rumors are not sufficient to provide proof of an occurrence. A **rumor** is nothing more than a story that has been repeated so often it is considered to be true. Probably one of the best known rumors is that of alligators living in the sewers of large cities complete with stories of dogs suddenly disappearing especially near sewer openings. Rumors are just that, rumors, and cannot be considered as evidence of scientific fact. And, finally, coincidence cannot be considered as evidence of fact. A **coincidence** is a sequence of events that although accidental seems to have been planned or arranged. For example, every time Jane wears her purple blouse, she gets a headache in school. She decides that the purple blouse is what gives her the headache. Does a purple blouse really cause headaches? Not generally. The cause of the headache is more likely to be the stress induced by the mathematics test given on Thursdays or the band practicing in the room next door. However, the error in thinking makes the blouse the cause.

Problems with Logical Thinking (Copi, 1978).   One of the scientific values is a respect for logic and, as science teachers, we attempt to help children gain in the ability to use logical thought processes. However, there are a variety of problems when it comes to working with logical thought you should be aware of.

Words.   The first problem in using logical thought is in the use of words. Some words carry connotations that can cause people to overlook rational thought and accept an argument because of the terms, analogies, or metaphors used. For example, in supporting creationism as an alternative to evolution, some creationists link evolution to atheism, communism, and lawlessness (Kirchner, 1982). Rather than look at the logic of arguments, listeners hear these emotionally charged words and draw their conclusions on the basis of the images words evoke.

Persons.   Secondly, logical thought can be disrupted when the argument used in drawing a conclusion considers the person making the claim rather than the support given for the claim. A famous film star states that pesticides used on apples is poisoning children. Rather than look at the evidence on which the claim is based, people look at the star. Surely someone who is so good an actor should be trusted? Not necessarily, not if the individual does not have the evidence to back up a claim. Because of the person or persons involved in the claim, false conclusions may be accepted or true conclusions may be rejected.

Authority.   Third, and closely related to this second problem in logical thought, is a tendency to overrely on authorities. Yes, the information presented by an authority in a particular field should be given more credence than that of an individual not in the field. However, simply because a person is an authority in one field does not mean he or she is an authority in all fields. A physicist may be an expert on atomic particles but may have no more information about the cause of the extinction of dinosaurs than the average person.

Either-Or Thinking. Fourth is the problem of considering every situation an either-or situation. In this case, any issue is seen as a dichotomy, as black or white, without the possibility of an in-between position or positions. Either a meteor hit Earth and caused the extinction of the dinosaurs or no meteor hit and extinction occurred slowly because dinosaurs had reached the end of their biological life span. If one can prove dinosaurs died out slowly, then the meteor could not have hit. If one shows a meteor hit, then dinosaurs couldn't have died out slowly. In reality, there is no clear-cut dichotomy like this. Many other possibilities exist between these two scenarios, but problematic logical thought may treat this as an either-or situation. In fact, this is frequently done in daily thought.

Circular Reasoning. Fifth is the logical problem of circular reasoning. Circular reasoning occurs when the conclusion drawn is simply a restatement of some of the supporting evidence. Consider the following conversation:

I read where oat bran is really good for you.

How do you know oat bran is really good for you?

Because I read it.

This is circular reasoning. The individual does not have, or perhaps cannot recall the actual evidence for oat bran being good and so simply reaffirms that it was read.

Jumping to Conclusions. In this case one is "jumping to conclusions" and often basing a conclusion on too little evidence or is allowing bias to point in the direction of the conclusion. Watching a film on shark attacks and then drawing the conclusion that "sharks are man-eaters and killing machines" is an example of jumping to conclusions. Far more evidence about sharks is needed before any kind of conclusion can be drawn about this diverse class of animals. And, in fact, it might be very difficult to draw a logical conclusion after viewing a film which shows so erroneous a picture of sharks that bias may also creep into any conclusion drawn.

Logical Reasoning in the Classroom. In the classroom setting, attention to logical thought processes, collecting evidence and drawing appropriate conclusions from that evidence, can often be used when considering sensitive issues in the classroom. By giving attention to logical thought and appropriate conclusions based on evidence, you can handle difficult topics in a way that maintains the integrity of science teaching while treating nonscientific and pseudoscientific ideas of students with respect.

In order to help students overcome these kinds of problems in thinking, problems that may lead to erroneous ideas and particularly to pseudoscientific thought, you should help students to do six things. First, help your students look carefully at the kinds of information they are considering as they draw conclusions. Ask for the origins of the information and for the kind of information. Biased information and anecdotal information can quickly result in erroneous ideas. Also help your students look at the source of the information (Beck and Doyle, 1992). Help them ask questions about the expertise of the individuals in the field and help them develop the ability to look past the characteristics of the person and only at the information. Second, remind your students that when there are unusual ideas, contrary to logic, they need to have a great deal of evidence to support them. If aliens really do visit Earth, a great deal of solid, factual information is needed to show this is true. Anecdotes by people who thought they saw little gray or green people is not enough. Simply stating forcefully or in print that flying saucers landed in New Mexico is not enough to allow that information to be accepted. Third, caution your students to look at scientific language and to make certain scientific terms are being used correctly. Many nonscientific ideas are carefully couched in scientific terms, and those terms need to be carefully analyzed. This includes statistical information. Fourth, help your students look at the other possibilities when it comes to considering theories or ideas. Many situations are presented as if the options given are the only possibilities. Look for alternative explanations that may not have been given originally. Fifth, have your students look for those emotional words that may be used to persuade one to a particular argument when no evidence supports the argument. And finally, in teaching use more than one activity to develop a concept, more than one source of information to support a concept, more than one viewpoint when appropriate. In this way you will be modeling the habits of mind you want your students to develop.

Logical thought is difficult for children to use and teacher modeling is highly appropriate as a teaching tool, so you should continually ask these questions:

Where did you get your information?

Who is the author of the information?

What evidence do you have for that?

Have you considered . . . ?

Developing Critical and Creative Thinking Skills

Much learning at the elementary school level is considered to be low-level learning, that is, learning designed to add to the store of factual knowledge held by students. As a consequence, students are frequently asked to simply memorize information without context and with the goal in mind of passing the test on Friday. Memorizing a list of the states and their capitals generally falls into this category. The difficulty lies in the fact that students need to have certain bits of information, information which is most efficiently, although not most effectively, learned through a memorization process. Being able to recall the names of the continents, the names of the oceans, the names of the presidents is important but only if that information is later applied to some further task. It is when students are asked to go beyond simple memorization to applying, analyzing, and evaluating the information they collect through their educational activities that they begin to think at higher levels (Collins and Mangieri, 1992).

Definition

Probably the broadest definition of thinking is **thinking** as a search for meaning. In this search, students try to make sense out of information, whether it is meaning assumed to exist in a document or searching for meaning within a set of data that seems to have no meaning. This search for meaning involves decision making, problem solving, conceptualizing, analyzing, synthesizing, distinguishing the relevant from the irrelevant, and reasoning. As a part of learning, thinking results in greater understanding of subject matter and so in more extensive learning of that subject matter. As teaching thinking within the subject matter areas increases understanding and application of the subject matter, in teaching thinking there is more interest in how students react to when they do not know an answer than in how many answers they can parrot back to the teacher (Beyer, 1987).

However, simply because thinking generates excitement within the classroom does not mean it is easy to teach thinking. One problem with the teaching of thinking is that our own feelings and concepts can interfere. It is easy, then, to measure the results of thinking activities not against outside criteria for good thinking but against whether the product of that thinking agrees with our own thoughts.

Thinking should be taught across all subject matter areas and all grade levels. But remember that thinking is a developmental process. The structures and contexts of any thinking operation and of thinking as a whole becomes more complex, more sophisticated as students develop and grow, as they accumulate experiences (Costa, 1985). A teacher cannot expect the same type of thinking or the same depth of thinking at the first grade level as at the sixth grade level, and so thinking requirements should be geared to the age and experiential background of the children. Teaching thinking gives a sense of excitement to the classroom as children learn to use information, to think critically, and to think creatively.

Whether thinking is taught to first graders or to eighth graders, three general assumptions hold true. First, begin with the assumption that all students can learn to think (Swartz and Parks, 1994). In the past the idea has been held that children from impoverished backgrounds have such deficits of academic skills that they need to have their education focus only on the acquisition of information. As a consequence of this idea, children have often been taught skills and lessons directed toward the knowledge level of learning. This erroneous idea should be discarded. Children from all socioeconomic, all ethnic, and all geographical areas need to learn thinking skills as well as content information. Second, keep in mind that students can think better than they are inclined to do on their own. Often teachers say, "these kids can't or don't or won't think." And they are often correct. That does not mean, however, that children cannot learn to use thinking skills well. Just as children must be taught to read or write or multiply, they must be taught to think using appropriately developed lessons and appropriate teaching techniques. No one expects a child to come into the world knowing the names of the continents or the location of the various European nations. No one should expect children to come into the world knowing how to think. And closely related to the first assumption is the last assumption. Teaching is for children of all intellectual levels and not simply for those who have been identified as intellectually gifted. In the past, thinking development programs have been part of programs for the gifted child. These children were generally pulled out of the regular classroom, given specific lessons in critical thinking, problem solving, and creative thinking and then returned to the classroom to continue with the daily routine. Such an approach is indefensible when it is acknowledged that children of all intellectual abilities are challenged to make decisions every day and so should be given the tools needed to make those decisions appropriately (Ruggerio, 1988).

Once commitment to teaching of thinking is developed, then there is a need to differentiate between two types of thinking: critical thinking and creative thinking.

Critical Thinking

In its simplest form, **critical thinking** is knowing when to question something as well as having the inclination to ask questions. In more sophisticated terms, it is teaching students how to recognize and construct sound arguments, apply the principles of formal and informal logic, and to avoid fallacies in their reasoning. Critical thinking does mean producing ideas, but it also means analyzing and evaluating those ideas in the light of available evidence. And critical thinking also involves problem solving (Ruchlis, 1990).

When it comes to critical thinking, the evaluation of ideas is just as important as the production of ideas. A solution to a problem may be practical. A solution to a problem may be based on perfect reasoning. A solution to a problem may even include the latest evidence. But even with all of this, others may not see the problem solution as particularly reasonable. Consequently, before any problem solution is suggested it should be evaluated according to stated, factual criteria. The products of critical thinking are evaluated by facts, not by opinions.

Critical thinking includes certain skills. The following list is not meant to be comprehensive but is illustrative of the range of critical thinking skills that children should learn to use:

1. Distinguishing among verifiable facts, opinions, and value claims.
2. Distinguishing relevant from irrelevant information, claims, or reasons.
3. Determining the factual accuracy of a statement.
4. Determining the credibility of a source.
5. Identifying ambiguous claims and arguments.
6. Identifying unstated assumptions.
7. Detecting bias.
8. Identifying logical fallacies.
9. Recognizing logical inconsistencies in a line of reasoning.
10. Determining the strength of an argument or claim.
11. Determining when a problem exists and determining what the problem is (Beyer, 1987; Costa, 1985).

Metacognition

In its essence, **metacognition** is thinking about one's own thinking. Metacognition is the ability to monitor other thinking processes. When using metacognition, students are able to plan a strategy for finding information, conscious of the strategies they use in problem solving, and able to evaluate their own thinking. Metacognition is a key attribute of formal operational thought, but students in other stages of development can be assisted in using metacognitive strategies (Astington and Olson, 1990).

Critical thinking has certain components and so does metacognition. The four major components of metacognition are (1) developing a plan of action, (2) maintaining that plan in the mind over a period of time, (3) reflecting back over the plan, and (4) evaluating the plan on completion. Each of these components gives a clue as to what you can do when working with children in order to help them develop metacognitive strategies.

First, before you have your students get involved in a problem-solving situation, take time to discuss strategies and steps for problem solving. Give the directions. State the time frame allowed. Give the rules under which they will be working. Discussing problem solving and problem-solving parameters with your students gets them to think about how they will solve a problem rather than simply working with trial and error strategies.

Second, as your students work at solving a problem, have them share their progress periodically with others in the class. Encourage your students to talk about how they reached the point at which they are working and especially about what they will do next. After the problem-solving session is over, have your students evaluate themselves, including how well they think they did in solving the problem. Have them look at the choices and decisions they made during the course of problem solving and how those choices affected their results. By looking at their decisions students have to explore not only their successes on the road to solving the problem but also their detours and their failures.

Third, as your students work, encourage them to ask their own questions rather than simply relying on your questions. The questions your students ask can often provide other problems for solution.

Fourth, help your students evaluate the results of their problem solving on the basis of established criteria. The criteria should be established by the students and can be subjective as well as objective.

Fifth, during activities help your students identify the kinds of materials and information needed for them to solve the problem. When students give you their ideas, use open-ended questions in order to get them to talk more about what they were thinking or trying. Try to have your students discuss one another's ideas. And, finally, help students learn to clarify their value statements. For example, students may say hunting as a means of population control for deer is bad. "Bad" is a value statement. Ask your students to tell you what they mean by the word bad in this situation. But clarifying is not simply describing or refining value statements; clarifying also means asking students where they got certain pieces of information. "They said" should never be enough. Ask students to clarify who "they" are, so they become more definite in their statements and use of supporting evidence. Third, encourage students to use operational definitions of terms. Using operational defin-itions is particularly important when a term can be defined in a variety of different ways. For example, the term *ecology* has a variety of different possible interpreta-tions, from the study of the interrelationships among the living and nonliving parts of the environment, to cleaning up the environment after oil spills and other cata-strophic events, to recycling, to environmental extremism. Until students agree on a particular definition, they may be discussing very different concepts. Fourth, encourage metacognition through role playing and simulations. When the role played requires a student to take a point of view opposite to his or her own, the result is thinking about his or her own thinking. Fifth, encourage metacognition in your students through journal writing. When students write in journals, they revisit and think about what they have learned and how their ideas have changed. And, finally, model metacognition. Use metacognitive strategies naturally as a part of your own thinking skills.

Using Critical Thinking in the Classroom

In using critical thinking skills in the classroom, always take into account the age and developmental level of the children involved in the lesson. Young children, kindergarten through second graders, can use critical thinking skills and can apply those skills provided the task selected is appropriate and the required cognitive skills are present. For example, in teaching first graders, one of the things my class did was plant seeds. Lima beans were easy for children to plant and generally sprouted without too much difficulty. However, there were always some seeds that simply did not grow and so some children were disappointed when green plants were growing in everyone's cups but their own. Naturally, they asked why all the seeds didn't grow. Rather than give an explanation, I asked my students what they thought. The children came up with four ideas:

The person who planted it didn't know how.
The seeds were just duds.
The seeds were too wet or dry.
The seeds needed more sunshine.

I asked them how we could decide which of these ideas was probably right. They ruled out the first one quickly by looking at the names on the cups. One of the cups had my name on it and they gave me the benefit of the doubt. I probably did know how to plant seeds. The last one was ruled out quickly as well. The first point was that all of the cups were in the same place. The second factor was more impor-tant. All of the seeds were under the dirt where they "couldn't tell if it was sunny or not." The other two possibilities took more consideration. They decided they could tell about wet or dry by looking at the cups. When they looked at one cup, without a plant growing, the dirt was so wet there was a layer of water sitting on the top of the dirt. Another cup was wet enough that the soil would pour out of the cup. But none of the cups without plants were overly dry. They ruled out dry. Finally, they decided they needed to look at the seeds in the cups that were neither too wet nor too dry but still had no plants. After dumping them out onto the table, they saw that the seeds were bigger than comparison bean seeds, but not one of them had done anything but get bigger. Their conclusion: seeds don't grow when they are too wet or when they are duds.

These first graders were engaging in high-order thinking skills, particularly analysis and evaluation, and did so successfully. The reason for the success was that the children were able to relate the problem solutions to things familiar to themselves. If we are going to have our students engaging in critical thinking, we need to be certain the experience is appropriate to the students. They should have the background they need in order to use their critical thinking skills. Consequently, critical thinking and creative thinking should be used in the context of subject matter rather than isolating a particular thinking skill and teaching it separately from the subject matter. For example, if you want your students to consider bias in information, have them look at a variety of sources of information on a topic under study and use questioning skills to help them look at the accuracy of the information and the biases that may be part of the information.

In addition to being certain your students have the background information necessary and you are working with critical thinking in context, the classroom atmosphere will be important in developing both critical and creative thinking. The classroom atmosphere must be such that students feel free to express their ideas and opinions. Your students need to know that they will be listened to with respect, that evaluation of ideas will come not during the presentation of those ideas but after all ideas have been given. Evaluation is the final step in both critical and creative thinking, not an ongoing process.

Using thinking skills in trying to decide why bean seeds did not grow is different from using thinking skills with sensitive issues. However, the same general ideas apply no matter what the situation. Consider the same sort of strategy applied to a topic like the controversial topic of all times: evolution.

In an eighth grade biology class, one of the chapters of the textbook dealt with biological evolution. The teacher presented the information in the chapter using as guest speakers a geneticist, a paleontologist, and an anthropologist from a local university. In addition, the teacher used films about Charles Darwin's voyage aboard the *Beagle* and took students on a field trip to a fossil location where students found their own fossils. As she began a summary discussion of what was learned during the unit, one of the students expressed the idea that the theory of evolution is only a theory and so should be taught not as something that is true but as something some scientists think is true. Once the first of the students showed skepticism, so did others until one of the students insisted that evolution was all wrong and anyone who believed in evolution can't possibly believe in God and so everyone else in the room is an atheist.

The teacher was at first shocked and then disturbed, but her students looked to her for guidance. The easiest thing would have been to dismiss the skeptics as having a religious concept whereas evolution is a scientific theory, but she decided that was not the way to help students weigh and evaluate ideas and issues.

She began by asking students to identify the problem. One of the students quickly stated that the problem is evolution is only a theory and so it shouldn't be presented as fact and that anyone who thinks evolution is true is an atheist. She then asked if there was one problem listed or more than one problem. The students identified more than one problem: what is a theory, are there only two ways of looking at the origins and development of life, and is anyone who believes in evolution automatically an atheist.

First the teacher asked the students what information would be needed to solve the three problems. The students decided they needed to know more about what is meant by a theory. Some of them expressed the idea that maybe the word *theory* is used differently in science than in other places. They also decided they needed to know if there are other explanations for the beginning and development of life on Earth. And finally, they decided they needed to know more about what different religions think about evolution. The students divided into groups to do some research.

Three days later, the teacher reconvened the total class to present their information. The group dealing with theories had come to the conclusion that a scientific theory is a great deal different than a "theory" as it is used everyday. They discussed the nature of a scientific theory and presented the evidence showing that evolution did indeed fit the concept of a scientific theory. The second group was excited about their results. They had discovered that almost every culture from the ancient Egyptians and earlier had explanations of how life started and how it got the way it was. Most of those myths, they had found, were based in the religion of the culture. They discussed many of the myths they discovered and then went on to a different type of information. They had also discovered that there were ideas in between strict evolutionary theory and strictly religious ideas. They presented their information in terms of a continuum. And, finally, the final group presented its information. They had been surprised to find that many of the religious groups in the United States see nothing wrong with evolutionary theory and others find it erroneous. It was not what they had expected to find. They had expected all of the different religious groups to agree.

At the end of the presentations, the teacher summarized what they discovered in their researches and asked the students to write in their journals about the information they had heard and researched.

This teacher took a very difficult and confrontational situation and handled it in a way that expanded ideas on all sides. Students had an opportunity to identify the problem areas, to present information on each of those problems, and to draw their own conclusions. Because the issue did have religious overtones, rather than have students publicly summarize information, she had them use their journals to react to what they had researched and discovered. She felt the strategy had worked well because of some of the comments she read. No one had felt coerced to believe or accept an idea that conflicted with religious or family values, but one of the most adamant skeptics wrote, "I never realized there were so many ways of looking at things. I don't agree with a lot of them, but I do see why people can get really upset and angry about some kinds of ideas."

Figure 12.2

Word Splash

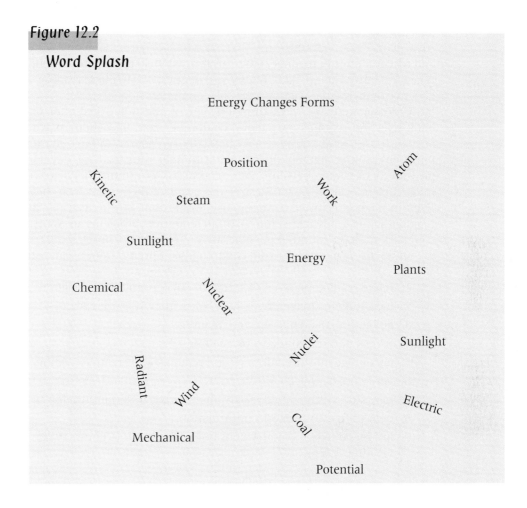

Critical Reading.   **Critical reading** involves evaluation. It asks the reader to make a personal judgment about the accuracy, value, or truthfulness of what is read. The reader is asked to interpret, apply, analyze, and synthesize information. This level of comprehension includes the ability to distinguish between fact and opinion, fantasy and reality, and to identify propaganda.

Creative Reading.   **Creative reading** asks the reader to come up with new or alternative solutions to those presented by the writer.

   Three means for assisting students to comprehend material are particularly helpful in the science classroom. The first is the use of semantic mapping strategies to help students recall what is already known about a particular topic prior to reading a new selection. Students who have considered their own concepts prior to reading are more likely to read with meaning. A second means for enhancing comprehension is to provide students with hands-on experiences that will help them develop the concepts contained in a text prior to reading the information (Santa and Alverman, 1991). A hands-on activity in which children develop a concept of action and reaction prior to reading about this law will help them comprehend written text when it is encountered. And, finally, use of questions to guide reading is particularly effective in increasing science textbook comprehension.

Unfortunately, the most common type of question asked after reading a textbook selection requires only literal comprehension, and children who are able to answer those literal questions are generally considered to have mastered the content found in the textbook. If you want to help your students develop more complex levels of comprehension, you need to ask questions that require students to infer, conclude, analyze, synthesize, and evaluate the information they are reading. Even in science, creative comprehension questions can be used. In this case, after reading about a possible solution to air pollution problems in a city, the teacher could ask students for other possible ways of solving the problem.

When using questions to aid children in comprehension, use questions to:

1. relate reading material to students' background knowledge.
2. help students make predictions before they start to read.
3. guide students while they are reading.
4. review and summarize after reading.
5. encourage interpretation, critical reading, and creative reading.
6. verify predictions.
7. help students find evidence from materials to support their answers.
8. help students summarize information.
9. intervene when comprehension is doubtful (Rubin, 1992; Pierson and Fielding, 1991).

Helping children comprehend the texts they read is an important aspect of using a science textbook. However, simply comprehending a text is not sufficient. Students should also be helped to remember the information in their textbooks and to develop the vocabulary presented by those textbooks. A widely used strategy for assisting students in recalling information from their textbooks is the SQ3R technique for study.

SQ3R Strategy

The **SQ3R strategy,** developed by Robinson (1970), is a widely used strategy for helping students learn to study and remember the information found in their textbooks. It consists of five easy-to-apply steps:

1. *Survey:* Students should get an overall sense of the information they will be reading and studying before they begin to look for details. In this first step, students skim the entire reading assignment to get some idea about the material and how that material is organized.

2. *Question:* Students look for the main headings and then change each of those headings into a question. The questions are then used to guide the reading done by the students.

3. *Read:* Using the questions for guidance, the students then read the information to answer the questions. While students read they should notice how the paragraphs are organized because this will help them remember the answers. Students can take notes on the key ideas so they can be used for future review.

4. *Recite or recall:* In this step, which is very important to the total strategy, students try to answer the questions they listed without referring to the textbook.

5. *Review:* Students take a few moments to review the major headings and subheadings of what they finished studying. In addition, students attempt to relate what they have just finished studying to what they have previously studied on the same topic before moving on to the next reading assignment.

Although this is an effective and easy-to-use strategy, children must be taught how to use it with their textbooks. In particular, students need to be helped to realize that although they can quickly skim through the material in step 1, that they need to slow down, concentrate, and read carefully as they read step 3. They also need to be helped to understand that recalling the answers to the questions they wrote is an important step. If they are unable to recall the answer to a question, they should go back and reread the material.

Strategies for Developing Science Vocabulary

Science textbooks and trade books are overflowing with vocabulary that is met with in few, if any other, places. Terms like *molecule, spectrum, generator, photosynthesis, tectonic,* and *arthropod* are unlikely to be found in most reading programs but these and many other terms are found in elementary science textbooks. Even though these words are not found in the typical child's reading program, the words are a vital aspect of science because they give precise names to the concepts and phenomena of science. Consequently, students must learn and use correct terminology, provided that terminology is meaningful to them.

With young children, kindergarten and early primary grade children, vocabulary cannot be taught with a glossary, dictionary, or formal explanation. With older children, vocabulary should not be taught with glossary, dictionary, or formal explanation. Instead, children should be given meaningful experiences that allow them to develop vocabulary which is meaningful. Meaningful vocabulary is not only remembered but used by children.

Science textbooks introduce new vocabulary to students at a rapid rate and often without providing a means for connecting new vocabulary to what is already known or for remembering that new vocabulary after it is learned. A variety of strategies exist for helping students remember vocabulary. Each of these strategies is discussed here.

Vocabulary Through Activities

One of the most productive ways to develop science vocabulary in children is through the science activities used to teach the content of science. Such activity allows students to develop the concept named by the new term before the term is introduced (Santa and Alverman, 1991). For example, in working with magnets, students discover through using paper clips and placing those paper clips in various locations on a magnet that the ends of the magnet hold more paper clips than anywhere else on the magnet. Students can then draw a conclusion that the ends of a magnet are stronger than the middle. You can then introduce the word *pole* as another name for the end of a magnet and then use the two terms—ends and poles—simultaneously until students have connected the term *pole* as meaning the area of greatest strength on a magnet, the ends of a bar or horseshoe magnet.

Semantic Mapping

Semantic mapping is one of those strategies that is useful in a variety of ways. It helps determine background information as well as introduce a new chapter or unit to students. Semantic mapping can also be used to introduce vocabulary to students. In this case the new word is put on the board, a sheet of paper, or the overhead. The word should be somewhat familiar to the students. The students then brainstorm individually the words they think of when they hear the new vocabulary word. After they have had a chance to brainstorm, they work together in small groups to develop a master list of all the possibilities. In the next step the children attempt to find a way to classify the master list terms into a few categories. With primary grade children, you should help determine the categories; older children can work in small groups to determine the categories for themselves. Once the categories are developed, the students continue to work in their small groups or as a class to develop their maps. Once the map is developed, the students use the map to write a definition for the new term. Their definitions can then be compared to dictionary or glossary definitions. In many case, the definitions written by the students are far more comprehensive and comprehensible than those formal book definitions. Figure 12.3 shows the use of a semantic map for developing a definition of soil after an activity in observing a soil sample.

Inferring Word Meanings

Inferring the meaning of a word requires a term that is totally unfamiliar to the class (Johnson and Pearson, 1984). It uses imagination, creativity, and fun to help children decide on the meaning of a totally new term. In the first step, the word is put on the board or overhead and the students are asked to guess at the meaning. No guess is rejected. All of the guesses are listed. The students have a chance as they give their guesses to tell why they think their definition is a good one. Once all of the possibilities are given, the word is presented in a series of increasingly more focused sentences. Each sentence is presented individually and the guesses considered in light of the information found in the sentence (Stahl and Karpinus, 1991).

Figure 12.3

Semantic Mapping for Developing a Definition

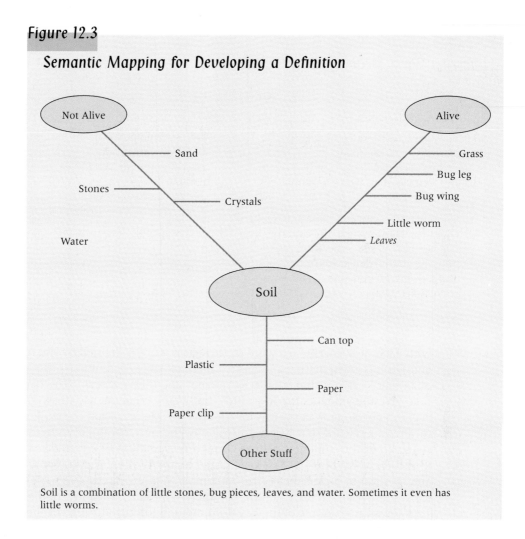

Soil is a combination of little stones, bug pieces, leaves, and water. Sometimes it even has little worms.

Some of the guesses are eliminated, and some new guesses may be added. After each of the sentences is presented, the possible meaning of the word is discussed. After all of the sentences have been presented, the students are asked to come to a consensus on the meaning of the word and then the definition is verified with a dictionary or with the glossary of the textbook. Figure 12.4 gives an example of using inferring word meanings to introduce vocabulary.

Helping Students Remember Vocabulary Terms

Using the Keyword Method. The **keyword method** (Johnson and Pearson, 1984) is a technique for helping students remember the definitions of new vocabulary terms. It is a memory strategy. In the keyword method, students are presented

Figure 12.4

Inferring Word Meanings

GRAYWACKE

Possible Meanings (brainstorming)

Somebody got hit with something gray.
The color gray went wacky.
Its the name of a horse.
It's a guy with gray hair who went nuts.

Clues

1. Sometimes you can find some graywacke when you take a walk in the country.
2. The collector picked piece of graywacke from the ground and looked closely at it.
3. The geologist identified the material as graywacke.

Possible Meanings (after seeing the clues)

1—It's a kind of flower.
3—It's a kind of rock.
1—It's something you can eat.
1—It's a crazy cow.
2—It's a piece of rock.
2—It's a piece of an arrowhead.

with each new vocabulary word in turn. The word is defined by the teacher or the definition is given by the students. In the next step, each new word is connected to a familiar keyword that sounds somewhat like the new term. The teacher may, at first, give the students the keywords, but as the students use this system they can begin to develop the keywords for themselves. Make certain the students can easily recall the keyword that belongs to each of the new vocabulary words. In the next step, you or the students create a visual representation that connects the new term to the keyword. In many cases the visual representation, the drawing, is humorous and the humor makes it easier to remember. Finally, the students use the keyword to recall the visual representation and then to recall the meaning of the term. Figure 12.5 shows an example of the keyword method for introducing vocabulary.

Figure 12.5

Using the Keyword Method

New Word	Definition	Keyword	Image
Crustacean	An invertebrate with a hard exo-skeleton, like a lobster.	**Crust**	A lobster breaking through the top crust of a pie.
Arthropod	An invertebrate with jointed legs, like a grasshopper.	**Arthritis**	A grasshopper with swollen joints walking with a cane.
Arachnid	An invertebrate with two body parts and eight legs, a spider.	**Rack**	A rack filled with wet spiders drying in the sun.

Using Acronyms. In some cases, it is necessary to recall a list of terms. These words may be recalled in a particular order, such as the colors that make up the visible light spectrum; in other cases the order makes no difference. In either case, the use of an acronym is a useful strategy for children to use (Johnson and Pearson, 1984). The colors of the visible light spectrum (red, orange, yellow, green, blue, indigo, violet) are remembered by the acronym Roy G. Biv, a name composed of the first letters of each of the colors. An **acronym** is a word or words composed of the first letters of the list of the terms being learned. When order is of no importance, the letters of the terms being learned can be rearranged into any order that spells a pronounceable word: real or made up.

Acrostics. An **acrostic** is similar to an acronym (Johnson and Pearson, 1984). The difference is that instead of using the first letter of each term to spell a word then used to recall the terms, a sentence is made using words that have the first letter of the words being recalled. This strategy is particularly useful for learning a list of words in a particular order. For example, the sentence "My very elegant mother just sat upon nine porcupines" is useful for recalling the names of the planets in order (Mercury, Venus, Earth, Mars, Jupiter, Saturn, Uranus, Neptune, Pluto), and two sentences "Queen Tess can jump to Peru. Can Duke Steve open canned peaches?" can be used to recall the geological eras (Quarternary, tertiary, cretaceous, jurassic, triassic, permian, carboniferous, devonian, silurian, ordovician, cambrian, precambrian). Acrostics are best when they contain an element of humor and when they are constructed by the students.

Pegwords. **Pegwords** are used to remember a list of items in a particular order by relating the items to a pegword (Johnson and Pearson, 1984). The pegwords are as follows:

> one is a bun
> two is a shoe
> three is a tree
> four is a door
> five is a hive
> six is a stick
> seven is heaven
> eight is a gate
> nine is a vine
> ten is a hen

Each time an item in a list is attached to a pegword, a picture or mental image should always be constructed to go with the pegword. When retrieving the list, the number is thought of first, followed by the pegword and then the image.

Children need to be given strategies for remembering the definitions for the new vocabulary terms they learn through the science class. Simply telling them to learn the definitions is ineffective. Giving them strategies for recalling those definitions is effective. Activity 12.3 focuses on including reading and vocabulary strategies in developing your unit plan.

Reading in Science Activity

Activity 12.3

Purpose   To incorporate vocabulary and reading development strategies into teaching.

Procedure
1. Return to the unit developed as a part of Chapter 8.
2. Make a list of all of the new vocabulary terms developed as a part of the unit.
3. Using the strategies developed in this section, show how you might teach the vocabulary in the most effective manner.

Appropriate Uses of the Science Textbook

According to *Science for All Americans,* 95 percent of teachers use their textbooks 90 percent of the time. Using the textbook simply as a reader is ineffective in teaching science. But using it in a variety of other ways is effective. A science textbook can be used effectively in the hands-on science program to develop unit plans, add additional information, check activity results, review information, and add terminology.

Developing Unit Plans

Unit plans are a means for organizing the curriculum in science. They allow the teacher to do long-range planning and to make decisions about the sequence, depth, and scope of the topics they will be teaching. In selecting the general content for a unit plan, the textbook is a good foundation. From the content of the textbook, you can make decisions about what to include, what to delete, and what to add to the content information. In addition, the textbook can provide a starting point to selecting science activities, for connections between and among subject matter areas, and for children's literature selections.

Adding Additional Information

The active involvement of students in the learning of science is a necessity if children are to understand not only science content but also the nature of science as inquiry. However, not all of the content we want students to learn can be learned through hands-on activity. Textbooks can be used effectively to provide the additional information that students may not be able to gain strictly through a hands-on program.

Checking Activity Results

Most elementary school science program use household materials and classroom-based activities rather than science laboratories and sophisticated science laboratory equipment. As a result, the data collected from an activity and the conclusions drawn from that data may be contrary to scientific knowledge. When this happens in the classroom, the textbook can be used to create a problem-solving situation. The children have drawn one conclusion. The teacher has the children compare their conclusion to the information found in the textbook. At this point the teacher can ask, "What do you think caused our results to be different from those found in your book?" In this way the teacher is challenging the students to consider their activities and to try to find where differences might have occurred. They are still being made familiar with the scientifically correct information, but they are also actively pursuing causes of differences.

Reviewing Information

Many units in textbooks can be effectively taught without ever opening the textbook. Units on magnets, simple machines, physical or chemical changes, characteristics of rocks and minerals, or weather can often be taught through direct hands-on experience. The textbook can then be used to help students review all of the information they have learned through direct experience, and to review it in a systematic manner.

Adding Terminology

As students are involved in hands-on activities, in the collection of results, and in the drawing of conclusions, they use their own words to express their ideas. The use of the children's own words adds both meaning and authenticity to the conclusions and the discussion of activity results. In many cases, however, the terms used by the students have equivalents in scientific terminology. Once students develop a concept using their own words in a conclusion statement, the textbook can be read and the connection made between the words used by the students and the scientific terminology in the textbook.

Science and Children's Literature

A strong movement within the elementary school curriculum is toward the development of literacy skills throughout the curriculum. This means the integration of reading, writing, listening, and speaking into all subject matter areas. In science, students have always been involved in these areas. They read their textbooks. They write the results of activities, keep journals of their investigations, and do research reports about topics of interest. They listen to others and present their own ideas in discussions of activities and reports. Reading in the science classroom, however, has tended to be limited to the textbook. This not only limits the information available to children but also gives an erroneous picture of science. The single textbook approach gives the impression that all of the knowledge about a certain topic can be, and is, collected into a single source and, by extension, that scientists can use a single source of information. It also gives the impression that there is little or no disagreement about particular topics when there may be a great deal of dissent and discussion. The inclusion of other sources of information in the classroom, particularly children's literature, can help alleviate these erroneous impressions.

Children's literature refers to nontextbook materials and can range from picture books to chapter books to children's magazines and newspapers. In general the use of children's literature in the science program involves either using literature as a supplement to a textbook program or using literature in lieu of a textbook program (Saul and Jagush, 1996).

Using Literature to Supplement the Textbook

Science textbooks attempt to include many diverse topics so that students are exposed to a variety of subject matter areas. The problem may be that there is little depth within those topics. Children's literature provides an opportunity for children to read about topics in greater depth (Scott, 1993). A paragraph about endangered species in a textbook can be expanded into books on whales, pandas, tigers, condors, whooping cranes, and hundreds of other endangered animals. A unit dealing with sound in a textbook may discuss the concepts of frequency, pitch, or volume, but children's literature can provide information on musical instruments, noise pollution, the effect of loud sounds on hearing, or communication. Probably one of the major reasons for including children's literature as a supplement to the science textbook in the classroom is that it increases the depth of the information included in the textbook.

A second advantage to the use of children's literature as a supplement to the science textbook is that it allows for a diversity of interests on the part of the children. A unit on animals as found in the textbook may talk about animal classification as vertebrates or invertebrates and then look in more detail at specific classes and orders of animals. Children's literature can allow students who are interested in tropical animals to read more extensively, students who are interested in extinct animals to add to their knowledge, and students who are interested in zoos to read about them.

A third advantage to the use of children's literature to supplement the science textbook is that it allows the teacher to provide materials on a variety of reading levels. Students who are having difficulty reading the textbook materials can be provided with books written at a lower readability level and students who read beyond the level of the textbook can be provided with materials at a higher level. In both cases, the students are still gaining the information presented in the textbook, but at a reading level more appropriate to their skills.

And finally, when children's literature is used as a supplement to the textbook, a more realistic picture of the role of reading in the scientist's world is given. Scientists do not go to a single source of information when planning an experimental study. Instead, they read from a wide variety of sources and gain supporting information from a variety of areas.

In using children's literature as a supplement to the textbook, you are still focusing on the content as suggested by the text but providing additional information of interest to the students and on an appropriate reading level.

Using Literature Instead of a Textbook

The advantages of using children's literature instead of a textbook begin with the same advantages found for using children's literature to supplement a textbook. A literature-based program allows for greater depth of study for a topic, for diversity of interests on the part of the students, for a variety of reading levels, and for a more realistic picture of reading within the world of the scientist. In addition, the use of children's literature in lieu of a textbook allows the teacher to develop a program appropriate to a particular class of children.

Textbooks are written for the mass market. In many cases the content in the textbook may not be relevant to a particular group of children. Inner-city children working through a chapter dealing with the ecology of a pond may not have the background information necessary to understand the concepts. Rural children looking at complex machines from the viewpoint of a city construction site may be equally at a loss. The use of trade books, of children's literature, allows teachers to take the basic concepts for a unit of work and to tailor those concepts to a particular group of children through the selection of appropriate books. In addition, teachers can select books that are more personal than the writing of many textbooks. Using fictionalized literature with strong scientific content can make a topic more relevant to children as they view that content through the eyes of the characters. The use of fictionalized accounts can also lead to an exploration of the emotional and social aspects of the science content.

Fact and Fantasy

The use of children's literature within the science program has distinct advantages over the sole use of a textbook series. However, as a teacher you need to use some caution in selecting literature to use in the classroom. Children's literature used to support the science program should be accurate, unbiased, and up to date.

One place in which a lot of caution needs to be taken is in the use of fantasy literature to support the science program. Some evidence indicates that the fantasy aspects of the literature may actually interfere with the development of accurate science content (Mayer, 1995). But fantasy literature also has some additional difficulties : anthropomorphism, teleology, and anthropocentrism.

Anthropomorphism is the giving of human characteristics to nonhuman living things. Peter Rabbit is an anthropomorphic book in that the characters in the story act like humans and are depicted in human settings. Anthropocentrism is the interpreting of animal behavior in terms of human motivations or human emotions. This occurs in books about animals in which tigers, lions, wolves or any carnivores are characterized as "vicious" because they prey on other animals. These animals aren't vicious, they're hungry!

Teleology is similar to anthropomorphism in that it gives human characteristics to the nonhuman. However, in this case, it is the giving of such characteristics to inanimate objects, particularly attributing wants or needs to those objects. Teleology occurs in writing where atoms bond with one another to form molecules because they "want to be neutral." Atoms don't *want* to be anything.

Anthropocentrism is the placing of humans at the center of all things and so looking at the world strictly from a human point of view. We characterize certain plants as *weeds,* a negative term, because they grow where humans do not want them, and certain insects as *pests,* also negative, because they occur where humans do not want them.

When selecting books for inclusion in a literature-based program, look carefully at the literature selected and avoid anthropomorphism or anthropocentrism. This does not mean, however, that books like *Peter Rabbit* or *The Hungry Caterpillar* cannot be effectively used within the science program. Such books, which are excellent children's literature but not so excellent in terms of science content, can be used as springboards for consideration through observation of the real behavior of rabbits or caterpillars and for a comparison of reality with fantasy.

Children's literature in the science classroom has strong roles to play. The teacher who chooses to allow it to play those roles is providing opportunities to make science more interesting, more exciting, and more relevant. Activities 12.4 and 12.5 address reading.

Reading in Science Activities

Activity 12.4

Purpose   To develop an annotated bibliography of children's books that could be used to supplement the elementary or middle school science program.

Procedure
1. Select a particular level to work with: early childhood, primary grades, intermediate grades, or middle school grades.
2. Using textbooks and/or course of study for the grade levels selected, develop a list of topics commonly taught in those grade levels.
3. Develop an annotated bibliography of books that could be used to supplement or form the basis of a science program for each of those topics.
   a. List the title of the book, author, appropriate grade level, and a brief description of the content.
   b. Organize the materials according to content so an individual book could easily be located.

Activity 12.5

Purpose To demonstrate how children's literature can be included in a discipline-oriented science unit plan.

Procedure
1. Return to the unit developed in Chapter 8.
2. Develop a list of children's books that could be used as a part of the unit.
3. Modify existing or develop new lesson plans that will incorporate the use of children's literature into the teaching of science content.

Summary

Because science textbooks form the basis for most elementary and middle school science teaching, their strengths and weaknesses need to be understood. Among the strengths of science textbooks are the scope, sequence, and teaching materials included in any series. Weaknesses include readability, concept density, background information, and kinds of strategies advocated for teaching.

Reading in a content area like science is more difficult than reading from a basal reader. Consequently, students need help to read and understand their textbooks. Strategies using semantic mapping can make textbooks more comprehensible, and the SQ3R strategy is a particular reading strategy effective with any kind of content reading. In addition to aiding in reading comprehension, techniques like word splash, keyword method, and use of acronyms can help students learn and recall vocabulary.

Finally, the use of children's literature can add another dimension to the science program by bringing in materials especially written for children to enhance the content found in textbooks or to form the basis of a textbook-free science program.

Chapter Vocabulary

The number following each term refers to the page on which the term is first introduced.

Applying the
CONCEPTS

1. You are teaching seventh grade science, but you discover that some of your students are unable to read at a seventh grade level. How could you use literature in order to help students overcome reading difficulties?

2. A second grade teacher in your school is using children's literature to help her students learn science. She has carefully selected the books she uses to be certain they have accurate, scientific information. Her strategy for using the books is to introduce each book using a semantic mapping technique and then to have the children read the book and write in their journals about what they have read. What could you suggest to this teacher to improve what she is doing in science?

3. You have begun to use children's literature as a part of your science program, and the children in your class are learning and enjoying it. Your principal gets a letter from concerned parents stating that you are not teaching the science curriculum mandated by the school system because you are not using the adopted textbook series. What would you do to alleviate the concerns of both parents and principal?

4. The students in your inner-city fourth grade class are about to begin a new unit of work in their science textbooks. The unit deals with machines, and the modular approach textbook organizes the study around a farm. What could you do to assure that your students will be able to learn from their textbook?

5. As you look through the textbook for your grade level, you find it is inappropriate to your students, both developmentally and in terms of background. What could you do?

References

Afferbach, P. P. 1990, Winter. The influence of prior knowledge on expert readers' main idea construction strategies. *Reading Research Quarterly* 25, 31–46.

American Association for the Advancement of Science. 1989. *Project 2061: Science for all Americans.* Washington, D.C.: Author.

Anderson, T. H., and B. B. Armbruster. 1984. Content area textbooks. In R. C. Anderson, J. Osborn, and R. J. Tierney (eds.), *Learning to read in American Schools: Basal readers and content texts* (pp. 193–226). Hillsdale, N.J.: Lawrence Erlbaum.

Armbruster, B. B. 1984. The problems of inconsiderate text. In G. G. Duffy, L. R. Roehler, and J. Mason (eds.), *Comprehension instruction: Perspectives and suggestions* (pps. 202–217). New York: Longman.

Association for Supervision and Curriculum Development. 1998, Fall. Science education: How curriculum and instruction are evolving. *ASCD Curriculum Update.* Alexandria, Va.: Author.

Davidson, J. L. 1982. The group mapping activity for instruction in reading and thinking. *Journal of Reading* 25, 52–56.

Forgan, H. W., and C. T. Mangrum. 1989. *Teaching content area reading skills* (4th ed.). Columbus, Ohio: Merrill.

Johnson, D. D., and P. D. Pearson. 1984. *Teaching reading vocabulary* (2nd ed.). New York: Holt, Rinehard and Winston.

Lapp, D., J. Flood, and N. Farnan. 1989. *Content area reading and learning.* Englewood Cliffs, N.J.: Prentice Hall.

Mayer, D. A. 1995. How can we best use children's literature in teaching science concepts? *Science and Children* 33(8), 22–25.

Myer, L. A., L. Crummy, and E. A. Greer. 1988. Elementary science textbooks: Their contents, text characteristics, and comprehensibility. *Journal of Research in Science Teaching* 25, 435–463.

Pearson, D. P., and L. Fielding. 1991. Comprehension Instruction. In R. Barr, M. L. Kamil, P. Mosenthal, and P. D. Pearson (eds.), *Handbook of reading research* (Vol 2). New York: Longman.

Robinson, F. P. 1970. *Effective study* (4th ed.) New York: Harper & Row.

Rubin, D. 1992. *Reading and study skills in content areas.* Boston: Allyn & Bacon.

Rubin, D. 1993. *A practical approach to teaching reading.* Boston: Allyn & Bacon.

Santa, C. M., and D. E. Alvermann (eds.). 1991. *Science learning: Processes and applications.* Newark, Del.: International Reading Association.

Saul, W., and S. A. Jagush (eds.). 1986. *Vital connections: Children, science, and books.* Portsmouth, N.H.: Heinemann.

Scott, J. (ed.). 1993. *Science and language links: Classroom implications.* Portsmouth, N.H.: Heinemann.

Singer, H., and D. Donlan. 1988. *Reading and learning from text* (2nd ed.). Hillsdale, N.J.: Lawrence Erlbaum.

Smith, N. B. 1969, December. The many faces of reading comprehension. *The Reading Teacher* 249–259, 291.

Stahl, S., and B. A. Karpinus. 1991, September. Possible sentences: Predicting word meanings to teach content area vocabulary. *The Reading Teacher* 45, 35–43.

Stepans, J. I., B. W. Saigo, and C. Ebert. 1995. *Changing the classroom from within: Partnership, collegiality, and constructivism.* Montgomery, Ala.: Saiwood.

U.S. National Research Center. 1998. *TIMSS United States.* URL: http//www.ustimss.msu.edu.

Woodward, A., and D. L. Elliot. 1990. Textbooks: Consensus and controversy. In D. L. Elliot and A. Woodward, (eds.), *Textbooks and schooling in the United States.* Chicago: University of Chicago Press.

CHAPTER THIRTEEN

SCIENCE AND THE TOTAL CURRICULUM: INTERDISCIPLINARY AND INTEGRATED APPROACHES

Chapter Objectives

Upon completion of this chapter you should be able to:

1 Define the terms *interdisciplinary* and *integrated* as they relate to science teaching and learning.

2 Differentiate between interdisciplinary and integrated approaches to science teaching.

3 Discuss the differences between traditional thematic teaching and conceptual thematic teaching.

4 Develop an interdisciplinary unit.

5 Develop an integrated unit.

6 Teach using an interdisciplinary approach.

7 Teach using an integrated approach.

Introduction

A paleontologist works in the mountains of central Pennsylvania carefully uncovering the evidence for a Devonian reef environment in those mountains. As she perches on the narrow ledge of rock above a road cut through the mountains, she uncovers a broad expanse of limestone showing corals, trilobites, crinoids, brachiopods, and a jawless fish. On maps, she notes the exact location of the rocks, photographs the area as a complete record of the find, then begins to make notes in her journal of the organisms in the rocks. As she writes, she also measures the sizes of the organisms, notes the location relative to other organisms, speculates about the species she is seeing, and begins to formulate an idea about conditions at the time of the scene she is now seeing in the rocks. She notes that she will need to look more into the chemical composition of the rocks, do some counts of the kinds of organisms found in order to determine relative abundances, and then at the location of the area she is uncovering in terms of the total rock formation. Later, after she has surveyed and recorded the area, she will begin to remove some of the fossils from the area so she can study them more fully in her lab.

In a third grade science class, Tamika dumps a sandwich bag with various kinds of rocks onto the floor and begins looking at them with a magnifying glass. As she looks at the rocks she begins to notice some interesting things about the rocks. Some are made of tiny pieces that shine. Some have three different colors. Some look as if they are made of only one kind of material; others look as if they have lots of different kinds of materials. Some have layers. Some are smooth. Some are rough. Some are harder than others and some weigh more than others. There are so many different things she notices about the rocks that she begins to write down what she sees and then decides it would be even better if she could draw pictures of the rocks instead. As she continues to observe the rocks from the bag, she begins to place them into piles so that all of the rocks in a pile are the same in some way. By the time Tamika has finished looking at the rocks and recording what she has seen, she is certain she could use some of the books in the classroom to name the rocks. That, she decides, is what she will do tomorrow.

The paleontologist on the rock face and Tamika in the classroom are both doing science. They are learning about the environment by studying rocks, by making notes about what they saw, by using the processes of science. But as they study about the rocks they are doing much more than what many teachers call "science." By recording information about the rock face or the rock samples they are using language skills and art skills. They are using mathematics skills to weigh and measure. Science investigation involves far more than simply "doing science." It involves many of the other traditional subject matter areas of the elementary school.

In order to better show that real science is much more than science facts and science process skills, you may want to organize your science program in a different way than the traditional "time for science" approach. As a teacher, you have two basic ways of organizing so you can show how science uses other subject matter areas and how other subject matter areas can be enhanced through science: an *interdisciplinary approach* and an *integrated approach*.

Interdisciplinary and Integrated Approaches

What do we mean by an integrated approach? What do we mean by an interdisciplinary approach? Both of these approaches have one thing in common. They both show that subject matter areas are not really separate, but overlap greatly. It is impossible to separate reading from social studies or science or language arts or mathematics. Children write and speak and listen in social studies, science, and mathematics, so the language arts are continually used. Children frequently use mathematics as part of a science or social studies lesson. And science and social studies overlap in the areas of geography, anthropology, and technology. Both interdisciplinary and integrated approaches to teaching recognize that subject matter areas are interrelated and use that interrelatedness so that one subject matter area is used to enhance learning in another. Where interdisciplinary and integrated teaching differ, however, is in the degree to which the subject matter areas are used to enhance one another. In general, an interdisciplinary approach combines fewer subject matter areas than does an integrated approach. Interdisciplinary approaches often consider combinations of two areas, whereas an integrated approach may combine all subject matter areas so that the lines separating one subject from another disappear.

Interdisciplinary Teaching

In Mrs. Green's sixth grade class, the schedule for the second six weeks of the school year does not show either science or social studies. Instead, she has a block of two hours listed on her schedule under the heading "Exploration." This is the title of the unit her students are studying. Within the unit they are studying about the move toward the west in the United States, the conquistadors in South America, and the exploration of Africa by Europeans. Rather than have a specific time for science and a specific time for social studies, the unit on exploration combines the two areas into one. As children study about exploration in various parts of the world they also study about rivers, plains, deserts, jungles, oceans, and mountains. In this unit, Mrs. Green is engaging in interdisciplinary teaching by combining two subject matter areas. In **interdisciplinary teaching,** two subject matter areas, and sometimes more than two, are combined in such a way that the lines separating one subject matter area from another are erased. The key to this type of teaching is the selection of the topic. It should be one that allows the two subject matter areas to be used purposefully. The most frequent combinations are science and mathematics, science and language arts, and science and social studies.

Interdisciplinary Science and Mathematics.   Of all of the areas that can be combined with science in an interdisciplinary manner, mathematics is the most natural. First, science continually uses mathematics as it attempts to describe the natural world. We look at the sizes of plants and animals. We look at the distances between the planets. We look at the time that has elapsed since dinosaurs existed on Earth. Scientists, and inquiring children, measure weight, time, growth rate, length, width, and height. Children and scientists make graphs and describe shapes. There is so much natural overlap between science and mathematics, so much *necessary* overlap between science and mathematics, that it is difficult to teach science without using mathematics. This overlap brings us to the second natural reason for an interdisciplinary approach to science and mathematics. If children use the process skills they are automatically using many mathematical skills as well: Observation, classification, using space-time relations, and using numbers are all science process skills that are also mathematical skills.

In general, if you are working with interdisciplinary science and mathematics, you are combining the two areas through the activities done by the children as they study a particular topic. Consider the following activity from a unit on magnets as it is done by two second grade classes.

In Mrs. Flynn's class the children are learning about magnets. In the first activity the children are given bar magnets and asked to move freely about the room trying to pick up objects. They make a list on paper of things the magnet will pick up or stick to and things the magnet will not. On the board, Mrs. Flynn makes two columns, one labeled yes and the other no, and collects the data from the activity. When the children have had an opportunity to classify the objects they tried, she has the children identify the material each item is made of. Finally, Mrs. Flynn has the children draw a conclusion about the kinds of objects picked up and the kinds of objects not picked up. The children conclude that magnets pick up some kinds of metals. One of the materials tried was paper clips. Mrs. Flynn asked the children where they think the most paper clips will stick. They decide it will be the ends and the middle. The children are then given paper clips and work with a partner to find out how many paper clips stick to each end and to the middle. Once again, Mrs. Flynn collects the information on the board. She has the children find out how many paper clips all together would stick to each end and to the middle. On the N end they had a class total of 79 paper clips. On the S end they had 81 paper clips. In the middle they had only 3 paper clips. After comparing the numbers, the children decide the number on each of the ends is about the same, but the middle doesn't work very well in picking up paper clips. The ends are much stronger.

In Mrs. Rosen's class, the children do the same activities. After the children have had a chance to try objects in the room, Mrs. Rosen collects the objects on the board and then has the children make a graph of the information collected. There are more objects in the "picked up" group than in the "not picked up" group. Then she has them count how many were in each group to confirm which had more. The children then move to the activity with the paper clips and magnets. The children collect their data for each pole and for the middle of the magnet and then add all three numbers together to see how many paper clips were picked up altogether.

In Mrs. Flynn's class mathematics was used purposefully in order to learn about magnets and their characteristics. They classified the items according to what was and what was not picked up and then drew a conclusion about the kinds of things magnets would pick up. In the second activity, they used counting and addition in a purposeful way as well. They used their addition to determine where the most paper clips would stick and drew conclusions about the magnets from the information collected.

Although Mrs. Rosen's class did the same activity, the children did not use mathematics as purposefully as they did in Mrs. Flynn's class. Although graphing is a good idea in many cases, in this one it only showed that the children happened to try more objects that were picked up. The graph did not add to an understanding of magnets or the kinds of materials attracted. In the second case, the children simply added together the numbers of paper clips. Once again, they used addition appropriately as a mathematical skill but it did not really contribute to an understanding of where magnets are strongest.

Figures 13.1 and 13.2 show the strategies used by Mrs. Flynn and Mrs. Rosen. A comparison of these diagrams shows that Mrs. Flynn used mathematics as part of the activities in order to enhance her students' understanding of mathematics; Mrs. Rosen included mathematics as a part of the activities but did not fully use mathematics to enhance and further her students' understanding of magnets.

Figure 13.1

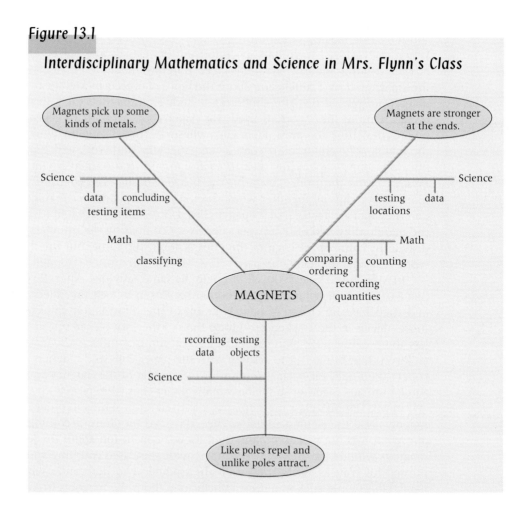

Interdisciplinary Mathematics and Science in Mrs. Flynn's Class

Figure 13.2

Interdisciplinary Mathematics and Science in Mrs. Rosen's Class

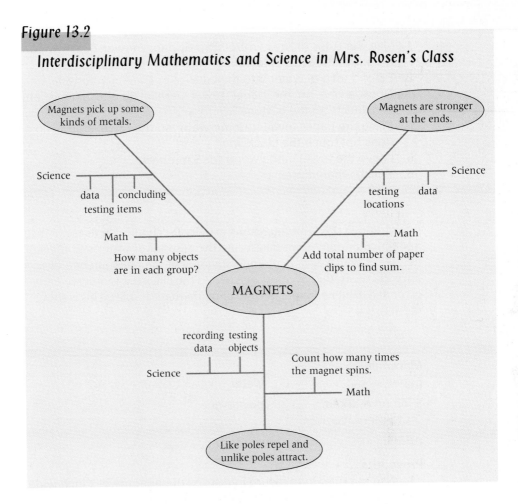

As a teacher, you want to utilize mathematics in an appropriate manner when using an interdisciplinary approach to science. Because this is best approached through hands-on activities, the best way to begin an interdisciplinary approach, after selecting the topic to use for the unit, is to consider an activity and its possibility for inclusion of mathematics.

As an example of how this can be done, consider the following activity.

Materials

paper   water

black felt tip marker   plastic cup

ruler   scissors

Procedure

1. Use the ruler to measure a strip of paper towel 1 inch wide and 6 inches long. Cut the strip of toweling from the entire towel.
2. Place 1 inch of water into the cup.
3. Draw a line on the paper towel parallel to the narrow end and about 2 inches from the bottom.
4. Place the paper towel into the water so the towel stands up and the water does not touch the black line.
5. Leave the towel in the water for 5 minutes.
6. Watch what happens.

Although this is an interesting activity for children, it does not include the use of mathematics other than measuring the amount of water and the size of the towel, neither of which add to an understanding of the phenomenon observed. However, once the separation of colors making up the black ink is observed, the activity can be extended to allow for greater use of mathematical skills. This is shown in the following activity:

Materials

paper	water
5 felt tip markers of different colors	plastic cup
ruler	scissors

Procedure

1. Use the ruler to measure five strips of paper towel 1 inch wide and 6 inches long. Cut the strips of toweling from the entire towel.
2. Place 1 inch of water into each of the cups.
3. Draw a line on the paper towel parallel to the narrow end and about 2 inches from the bottom using one of the markers.
4. Place the paper towel into the water so the towel stands up and the water does not touch the marker line.
5. Leave the towel in the water for five minutes.
6. List the colors as they are shown on the towel. Remove the towel from the water and lay it flat on the table.
7. Repeat steps 3 through 6 using a different color of marker each time.
8. Make a graph of the colors shown on each of the paper towel strips. Which color is used most frequently in the inks tested? Which color is used least frequently?
9. Measure the width of each of the color bands on each of the paper towels. How do you think the width of the color band relates to the amount of the color included in the ink? Why? How could you test your prediction?

In the first description, the students simply used measurement to cut the toweling to size. In the second version of the activity, the students used mathematics to develop a graph of the colors of ink used. They then used measurement to see if they could determine any relationship between the width of the color band and the amount of that color included in the ink. In this way, mathematics is being used in a purposeful manner.

As an additional example of the interdisciplinary approach to mathematics and science, consider the following pair of activities. The first shows the original activity.

Materials

book	marble
ruler with a groove	pencil
1-inch wooden block	

Procedure

1. Place one end of the ruler on the pencil so about 1 inch of the ruler sticks out over the pencil and the other end rests on the table.
2. Place the block on the table so it touches the end of the ruler.
3. Roll the marble down the ruler. Watch how far the block moves.
4. Remove the pencil and place the end of the ruler on the book. Return the block to the end of the ruler.
5. Roll the marble down the ruler. Watch how far the block moves.
6. Which time did the block move further?

Although this activity has the possibility of the inclusion of mathematics, there is no actual use of mathematics in the activity. The activity could be easily rewritten, however, so students are far more involved in interdisciplinary mathematics and science.

Materials

5 books	marble
ruler with a groove	pencil
1-inch wooden block	drawing paper
tape	meterstick

Procedure

1. Tape the sheet of drawing paper to a flat surface.
2. Place the first book flat on the table so it just touches the edge of the paper. Place the ruler so one end overlaps with the book by about an inch and the other end is on the paper.

3. Place the block at the end of the ruler on the paper and draw around it with the pencil. Remove the block and draw two diagonals through the pencil outline so you find the center of the block.
4. Roll the marble down the ruler so it hits the block. Draw around the block and again find the center point. Measure how far the block traveled from center point to center point. Record the distance.
5. Repeat step 3 two more times. Find the average distance the block moved for the three tries.
6. Repeat steps 2, 4, and 5 four more times using two books, then three books, then four books, and finally five books. Pile the books one on top of the other so the height is always increased.
7. Make a graph showing the number of blocks used and the average distance the block traveled.
8. What relationship exists between the height of the books and the distance the block moves?

In this second version of the activity, the students are engaged in three mathematical skills that are purposeful to the activity. First, they measure the distance the block traveled with each change of height. Second, because the blocks do not travel a consistent distance each time they are hit, they have used averages to find the mean distance traveled. And third, they have used graphing in order to determine the relationship between height and distance. After the students have had an opportunity to investigate and use mathematics to help find relationships the teacher can easily use the activity to discuss potential and kinetic energy.

In creating an interdisciplinary approach revolving around science and including mathematics, the key is to look at the activities found in textbooks or activity books and to extend those activities so students are using their mathematical skills to increase their understanding of the science content shown in the activity. In including mathematical skills within a science topic, the children should already have studied the mathematical skill in their mathematics classes so it can be applied easily to the activity. If the children are trying to both learn a new mathematics skill and to apply it in a new situation, frustration can result and with that frustration not only errors in mathematics but also poor attitudes can develop.

It is also possible to begin with a mathematical topic and use science to add to that topic. In this case, we might begin with mathematical concepts such as mean, median, and mode. It is easy to teach these ideas by having children work strictly with numbers, but not particularly interesting. The calculation of mean, median, and mode, however, are often used in the sciences. For example, children are always interested in themselves. Because mean, median, and mode are descriptive statistics, they can be used to help describe a seventh grade class.

In Mr. Gonzales's seventh grade mathematics class, the new topic is statistics. Although it would be easier to define the three terms and then show the students how to find the three averages mentioned previously, Mr. Gonzales decides to get the students involved in an activity that will not only help them understand these three statistics but also contribute to their understanding of themselves. To start his unit "Statistics," Mr. Gonzales asks the students to answer some questions and make some predictions about their class:

1. Which students do you think will be taller, boys or girls?

2. How tall do you think most students will be?

3. If you wanted to tell someone which student in our class was the most typical in height, who would you say it was?

4. If you wanted to define the terms *tall* and *short*, how would you do it?

5. Do you think our class will be similar to other classes? How could we find out?

After working in small groups to answer the questions, the students measured the heights of all the students in the class. All 26 heights were listed on the board and the students tried to use the unorganized information to see if their height predictions were correct or not. They found it difficult to use all of the information as it was listed to check those predictions. With Mr. Gonzales's help, they organized the information in order from the tallest to the shortest and then recorded the distribution of each height. They could now answer question 2. Mr. Gonzales then defined the term *mode* as the measurement that occurred most often. They then decided how they could decide who to categorize as short and who to categorize as tall. They found the height that had half of the class above it and half of the class below it. This Mr. Gonzales labeled the median. Now they could answer question 3. And, finally, they calculated the average height for the class and termed this the "mean" height. After doing means for both boys and girls, they were able to answer question 1. After some discussion of the three averages, they decided that question 5 could be answered by collecting the heights of children in the other seventh grade classes and finding the mean, median, and mode for each class and each gender. This class was learning the mathematics as they investigated themselves. However, they were also learning science as they engaged in a variety of science process skills and also engaged in drawing conclusions from their activities related to the study of the human body. Figure 13.3 shows the semantic map used for developing this interdisciplinary mathematics/science topic of statistics.

In working with mathematics as the starting point for an interdisciplinary approach to science and mathematics, it is important to select a mathematics topic that can be developed easily through purposeful science activities.

Mathematics and science can easily be combined in an interdisciplinary approach. Science and social studies are also easy to combine, particularly in the areas of anthropology and geography, although history and sociology can also be effectively used in combination with science. Activities 13.1 and 13.2 allow you to consider an interdisciplinary approach to science and mathematics teaching.

Figure 13.3

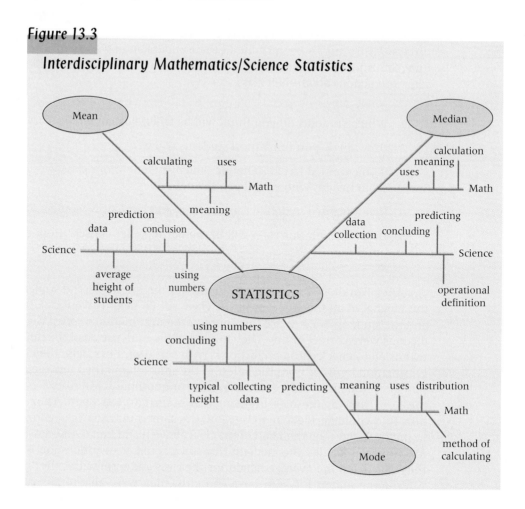

Interdisciplinary Mathematics/Science Statistics

Interdisciplinary and Integrated Curriculum Activities

Activity 13.1

Purpose To demonstrate how mathematics can be purposefully included in science activities.

Procedure
1. Select three activities from a science textbook or science activity book. One activity should come from the biological sciences, one activity from the physical sciences, and one activity from the earth-space sciences.

2. Rewrite each of the activities to include the purposeful use of mathematics as a part of the activity. The use of mathematics should be appropriate to the grade level of the students who would be using the activity.

Activity 13.2

Purpose   To demonstrate how science activities can be used to teach mathematics concepts.

Procedure
1. Locate a mathematics textbook or course of study for any grade level from first through eighth grade.
2. Select one of the topics taught at the grade level suggested, (e.g. graphing).
3. Design a teaching strategy that could be used to teach the selected mathematics topic through the use of science activities.

Interdisciplinary Science and Social Studies.   Creating an interdisciplinary approach that combines science and social studies can contribute a great deal to both subject matter areas. Science occurs in a social context. It is often a product of its time, and knowing what society was like at the time scientific laws, theories, principles, and theories were developed can contribute a great deal to an understanding of the topic. For example, many textbooks describe the trouble Galileo got into because of his insistence that Earth traveled around the Sun rather than the Sun around Earth. Few science books for elementary or middle school students describe why this was so troublesome a theory. By considering the time in which Galileo was working, the teacher can not only combine science with social studies but also can show why Galileo's theory was so controversial when it developed.

As a second example, we often discuss how ancient peoples used astrology in making decisions and we tell students that astrology was the forerunner of astronomy. By combining social studies with science we can also look at why astrology was considered a science, at how astronomy developed out of astrology, and at how we now know astrology is a foolish means for predicting the future.

In creating an interdisciplinary approach to science and social studies, the key is not so much in the selection of activities, but in the selection of topics or concepts. In order to develop an interdisciplinary science and social studies program, select a unit topic in which both science and social studies can be combined purposefully. It is not necessary to force one subject matter area into another. For example, if a class is studying how laws are enacted at the federal level, it is probably not an appropriate place to include science concepts. True, one could have a bill that deals with a science topic, but such a means of introducing science does little to really help students understand science. It is simply an added attraction so science is present. However, there are far more social studies topics that include science than those that do not. Consider the following two examples of creating an interdisciplinary science and social studies program. In the first example, the teacher begins with a topic from

Figure 13.4

Semantic Map for an Interdisciplinary Unit on Kenya

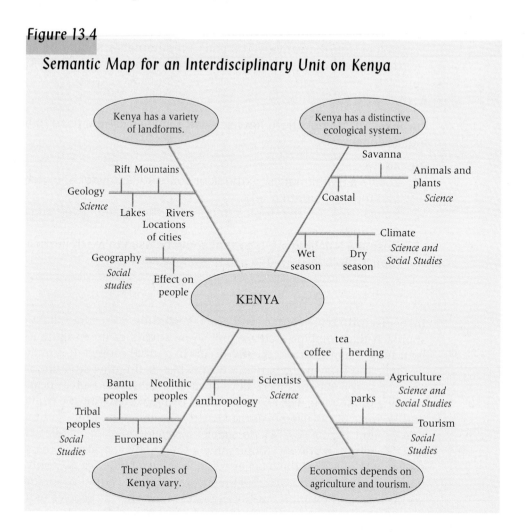

social studies and in the second the teacher begins with a topic from science. Both reach the same conclusion: a purposeful program that combines science and social studies in an interdisciplinary manner.

Mr. Jefferson and Mrs. Kent, eighth grade teachers, decide to do an interdisciplinary science-social studies unit on East Africa, focusing on Kenya. As a starting point for developing the unit, they drew the semantic map shown in Figure 13.4.

By looking at the map, you can see the concepts these teachers would like to have their students learn and the main subject matter area, science or social studies, concerned with that area. As they prepare to teach the unit, Mr. Jefferson and Mrs. Kent work together to teach about Kenya rather than to teach science or social studies. By team teaching and using a theme like Kenya as the basis for that team teaching, these teachers are creating an interdisciplinary approach.

In the second example, Mrs. Cohn, a fifth grade teacher, uses the science topic "Force and Motion" to create an interdisciplinary approach to science and social

Figure 13.5

Semantic Map for an Interdisciplinary Unit on Force and Motion

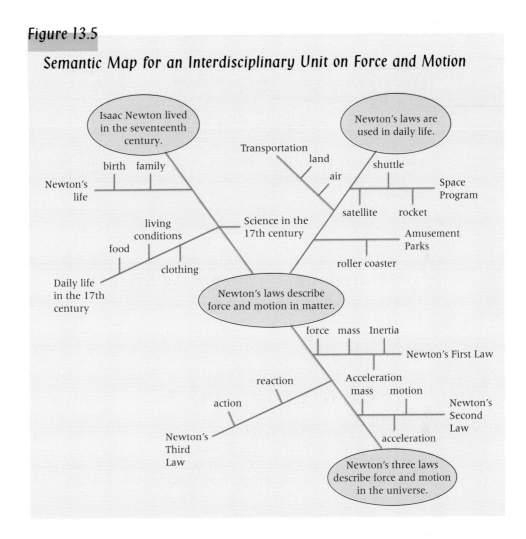

studies. Figure 13.5 shows the map Mrs. Cohn used to develop her interdisciplinary unit.

The science aspect of this unit is immediately evident because the study of forces and motion is a major part of the study of physics. Consideration of simple and complex machines also focuses on the study of science. The focused study of Newton's three laws of motion and the concepts related to those laws, however, is expanded in this unit through consideration of the time period in which Newton lived and developed these laws, through application of the laws to today's space program, and by considering how the concepts studied are used in daily life in the city. Had the school been in a rural environment rather than in a city environment, the applications of the concepts would be to life in the country rather than in the city.

Whether working with the eighth grade topic of Kenya or the fifth grade topic of force and motion, once the concepts have been selected, the remainder of the procedure for developing an interdisciplinary science/social studies unit is the same as for developing a discipline-centered unit. Once the concepts are known, the subconcepts are developed. From the subconcepts come the objectives and from the objectives come the lessons for the unit. The main difference is that the lessons include science and social studies rather than only science.

Whether science is used as the starting point or social studies is used as the starting point for the development of an interdisciplinary unit, the outcome is the same. The subject matter areas are combined in such a way that both science and social studies contribute to the student's understanding of the topic. Activities 13.3 and 13.4 develop your ability to include science and social studies in an interdisciplinary format.

The final combination that is easily developed in an interdisciplinary approach is a combination of science and language arts.

Interdisciplinary/Integrated Science Curriculum Activities

Activity 13.3

Purpose To demonstrate the inclusion of science and social studies in an interdisciplinary approach based on science.

Procedure
1. Locate a science textbook for any grade level from first through eighth and select one topic from that textbook.
2. Show how social studies could be integrated into the selected science topic by drawing a semantic map that could be used as the basis for unit development.

Activity 13.4

Purpose To demonstrate the inclusion of science and social studies in an interdisciplinary approach based on science.

Procedure
1. Locate a social studies textbook for any grade level from first through eighth and select one topic from that textbook.
2. Show how science could be integrated into the selected social studies topic by drawing a semantic map that could be used as the basis for unit development.

Interdisciplinary Science and Language Arts. Language arts is constantly used within a science program. Students talk to one another as they are involved in activities. Students make written records of their activities. Students read activity directions to know how to conduct an activity or experiment. Students read science textbooks and trade books to find more science information. In all of these cases, the students are using language arts as a part of the science program. An interdisciplinary approach that includes science and language arts, however, goes beyond the simple use of language skills in the science program to the use of science content as a means for advancing important concepts from the language arts program.

Research Papers.   Language arts programs include the development of research skills, so that students develop their ability to write a coherent and well-developed research paper. In doing so, students are asked to use multiple sources of information, to document correctly where information was found, and to present that information in a clear and concise manner. Although teachers can teach children the individual skills of library research, note taking, bibliographic citation, and writing, the use of those skills in context is a far more appropriate way of teaching because it gives purpose to learning the research paper process.

There are many science topics that allow children to use research skills in a particularly meaningful way. Such topics include endangered species, ecological biomes, pollution, energy production and use, careers in science and technology, the history of science, and biographies of scientists. Many other topics, of course, are also possible, but these tend to lend themselves to using multiple sources of information rather than a single source.

Consider the topic of endangered species. In helping students begin to write a research paper on this topic, a brainstorming session could be used. In this session, students can list all of the endangered species they can. Once the list is completed, they can go to other sources to add to the list. Sources might include books on endangered species, biologists, films and videos, or the Internet where complete lists of endangered species can be found. Once there is a fairly lengthy list of species, students can begin the research process by using a semantic web.

The teacher working with a class using a web as the beginning of a research paper begins by modeling the use of a web. The first step, as with the use of any webbing technique, is to write the topic on the board and draw a circle around it. In this case, the topic would be the name of a particular endangered species. As an example, let's consider the California condor.

After writing the words "California condor" on the board, the teacher asks the students what they would like to know about that particular animal and gives the children time to write down some of the questions they would like to have answered. In most cases children will write down questions based on their past experiences with animals, and in this case, with birds.

Once the teacher has modeled the development of questions like these, the questions can then be grouped into broader categories. For example, questions on the characteristics of a California condor can be grouped under the topic "Characteristics of California condors." The teacher helps the students decide what questions can be grouped and how the topic can be named.

Figure 13.6 shows a beginning map for a research paper on the California condor. This figure shows the broad topics that would be considered in the research

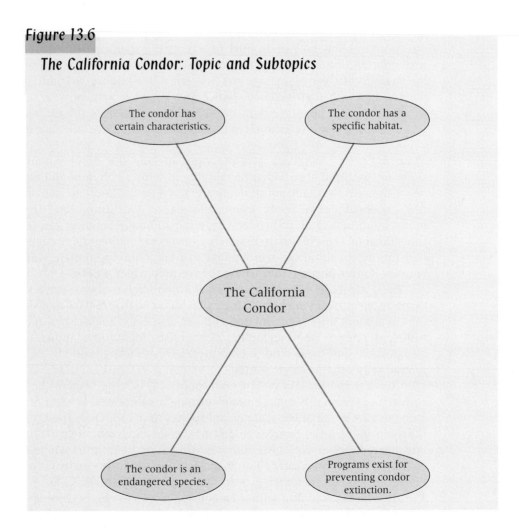

Figure 13.6

The California Condor: Topic and Subtopics

paper. Once the broad topics have been gained, the teacher and the children together can decide on the specific information or questions that should be answered under each topic. For example, under characteristics of California condors, students might look for size of adults, number of eggs laid, when eggs are laid, coloration of adults and children, kinds of foods eaten, where nests are built, whether or not they migrate, and so on. These specifics can then be added to the web to guide in the research process. Figure 13.7 shows this next step in the development of a web. Finally, the teacher can help the students decide on the order in which they should present the information in the final paper. The easiest way to do this is to simply number the topics on the map in the order in which the presentation would make the most sense to the reader. Figure 13.8 shows this next step.

Once the teacher has modeled the development of a web with the class, the students select the animal they will research and use a similar process. Although most of the webs will be similar, if not identical, to the modeled web, this gives the chil-

Figure 13.7

The California Condor: Specific Areas

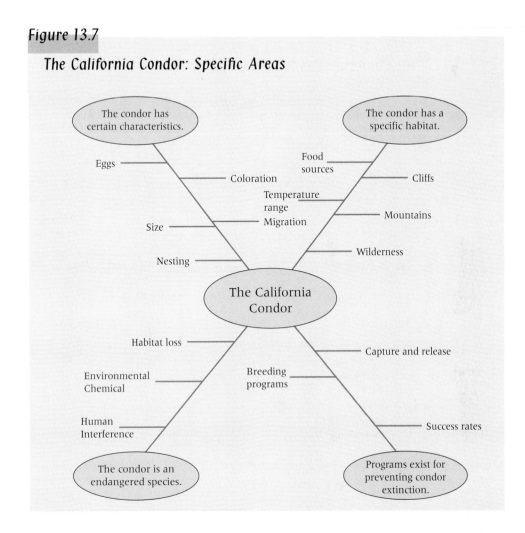

dren an opportunity to practice the webbing procedure. This technique can then be used as students write research papers in other areas and on other topics. In particular, the children will have a way of focusing in on the information they need and of determining what they want to find out about each individual topic.

Once the students have developed their webs, the next step is to help the students decide where they could find the information they need. Children immediately want to go to encyclopedias, either paper or electronic, to find the information they need for a research paper. In many cases, they do not know where else to go to find the kind of information they need. By helping students brainstorm sources of information beyond the standard encyclopedia, the teacher is helping the students develop the ability to use a variety of sources. The brainstormed list can include trade books, textbooks, resource persons, museums, CD-ROM, Internet sites, magazines, television programs, and, yes, even encyclopedias. Once the list is made, the teacher and students need to discuss the kinds of information that can be

Figure 13.8

The California Condor: Order for Research

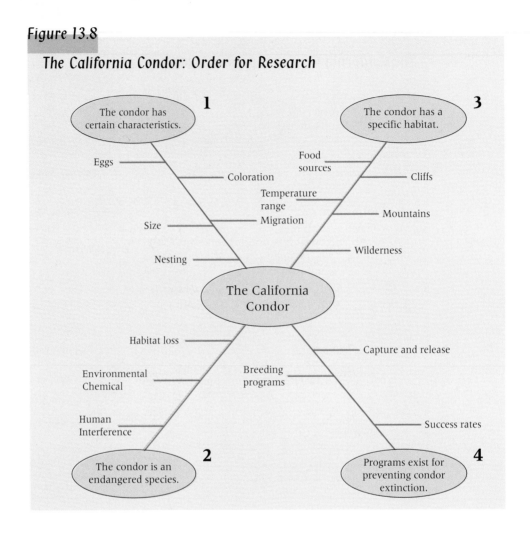

found in each source and how to determine whether the information is accurate and up to date.

At this point, students are ready to use their language arts skills of researching, note taking, and writing in a purposeful manner to write a research paper. Language arts and science are combined in an interdisciplinary manner through the research paper.

Other Strategies for Interdisciplinary Science/Language Arts.   Although the research paper is an easy way to develop an interdisciplinary approach to science and language arts, it is not a particularly creative means of doing so. To allow for more creativity, language arts and science can also be combined in an interdisciplinary approach through creative writing, through developing a student science magazine, through writing plays and skits, and through the development of multimedia presentations for the class, other classes, or for parents.

Studying about the galaxy, the solar system, and space travel provides the perfect opportunity for creative writing: science fiction stories. In order to combine science with language arts, students can read science fiction stories written specifically for children, discuss what it is that makes a story both science and fiction, and then write their own stories. The writing, proofing, editing, and rewriting process is used and students produce a story that can be included in a class anthology, bound, and made available through the library to other classes.

Using other science topics, the same writing process can be put into play by creating a classroom science magazine in which students write articles, take photographs or make drawings, and eventually develop their own magazine for circulation through the school or grade level.

The lives and discoveries of scientists can provide the basis for writing a play or skit about that scientist and his or her discoveries. In addition to engaging in the total writing process, students are also involved in acting, producing, and advertising, all of which heavily involve the use of language skills.

And finally, students with access to video cameras and computer systems can develop multimedia presentations involving live action, film, and computer-generated images to show what has been studied and learned in the science class.

With the language arts, the key to creating an interdisciplinary program is to utilize the language arts skills in a manner that helps students learn the science content while utilizing their language arts skills purposefully. Activity 13.5 focuses on integrating language arts into a science topic.

Interdisciplinary/Integrated Curriculum Activities

Activity 13.5

Purpose   To demonstrate how language arts could be integrated into a science topic.

Procedure
1. Locate a science textbook for any grade level from fourth through eighth and select one chapter from that textbook.
2. Select one topic from the chapter that could be used to engage students in library research.
   a. Create a semantic map that could be used to assist students in developing a research paper.
   b. Make a list of resources that could be used by students as they research the topic. Include the specific titles of books, CD-ROM databases, and other materials.
3. Consider the entire chapter. How could science learning be enhanced through the use of language arts? Give specific examples.

Interdisciplinary teaching frequently involves the combining of two broad subject matter areas in a way that both areas are enhanced. Science and mathematics, science and social studies, and science and language arts all can be easily and successfully combined in an interdisciplinary program. The same kind of procedure used for developing an interdisciplinary science–social studies program can also be used in those cases where science can be combined with the fine arts such as music or art or with physical education. When more than one subject matter area is combined, and particularly when all subject areas are subsumed under one umbrella topic, the curriculum is no longer interdisciplinary. Instead, the curriculum has become integrated.

Integrated Teaching

In a truly **integrated approach** to teaching, the subject matter areas no longer exist as distinct entities. There is no longer a time for science, for math, for social studies, for music, art, or reading. Instead, the subject matter areas are used, as appropriate, to develop an understanding of a particular conceptual theme.

Thematic Approach.   A thematic approach has often been used as a means of organizing a curriculum. However, most thematic approaches are not truly integrated approaches. In a thematic approach, the theme or topic of the unit is used as an organizing pattern. The subject matter areas kept distinct from one another, but all areas use the theme. For example, a theme could be developed around the science topic of dinosaurs. In science, the students read about and create models of various types of dinosaurs. In reading, they read stories about dinosaurs, both factual and fiction. In mathematics, they do word problems with dinosaurs as the characters in the problems. In social studies, they study about the states in which dinosaur fossils are found. In art, they draw pictures, of dinosaurs, in music, they sing a song about dinosaurs, and in physical education, they play "dinosaur tag." In each case, dinosaurs appear in the subject matter areas, but some of the areas contribute to an understanding of dinosaurs while others do not. Simply doing word problems using the names of dinosaurs does not really contribute to understanding dinosaurs and their characteristics. Singing a song about dinosaurs does little to advance knowledge, nor does dinosaur tag. In the case of many thematic approaches, the theme is used to organize the classroom but the subject matter areas remain distinct from one another.

Integrated Approach.   In a truly integrated program, the subject matter areas disappear. There is no particular time for mathematics or science or reading, but rather those subject matter areas come into play as the students learn about the particular topic. And in an integrated approach the topic is used as a means for determining the concepts that will be taught to the students rather than as a means for organizing the classroom. Figure 13.9 shows a map for developing a thematic unit on dinosaurs, and Figure 13.10 shows a map for developing an integrated unit on dinosaurs.

Figure 13.9

Thematic Approach to Dinosaurs

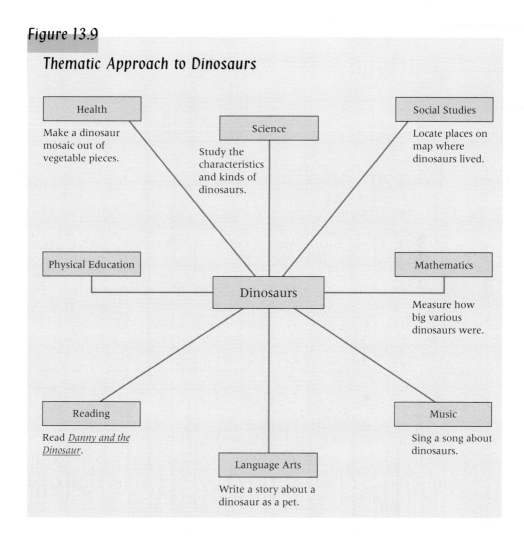

In comparing the two figures, notice that in the thematic approach diagram, the subject matter areas are listed and the topic of dinosaurs is used within each of the subject matter areas. Scientific content on dinosaurs is most likely covered in the subject matter area of science. In reading, students may read books about dinosaurs, but the main purpose of the lesson is the development of reading skills rather than the development of additional scientific content about dinosaurs. In mathematics, dinosaurs are simply used as a topic of word problems dealing with addition, whereas in language arts, dinosaurs are used as the starting point of an imaginative story, for creative writing, so information on dinosaurs is not necessarily increased or scientifically accurate. The social studies do indeed extend knowledge of dinosaurs: Students look at the geography of the area in which many dinosaur fossils are found. Drawing dinosaurs, singing a song about dinosaurs, and playing

Figure 13.10

Integrated Approach to Dinosaurs

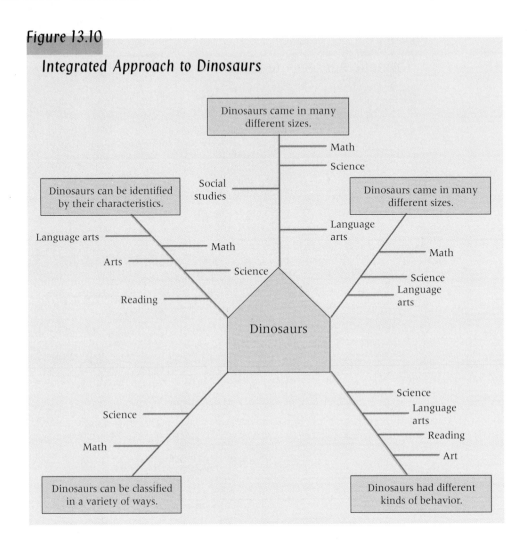

dinosaur tag allow the theme to be an organizing principle for all of the other curricular areas. Thematic approaches to the integration of the curriculum are appropriate and often excellent ways of motivating children through the use of a favorite topic, but often the overlying thrust of including all of the subject matter areas within a particular theme results in nonpurposeful inclusion of the topic. Knowledge of the theme is not enhanced through each of the subject matter areas. Instead the theme is forced into the areas simply so they can be included.

In contrast, the integrated approach shown in Figure 13.10, shows the topic of dinosaurs as organized around the concepts the teacher wants his or her students to learn. When the concepts are known, the teacher can decide on the kinds of activities necessary to teach those concepts. Once the activities are known, the teacher determines which of the subject matter areas are being used during the study of the topic. The subject matter areas, then, disappear into the topic itself and are used as a means for learning. The subject matter areas become a means for learning rather than an end point for learning. In addition, only the subject matter areas appropriate to the topic are utilized. There is not attempt to force the topic into all of the subject matter areas. Music and physical education may not be included in an integrated study of dinosaurs, but both of these areas can be prominent in a study of sound.

Planning an Integrated Approach to Science Teaching

Selecting the Topic.   Any integrated approach begins with a topic. The topic should be broad enough that a number of concepts are considered during the study but not so broad it includes an entire field of study. For example, the topic "Animals" is so broad it is often studied as an entire year's worth of science at the college level. Better topics would be "Vertebrate Animals" or "Invertebrate Animals." These topics could be narrowed further to "Mammals," "Reptiles and Amphibians," "Insects," or "Arthropods." Even specifying the particular phylum or class of animals still leaves a broad topic for study. Within the physical sciences, a topic such as "Matter" sounds broad but may be too narrow in focus depending on how the topic is defined. "The States of Matter" is a narrow topic as it is usually considered because the characteristics of solids, liquids, and gases form the focus. However, the topic "Matter" can be more than broad enough if it includes not only characteristics of solids, liquids, and gases, but also elements, compounds, solutions, mixtures, and chemical and physical changes. As with any topic chosen for use in the elementary school science program, always consider whether or not the topic is developmentally appropriate. Whatever the topic, write it in the center of a sheet of paper and draw a circle around it. As an example of developing an integrated approach to teaching, we'll use the topic mammals.

Developing the Concepts.   Once the topic for the integrated approach has been selected, determine the concepts for the unit. There are a number of ways of determining the concepts for the topic. First, consult written documents. Look at the textbook and see what concepts the textbook series considers appropriate. Look at the state or school system course of study in the science area. This document lists the concepts the state or school system thinks should be taught at a particular grade level. Once you have considered these two sources, you might also consult *Benchmarks* and the *Standards* for additional insight into the kinds of concepts children at a particular grade level should be learning. Written documents such as these often list the minimum requirements and are only a starting point for determining concepts. When you use these kinds of documents, look carefully at the concepts included to determine whether they are developmentally appropriate, whether they are appropriate to the particular school or class, and whether there are other concepts to add. A second source for determining the concepts to be taught as a part of the integrated approach is the children. Asking the children in your class what they would like to learn about a topic is always a good strategy. Your students will feel greater ownership of the topic and see it as more relevant if they have had the opportunity to contribute their ideas about what they will be learning. Usually, the suggestions made by the children are in addition to the concepts mandated by the state or school or suggested by other documents. And, finally, the third source for concepts for an integrated approach is you, the teacher. Your understanding of subject matter, of children, or the community is always a good source of concepts for study. Using your own knowledge allows for a more personalized approach to the topic.

Each of the concepts determined should be written in sentence form so the information the students will learn is stated clearly and concisely. The concepts are added to the sheet of paper with the topic and connected to the topic with lines. This is the beginning of the web used to develop the integrated approach.

After the concepts have been listed, the specific information developed through each of the concepts is added to the web. In this way, it becomes clear exactly the content to include as a part of the integrated topic. See Figure 13.11 for the beginning stages of a web planning an integrated approach for the topic "Mammals," which could be taught at the sixth, seventh, or eighth grade level.

Figure 13.11

Integrated Unit on Mammals: Concepts

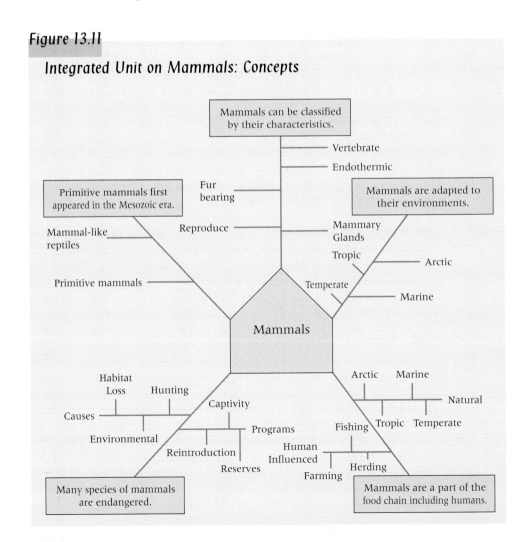

Selecting the Activities. Selecting the activities for an integrated approach involves three stages. In the first stage, the activities are selected to meet the content objectives. This should sound self-evident, but it has a particular meaning. In a traditional thematic approach, you select the activities according to the subject matter areas. So you select an activity that allows you to use the topic in science, in math, in social studies, and so on. In an integrated approach, you select the activities without consideration to the subject matter areas included. The main criterion for selection, beyond that of developmental appropriateness, is whether or not the activity will help your students to reach the concept. While you are selecting the activities to teach the concepts, also remember one other thing. Neither children nor adults learn a new concept through only one experience. It takes a number of encounters with the same concept for a child to truly comprehend the new concept. So, select more than one activity for teaching any particular concept, and make sure the activities show a variety of approaches to the same concept. The more times the concept is met and the more different ways the concept is shown, the better. Figure 13.12 shows the inclusion of the activities on the web.

In the second stage of activity selection, you need to scrutinize the activities closely to determine the subject matter areas that are being used as a part of the activity. In a topic like "Mammals," science is going to be used in the vast majority of the concepts. However, if students investigate how mammals are classified, they are also going to use mathematics and language arts. The mathematics comes in as they consider sizes, dentition, and general concepts of classification. The language arts comes in as the students plan their activities, write their descriptions, and create their own classification systems. Art can be used as students illustrate the kinds of animals found within each of the classifications. In looking at how animals are adapted to their environments, they need to look at geography. They will also be involved in reading in the search for information and in language arts as they prepare written reports. Social studies is included as students look at how human beings use mammals, including some of the controversies that are arising from environmental activists. Student can use their artistic skills as they create dioramas, posters, and murals showing animal use and misuse.

Once the activities are selected, you move to stage 2 where you look at each of the activities and determine the subject matter areas being used. Always keep in mind that it is not necessary to include every subject matter area in every integrated unit. In fact, only those subject matter areas that students naturally use as a part of the activities should be included. Do not use the subject matter areas as a starting point for the activities. Rather, use the activities as a starting point for the subject matter areas. See Figure 13.13 for the subject matter areas included within the activities.

In stage 3 of activity selection, consider the grouping arrangements for the activities. As with the kinds of activities, the groupings should show variety. Some of the activities should allow students to work alone to pursue their own information and their own interests. Other activities should allow students to work in partnerships, in small groups, or as a total group. Variety in activities and variety in grouping procedures helps in matching the learning styles of children. And variety also helps in maintaining student interest and motivation. See Figure 13.14 for the types of groupings used.

Figure 13.12

Integrated Unit on Mammals: Subject Areas

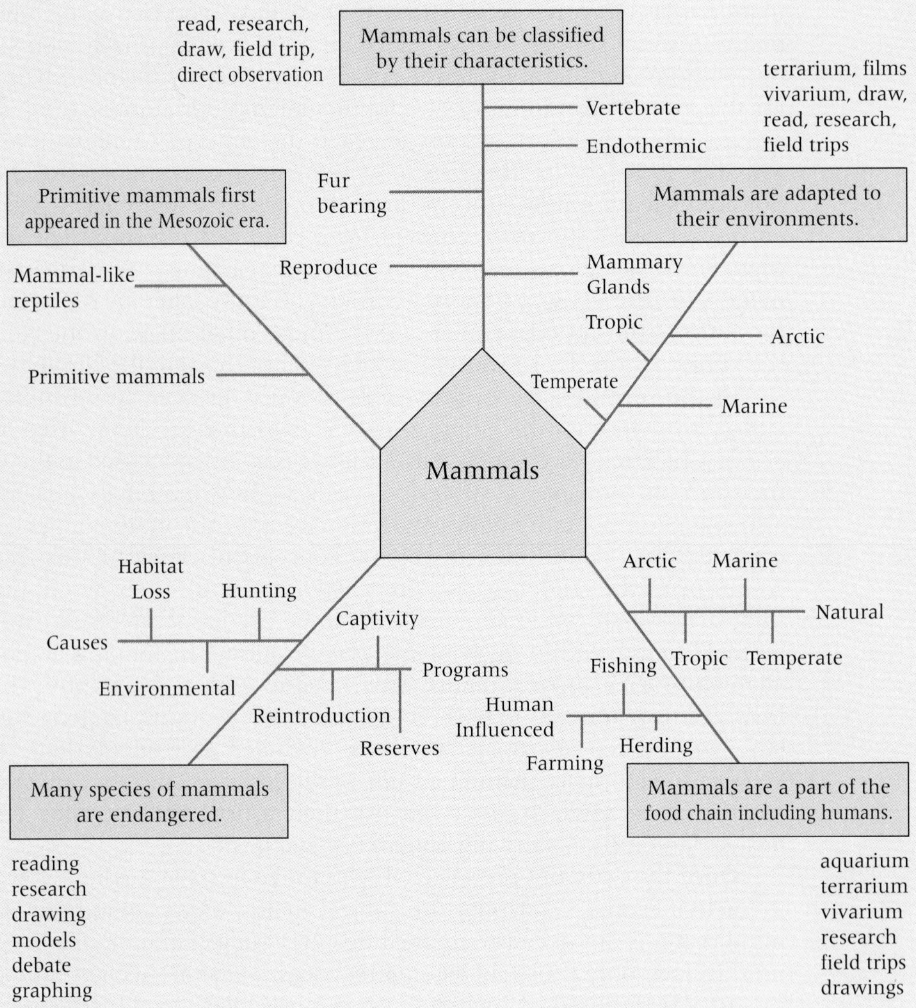

read, research,
draw, field trip,
direct observation

Mammals can be classified
by their characteristics.

terrarium, films
vivarium, draw,
read, research,
field trips

Vertebrate

Endothermic

Fur
bearing

Primitive mammals first
appeared in the Mesozoic era.

Mammals are adapted to
their environments.

Mammal-like
reptiles

Reproduce

Mammary
Glands

Primitive mammals

Tropic

Arctic

Temperate

Marine

Mammals

Habitat
Loss

Hunting

Arctic   Marine

Natural

Causes

Captivity

Programs

Fishing   Tropic   Temperate

Environmental

Reintroduction

Human
Influenced

Reserves

Farming

Herding

Many species of mammals
are endangered.

Mammals are a part of the
food chain including humans.

reading
research
drawing
models
debate
graphing

aquarium
terrarium
vivarium
research
field trips
drawings

Presenting the Integrated Approach

Scheduling. Integrated teaching generally requires a different approach to class-room scheduling. In many schools and school systems, teachers schedule according to the subject matter areas and assign a particular number of minutes for instruction in each of those areas. Within an integrated approach, a large block of time is needed so that students have the opportunity to pursue a variety of activities, many of them lengthy, and have the opportunity to use the subject matter areas effectively in their pursuits.

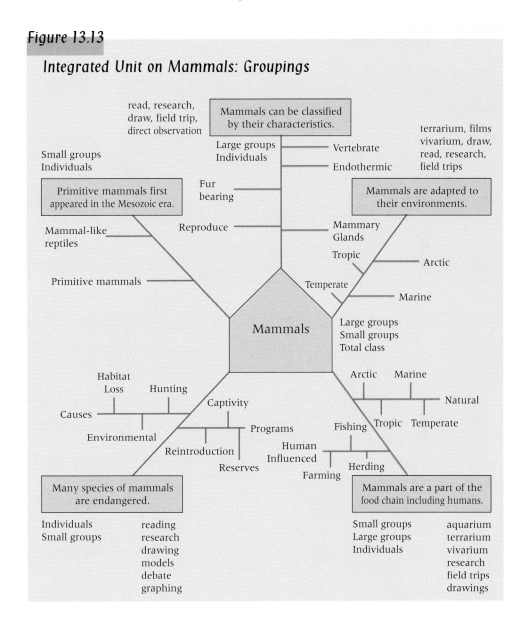

Figure 13.13

Integrated Unit on Mammals: Groupings

Implementation.   When students begin to work within the integrated approach, they have the opportunity of selecting the areas in which they will work at a particular time. Consequently, while some students are researching the life and times of Isaac Newton, others will be planning a model of an amusement park, and still others will be working with the teacher to plan and conduct activities or experiments dealing with force, motion, gravity, and simple machines. Student choice is important in the use of an effective integrated approach. When you introduce the topic for study, you give an overview of the entire area of study and then detail the kinds

Figure 13.14

Integrated Unit on Mammals: Subject Areas

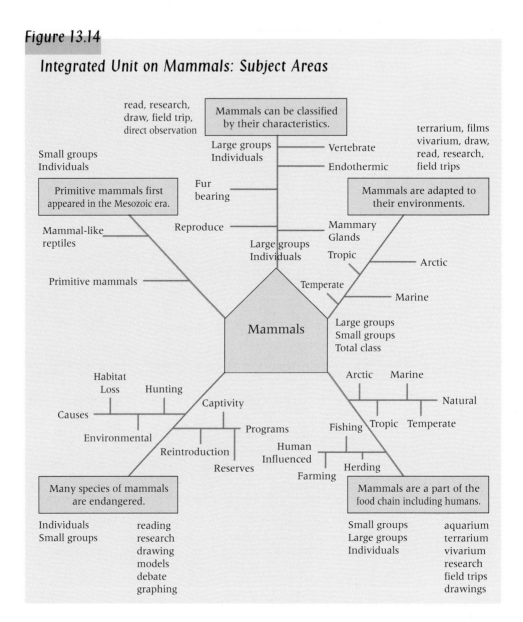

of activities the students can select. As the teacher you need to make it clear how many of the activities must be completed or if all of the activities must be completed.

Organizing the Classroom.   Because the activities used in an integrated approach can require a variety of grouping procedures and children can be engaging in a variety of activities and projects at the same time, the classroom needs to be organized to allow for this kind of variety. Areas for independent group work need to be established. For example, if students are working on a model of an amusement park to demonstrate the application of laws of motion, they should be near the area where the materials needed for the project are stored. Students doing research using books and other sources need to be in a quiet area where they can read and write or use computers for research or authoring. If, you are assisting the students in developing and carrying out particular experiments, there should be an area with enough space for children to work. Don't neglect the possibility of using the floor or hallway as areas for students to use. Because activities and experiments dealing with motion often require a lot of space for objects to move, a hallway is a great place for students to work.

Management. An integrated approach can appear to be chaotic to outsiders simply because so many different activities are going on at the same time and the teacher is not standing in front of the classroom leading the total class in an activity. The key is that the chaos only be one of appearance. When children are working at a variety of activities and projects as the same time, one of your first chores is to establish the working rules for the classroom. Things to be considered include when to move from one activity to another, how to approach the teacher, for assistance when he or she is engaged in working with a group or with a single student, who is responsible for cleaning up, how many students may be working at a particular area at a time, and what signal will be used if the teacher or a student wishes to get the attention from the entire class.

Often a concern of teachers in a classroom setting as active as this is the possibility for students getting out of control. For the most part this is not a particular problem. Students in an activity-oriented, integrated approach are engaged in activities of interest to them that are developmentally appropriate. When these two criteria are met, students are generally so actively engaged in their learning that they are less likely to get out of hand than they are in a teacher-directed activity that is developmentally inappropriate. The one area that can be of concern is the noise level. The sound of active, productive learning is louder than the sound of students reading and writing. So long as the level of noise is not so great it disturbs other classes or the students attempting to research and write, so long as the noise is productive, let the children work. However, if the noise level becomes too loud, have some signal that allows you to get the attention of the students and brings them back to a more acceptable level. It is not appropriate for students who are actively involved in group and individual work to be silent.

Assessment. In assessing the learning taking place in an integrated approach, pencil and paper tests are probably not the best choice. Instead, the learning is assessed through the outcomes of the activities and projects undertaken by the students. Children who have constructed models of simple and complex machines can be assessed according to how well their models meet the objectives for that activity. Children who are writing papers can be assessed on the content of the paper and on the dynamics of writing. Children who have drawn murals to demonstrate their understanding of a particular concept can be assessed on the content as well as the artistic value. When assessing the outcome of an integrated approach, the learning is assessed both in terms of the concept but also in terms of the contributing subject matter areas. For example, if students have engaged in an experiment in which they had to use mathematical skills, the activity can be assessed in terms of the science content learned through the experiment, the accuracy of the mathematics used, and the writing involved in presenting the results. The key is to be certain the students realize all of the areas will be considered before they begin to work on the activity or project. Activity 13.7 is designed to help you develop a plan for interdisciplinary teaching.

Interdisciplinary/Integrated Curriculum Activity

Activity 13.6

Purpose To develop a plan for an interdisciplinary approach to science teaching.

Procedure
1. Select any science topic from a first through eighth grade textbook series. Identify the concepts being considered.
2. Using the steps described in the preceding paragraphs, develop an interdisciplinary approach to the topic including the semantic maps necessary for the development of the topic.
3. Discuss how you would implement the interdisciplinary strategy developed at the grade level for which it was planned.

Summary

Science teaching can contribute to the rest of the elementary school curriculum, and the rest of the elementary school curriculum can contribute to science teaching through the use of interdisciplinary or integrated approaches.

In an interdisciplinary approach, subject matter areas are combined so that both areas are being used within a particular topic. Mathematics is probably the easiest area to combine with science in an interdisciplinary approach. Other areas that are easy to combine are social studies and language arts. The trick to working with an interdisciplinary approach is to be certain the subject areas are contributing equally to an understanding of the science topic.

Integrated teaching goes a step beyond interdisciplinary teaching in that the subject matter areas disappear and the concepts to be learned become far more important than science, mathematics, social studies, or any of the other disciplines. The traditional way of looking at curriculum integration is through a thematic approach. In a thematic approach the theme is used as an organizing topic and the theme is then used in each of the subject matter areas. In some cases, the theme does not lend itself easily to the inclusion of all subject matter areas and it becomes necessary to force the theme into particular disciplines. In other cases, the theme naturally allows the inclusion of all areas. In the traditional thematic approach, the subject matter areas remain distinct.

In the integrated approach, the subject matter areas disappear into the topic of study so the subject matter areas become tools for study rather than ends in themselves. In planning for an integrated approach, the teacher begins by developing the concepts he or she wants the students to learn and ends by considering the specific subject matter areas used in the study. The subject matter areas are used to develop the concepts and so are used purposefully. No attempt is made in an integrated approach to force all of the subject matter areas into every topic of study.

Vocabulary Terms

The number following each term refers to the page on which the term is first introduced.

Integrated approach, 376   Interdisciplinary approach, 394

1. You want to begin using an interdisciplinary approach to teaching. As work on units combining science and mathematics, science and social studies, you are told by another teacher that you can't do it. You are required to teach science and social studies for 40 minutes a day and mathematics for 60 minutes a day. How could you demonstrate to individuals concerned about the number of minutes a subject matter area is taught per day that you are meeting or exceeding those requirements?

2. You are visiting a middle school using an interdisciplinary approach. Each of the three grade levels in the school, sixth, seventh, and eighth, uses a different topic to organize the curriculum. In seventh grade, the topic is the Middle Ages. When you go into the science class, the teacher tells you this is the day they do their interdisciplinary study. He then begins by telling the students they will not be continuing their study of simple machines that day, but instead will be making shields as a part of their study of the Middle Ages. This is their usual means for working with an interdisciplinary program. How would you answer the principal of this school when she asks what you think of their program?

3. You have been asked to serve on a committee for a new science-mathematics-technology magnet elementary school. The decision has already been made to use an interdisciplinary approach in the school. What suggestions would you make as to how to do this?

References

Allen, H., F. Spittgerberge, and M. Manning. 1993. *Teaching and learning in the middle level school.* New York: Merrill.

Bean, J. 1992. Creating an integrative curriculum: Making the connections. *National Association of Secondary School Principals Bulletin* 16(11), 46–54.

Charnpmmear, M., and B. Reider. 1995. *The integrated elementary classroom: A developmental model of education for the 21st. century.* Boston: Allyn & Bacon.

Drake, S. 1993. *Planning integrated curriculum.* Alexandria, Va.: Association of Supervision and Curriculum Development.

Fogarty, R. 1991a. *How to integrate the curricula.* Palatine, Ill.: IRI/Skylight.

Fogarty, R. 1991b. Ten ways to integrate curriculum. *Educational Leadership* 49(10), 24–26.

Fredericks, A. 1992. *The integrated curriculum.* Englewood, Colo.: Teacher Ideas Press.

Gherke, N. 1991. Explorations of teachers' development of integrative curriculums. *Journal of Curriculum and Supervision* 6(2), 107–117.

Jacobs, H. H. 1989. Interdisciplinary curriculum: Design and implementation. Alexandria, Va.: *Association for Supervision and Curriculum Development.*

Jacobs, H. 1991. On interdisciplinary education: A conversation. *Educational Leadership* 49(10), 24–26.

Kivalic, S. 1993. *ITI: The model: Integrated thematic instruction.* Village of Oak Creek, Ark.: Books for Educators.

Lapp, D., and J. Flood. 1994. Integrating the curriculum: First steps. *The Reading Teacher* 47(5), 416–419.

Lipson, M., S. Valencia, K. Wixon, and C. Peters. 1993. Integration and thematic teaching: Integration to improve teaching and learning. *Language Arts,* 70(4), 252–263.

Martinello, M., and G. Cook. 1994. *Interdisciplinary inquiry in teaching and learning.* New York: Merrill.

Marzano, R. J., D. Pickering, and R. Brandt. 1990. Integrating instruction programs through dimensions of learning. *Educational Leadership* 47, 5.

McDonald, J., and C. Czerniak. 1994. Developing interdisciplinary units: Strategies and examples. *School Science and Mathematics* 94(1), 5–10.

Stice, C., J. Bertrand, and N. Bertrand. 1995. *Integrating reading and the other language arts.* Belmont, Calif.: Wadsworth.

Willis, S. 1995. Making integrated curriculum a reality. *Association for Supervision and Curriculum Development Education Update* 37(4), 4.

Wilson, L., D. Malmgren, S. Ramage, and L. Schultz. 1993. *An integrated approach to learning.* Portsmouth, N.H.: Heinemann.

Wolfinger, D. M., and J. W. Stockard. 1997. *Elementary methods: An integrated curriculum.* New York: Longman.

CHAPTER FOURTEEN

TECHNOLOGY AND SCIENCE TEACHING

Chapter Objectives

Upon completion of this chapter, you should be able to:

1 define technology for science teaching.

2 discuss the appropriate use of technology in the classroom.

3 discuss the benefits of technology use in the classroom.

4 differentiate between technology as a tool for the teacher and technology as an aspect of instruction.

5 differentiate among tutorials, drills, simulations, and tool applications.

6 discuss the use of computer interface instruments in the hands-on science program.

7 discuss the use of databases, including Internet, within the science classroom.

8 discuss cautions on the use of technology within the classroom.

Introduction

Ms. Grant uses technology in her classroom. She has a computer on her desk that she uses for keeping student records. Her computerized grade book makes it easier for her to keep student grades and for her to calculate the grades at the end of each grading period. In addition to the computer grade book, Ms. Grant also uses a program to help her with writing lesson plans. She finds it much easier to make and keep her plans on her computer than to use a standard teacher planning book. And she also uses her classroom computer to e-mail other teachers in the building, to keep in touch with the principal, and in many cases to keep in touch with parents.

Mr. Roth also uses technology in the classroom. He has a computer center, with four computers, set up in an area of the classroom away from his main instructional area. Students having difficulty with a particular concept can go to the computer center and work on the concept presented in the regular class setting. Students who complete work quickly also have an opportunity to use the computer center. These children can go to the center when work has been completed to play educational games, often in competition with one another, and so the computers are a reward for work well done.

In Mrs. Sanchez's class, four computers are set up in a learning center. Three of the four computers are used every day by the children. Each morning, Mrs. Sanchez starts the computers and opens a particular program for the children to use to reinforce a previous lesson. Then, during the day, the children go to the computer center on a rotational basis to work with the information on the program. All of the children have a chance to go to the center. The third computer is set up with a word processing program. Mrs. Sanchez uses this computer for her own work, but also uses it as a reward for children who have written particularly good stories during her language arts program. Those children can use the word processing capabilities of the computer to make a finished copy of the story for display in the classroom.

Mr. Wong also has computers in his classroom. Some of the children use the computers for review and reinforcement of previous lessons. Others are using the computers to learn more about a topic through CD-ROM technology or through Internet access. During his science lessons he uses instrument interfacing: Students use probes connected to a microcomputer to collect data during an activity dealing with temperature changes during chemical reactions, data dealing with temperature or velocity or light intensity.

All four of these teachers are using technology in their classrooms; that is, they are using computers in the classroom. And yet, all four have a different approach to the use of technology.

No single approach to the use of computers in the classroom is correct, but some ways of including computer technology make better instructional use of the computer than others. In Ms. Grant's classroom the computer has become a tool to make the life of the teacher a little easier. In both Mr. Roth's and Mrs. Sanchez's classrooms, computer technology is an adjunct to the traditional teaching they do in their classrooms, and is sometimes a reward rather than a teaching tool. And in Mr. Wong's classroom, the computer has become an integral part of daily instruction.

If you want to move toward integrating instructional technology into the science classroom, you need an understanding of what technology is, how it can be used, and the kinds of benefits that can accrue from its use.

Computer Technology for the Classroom

Technology in the classroom tends to mean one thing: computers. For many teachers, the words *computers* and *technology* have become synonyms, and, therefore, bringing technology into the classroom has come to mean bringing computers into the classroom. But simply bringing computers into the classroom for teacher or student use is not enough to assure those computers will contribute to the education of the children in that classroom. If computers are to have a positive impact on the learning that takes place in the classroom, then they should help students apply knowledge, seek out new knowledge, solve practical problems, and extend their capabilities. All of these uses of computers contribute to academic learning time and so present positive ways to enhance student learning.

Academic Learning Time

Academic learning time is the amount of time a student gives to an appropriate and purposeful academic task while accomplishing that task with a high rate of success (Berliner, 1984; Caldwell, Huitt, and Graeber, 1982). Think for a moment about three eighth graders working to develop a graph of the data they collected for an experiment dealing with the effect of mass on acceleration. They decide on the format, develop the scales, graph the data, and draw a conclusion from that data. Their work is focused and productive. These students have made excellent use of academic learning time. Now think about a group of second grade students attempting to develop a hierarchical classification system for a variety of "junk box" materials. After working for a few minutes at this developmentally inappropriate task, they find it impossible and begin using the materials to see how high a tower they can build. Although they may be having fun, they are no longer engaged in an activity leading to a particular objective. Their use of academic learning time is not particularly effective.

The more time our students spend focused productively on an educational task, the more they achieve. One of the ways of helping students remain focused and purposefully engaged, and so to enhance academic learning time, is to use computers in ways that are purposeful and focused. Vockell and Schwartz (1992) identified three ways in which we can use computers effectively to enhance academic learning time. The first way is by allowing students to acquire specific information or to practice specific skills. Students engaged in using computers in this way may be using a computer to learn more about mammals or sound or volcanoes by working with a CD-ROM database or they may be reviewing vocabulary terms dealing with flower parts as they play a game. A second way of using computers to enhance academic learning time is in helping students develop basic tools of learning that they can then apply in a wide variety of settings. In this use, students may be learning to use a word processing program, learning how to use Hypercard stacks to organize and present information, or learning to use a spreadsheet to help them do calculations quickly and interpret information. Once the students have learned to organize data through Hypercard, they can use that program to present information using text, pictures, QuickTime movies, sound, and connections from one set of data to another. Once students have learned to use word processing or spreadsheets, they can present or store information in organized and effective ways. These skills can then be used in any subject matter area. Third, and finally, we can use computers in the science class to help students focus their attention more completely and for a longer time. Here academic learning time is enhanced by CD-ROM programs and interactive videodisks that present information in a highly motivating manner through sights and sounds or through Internet searches.

If we are going to use computer technology effectively in the classroom, we do not do it simply by having computers in the classroom or by using computers as a part of instruction, but rather by using computer technology to help our students meet our instructional objectives in a better way. Consider a group of third graders working in a unit on rocks and minerals. They have collected rocks and minerals from their local environment, they've taken a field trip to a local college museum to see the rock and mineral collection there, they have had a geologist come in to talk to them about geology and what it means to be a geologist, and they have taken a trip to a local jeweler to see how rocks and minerals, in the form of precious and semiprecious stones and metals like gold and silver, are turned into jewelry. This is a highly effective way of teaching children about rocks and minerals. Teaching this same unit would not be nearly as effective if students are placed before computer screens where they can only look, read, and hear but not touch and collect rocks and minerals. In other words, computers in the classroom should be used not just for the sake of using computers but when those computers can accomplish the instruction in a way that is more effective than traditional teaching techniques.

However, computers in the classroom can contribute to the total science program in many ways. Computer programs can be used effectively to simulate experiences that would otherwise be far too dangerous, expensive, time consuming, or for some other reason impossible to carry out in the classroom. The computer can provide superb alternatives to traditional instruction (Trollip and Alessi, 1988). Few schools have the funds or the opportunity to take students to watch a space shuttle take off, to a location where a dinosaur skeleton is being removed from the surrounding rock, or to a nuclear reactor. Through computer technology, students can view all of these events and can often interact with shuttle crew, paleontologists, or nuclear engineers. Through computer technology, students can simulate the dissection of a frog or look into the human body. These kinds of experiences may not be available to students in a particular school. These kinds of experiences cannot be simulated through still pictures and written words in a textbook. Computer technology can, however, provide these kinds of experiences.

But even though computers can provide this type of experience, it is highly unlikely that a computer will replace real live teachers. Even when computers are used effectively, good science teaching and learning takes place when learning takes place in a human-oriented, teacher-facilitated learning environment. The computer is merely a tool for extending your teaching ability. Because you are so important in the success or failure of computer instruction in the classroom, you need to why, when, and how you can use computers as tools to support effective instruction. A good computer system in the hands of a great teacher does more to enhance classroom learning than a great computer system in the hands of a poor teacher. Computer technology in the classroom should supplement, not supplant the hands-on aspects of science teaching and learning. Activity 14.1 develops your understanding of the use of technology in local classrooms.

Technology in the Classroom Activity

Activity 14.1

Purpose   To interview teachers about the use of technology in their classrooms.

Procedure
1. Arrange to interview three or four teachers working at a single grade level.
2. Interview the teachers to find the answers to the following questions:
   a. What kinds of computer technology do you have available in your school? In your classroom? (Consider both hardware and software.)
   b. How do you use the computer technology available to you?
   c. What are the benefits to you and your students of computer technology in the classroom?
   d. What are some of the problems you run into using computer technology in the classroom.
   e. What would help you overcome the problems?
   f. What kinds of computer technology would you like to have available to you in your classroom.

Impacts of Computer Instruction

When computers are used effectively in the classroom, when they are used appropriately by teachers with particular goals and objectives in mind, those computers can make a difference in four basic areas: retention, learning time, achievement, and student attitudes (Lillie, Hannum, and Stuck,1989).

Retention.   Computer technology is most effective in improving retention at the knowledge and comprehension levels. This may be because computers can present information in a number of different formats, including written, spoken, pictures, and photographs. Computers, therefore, can be highly effective in helping students learn factual information and vocabulary within a particular field of science. Game formats make learning knowledge-level information enjoyable and offer the opportunity to practice the material over and over again with an infinitely patient teacher, the computer program, which enhances retention of basic information.

Learning Time.   Computer technology is useful in decreasing the amount of time necessary for children to learn. As with retention, this is especially true when the learning objectives are at the lower levels: knowledge and comprehension. Probably the reduction in learning time is tied to motivation. Students are interested in computers and so they find the material more interesting. In addition, computers can provide multisensory experiences to engage attention and match various learning styles or intelligence. And, finally, computer programs at the knowledge and comprehension levels, provide immediate feedback to the students. All of these factors contribute to faster learning of low-level information.

Achievement.   Students who use instructional technology in learning tend to score higher on objective tests than students who have traditional text and lecture format teaching. This may be due to the fact that teachers often use drill and practice software with students who are having difficulties with a particular science concept. In this case, computer technology supports mastery learning by providing additional practice and feedback to students having problems with a concept or skill. In addition, computer technology can be used when a student wants to use it and at a learning pace appropriate to the individual learner.

Computer technology can also increase the achievement of children with learning disabilities, children coming from lower socioeconomic levels, and average children in need of remediation. But it is not only the child in need of additional instruction who is assisted by the computer in the classroom. Students who are gifted and talented can use the computer to pursue more advanced information and problem-solving skills.

Attitudes.   Computer technology in the classroom also contributes to positive attitudes toward learning on the part of children. Because the computer is endlessly patient in working with students, because computers teach and reteach, because computers present information over and over until children learn, and because computers give feedback consistently to children, those children learn effectively and feel good about their ability to learn. Not only do computers develop positive attitudes due to infinite patience in the reteaching and teaching process, but computers, because of their association with games in the minds of many children, are viewed as more fun than the traditional teacher in front of the classroom. The use of colorful visuals, animation, sounds, and generally multimedia approaches also engenders positive attitudes in children. And, because computers provide constant reinforcement in a neutral atmosphere, students gain in self-confidence and also gain a sense of accomplishment.

How do we gain these benefits in our classrooms? One of the main ways is by selecting instructional programs that are appropriate to our objectives. The best instructional packages are, first of all, appropriate for both multicultural classrooms and a wide range of learner abilities. Second, they present information in an interesting and motivating manner while avoiding redundance with an equally or more effective way of providing the information or instruction. Third, an effective instructional package meets the objectives of the curriculum with material or experiences that might not otherwise be accessible to students. Fourth, good program packages are easily learned, work with the hardware already available in the classroom, and fit into the class schedule. Fifth, and finally, good instructional packages are flexible. They connect several topics, concepts, or themes and allow for use in a variety of settings: by individuals, by small groups, or by the whole class. Flexibility also means there are opportunities for students to use the package in beginner or advanced modes. The more flexible a program, the more likely it will be used in a classroom setting by a variety of students (Reynolds and Barba, 1996).

Modes of Learning

Once the computer technology has been brought into the classroom, learners can interact with that technology in four basic modes: instructional, revelatory, conjectural, and emancipatory (Vockell and Schwartz, 1992).

Instructional Mode. In the **instructional mode,** the computer serves as a means for delivering information to the student. In essence, the computer used in this manner is filling the traditional role of the classroom teacher. The instructional mode includes drills and tutorials. When computers are used in the instructional mode, always keep in mind that simply because a computer can deliver a unit of instruction does not mean the computer should deliver that unit of instruction. In the instructional mode, your question should always be, Does the program do this better than another commonly used method? If the answer is yes, use the computer as the teaching method.

Revelatory Mode. In the **revelatory mode,** the computer provides a bridge between the student and a model of the real world. In science classes, revelatory programs supplement hands-on laboratory experiences or take the place of direct experiences when those experiences are too time consuming, expensive, dangerous, technical, or remote to be practical. The relevatory mode includes simulations and role playing. When used in the relevatory mode, computers can help students learn and apply higher order thinking skills as well as develop accurate conceptions of phenomena that would otherwise be difficult to study in the classroom. Sometimes good simulations are not tied directly to specific topics or content. Instead, these simulations help students focus on a basic strategy or thinking skill. For example, a computer simulation engaging students in using the scientific method is not only more effective than reading about the scientific method but can cut across the traditional division of science content and so be appropriate to biology, physical science, or earth-space science. Role-playing situations can allow students to become a part of the story situation and so make decisions and find the effects of those decisions.

Conjectural Mode. In the **conjectural mode,** the computer enables the learner to explore "what if" questions and so helps the learner build interactive models of various phenomena. The learner asks "what if" questions, establishes hypotheses, and then tests those hypotheses to determine the answers to the questions.

Emancipatory Mode. In the **emancipatory mode,** the computer frees the learner from tiresome learning tasks and so allows that time to be used for more important learning activities. What are these tiresome learning tasks? Tasks such as repetitive calculations, technical setups, or organization of data into productive patterns such as graphs come under this category. The student is freed from these tasks because the emancipatory mode includes spreadsheets, word processing programs, database management programs, microcomputer-based laboratories, and telecommunications.

The student, however, is not the only person emancipated by use of classroom computer technology in this mode. Computerized tools also free the teacher to be more creative and productive. Use of databases to research and support teaching, computerized grade books, word processing programs, lesson planning packages, and computerized test generators can all assist the teacher in the classroom.

The modes of computer use lead directly into the types of computer programs and uses within the classroom. The following sections discuss the applications of computer programs: tutorial, drill, simulation, microcomputer-based labs, technology-based information systems, and tools.

Computer Applications in the Classroom

Computerized Tutorials

In Mr. Johnson's seventh grade biology class, the students are studying classification of vertebrate animals. He has been working with students to observe various kinds of vertebrates in the local parks as well as at the zoo. The students have been reading their textbook and watching films about vertebrates. Although they are having no difficulty identifying the characteristics of individual animals, they are still having some difficulty with classifying the animals correctly. He decides to use his classroom computers to provide additional information about classification and so chooses to use a computer-based tutorial.

A **computer-based tutorial** is basically the same as a teacher with a textbook. However, unlike the teacher and the textbook, the computer-based tutorial allows a student to proceed at his or her own pace. Tutorials are helpful especially in reviewing information that has not previously been mastered by the students, providing reinforcement of a skill learned, or in providing additional time with a skill or idea. The same information could be presented in a textbook, but students often find computer-based tutorials more motivating because of the use of animated graphics, photographs, and sound. And immediate feedback is always provided to the students.

As he looks for an appropriate tutorial, Mr. Johnson keeps in mind some of the characteristics of good tutorial programs and looks for a tutorial based on branching programmed instruction. In this type of format, the learner's response to a particular item triggers the computer's next response. If the student using the tutorial answers correctly, the computer program goes to the next item of information in the program. If the student gives an incorrect response, the program provides remediation. It presents information to the student so he or she can review it before attempting to answer new questions. And if it is a really good tutorial program, the computer has a number of different alternatives for explaining the same information. The program does not simply return the student to the same information over and over again. If a student indicates he or she needs help before even trying to answer a question, a good tutorial program assists that student by providing definitions, clarification, or other information needed to solve a particular problem.

If possible, Mr. Johnson will use a tutorial that involves CD-ROM technology and interactive laser discs. This type of technology can provide his students with a vast amount of information, using still and moving pictures within the tutorial, by including diagrams as well as text, and including sound features. These kinds of features will help his students maintain their motivation as they learn.

Mr. Johnson also realizes there are some difficulties with using computer-based tutorials with his students, and so even when they are working with tutorials he maintains close watch over what is happening. Tutorials can sometimes be frustrating, especially to students who need to go back and review information presented before going on. With a textbook it is easy to flip back and forth among the pages to find information. It is very difficult to flip back and forth in a computer tutorial to find information. He wants to be on hand to provide information if it is needed. The second problem he wants to watch for is "electronic segregation," that is, assigning students to work independently at a computer terminal where he or she is isolated from peers. This type of assignment can cause a student to be physically, socially, and educationally separated from mainstream learning activities (Vockell and Schwartz, 1992).

Technology in the Classroom Activities

Activity 14.2

Purpose To review and critique a tutorial program designed for use in science teaching.

Procedure
1. Review the material presented here on the characteristics of good tutorial software.
2. Locate a tutorial program for use in elementary or middle school science teaching.
   a. Use the program yourself. If possible, observe a student at the appropriate grade level using the program.
   b. Critique the program for its strengths and weaknesses.

Activity 14.3

Purpose To develop a file of tutorial programs for use in elementary or middle school science teaching.

Procedure
1. Using a variety of resources including catalogs, computer magazines, science education journals, textbooks, and teacher referrals, develop a file of tutorial programs for science teaching.

2. Include in the file the title of the program, the subject matter included, the suggested grade level use, any review comments, and the original source where the program was found.

Drill and Practice Programs

In her third grade class, Mrs. Phillips has some students who are having difficulty learning the names of the parts of a flower. Although she has had the students in her class observe flowers and draw them, has had them dissect flowers to look at the parts, and has used visual aids to show the parts, some of the children are still finding it hard to identify the pistil and stamens, as well as other parts. Because most of the students can identify the parts, she decides not to reteach herself but to use her classroom computers. She selects a drill and practice program that shows the vocabulary she wants her students to practice in a variety of different ways and in a game format that makes the practice fun to do.

A **drill and practice program** provides repeated practice and feedback to help students reach a particular objective. Consequently, a good computer drill and practice program focuses clearly on the teacher's instructional objectives. The program states the problem or question so the student knows exactly what to do but refrains from giving the student irrelevant clues. A good drill and practice program gives students immediate feedback for responses as they practice skills or concepts previously taught. And, when necessary, a good drill and practice program provides remediation if it is necessary.

The questions presented and the format for the presentation of those questions is particularly important to a drill and practice program. Good programs have different levels of questions with the easier questions appearing early in the program and harder questions appearing after the students begin to show mastery. In addition to the sequence of the questions from easy to difficult, good drill and practice programs present the questions randomly so students cannot simply memorize the sequence of the answers rather than really learning the information.

By deciding to use a drill and practice program at this point in her teaching, Mrs. Philips is using the program appropriately. Drill and practice programs should be used after material has been taught rather than as a way of presenting new information to students. She realizes that having students drill on information they do not understand is not going to result in their development of understanding. In fact, placing children in front of computers to work with information they have never encountered may result in frustration. They may even decide the material is simply too hard for them and quit trying to learn. And finally, Mrs. Phillips realizes drill and practice programs are meant to be used with students who need them and not with the entire class.

A good computerized drill, used appropriately, can provide excellent opportunities for practice and feedback about important concepts, principles, and skills. At their best, drills help students learn to perform skills or recall information so automatically that those skills or that information can then be used in pursuing higher level activities. At their worst, drills trivialize subject matter by making students focus on lower level activities to the exclusion of applying those skills and concepts to the higher level activities that the subject matter is really about. Activity 14.4 provides you with an opportunity to evaluate drill and practice programs. Activity 14.5 adds to your developing file of software for science teaching using technology.

Technology in the Classroom Activities

Activity 14.4

Purpose To put into practice the criteria developed here for a good drill or practice program.

Procedure
1. Review the criteria presented here for a good drill or practice program.
2. Develop a checklist based on the given criteria that could be used to evaluate a drill or practice program appropriate for science education.
3. Locate a drill or practice program appropriate for use in elementary or middle school science.
   a. Try the program yourself. If possible, observe while a student at the appropriate grade level uses the same program.
   b. Evaluate the program according to the developed criteria. What are the strengths and weaknesses of the program?

Activity 14.5

Purpose To develop a file of drill or practice programs for use in elementary or middle school science teaching.

Procedure
1. Using a variety of resources including catalogs, computer magazines, science education journals, textbooks, and teacher referrals, develop a file of drill or practice programs for science teaching.
2. Include in the file the title of the program, the subject matter included, the suggested grade level use, any review comments, and the original source where the program was found.
3. Add the drill or practice programs to the file of tutorial programs.

Simulations

In Ms. Farrag's fifth grade class, the students are studying ecology. They have worked with the ideas of food chains through an aquarium and a terrarium and have considered the idea of a food web by investigating a local lake and then taking an extended field trip to the seashore. Although she can discuss the effects of changes in an ecosystem on the plants and animals living there, she cannot really have the children see firsthand the results of changes. Films about oil spills and other disastrous effects on the environment are giving her students the idea that only momentous changes cause the environment to change. She decides to involve her students in a computer simulation that will allow them to make changes in a forest system and then see the results of those changes.

Simulations allow students to enter into a fictitious world with specified boundaries and to interact with that world. A simulation could allow students to travel the world's oceans, to test the effects of environmental changes on a pond, or to probe the internal structure of the human body. Many simulations involve problem solving and many allow the user to be in a location that would be too dangerous, too expensive, unethical, impractical, or otherwise impossible to visit. Simulations have the advantage of controlling the number of variables in the environment so patterns and relationships become easier to grasp.

As she looks for a computer simulation to use with her class, Ms. Farrag first considers the appearance of the simulation. A simulation should look interesting with appropriate graphics, but she also realizes the simulation should not be chosen simply for its graphics, and particularly not simply because it looks like fun. A simulation that provides too much fun may be treated more like a game than a serious learning experience.

The second thing Ms. Farrag considers in selecting her computer simulation is the accuracy of the simulation. She wants it to be an accurate model of an ecosystem, but not one that is so complicated her students will not be able to use it. A good simulation often simplifies the situation so that students can focus on the important principles involved without being overwhelmed by too much information and too many variables. Too many variables may result in confusion on the part of the students trying to use it.

The kind of simulation Ms. Farrag is looking for is one that involves her students in problem solving. This kind of simulation generally presents a problem or challenge and then has students get involved in using their background information along with provided information to solve the problem. It involves making decisions and testing those decisions. Before having her students use the simulation, Ms. Farrag wants to try it herself. In this way she can determine whether or not it is bringing out the concepts she wants her students to develop, and she can also determine whether her students will have the information and thinking skills needed to use the program successfully. Activity 14.6 asks you to evaluate a simulation program according to established criteria. Activity 14.7 continues to develop your file of appropriate science software.

Technology in the Classroom Activities

Activity 14.6

Purpose   To put into practice the criteria developed here for an effective simulation program.

Procedure

1. Review the criteria presented here for an effective simulation program.
2. Develop a checklist based on the given criteria that could be used to evaluate a simulation program appropriate for science education.
3. Locate a simulation program appropriate for use in elementary or middle school science.
   a. Try the program yourself. If possible, observe while a student at the appropriate grade level uses the same program.
   b. Evaluate the program according to the developed criteria. What are the strengths and weaknesses of the program?

Activity 14.7

Purpose   To develop a file of simulation programs for use in elementary or middle school science teaching.

Procedure

1. Using a variety of resources including catalogs, computer magazines, science education journals, textbooks, and teacher referrals, develop a file of simulation programs for science teaching.
2. Include in the file the title of the program, the subject matter included, the suggested grade level use, any review comments, and the original source where the program was found.
3. Add the simulation programs to the file of tutorial and drill or practice.

Microcomputer-Based Labs

Mr. Harris teaches in a **microcomputer-based lab.** His students carry on hands-on activities directly using science equipment, but at times they need more than the standard balances, test tubes, bulbs and batteries. At times, he wants them to carry out experiments that require more than the simple use of the five senses and sometimes require more time than is available. His lab allows him to carry out a variety of experiments and investigations that might not otherwise be available to his students. In addition to promoting higher order thinking skills, microcomputer-based labs also allow teachers to present information in a variety of different ways, allow them to focus on concepts rather than procedures, and provide students with real-world applications of classroom knowledge (Reynolds and Barba, 1996).

In his lab, Mr Harris has a variety of tools he can use. Two particular categories are used to classify these instruments. The first includes instrument interfaces and the second includes vision extenders.

Instrument Interfaces.   Mr. Harris's microcomputer-based lab uses instruments consisting of sensors interfaced with the computer through the input/output port. These instruments require a probe, a way of connecting the probe to the computer, and the software to manage the probe's input. The most common kinds of sensors include photoresistors for sensing light, thermoresistors for sensing heat, microphones for sound, infrared sensors for infrared waves, and potentiometers attached to a mechanical device for angular movement. The sensor is activated, partially activated, or not activated by incoming energy which affects the resistance of the electric current. The current is then "read" by the computer's software and turned into an on-screen display.

Mr. Harris uses light sensors to have his class measure brightness, light absorption by variously colored surfaces, speed of an object, or heart rate by detecting a pulse of blood through a translucent object. He uses temperature sensors to monitor changes in temperature, compare temperatures in differing locations or under differing conditions, and measure heat from such biological phenomena as rotting leaves or seed germination. And he uses sound sensors to measure loudness and pitch as well as underwater sounds, and a motion sensor to measure distance and motion.

Vision Extenders.   In Mr. Harris's microcomputer-based lab, students collect information from sources that might not otherwise be possible due to the limitations of their senses or to the limitations of their patience. In addition to the probes used as a part of the microcomputer-based lab, Mr. Harris's students use sensory extenders, particularly those that extend the limits of vision. The students use familiar devices such as video cameras and microscopes attached to video cameras interfaced with a computer or used separately from a computer to extend their senses and make the collection of data easier and more accurate.

Students in the microcomputer lab also use a video camera for unobtrusive viewing so they can monitor an activity that could be disturbed by their own presence. They have observed a nest full of hatchling robins, a bird feeder, and a rabbit run. They have also used video cameras to take closeups that they then projected for all to see, have filmed demonstrations for repeated viewing, and have even used slow motion and time-lapse photography. They used time-lapse photography to speed up, at least for watching, the lengthy process of a chick hatching from an egg and they slowed down the fall of a ball from a second floor window so they could measure the distance the ball fell with each second of elapsed time.

In teaching biology, Mr. Harris has connected a microscope to a video camera so the entire class could see the same microscopic scene and he could point out the objects and organisms of interest rather than relying on students for correct identification of items never before seen.

Mr. Harris has found that using microcomputer-based labs improved his students' understanding of science activities over traditional methods of teaching, perhaps because of the motivation and interest generated by the techniques.

Technology-Based Information Systems

"I used to be able to open my textbook and teach my kids what was in that book. If we needed more information we went to the library and looked up the information in an encyclopedia. The only real problem I had was that when kids wrote reports, they copied the information word for word out of the encyclopedia. Now, I don't have them copying information. I have them printing out pages from an electronic encyclopedia. Yesterday I got a report on volcanoes that consisted of a beautiful cover and 17 pages of printed information right out of a multimedia encyclopedia. I also got a report on volcanoes that had the information printed right from a site on the Web. It even had the little logo that told me I could go back to the main menu if I wished. I can help them understand that printing out information and calling it your own is not right. What I'm not sure I can do is help them use electronic information. In fact, the whole idea of electronic information is overwhelming."

This fifth grade teacher was expressing the feeling of a great many teachers at all grade levels. She was being confronted with a new, vast source of information for her students, but was uncertain how to help her students use that information.

Databases.   The vastness of information, particularly that available on the Internet, can be overwhelming. But the teacher just cited makes an interesting point. Her students were using electronic information sources just as they had used encyclopedias. If we consider the new electronic sources of information as similar to the old paper- and book-based sources of information, then perhaps they will not be so intimidating.

Textbooks, dictionaries, encyclopedias, and libraries are databases housed in paper format. CD-ROM and laser discs as well as the Internet are also databases housed in electronic format. A **database,** therefore, is a source of information. Both types of databases can be searched in similar ways, although electronic sources seem to have even more possibility for tangential searches than do paper sources. It is easy to get lost in the E volume of an encyclopedia as one roams through Eisenhower, elephants, emancipation, emus, Everest, evergreens, and a hundred other possibilities. It is easy to go off on tangents, reading information on Eisenhower even when the search is for information on emus. And if it is easy to get lost in a single volume of an encyclopedia, then it is ten thousand times easier to get lost within the realms of cyberspace when a search results in hundreds or thousands of sources of information. Thus students must have good search skills when they begin to use electronic databases.

CD-ROM Databases.   A **CD-ROM** is a virtually indestructible laser optical disc that can store a tremendous amount of information. When combined with a laser disc, in a tool known as interactive video, it becomes possible for students to access various combinations of moving pictures, still pictures, text, and sound almost instantaneously.

Students using CD-ROM and laser disc technologies tend to have greater success in working with these sources of massive amounts of information when they have a specific problem to solve or question to answer, a problem that requires the student to pursue information from a variety of sources, to compare varying authorities, and to draw conclusions from the information found. Students who simply use CD-ROM technology as a glorified encyclopedia are not taking advantage of the possibilities of this technology.

If you are going to help your students make the most effective use of technological databases, you first need to assist your students to define the problem they want to solve or the questions they want to answer during the investigation. Once your students have identified the question or problem, have them do some preliminary work in the library, narrowing down the question or providing possible solutions for the problem and determining what other kinds of information might be needed if they are to fully answer the question or solve the problem.

Once the students have determined the precise question or problem, have them go to their CD-ROM sources. Once they get to this electronic database, rather than having students attempt to survey the entire database at one sitting, help them break the question or problem down into smaller areas and research one area at a time. For example, students researching endangered species might begin by looking for sources naming endangered species and then go from there to endangered species in their area and finally to causes for endangerment. Trying to investigate all of the subquestions and all of the areas of a database is too much for a single search and a single sitting. Breaking complex problem-solving tasks into simpler steps is a problem-solving strategy that is particularly appropriate to the use of electronic databases.

Once your students have planned the search for information using the smaller subquestions or subproblems as a basis for dividing the search, the next step becomes that of gathering the data. At this stage, your students may need help in differentiating between those sources of information appropriate at that time and those sources of information helpful at another time and for another topic. Information of pandas and why pandas are endangered may be fascinating, but hardly pertinent to research on endangered species in the southeastern United States. Help your students see that the information is not relevant at that time but could be accessed at another time. Your job as a teacher does not end when your students begin to use electronic databases. Their vastness requires you to be present to assist students in their use.

If strategies like narrowing a topic, refining the research question, and searching for appropriate information are needed for using CD-ROM databases, those strategies are even more needed when it comes to using the greatest database of all: the Internet. Activity 14.8 involves you in the use of a CD-ROM database in researching a science topic while activity 14.9 continues to develop your file of technology based teaching materials.

Technology in the Classroom Activities

Activity 14.8

Purpose   To use a CD-ROM database to research an identified science topic appropriate to the elementary or middle school science program.

Procedure
1. Consider the topic of the unit developed as a part of Chapter 8 or a topic taken from a science textbook for grades 1 through 8.
2. Locate one or more CD-ROM databases related to your topic.
   a. Review the databases for content.
   b. Develop a plan for use with elementary or middle school students for researching the identified topic.

Activity 14.9

Purpose To develop a file of CD-ROM database materials for use in elementary or middle school science teaching.

Procedure
1. Using a variety of resources including catalogs, computer magazines, science education journals, textbooks, and teacher referrals, develop a file of CD-ROM database materials for science teaching.
2. Include in the file the title of each item, the subject matter included, the suggested grade-level use, any review comments, and the original source where the item was found.
3. Add the CD-ROM materials to the file of tutorial, drill or practice, and simulations.

Internet Databases. The Internet is a database of incredible proportions, a database that can allow students in Canada to access information in China and students in Kansas to access information in Kenya. Electronic networks like the Internet make it possible for students to become actively involved in social issues by communicating and interacting with people in communities other than their own. Similarly, contact with schools and classrooms around the world can provide students with data for investigations that might not be possible otherwise. Communicating with children in Hawaii about volcanic eruptions, children in Japan about a typhoon, children in Australia about the reversal of seasons between the Southern and Northern Hemispheres, children in Tanzania about problems of poaching, or children in Brazil about rain forests add a dimension not available through textbook, film, or CD-ROM database.

The main way of using the Internet is for information. However, teachers can also effectively use the e-mail aspect of the Internet in a variety of educationally useful ways. In the following paragraphs, the use of the Internet for finding and locating information as well as the use of e-mail in the classroom are discussed.

Searching the Internet Database. In using the Internet as a database, two kinds of searches can be conducted. The first are considered to be structured searches and the second are called by the descriptive name surfing. **Structured searches** have a particular area of information in mind and the database user structures the search to locate that particular information. You might look at structured searches as going to the encyclopedia and selecting the P volume and then opening it to the planet Pluto and reading the information. In **surfing,** the database user has a broad area of interest and uses the Internet to see what can be found on the topic. Surfing might be likened to walking into a library to find out something about astronomy and then looking around to see what is available.

Conducting an Internet Search. The first step in conducting an Internet search is to access the Internet through whatever server is providing Internet access at your school. Commercial servers include Compuserve, Prodigy, and America On-Line.

Schools are more likely to be connected to the Internet through a server such as Microsoft Network or Netscape. Once you are connected to the server, you have two choices for locating information.

The first choice is the easiest by far. If you know the address for the particular site you want to access, simply type in the URL (Uniform Resource Locator) in the proper box, press enter, and wait until the information appears on the screen. For example, if you want to learn more about classroom safety you might want to access the National Science Teachers Association's position on safety by typing in the URL: http://www.nsta.org/ or if you want to find more information on software, and particularly reviews of software for students, you might try the URL: http://www.microweb.com/pepsite/Revue/Softnews. Simply providing the server with the address for the information you want to locate is the simplest possible way of conducting a structured search. If you do not know the address for the particular site you want to locate, you might try the *Internet Yellowpages.*

But in some cases, you want to access a variety of sources of information, or just see what you can find about a particular topic. In order to conduct searches of this type, you need to access a search tool. The most commonly used search tools and their URLs are as follows:

All-In-One: http://www.albany.net/allinone/

Alta Vista: http://altavista.digital.com/

CUSI: http://pubweb.nexor.co.uk/public/cusi/cusi.html

Excite: http://www.excite.com/

InfoSeek: http://www2.infoseek.com/

Lycos: http://www.lycos.com

Wandex: http://wandex.netgen.com/cgi/wandex

World Wide Web Worm: http://www.cs.colorado.edu/www

Yahoo: http://www.yahoo.com/

Begin your search by typing in the URL for one of these search tools. The result will be the home page, the starting page, for that particular tool. Your screen will show you two options. The first is a box into which you can type the topic for which you wish to search. The second is a list of generic topics such as arts, entertainment, sports, recreation, science, and so on. The first option allows you to conduct a more structured search than the second.

In conducting a structured search, type into the box the topic you want to research. This term needs to be selected carefully. If you type in the word astronomy you will get anything the search tool has on this particular topic. It could run into the thousands or even hundreds of thousands of possibilities. Rather than asking for a search on astronomy, be more specific. If you want to see photographs taken by the Hubble Space Telescope, type in "Hubble Space Telescope." The result will be a list of possibilites, each with a brief description of the information at the particular location. Select the site you want to visit by clicking on it to open it. Providing there are not too many others looking for information at that site, it will soon appear. At times, the message received is not the information but a message reading "connection refused by host." Do not take this message personally. It's like a busy signal. Try again later. If you reach a site, you have the information at your fingertips to save or to print for later use. It is usually easier and more efficient to skim the material than save or print the information you would like to consider more fully.

A request for information about the Hubble Space Telescope is likely to give you specific information. At other times, a term may give you a variety of sites that seem to have little or no relationship to the information you want to research. For example, you may have asked for information on AIDS. Your list of possible sites includes information on Senate aides, teacher aides, Red Cross programs to aid flood victims, and aids for improving your golf swing as well as AIDS. In this case the easiest remedy is to spell out the words behind the acronym AIDS. In other cases, you may want to indicate, as Yahoo will allow, that you are looking for a site containing the complete word. For example, if you are looking for information on books and you end up with information on bookworms, bookcases, bookings, and beekeeping, select the complete word option to limit your search to the word *book.*

The second option at most search tool home pages is the list of generic topics. These topics lend themselves to surfing rather than to more structured searches. For example, clicking on the term *science* from the list on the Yahoo home page gives a list of sciences that can be accessed: biology, chemistry, anthropology, engineering, paleontology, astronomy, and so on. Clicking on any of those sciences then gives another list of relatively broad possibilities. Finally, however, you arrive at particular sites and information. The fun of this type of search is opening a site that looks interesting and finding it leads to other sites and other sites and other sites. This is surfing. You may have started looking under science and paleontology and you may end up in Mongolia looking at the latest information on dinosaur finds in the Gobi Desert. Surfing the Internet for information can bring new concepts and images to children, can encourage their learning, and can develop their imaginations. As children surf the Internet, encourage them to keep a record of the locations they have visited. Such records kept in a classroom file can then be used as sources of sites for other children interested in a particular topic or can even be used at later times as sources of information for structured searches.

Conducting a Web search is an always interesting, sometimes time consuming, and sometimes frustrating activity. There is a great deal of information available, some of it worth reading and some of it worth ignoring. If you are working with your students to conduct Web searches, you need to keep some caveats in mind.

Conducting Searches with Students. Children at the elementary and middle school levels will, first, need to be guided to appropriate locations on Internet servers. When URLs for particular sites are known, the server used makes little difference. When students are making less focused searches, you will need to be aware of where your students are going as they search the net. There is information on the Internet that is both appropriate and inappropriate for elementary students.

Second, elementary and middle school students need to be assisted in narrowing and focusing their searches. When using the Internet for particular searches of information, children might be encouraged to begin the search with the school or local library to find information and with CD-ROM databases. Both are more manageable databases that can help students narrow down their Internet search to specific topics. In addition, they should be helped to enter appropriate descriptors when conducting searches. "Dinosaurs" results in a huge number of sites. "Tyrannosaurus Rex" results in far fewer sources and far more focused information.

Third, as your students locate information, encourage them to download that information onto a disc or to print it out so they can review and analyze the information at a later time rather than trying to search, read, and analyze at the same setting.

Fourth, your students will need assistance in evaluating the information taken from the Internet. As students begin to read and analyze the information they gather on the Net, they should be asking themselves questions, particularly questions about the sources of the information. Assist students in determining when information in biased and when information is being presented in a neutral manner. This requires the use of higher order thinking skills, particularly at the analysis and evaluation levels of the cognitive domain as well as critical and logical thinking skills.

And finally, whether using the Internet or CD-ROM databases, students should be alerted to the facts of plagiarism. Materials in electronic databases are protected through copyright laws in the same way as paper databases. Copying the work of others, whether on-line or on paper, and presenting those ideas as one's own is plagiarism. Students can print out information from both types of electronic database. Use of that information requires the use of footnotes or other types of citations. Activities 14.10 develops your ability to conduct an Internet search on a particular science topic. Activity 14.11 considers the use of the Internet in local schools.

Technology in the Classroom Activity

Activity 14.10

Purpose   To conduct an Internet search on a particular topic.

Procedure
1. Identify a topic in science you would like to learn more about.
2. Using one of the common search engines as a starting point, do an Internet search for information about the topic.
   a. How many hits did you get from your first identification of the topic?
   b. How appropriate were the hits?
      (1) List the addresses of five to ten of the most appropriate sites.
      (2) List the addresses of five to ten of the least appropriate sites.
         (a) Why do you think these sites were included in your search results?

c. Investigate five to ten of the most appropriate sites.
   (1) What kinds of information did you find?
   (2) What additional sites did your appropriate sites lead you to?
   (3) What tangents did you investigate?

Activity 14.11

Purpose   To investigate the use of the Internet in schools.

Procedure
1. Arrange to interview three or four teachers at the elementary or middle school levels about their use of the Internet with students in heir classrooms.
2. In the interviews determine:
   a. Current access in the school and/or classroom.
   b. How the Internet is currently being used in the classroom.
   c. The kinds of difficulties found in using the Internet.
   d. The most successful uses of the Internet.
   e. The extent of Internet access to children at home.
3. Access the Internet and do a search for information on national use of the Internet in elementary and middle schools.
   a. How does the information from the interviewed teachers compare to national use of the Internet in teaching?

Problems in Internet Use.   Two problems exist with the use of the Internet in schools. First, public search engines such as Yahoo, Lycos, Gopher, Archie, and Veronica can result in children reaching sites that are basically infomercials or electronic ads, neither of which contribute to the student's search for information. And such search engines have the possibility of children reaching sites that are inappropriate. Although technology does exist for blocking children from reaching inappropriate sites, there are still times when they will manage by accident or on purpose to access those sites. In the first case, you want to help your students use their critical thinking skills to analyze and evaluate the sites they reach. In the second case, you want to monitor your students as they use the Internet.

E-Mail in the Classroom.   Although the main use of the Internet is as an electronic database of incredible proportions, the Internet also provides a unique opportunity in communication. Through electronic mail, or e-mail, teachers can communicate easily with one another to share ideas and information. But e-mail has greater possibilities than simple teacher-to-teacher communication.

Student-to-Student Communication.   Students can use the Internet to communicate with students in classrooms across the country and around the world. Students studying the same science topics can share what they are learning, pool data collected from similar investigations or experiments, or obtain information about settings they cannot visit. Students in Japan and California can communicate with one another about earthquakes. Students in Australia can communicate with students in Maine about differences in seasons. And as was previously described, students in various locations can collect data about magnets and answer questions.

Students to College Students.   Students at the elementary and middle school levels can often benefit from having mentors as they research topics, create science projects, or simply struggle with their learning. E-mail provides a way for students at the elementary level to communicate with college or high school students interested in science and interested in working with younger students.

Students to College Faculty.   Students and teachers at the elementary and middle school levels often have questions that cannot be easily answered. Having a scientist or science educator to query can often be useful for both the teachers and the students.

Using e-mail to enhance communication on all levels is a simple use of Internet technology at the elementary and middle school levels.

Tool Applications of Computer Technology

Each of the uses of computer technology in the classroom described here involves students directly with the material that is part of the academic program. Tutorials attempt to teach students new science content. Drill and practice programs ask students to practice previously learned information. Simulations ask students to use problem solving and decision making within a particular area of science content. Microcomputer-based labs help students collect and analyze data from activities and experiments. And CD-ROM and Internet databases aid students in their researches. These uses of computer technology are designed to enhance the academic instructional parts of the total science program.

In a different kind of use, computer technology is used in a slightly different way. Rather than as a means for increasing information, the computer becomes a tool. This is known as the tool application aspect of computer technology in the classroom.

Word Processing.   One common form of tool application is the word processing program. Word processing programs assist your students in writing and preparing reports without the tediousness of recopying edited work. Students who use word processing programs are more likely to edit work for grammar, spelling, syntax, and content than are students who do not have access to word processing. It is far easier to make corrections on a computer than it is to make them on paper and then have to recopy the correct materials. The time needed for recopying can be put to better use in editing.

Drawing and Painting.   Drawing and painting programs are also tools that can be used easily by your students to create attractive additions to reports and projects.

The addition of clip art, available with draw and paint programs or over the Internet, can add another dimension to the final product.

Spreadsheets.   Spreadsheets are tools that your students can use for organizing and presenting information and to do repetitive calculations easily and quickly. Spreadsheets often require students to develop their own mathematical formulas, so students are not only manipulating data but also telling the computer how to go about those manipulations. In addition, spreadsheets may also have graphing capabilities that present data in such a way that students can use the information to determine patterns within the data and so draw conclusions.

In addition to computer tools that can be used by the students, programs also exist for the use of the teacher. Teachers can use computer tools for developing multimedia presentations for use in lessons, for keeping grades and other records, and for developing lesson plans.

Computer Technology in the Classroom

Computer technology has a great deal to offer to the science teacher in the elementary or middle school. It can make life easier for the teacher in the form of computer tools, can bring to students situations that might not otherwise be possible through simulations, can aid students in gathering information during a laboratory experience, or provide new information or practice with old information. In general, the uses of computers in the classroom are positive, but the teacher needs to make a decision about when and where to use computer technology in the classroom.

Let's return for a moment to the four teachers described at the beginning of this chapter.

Ms. Grant uses technology in her classroom. She has a computer on her desk that she uses for keeping student records. Her computerized grade book makes it easier for her to keep student grades and for her to calculate the grades at the end of each grading period. In addition to the computer grade book, Ms. Grant also uses a program to help her with writing lesson plans. She finds it much easier to make and keep her plans on her computer than to use a standard teacher planning book. And she also uses her classroom computer to e-mail other teachers in the building, to keep in touch with the principal, and in many cases to keep in touch with parents. Ms. Grant is making use of the computer in the classroom as a tool. Although this use makes her life as a teacher a little, or even a lot easier, she is not taking full advantage of computer technology.

Because Ms. Grant seems to see computer technology as a way of making life in the classroom easier, she may want to look into including some tutorial programs to enable students to gain information on their own or some drill and practice programs so students who are having difficulty can gain additional practice. She may even want to consider using CD-ROM databases to assist her students in research.

All three of these would be in keeping with her view of the computer as a tool. And success in these uses may encourage her to consider other classroom uses.

Mr. Roth also uses technology in the classroom. He has a computer center, with four computers, set up in an area of the classroom away from his main instructional area. Students having difficulty with a particular concept can go to the computer center and work on the concept presented in the regular classroom setting. Students who complete work quickly also have an opportunity to use the computer center. These children can go to the center when work has been completed to play educational games, often in competition with one another, and so the computers are a reward for work well done.

Mr. Roth is using the computer as a tutorial and as a reward. Like Ms. Grant, he is not yet using the classroom computer to its full potential. In addition to tutorials, Mr. Roth may want to look into the use of simulations in his classroom. He appears to be convinced of the use of computers as gaming possibilities, and the interactive and often game format of simulations would extend his use of computers in a way that would be appropriate. Once again, success in adding simulations may result in additional use.

In Mrs. Sanchez's class, her four computers are set up in a center. Three of the four computers are used every day by the children. Each morning, Mrs. Sanchez starts the computers and puts on them a particular program for the children to use to reinforce a previous lesson, to provide practice. Then, during the day, the children go to the computer center on a rotational basis to work with the information on the program. All of the children have a chance to go to the center. The third computer is set up with a word processing program. Mrs. Sanchez uses this computer for her own work, but also uses it as a reward for children who have written particularly good stories during her language arts program. Those children can use the word processing capabilities of the computer to make a finished copy of the story for display in the classroom.

Mrs. Sanchez is using her computers in two ways, as a drill and practice setting and as a tool. If the use of programs for drill and practice is seen as successful, then Mrs. Sanchez may want to branch into tutorial programs and into databases for her students to use. She may also want to consider greater use of computers as a word processing tool, encouraging use by students who have difficulty with the writing process as well as students who are already highly successful. Finally, she may want to look into the use of other computerized tools: drawing and painting or spreadsheet.

Mr. Wong also has computers in his classroom. Some of the children use the computers for review and reinforcement of previous lessons. Others are using the computers to learn more about a topic through CD-ROM technology or through Internet access. During his science lessons, he uses instrument interfacing to have the children work with science activities involving the collection of data dealing with temperature or velocity or light intensity.

Mr. Wong is using most of the readily available technology to his advantage. The addition of computer tools might make it easier for him to keep track of his uses and the progress of his students and may make it easier for his students to prepare certain kinds of reports and presentations.

In each of the cases, teachers are using technology in the classroom. They have made decisions on the basis of their preferences for technology and perhaps on their knowledge of computer technology. Each teacher needs to make similar decisions. Every teacher is not ready to use every type of computer technology in the classroom. In fact, teachers should probably start small and work toward increasing use of technology. It is not just important to have technology in the classroom, but also to use that technology in an appropriate manner. Moving from the use of tutorials to the use of databases may be a logical step. Moving from the use of drill and practice programs to the use of tutorials may also be a logical step. Effectively integrating all types of technology into the classroom setting involves choices on the part of the teacher. Effectively integrating technology into the classroom may also involve a change in the teaching strategies used by a particular teacher. Teachers who consistently use large group instruction may find it difficult to have students working individually on tutorials or in drill and practice. Teachers who use a great deal of small group work may find it difficult to have individuals working with databases or in drill and practice programs. Teachers who consider it important for students to check spelling in a dictionary, to do paper and pencil editing and recopying, or to do simple mathematical calculations and hand-plot graphs may find it difficult to integrate computer tools into the classroom setting. And teachers who find computers daunting, laserdiscs intimidating, and the Internet downright terrifying may find integration of any type of technology into the curriculum appropriate for someone else entirely. The point is to begin slowly, to experience success, and then add to the classroom the technology that will most likely enhance academic learning time for a particular group of students.

Summary

Technology in the classroom has been shown to be effective when it enhances academic learning time, that is, it increases the amount of time students actually spend in the learning process. The most common form of technology in the classroom involves the use of computer technology.

Computer technology can take a variety of forms. Drill and practice programs allow students to practice information that has already been taught; tutorials assist students in learning new information. Simulations engage students in a problem-solving format. Microcomputer-based labs assist students in the inquiry process by helping them collect and analyze data they may not be able to collect through the use of normal senses or for experiments that may be too expensive or dangerous for students to performs. Databases such as the Internet and CD-ROM formats can assist students in exploring the world, solving problems, and discovering new information and new ideas. And, finally, computer tools simply work for both teacher and student through word processing. spreadsheets, and draw or paint programs.

Computer technology in the classroom, should enhance the learning process. As such the teacher needs to make decisions about what sorts of computer technology to use and how to use it. Rather than attempt to include all forms of technology in a classroom setting, the teacher needs to begin with types of materials that are comfortable to the teacher and students, and then, on the basis of successful use, expand into other areas.

Chapter Vocabulary

The number following each term refers to the page on which the term is first introduced.

Academic learning time, 409
CD-ROM, 421
Computer-based tutorial, 414
Conjectural mode, 413
Database, 421
Drill and practice program, 416
Emancipatory mode, 414

Instructional mode, 413
Microcomputer-based labs, 419
Revelatory mode, 413
Simulations, 418
Structured search, 423
Surfing, 423

Applying the CONCEPTS

1. You have been asked to serve on a committee for your middle school or elementary school to determine how you can better incorporate computer technology into the academic program. How would you suggest this committee go about its work? How would you base your decisions on how to incorporate computer technology into the academic program?

2. You are effectively using computer technology in your third grade classroom, so your principal has asked you to talk with Mrs. Greene about the fact that she has computers in her classroom she never turns on. Your principal wants Mrs. Greene to use the computers available to her. How might you work with her?

3. As you are working with your eighth graders on doing an Internet search, you notice a group of your students clustered around one of the computer screens. They have managed to find one of the more inappropriate sites on the Net and are very interested in the pictures they've obtained. How might you handle this situation?

4. As you read the reports on plants turned in by your fourth graders, you come across one that is simply printed pages from an Internet site. You give it a failing grade. Naturally, the student's parents are upset about the grade and want to know why you have given the report a failing grade when it is (a) complete, (b) used the computer, and (c) in color. How would you handle this situation?

References

Alessi, S. M., and S. R. Trollip. 1991. *Computer-based instruction: Methods and development* (2nd ed.). Englewood Cliffs, N.J.: Prentice Hall.

Assetto, E R., and E. Dowden. 1988. Getting a grip on interfacing. *The science teacher* 55(6), 65–67.

Berliner, D. 1984. The half-full glass: A review of research on teaching. In P. Hosford (ed.). *Using what we know about teaching.* Alexandria, Va.: Association for Supervision and Curriculum Development.

Caldwell, J. H., W. G. Huitt, and A. O. Graeber. 1982. Time spent in learning: Implications from research. *Elementary School Journal* 82, 471–480.

Cannings, T. R., and L. Finkel. 1993. *The technology age classroom.* Wilsonville, Oreg.: Franklin, Beedle, and Associates.

D'Ignazio, F. 1994. Electronic highways and the classroom of the future. In T. R. Cannings and L. Finkel (eds.), *The technology age classroom* (pp. 632–638). Wilsonville, Oreg.: Franklin, Beedle, and Associates.

Gertler, N. 1994. *Multimedia illustrated.* Indianapolis, Ind.: QUE.

Hannafin, M. J. 1985. Keeping interactive video in perspective. In E. Miller (ed.), *Educational media and technology yearbook 1985.* Littleton, Col.: Libraries Unlimited.

Krendl, K. A., and D. A. Lieberman 1988. Computers and learning: A review of recent research. *Journal of Educational Computing Research* 4, 388.

Lillie, D. L., W. H. Hannum, and G. B. Stuck. 1989. *Computers and effective instruction.* New York: Longman.

Lockard, K. A., P. D. Abrams, and W. A. Many. 1987. *Microcomputers for educators.* Boston: Little, Brown.

Mayer, V. J. 1990. Teaching from a global point of view. *The Science Teacher* 57(1), 47–51.

Mokron, J. R. 1986. The impact of microcomputer-based labs on children's graphing. *YERC Technical Report* 2, 7.

Nachmias, R., and M. C. Linn. 1987. Evaluations of science laboratory data: The role of computer presented information. *Journal of Research in Science Teaching* 24(5), 505.

Reynolds, K. E., and R. H. Barba. 1996. *Technology for the teaching and learning of science.* Boston: Allyn & Bacon.

Rogers, R. T. 1987. The computer-assisted laboratory. *Physics Education* 22, 223.

Rubba, P. A. 1987. Perspectives on science-technology-society instruction. *School Science and Mathematics,* 87; 181–189.

Schwier, R. 1992. A taxonomy of interaction for instructional multimedia. Paper presented at the Annual Conference of the Association for Media and Technology, Vancouver, British Columbia, Canada. Review in *Journal of Educational Multimedia and Hypermedia* 3(1), 112–113.

Trollip, S. R., and S. M. Alessi. 1988. Incorporating computers effectively into classrooms. *Journal of Research on Computing Educations* 21,(1), 70–81.

Vockell, E. L., and E. M. Schwartz. 1992. *The computer in the classroom* (2nd ed.).Watsonville, Calif.: McGraw-Hill.

Vockell, E. L., and M. Simonson. 1994. *Technology for teachers.* Dubuque, Iowa: Kendall/Hunt.

Wheatley, G. H. 1991. Constructivist perspectives on science and mathematics learning. *Science Education* 75(2), 9–21.

Wise, K. 1989. The effects of using computing technologies in science instruction: A synthesis of classroom-based research. In J. D. Ellis (ed.), *Information technology and science education.* Columbus, Ohio: ERIC.

Woerner, J. J., R. H. Rivers, and E. L. Vockell. 1991. *The computer in the science curriculum.* Watsonville, Calif.: McGraw-Hill.

Appendix A

The National Science Education Standards
Teaching Standards

The teaching standards describe what teachers of science at all grade levels should understand and be able to do. In particular, the teaching standards highlight the importance of teachers in science education. The teaching standards are found in Chapter 3 of the *Standards* (pp. 27–53).

Teaching Standard A   Teachers of science plan an inquiry-based program for their students. In doing this teachers:

- Develop a framework of year-long and short-term goals for students.
- Select science content and adapt and design curricula to meet the interests, knowledge, understanding, abilities, and experiences of students.
- Select teaching and assessment strategies that support the development of student understanding and nurture a community of science learners.
- Work together as colleagues within and across disciplines and grade levels.

Teaching Standard B   Teachers of science guide and facilitate learning. In doing this teachers:

- Focus and support inquiries while interacting with students.
- Orchestrate discourse among students about scientific ideas.
- Challenge students to accept and share responsibility for their own learning.
- Recognize and respond to student diversity and encourage all students to participate fully in science learning.
- Encourage and model the skills of scientific inquiry, as well as the curiosity, openness to new ideas and data, and skepticism that characterize science.

Teaching Standard C   Teachers of science enagage in ongoing assessment of their teaching and of student learning. In doing this, teachers:

- Use multiple methods and systemactically gather data about student understanding and ability.
- Analyze assessment data to guide teaching.
- Guide students in self-assessment.
- Use student data, observations of teaching, and interactions with colleagues to reflect on and improve teaching practice.

- Use student data, observations of teaching, and interactions with colleagues to report student achievement and opportunities to learn to students, teachers, parents, policy makers, and the general public.

Teaching Standard D   Teachers of science design and manage learning environments that provide students with the time, space, and resources needed for learning science. In doing this, teachers:

- Structure time available so that students are able to engage in extended investigations.
- Create a setting for student work that is flexible and supportive of science inquiry.
- Ensure a safe working environment.
- Make the available science tools, materials, media, and technological resources accessible to students.
- Identify and use resources outside the school.
- Engage students in designing the learning environment.

Teaching Standard E   Teachers of science develop communities of science learners that reflect the intellectual rigor of scientific inquiry and the attitudes of social values conducive to science learning. In doing this, teachers:

- display and demand respect for the diverse ideas, skills, and experiences of all students.
- Enable students to have a significant voice in decisions about the content and context of their work and require students to take responsibility for the learning of all members of the community.
- Nurture collaboration among students.
- Structure and facilitate ongoing formal and informal discussion based on a shared understanding of rules of scientific discourse.
- Model and emphasize the skills, attitudes, and values of scientific inquiry.

Teaching Standard F   Teachers of science actively participate in the ongoing planning and development of the school science program. In doing this, teachers:

- Plan and develop the school science program.
- Participate in decisions concerning the allocation of time and other resources to the science program.
- Participate fully in planning and implementing professional growth and development strategies for themselves and their colleagues.

Appendix B

The National Science Education Standards
Content Standards

The content standards outline what students should know, understand, and be able to do in the natural sciences. Although the content standards are a complete set of outcomes for science, they are not a curriculum. The content standards for grades kindergarten through 8 are found in Chapter 6 of the *Standards* (pp. 103–113).

Category One: Unifying Concepts and Processes in Acience
- Systems, order, and organization.
- Evidence, models, and explanation.
- Change, constancy, and measurement.
- Evolution and equilibrium.
- Form and function.

Category Two: Science as Inquiry
- Engaging students in inquiry in order to develop an understanding of science concepts and of the nature of science as they become independent inquirers.

Category Three: Physical Science
- Subject matter focuses on the science facts, concepts, principles, theories, and models that are important for all students to know, understand, and use.

Category Four: Life Science
- Subject matter focuses on the science facts, concepts, principles, theories, and models that are important for all students to know, understand, and use.

Category Five: Earth and Space Science
- Subject matter focuses on the science facts, concepts, principles, theories, and models that are important for all students to know, understand, and use.

Category Six: Science and Technology
- Establishes connections between the natural and designed worlds and provide students with opportunities to develop decision-making abilities.

Category Seven: Science in Personal and Social Perspectives
- Gives students a means to understand and act on personal and social issues.

Category Eight: History and Nature of Science
- Develops an understanding that science reflects its history and is an onging, changing enterprise.

Appendix C

The National Science Education Standards
Content Standards: Standards for K–8

The content standards outline what students should know, understand, and be able to do in the natural sciences. Although the content standards are a complete set of outcomes for science, they are not a curriculum. The content standards for grades kindergarten through grade 4 are found in Chapter 6 of the *Standards* (pp. 121–141). The content standards for grades 5 through 8 are found in Chapter 6 of the *Standards* (pp. 143–171).

I. Kindergarten through Grade Four

   A. Science as Inquiry Standards

      1. Abilities necessary to do scientific inquiry

         a. Ask questions about objects, organisms, and events in the environment

         b. Plan and conduct a simple investigation

         c. Employ simple equipment and tools to gather data and extend the senses

         d. Use data to construct a reasonable explanation

         e. Communicate investigations and explanations

      2. Understandings about scientific inquiry

   B. Physical Science Standards

      1. Properties of objects and materials

      2. Position and motion of objects

      3. Light, heat electricity, magnetism

   C. Life Science Standards

      1. Characteristics of organisms

      2. Life cycles of organisms

      3. Organisms and environments

   D. Earth and Space Science Standards

      1. Properties of Earth materials

      2. Objects in the sky

      3. Changes in Earth and sky

   E. Science and Technology Standatds

      1. Abilities to distinguish between natural objects and objects made by humans

      2. Abilities of technological design

      3. Understanding about science and technology

    F. Science in Personal and Social Perspectives Standards
       1. Personal health
       2. Characteristics and changes in populations
       3. Types of resources
       4. Changes in environments
       5. Science and technology in local challenges
    G. History and Nature of Science Standards
       1. Science as a human endeavor

II. Fifth Through Eighth Grades
    A. Science as Inquiry Standards
       1. Abilities necessary to do scientific inquiry
       2. Understanding about scientific inquiry
    B. Physical Science Standards
       1. Properties and changes of properties in matter
       2. Motions and forces
       3. Transfer of energy
    C. Life Science Standards
       1. Structure and function in living systems
       2. Reproduction and heredity
       3. Regulation and behavior
       4. Populations and ecosystems
       5. Diversity and adaptations of organisms
    D. Earth and Space Science Standards
       1. Structure of Earth system
       2. Earth's history
       3. Earth in the solar system
    E. Science and Technology Standards
       1. Abilities of technological design
       2. Understanding abut science and technology
    F. Science in Personal and Social Perspectives Standards
       1. Personal health
       2. Populations, resources, and environments
       3. Natural hazards
       4. Risks and benefits
       5. Science and technology in society
    G. History and Nature of Science Standards
       1. Science as a human endeavor
       2. Nature of science
       3. History of science

APPENDIX D

PROGRAMS AND PROJECTS IN SCIENCE EDUCATION

Activities to Integrate Mathematics and Science (AIMS)

This project publishes materials for integrating methematics and science in grades kindergarten through 9. The materials consist of teacher manuals that were produced by teachers and have been tested in classroom situations. The AIMS Organization, based in Fresno, California, offers workshops and seminars in the project. Some of the titles include *The Sky's the Limit; Pieces and Patterns; Jaw Breakers and Heart Thumpers; Our Wonderful World; Spring into Math and Science; Water, Precious Water;* and *Floaters and Sinkers.*

Explorations in Science

This project provides middle school students with lessons in biological science, physical science, and earth sciences through CD-ROM and computer network technology. The computer-simulated activities are appropriate for grades 6 through 9 and focus on concept development and critical thinking skills. This program is available through Jostens Learning Corporation in San Diego, California.

Arkansas's Project MAST: Mathematics and Science Together

This project presents integrated mathematics and science materials for grades 2 through 6. The focus of the program is on critical thinking skills and the use of technology. This project combines materials that had previously existed with new materials developed for the projects.

Elementary Science Study (ESS)

The Elementary Science Study consists of 56 units that can be used as a total curriculum or as supplemental materials. The units were extensively tested and have been revised for commercial purposes. Some of the available units include *Animals in the Classroom, Balloons and Gases, Bulbs and Batteries, Brine Shrimp, Changes, Butterflies, Colored Solutions, Drops, Earthworms,* and *Microgardening.* The life sciences, earth sciences, and physical sciences are all represented in these kindergarten through eighth grade units available through Delta Education.

Full Option Science System (FOSS)

Developed through the Lawrence Hall of Science in Berkeley, California, and distributed by Encyclopedia Britannica Educational Corporation, this project, for grades 3 through 6, includes student equipment kits and print materials. The assessments included are innovative and authentic. The project includes biological, physical, and earth sciences.

Project WILD and Project Aquatic

These projects emphasize wildlife and aquatic life, respectively, and are unique because they emphasize an interdisciplinary approach to teaching that includes the major school subjects and skills. This interdisciplinary approach is carried out by involving students in firsthand and simulated experiences with wildlife. Both programs include outdoor experiences and experiences for bringing the outdoors into the classroom. These projects are appropriate from grades kindergarten through 12. Information can be obtained by contacting Project WILD, P. O. Box 18060, Boulder, CO 80308.

Project Learning Tree

Project Learning Tree is similar to Project WILD and Project Aquatic. The emphasis, however, is on plant life rather than on animal life. This kindergarten through grade 12 program begins with simple concepts about trees for younger children and develops concepts of forests and forestry issues for older students. Information about Project Learning Tree is available from the American Forest Council, 1250 Connecticut Avenue NW, Washington, DC 20036.

Great Explorations in Math and Science (GEMS)

This program is designed to integrate mathematics with biological, physical, and earth sciences for grades kindergarten through 12. The materials consist of presentation guides, teacher guides, and exhibit guides written for teachers with little knowledge of mathematics and science. The 24 publications include *Animals in Action; Bubble-ology; Chemical Reactions; Fingerprinting; Earth, Moon, and Stars; Ooblik;* and *Paper Towel Testing.*

JASON Project

The instructional materials for this project integrate science and social science through on-line investigations undertaken by the underwater robot JASON. The units are thematic in nature and can stand alone as units with such topics as *Journey to the Center of the Earth, Adapting to a Changing Sea, The Galápagos Islands,* and *The Mediterranean Sea.* The teacher is provided with guides, lesson plans, and posters to prepare students for their on-one links with JASON.

GLOSSARY

Academic Learning Time—Amount of time a student gives to an appropriate and purposeful academic task while accomplishing that task with a high rate of success.

Acronyms—Memory device in which the first letter of each word to be remembered is formed into an easily remembered word (e.g., Roy G. Biv).

Acrostics—Memory device in which the first letter of each term is used as the first letter of a word forming a sentence (e.g., Every good boy does fine).

Activity—Hands-on aspect of a discovery lesson; either an experiment or an investigation.

Activity Results—Data collected during a student investigation or experiment: used to evaluate student success in working in a hands-on manner.

Advance Organizer—Verbal device that provides relevant introductory material and serves as a cognitive anchor for new material presented in the lesson.

Analysis Level—Fourth level of the cognitive taxonomy in which the separation of material into its constituent parts and detection of the relationships between those parts is emphasized.

Analysis of Elements—Sublevel of the analysis level of the cognitive domain at which the student should be able to identify both the clearly stated facts of a written piece and the underlying assumptions of the author.

Analysis of Organizational Principles—Sublevel of the analysis level of the cognitive domain that asks students to analyze the organization of a piece of written material.

Analysis of Relationships—Sublevel of the analysis level of the cognitive domain that asks students to determine relationships among the parts of a piece of writing.

Anecdotal Information—Information collected outside of experimental procedures including memories, stories, and personal experience that have been neither verified not replicated.

Anecdotal Records—Means of informally observing students at work in order to determine student progress.

Animism—Form of precausality in which all events and phenomena are seen as alive.

Anthropocentrism—Placing humans at the center of all things and so looking at the world strictly from a human point of view.

Anthropomorphism—Giving of human characteristics to nonhuman living things.

Application Level—Sublevel of the comprehension level of the cognitive domain that asks students to go beyond the limits of information and apply that information to problems not actually included in the original material.

Application Level—Third level of the cognitive domain in which students are asked to use content correctly in a situation where no method for solution for the problem is given.

Applied Science—Information within the broad field of science that has immediate, practical application. Also known as technology.

Artificialism—Form of precausality in which events and phenomena are the result of human activity.

Authentic Evaluation—Evaluation based on the activities and work of the students as they interact with materials, with the teacher, and with one another.

Autism—Category of disability in which children show a lack of social responsiveness beginning at a very early age.

Bar Graph—Graph in which the length of the bar demonstrates some quantity.

Basic Processes—The science process skills fundamental to any science activity: observation, classification, communication, using numbers, using space relations, and operational questions.

Biological Science—Branch of science including information on the five kingdoms of living things: monera, protista, fungi, plants, animals.

Bodily Intelligence—One of Gardner's eight intelligences that focuses on bodily movement.

Cartesian Coordinate Graph—Graph employing an X and Y axis on which data is plotted and trends shown through lines connecting data points.

Cause and Effect—Ability to determine which of two or more factors came first in a sequence and to correctly attribute some result to this factor.

CD-ROM—Laser optical disk frequently holding a database that is a combination of text, sound, pictures, and film.

Centering—Tendency in preoperational children to look at only one characteristic of an object at a time.

Chaos—Random component of any change.

Charts—Device for recording and organizing data.

Checklists—Standardized form of teacher observation in which specific items are listed and assessed.

Class Discussion—Method of preassessment involving an entire class in a discussion of a problem situation.

Classification—Ability to place objects into groups on the basis of the characteristics that those objects do or do not possess.

Cognitive Anchor—According to Ausubel, a piece of information already in cognitive structure and used to help remember new information in a meaningful manner.

Cognitive Domain—The knowledge domain including such activities as remembering and recalling knowledge, thinking, applying material, solving problems, creating new ideas, and evaluating information.

Coincidence—Sequence of events that although accidental seems to have been planned or arranged.

Collaborative Program—Means of developing appropriate programs for disabled students through team work involving teachers, special educators, parents, counselors, and paraprofessionals.

Collective Monologue—Conversation among preoperational children in which the children appear to be talking to one another but the successive sentences are not related to one another.

Combinatorial Reasoning—Form of reasoning used in the formal operational stage of development in which attention is given to all possible combinations.

Communication—Any means for passing information from one individual or group of individuals to another.

Communication Style—Way in which individuals from a particular culture interact with one another.

Comparative Organizers—Advance organizer that compares new information to material already known in a way that highlights the similarities between the two and also indicates what information is to come.

Complexes—The second stage in concept development according to Vygotsky in which relationships between and among objects are developed.

Comprehension Level—Second level of the cognitive domain that is concerned with understanding of information.

Computation—Use of basic computation skills—addition, subtraction, multiplication, and division—to manipulate the data collected during investigations or experiments.

Computer-Based Tutorial—Computer program that functions similarly to a teacher with a textbook.

Concept Development—Concept development, according to Vygotsky, occurs when words that are first used in developing concepts come to be used as a symbol for a concept.

Conceptual Change Model—Constructivist teaching strategy that encourages students to confront their misconceptions and then to change their conceptual framework to incorporate information gained directly from an activity which conflicts with the misconception.

Conceptual Models—Analogies or metaphors based on some attribute or similarity to the real thing.

Conclusion—Special form of inference that is stable and unlikely to change with the collection of additional data.

Concreteness—The reality of an object.

Concrete Objects Graph—Graph developed from actual objects.

Concrete Operational Stage—Stage in cognitive development, according to Piaget, and defined as (1) from about 6.5 years to about 11 or 12 years, or (2) from conservation of number to conservation of volume.

Concrete Predictions—Prediction based on direct experiences with concrete materials.

Concrete System—System in which the components are all easily visible or easily sensed concrete objects.

Conjectural Mode—Mode of computer use in which the computer enables the learner to explore "what if" questions and so helps the learner build interactive models of various phenomena.

Conservation—Ability to realize that a change in the appearance of an object does not change the quantity of the object.

Consideration of Consequences—Scientific value that causes scientists to look at the effect their discoveries might have on society.

Consideration of Premises—Scientific value that results in scientists looking at the foundation on which their ideas, hypotheses, and theories are built.

Constancy—Scientific theme that considers ways in which systems do not change.

Constants—All factors kept the same during an experiment.

Constructivist Teaching Strategy—Teaching strategy in which students construct knowledge for themselves based on their own conceptualization rather than being presented knowledge by the teacher.

Control Group—Comparison group that receives no experimental manipulation but otherwise has the same characteristics as the experimental group.

Convergent Question—Question for which a single answer is the correct answer to the question.

Counting—Cardinal and ordinal enumeration of objects.

Creative Reading—Fourth level of reading comprehension in which the reader is asked to determine alternative solutions to those presented by the writer.

Creative Thinking—Form of thinking that is divergent and generates something new.

Critical Reading—Fourth level of reading comprehension in which the reader is asked to make a personal judgment about the accuracy, value, or truthfulness of what is read.

Critical Thinking—Knowing when to question something as well as having the inclination to ask questions.

Curiosity—Spontaneous desire to explore the environment to learn about and investigate its phenomena.

Cycles—Sequences of changes that happen over and over again.

Data—Information collected during experiments or investigations, generally in the form of verbal observations and or measurements.

Database—Source of information such as encyclopedias, CD-ROM, and Internet.

Deductive Discovery—Form of discovery in which students investigate a generalization in order to find specifics about it.

Deductive Reasoning—Form of logical reasoning in which the reasoning moves from generalization to specifics.

Demand for Verification—Scientific value that requires experimental results be replicated by other scientists before they are accepted.

Dependent Variable—Factor in an experiment that changes as a result of a change in the independent variable.

Derivation of a Set of Abstract Relations—Sublevel of the synthesis level of the cognitive domain in which the student is asked to derive a statement to explain or classify a set of data.

Developmental Stage—One of the four stages in the developmental psychology of Jean Piaget showing predictable changes in children's thought processes.

Discipline-Centered Unit—Unit plan using as its basis a topic from the biological, physical, or earth-space sciences.

Discovery—General teaching strategy in which children utilize materials in order to develop understanding of science content for themselves.

Discovery Demonstration—Demonstration teaching strategy used to develop problem-solving skills.

Discovery Stage—Final stage in Learning Cycle in which children test the concept learned during the invention stage through experimentation and explanation.

Discrepant Events—Demonstration or activity that has an unexpected result and so generates curiosity.

Discussion—(1) The final step in a discovery lesson in which students draw the lesson conclusion from the data collected; (2) An open forum in which students can express their opinions as well as review factual material.

Divergent Questions—Questions in which the student is asked to use background material as well as personal experiences to answer questions having many equally valid answers.

Drill and Practice Program—Computer program that provides repeated practice and feedback to help students reach a particular objective.

Earth-Space Science—Branch of science including geology, astronomy, and meteorology.

Egocentric Speech—External language, according to Vygotsky, which is used by young children in problem solving.

Egocentrism—Cognitive trait in pre-operational children that allows them to view the world only from their own point of view.

Elementary Science Study—Curriculum project begun in the 1960's and which focused on science content through the use of multi-grade-level units.

Emancipatory Mode—Mode of computer use in which the computer is used to free the learner from tiresome learning tasks (e.g., editing and repetitive calculations).

Equilibrium—Balance within a system.

Essay Questions—Questions used on a test or quiz that require students to compose an answer in written form.

Evolution—General concept that the present arises from the materials and forms of the past in explicable ways; one of the themes of science.

Exhaustive Sorting—Ability to classify all objects in a set.

Experiment—(1) Form of student activity in which students gain evidence to support or refute a hypothesis; (2) Tool used by scientists to gain the evidence to support or refute a given hypothesis.

Exploration—The first stage of Learning Cycle in which students freely explore materials without the constraint of learning a particular concept.

Exploration Stage—The first stage of Learning Cycle in which students explore materials, identifying problems and questions for later investigation.

Expository Organizer—Advance organizer that presents several broad generalizations to which detail will be added.

Expository Teaching—Verbal teaching strategy in which the teacher or other source presents information to students.

Evaluation Level—Sixth and highest level of the cognitive domain in which the student is asked to make judgments according to some established criteria.

Field Trip—Any educational experience that takes children out of the classroom.

Formal Measurement—Measurement using standard units: meters, kilograms, seconds, and so on.

Formal Operational Stage—Cognitive developmental stage according to Piaget and defined as (1) beginning at 11 or 12 and continuing throughout adulthood, or (2) beginning with the attainment of conservation of volume.

Formulas—Expression of a highly abstract numerical relationship that can be applied in a variety of situations.

Formulating Hypotheses—Experimental process in which a testable hypothesis in the form of an if . . . then statement is developed.

Genuine Concepts—Fourth stage in Vygotsky's theory of concept development in which students develop the abstract and systematic knowledge common to their culture.

Graphing—Visual means for organizing and presenting numerical data.

Group Structured Experiments—Experiment designed by a group of students to test a hypothesis written by the teacher.

Heaps—Vygotsky's first stage in concept development in which objects in the environment are grouped into random categories.

Hierarchical Classification—Sophisticated form of classification involving the use of sets and subsets arranged in hierarchical format.

Histogram—Bar graph showing a frequency distribution.

Honesty—Scientific attitude involving reporting the true outcome of an investigation or experiment, maintaining records which show all of the data collected not simply a sample of that data, and reporting what is observed rather than what one wishes to observe.

Hypothesis—An if . . . then statement making a prediction and used in testing a theory through experimentation.

Inclusion—Bringing together all children into the regular classroom setting.

Independent Variable—The variable purposely changed by the experimenter in order to determine its effect on the rest of the system.

Individual Education Program—Plan developed for an individual child that shows the goals, teaching strategies, and evaluative measures that will be used to help the student reach a particular learning or behavioral need.

Inductive Discovery—Form of discovery in which students collect specific data and develop a generalization from that data.

Inductive Reasoning—Form of logical reasoning that moves from specifics to generalizations.

Inference—An interpretation of observations.

Informal Measurement—Measurement using nonstandard units such as footsteps, body lengths, pencil lengths, and so on.

Inner Speech—Internal speech as used by adults.

Instructional Mode—Mode of computer use in which the computer serves as a means for delivering information to the student.

Interactions—Relationships between and among the various parts of a system.

Integrated Approach—Curriculum pattern in which distinct subject matter areas no longer exist.

Interdisciplinary Teaching—Curriculum pattern in which two or more subject matter areas are combined in a way that the lines separating one subject matter area from another are erased.

Interpersonal Intelligence—One of Gardner's intelligences used to understand the feeling, desires, and ideas of others.

Interpretation—(1) A sublevel of the comprehension level of the cognitive domain that asks the student to give a total view of the essential meaning of a concept; (2) The second level of reading comprehension in which the reader is asked to consider information suggested or implied by the textual material.

Interpreting Data—Ability to perceive patterns in the information collected from an experiment and to express those patterns as a conclusion that either supports or refutes the hypothesis of the experiment.

Interpreting Graphs—Drawing conclusions and making predictions from graphed data.

Interview—Means of assessing background information through a one-on-one conversation between teacher and student.

Intrapersonal Intelligence—One of Gardner's eight intelligences that is concerned with the self.

Invention Stage—Second stage of the Learning Cycle in which students are introduced to new concepts.

Investigations—Activities using basic and causal processes and resulting most usually in descriptive rather than numerical data.

Journal—Means of combining science with language arts in a way that enables students to present information in an open-ended, personalized manner.

Judgment in Terms of External Evidence—Sublevel of the evaluation level of the cognitive domain in which students use prerequisite knowledge in making judgments.

Judgment in Terms of Internal Evidence—Sublevel of the evaluation level of the cognitive domain in which students determine the accuracy of particular statements.

Keyword Method—Technique for re-calling vocabulary in which students connect new vocabulary with a familiar word and an image.

Knowledge Level—Lowest level of the cognitive domain that emphasizes the recall or recognition of factual information.

Knowledge of Specifics—Sublevel of the knowledge level of the cognitive domain that deals with recall of specific bits of information.

Knowledge of Ways and Means of Dealing with Specifics—Sublevel of the knowledge level of the cognitive domain that consists of knowledge of how informa-tion is organized, studied, judged, and criticized.

Knowledge of Universals and Abstractions in the Field—Sublevel of the knowledge level of the cognitive domain that deals with principles, generalizations and theories used to organize the content of science.

Lack of Superstition—Scientific attitude of looking for logical, physical causes for phenomena rather than for explanations based on paranormal or unproven phenomena.

Language—The child's use of the dominant language of the classroom.

Law—Broad statement of fact often considered to be a universal generalization.

Learning Cycle—The three-stage learning strategy originally developed in *SCIS* and consisting of three stages: exploration, invention, and discovery.

Learning Disabled—Students characterized by problems in information processing.

Learning Style—The way individuals receive and process information.

Least Restrictive Environment—Most appropriate learning environment for a disabled student; mandated by P.L. 94-142.

Linguistic Intelligence—One of Gardner's eight intelligences that focuses on language use.

Literal Comprehension—Lowest level of reading comprehension in which understanding is geared toward information directly stated in the text.

Logical Intelligence—One of Gardner's eight intelligences that focuses on reasoning and logic.

Longing to Know and Understand—Scientific value that causes the scientist to want to develop the theories that explain how the universe operates.

Mathematical Intelligence—One of Gardner's eight intelligences that focuses on thinking about the physical world and its properties.

Mathematical Modeling—Form of model building that uses mathematics to find a mathematical relationship and allows behavioral prediction in the physical world.

Mathematics—Branch of science including measurement, computation, modeling, and statistics.

Measurement—Part of the basic process of space relations looking at quantities such as length, area, weight, volume, and time.

Mental Models—Conceptualization of an object or phenomenon that can be tested.

Mental Retardation—Category of disabled student in which children experience learning problems in all academic areas.

Microcomputer-Based Lab—Lab setting using a combination of hardware and software to enable students to collect, tabulate, and analyze data.

Modeling—Method for teaching that uses the actions of the teacher rather than direct instructional strategies.

Models—(1) A physical, mental, or mathematical representation of an object or phenomenon; (2) A form of communication that allows children to communicate their ideas through three-dimensional objects.

Modular Approach—Approach to curriculum organization in which each topic is treated as a separate set of materials.

Movement—Form of communication using bodily movement.

Multiple Choice Item—Item on a test or quiz consisting of a stem and a list of possible responses from which the students select a response.

Multiple Disabilities—Category of disability including children with more than one disabling condition.

Multiple Inferences—Various inferences that can be made based on the same set of data.

Multiple Intelligences—Gardner's theory that intelligences can come in many forms: interpersonal, intrapersonal, spatial, musical, bodily, logical, linguistic, mathematical.

Multiple Traits—Classification according to two or more traits at a time.

Music—Form of communication using songs and musical forms.

Musical Intelligence—One of Gardner's eight intelligences that focuses on thinking through musical sounds.

Newsletter—Brief written report prepared for a special group.

Nonconcrete Systems—Systems in which the major components are phenomena rather than concrete objects.

Nonconserver—Cognitive trait resulting in an inability to see quantity as unchanging when the appearance of an object changes.

Nontraditional Evaluation—Form of evaluation based on the idea that all students should learn certain things but may learn those things at differing rates and may demonstrate their learning in different ways.

Null—Hypothesis stated in a form predicting no change.

Number Relations—Basic process of using numbers to describe the outcomes or occurrences of an activity: computation, counting, charts, graphs, and formulas.

Numerical Relationships—Using such concepts as rate, mean, median, and mode as a part of an investigation or experiment.

Objective—Statement detailing what will be learned in the context of both the content and outcomes of the learning process.

Objectivity—As a scientific attitude, objectivity asks the scientist to begin with a neutral position and attempt to determine what will happen in a particular situation or which position on a topic is most valid.

Observation—Piece of information learned directly through the senses.

Observational Consequences—Statements whose accuracy can be determined through observation.

Open Discussion—Discussion that occurs spontaneously and without prior planning by the teacher.

Open Inquiry—Constructivist teaching strategy most appropriate for preoperational children.

Operation—Action that can return to its starting point and be integrated with other actions also possessing this feature of reversibility.

Operational Definition—Definition developed by the experimenter to satisfy a new experience during the planning and carrying out of an investigation or experiment.

Operational Question—Questions asked by students that can be answered through direct manipulation of concrete materials.

Oral Communication—Communication through speech.

Ordinary Demonstration—Demonstration used to teach science content through the use of process skills.

Orthopedic Impairment—Category of disability including functional limitations such as body control, hand use, or mobility.

Other Health Impairment—Category of disability including children with illnesses or disorders that have an impact on learning.

Parallel Play—Characteristic of preschool children in which they play beside one another but not necessarily with one another.

Partially Concrete System—System in which the components are both concrete objects and inferred phenomena.

Patterns—Form of classification used by young children in which they classify objects by making pleasing arrangements.

Patterns of Change—Regularities in the physical world that allow for prediction, analysis, and control of change.

Peer Review—Component of a portfolio showing assessment of one student's work as reviewed by other students in the class.

Pegwords—Memory device used to recall a list of words in a particular order based on a list of words and imagery created.

Phenomenism—Form of precausal explanation in which anything can cause anything.

Physical Model—Physical representation of an object; generally on a smaller scale than the original.

Physical Science—Branch of science involving the study of matter and energy.

Pictures—(1) Form of classification used by young children in which they classify the objects by making pictures; (2) Form of communication based on drawings or paintings.

Plane Geometric Forms—Two-dimensional shapes including square, rectangle, circle, triangle, ellipse.

Planned Discussion—Discussion in which the teacher determines the topic, plans the questions, and guides the students toward a particular predetermined goal.

Portfolio—Collection of a student's achievements over a period of time as shown by a variety of different examples of student work.

Positive Approach to Failure—Scientific attitude which states that each testing of a hypothesis, whether supportive or non-supportive, yields some new information a scientist can incorporate into further experimentation.

Potential Concept—Third stage in Vygotsky's theory of concept development: begins at school age and shows a transition from concrete to abstract concepts.

Prediction—Special form of inference based on data collected that attempts to determine what will happen in the future.

Preoperational Stage—Developmental stage, according to Piaget, and defined as (1) approximately 18 months to 6.5 years or

(2) from the onset of language to the development of conservation of number.

Pretest—Short test of the information contained in a unit designed to determine how much of the information in a unit or textbook chapter the students already know.

Private Speech—Egocentric speech as defined by Vygotsky.

Problem—The start of a discovery lesson that gives a purpose to the lesson.

Processes—Techniques or methods used by scientists as they gather, interpret, and disseminate information.

Production of a Plan—Sublevel of the synthesis level of the cognitive domain that focuses on the development of a particular plan of operation.

Production of a Unique Communication—Sublevel of the synthesis level of the cognitive domain that focuses on the communication of ideas, feelings, or experiences of others.

Propositional Thinking—Thinking through the manipulation of assertions or statements. A characteristic of formal operational thought.

Pseudoscience—False science; an area that claims to have scientific backing but does not.

Psychological Causality—Preschool child's type of cause and effect in which magic is possible.

P.L. 94-142—Education for the Handicapped Act (1975) establishing guidelines for special education services including the concept of least restrictive environment.

Pure Science—Information resulting from the pursuit of knowledge for its own sake.

Purposeful Activity—Activities used as the primary learning experience.

Qualitative Research—Form of research in which observations are used to confirm or refute a particular hypothesis.

Quantitative Research—Research based on controlled experimental design and with numerical data as the most frequent type of observation.

Questioning of All Things—Scientific value that causes the scientist to ask and investigate questions. Includes the idea that anything and anyone can be questioned.

Rating Scale—Component of a portfolio in which each behavior is rated on a continuum from lowest to highest level.

Revelatory Mode—Mode of computer use in which the computer provides a bridge between the student and a model of the real world.

Rubrics—Wholistic grading device particularly appropriate for assessing projects and investigations in a wholistic manner.

Replicated—An experiment is replicated when an independent scientist repeats an experiment and obtains the same results as the original experimenting scientists.

Resemblance Sorting—Classification used by young children in which two objects are matched according to a trait.

Respect for Logic—Scientific value that requires scientists to consider data logically and to use logic in drawing conclusions.

Respect for the Environment—Scientific attitude based on the idea that all aspects of the environment are interrelated and plants and other animals inhabiting our environment are worthy of our respect.

Reversibility—The ability to trace one's thought processes backward to the starting point.

Rumors—Story that has been repeated so often it is considered to be true.

Scaffolding—According to Vygotsky, gradually removing the prompts or hints a child needs in order to accomplish a particular task.

Scale—Scientific theme referring to size and particularly to the magnitude of size.

Science—The active pursuit of understanding.

Science: A Process Approach—Federally funded science curriculum project begun in the 1960s that focused on teaching students science processes.

Science Content—The stuff of science; all of the information contained in textbooks for the various branches of science.

Science Curriculum Improvement Study—Science curriculum project begun in the 1960s that used process skills to teach content through the use of the Learning Cycle instructional strategy.

Science Processes—Skills of investigation and data collection used by students to develop concepts in a direct, personal, and active manner.

Scientifically Correct—Content conclusions drawn from activity results that show the same results as are generally found.

Scientifically Dishonest—Content conclusions resulting from an activity that are scientifically accurate but do not reflect the data collected.

Scientifically Incorrect—Content conclusions based on activity results that fit the data collected but do not reflect commonly held scientific thought.

Scientific Attitudes—Scientific thinking skills that guide the behaviors seen in children as they investigate in the classroom and beyond.

Scientific Literacy—Knowledge and understanding of scientific concepts and processes required for personal decision making, participation in civic and cultural affairs, and economic productivity.

Scientific Values—Principles common to the behavior of scientists which govern that behavior.

Scientists—Men and women in every nation who attempt to extend understanding of our universe through active investigation.

Scope—Totality of the information covered in the science program.

Search for Data and Their Meaning—Scientific value that results in the collection and interpretation of data.

Semantic Mapping—Visual means for determining the conceptions and misconceptions of a group of students.

Sensitive Issue—Any topic in the science curriculum is controversial and so can cause parents to become concerned about what their children are learning.

Sensorimotor Stage—Developmental stage, according to Piaget, defined as (1) birth to approximately 18 months, or (2) birth to the beginning of language.

Sensory Impairment—Category of disability including children with visual, speech, or language impairments and deaf-blind children.

Sequence—Order in which topics are presented in a science program.

Serious Emotional Disturbance—Category of disability in which children have serious difficulty with interpersonal relationships.

Simulations—Computer programs that allow students to enter into a fictitious world with specific boundaries and interact with that world.

Skepticism—Scientific attitude of maintaining a doubting, questioning stance.

Solid Geometric Form—Three-dimensional shapes including sphere, cube, prism, pyramid, cylinder, cone.

Space Relations—Basic process that uses the plane and solid geometric shapes as well as measurements in making observations.

Spatial Intelligence—One of Gardner's eight intelligences that focuses on spatial relations.

Spiral Approach—Approach to curriculum development in which a topic is presented at one grade level and then expanded at subsequent grade levels.

SQ3R Strategy—Widely used study strategy based on five steps: survey, question, read, recite(recall), review.

Structured Search—Database search in which the searcher attempts to locate specific, predetermined information.

Student Structured Experiments—Experiments fully developed by the students individually or in small groups.

Student Reflection—Component of a portfolio showing a student's own evaluation of his or her work samples.

Surfing—Database search in which the searcher has a broad area of interest and uses the database to see what is available on the topic.

Synthesis Level—Fifth level of the cognitive domain that involves the production of a plan or creative use of information.

System—Collection of things that have some influence on one another and which appear to make up a unified whole.

Teacher Observation—Informal means of assessment in which the teacher watches the interactions occurring among and between students.

Teacher Structured Experiments—Experiment fully designed by the teacher for use in a class.

Technology—Ability to cut, shape, or put together materials; to move things from one place to another, to reach farther with one's hands, voice, and senses.

Teleology—Giving of human characteristics to inanimate objects, particularly attributing wants and needs.

Tests and Quizzes—Standard pencil and paper forms of traditional evaluation.

Theoretical Predictions—Prediction based on either a combination of data drawn from concrete experience and reading matter or on reading matter alone.

Theory—Bundle of statements that can be used to explain events and can be supported or weakened by the observations made in testing predictions.

Thinking—Search for meaning.

Traditional Evaluation—Form of evaluation based on the concept that students should learn certain things by a certain point in time.

Transductive Reasoning—Cognitive trait in preoperational children resulting in reasoning from specific to specific without drawing a generalization.

Translation—Sublevel of the comprehension level of the cognitive domain in which a student is asked to tell what a word, definition, or concept means in his or her own words.

Traumatic Brain Injury—Category of disability including children who have experienced serious head injuries.

True-False Items—Item on a test or quiz in which the student determines whether a statement is accurate or not.

Unit Plan—Method for organizing teaching over an extended period of time.

Variables—All of the factors within a quantitative experiment that may be changed by the experimenter, may change because of a change made by the experimenter, or are kept the same because the experimenter wishes to rule them out as the cause of a change.

Verbal Teaching Strategy—Teaching strategies using formats such as lecture, reading, film, filmstrip, guest speaker, or research involving written sources of information.

Wait Time—Strategy used in questioning developed by Mary Budd Rowe that provides time between the end of a question and the expectation of a response.

Willingness to Suspend Judgment—Scientific attitude which requires that an individual wait until all of the facts are in before any judgment is made or conclusion drawn.

Work Sample—Main component of a portfolio, including writing samples, drawings, photographs of projects, and so on.

Zone of Proximal Development—According to Vygotsky, the area where a child can solve a problem with the help of others but not alone.

REFERENCES

Afferbach, P. P. 1990, Winter. The influence of prior knowledge on expert readers' main idea construction strategies. *Reading Research Quarterly* 25, 31–46.

Aicken, F. 1991. *The nature of science*. Portsmouth, N. H.: Heineman.

Airasian, P. W., and M. E. Walsh. 1997. Constructivist cautions. *Phi Delta Kappan* 78(6), 444–449.

Alessi, S. M., and S. R. Trollip. 1991. *Computer-based instruction: Methods and development* (2nd ed.). Englewood Cliffs, N.J.: Prentice Hall.

Algozzine, B., C. V. Morsink, and K. M. Algozzine. 1988. What's happening in self-contained special education classrooms? *Exceptional Children* 55, 259–265.

Allen, H., F. Spittgerberge, and M. Manning. 1993. *Teaching and learning in the middle level school*. New York: Merrill.

American Association for the Advancement of Science. 1975. *Science—A process approach*. Lexington, Mass.: Ginn.

American Association for the Advancement of Science. 1993. *Benchmarks for science literacy*. New York: Oxford University Press.

American Association for the Advancement of Science. 1989. *Project 2061: Science for all Americans*. Washington, D.C.: Author.

Anderson, C., and D. Butts. 1980. A comparison of individualized and group instruction in a sixth grade electricity unit. *Journal of Research in Science Teaching* 17,2.

Anderson, G. J. 1970. Effects of classroom social climate on individual learning. *American Educational Research Journal* 7, 135–152.

Anderson, O. R. 1992. Some interrelationships between constructivist models of learning and current neurobiological theory, with implications for science education. *Journal of Research in Science Teaching* 29(10), 1037–1058.

Anderson, T. H., and B. B. Armbruster. 1984. Content area textbooks. In R. C. Anderson, J. Osborn, and R. J. Tierney (eds.), *Learning to read in American schools: Basal readers and content texts* (pp. 193–226). Hillsdale, N.J.: Lawrence Erlbaum.

Andre, T. 1979. Does answering high-level questions while reading facilitate productive learning? *Review of Educational Research* 49, 280–318.

Armbruster, B. B. 1984. The problems of inconsiderate text. In G. G. Duffy, L. R. Roehler, and J. Mason (eds.), *Comprehension instruction: Perspectives and suggestions* (pps. 202–217). New York: Longman.

Arnold, D. S. 1975. An investigation of relationships among question level, response level, and lapse time. *School Science and Mathematics* 73, 591–594.

Aspy, D. N., and F. N. Roebuck. 1982. Affective education: Sound investment. *Educational Leadership* 39, 7.

Assetto, E R., and E. Dowden. 1988. Getting a grip on interfacing. *The science teacher* 55(6), 65–67.

Association for Supervision and Curriculum Development. 1998, Fall. Science education: How curriculum and instruction are evolving. *ASCD Curriculum Update*. Alexandria, Va.: Author.

Astington, J. W., and D. R. Olson. 1990. Metacognitive and metalinguistic language: Learning to talk about thought. *Applied Psychology* 39, 77–87.

Ausubel, D. P. 1960. The use of advance organizers in the learning and retention of meaningful verbal learning. *Journal of Educational Psychology* 51, 267–272.

Ausubel, D. P. 1963. *Psychology and meaningful verbal learning*. New York: Greene and Straton.

Bailey, D. B., V. Buysse, R. Edmonson, and T. M. Smith. 1992. Creating family-centered services in early intervention: Perceptions of professionals in four states. *Exceptional Children* 58, 298–309.

Ballard, J., B. Ramirez, and K. Zantal-Weiner. 1987. *Public Law 94–142, Section 504 and Public Law 99-457: Understanding what they are and are not*. Reston, Va: Council for Exceptional Children.

Barone, T. 1989. Ways of being at risk: The case of Billy Charles Barnett. *Phi Beta Kappan* 71, 147–151.

Barrow, L. H. 1979. The basics-communicating, thinking, and valuing. *School Science and Mathematics* 70, 8.

Baska, L. K. 1989. Characteristics and needs of the gifted. In J. Feldhusen, J. Van Tassel-Baska, and K. Seeley (eds.). *Excellence in educating the gifted*. Denver: Love.

Bauer, A. M., and T. M. Shea. 1989. *Teaching exceptional students in your classroom*. Boston: Allyn & Bacon.

Baust, J. A. 1981. Spatial relationships and young children. *Arithmetic Teacher* 29, 1.

Baust, J. A. 1982. Teaching spatial relationships using language arts and physical education. *School Science and Mathematics* 82, 7.

Bean, J. 1992. Creating an integrative curriculum: Making the connections. *National Association of Secondary School Principals Bulletin* 16(11), 46–54.

Beane, J. A. 1982. Self-concept and self-esteem as curriculum issues. *Educational Leadership* 39, 7.

Beck, I. L., and J. A. Dole. 1992. Reading and thinking with history and science text. In C. Collins and J. N. Mangieri (eds.), *Teaching thinking: An agenda for the 21st century.* Hillsdale, N.J.: Lawrence Erlbaum.

Bellamy, M. L. 1983. What is your theory? *Science Teacher* 50, 2.

Berk, L. E. 1986. Relationship of elementary school children's private speech to behavioral accompaniment to task, attention, and task performance. *Developmental Psychology* 22(5), 671–680.

Berliner, D. 1984. The half-full glass: A review of research on teaching. In P. Hosford (ed.). *Using what we know about teaching.* Alexandria, Va.: Association for Supervision and Curriculum Development.

Beveridge, W. I. B. 1950. *The art of scientific investigation.* New York: Vintage Books.

Beyer, B. K. 1987. *Practical strategies for the teaching of thinking.* Boston: Allyn & Bacon.

Bilken, D., C. Corrigan, and D. Quick. 1989. Beyond obligations: Student's relations with each other in integrated classes. In D. K. Lipsky and A. Gartner (eds.) *Beyond separate education: Quality education for all* (pp. 207–221). Baltimore: Brookes.

Bivens, J. A., and L. E. Berk. 1990. A longitudinal study of elementary school children's private speech. *Merrill-Palmer Quarterly,* 36, 443–463.

Blank, M., and S. J. White. 1986. Questions: A powerful but misused form of classroom exchange. *Topics in Language Disorders* 6, 1–11.

Blankenship, T. 1982. Is anyone listening? *Science Teacher* 49, 9.

Bloom, B. S. 1956. *Taxonomy of educational objectives: The classification of educational goals. Handbook I: The cognitive domain.* New York: McCay.

Blosser, P.E. 1975. *How to ask the right questions.* Washington, D.C.: National Science Teacher's Association.

Bogdan, R., and S. Biklen 1982. *Introduction to qualitative research in education.* New York: Aldine.

Bonnwell, C. C., and J. A. Eison. 1991. *Active learning: Creating excitement in the classroom.* Washington, D.C.: ASHE-ERIC Higher Education Report.

Boulanger, F. D. 1980. Instruction and science learning: A quantitative synthesis. *Journal of Research in Science Teaching* 18, 4,.

Brandwein, P. F., E. K. Cooper, P. E. Blackwood, M. Cottom-Winslow, J. A. Boeschen, M. G. Giddings, F. Romero, and A. A. Carin. 1980. *Concepts in science.* New York: Harcourt, Brace, Jovanovich.

Brooks, J. G. 1990. Teachers and students: Constructivists forging new connections. *Educational Leadership* 47, 68–71.

Brophy, J. 1992. Probing the subtleties of subject-matter teaching. *Educational Leadership* 49(7), 4–8.

Brown, A., and J. Campione. 1994. Guided discovery in a community of learners. In K. McGilly (Ed.), *Classroom lessons: Integrating cognitive theory and classroom practice* (pp. 229–270). Cambridge, Mass.: MIT Press.

Bruni, J. V. 1982. Problem solving for the primary grades. *Arithmetic Teacher* 29, 6.

Burns, M. 1982. How to teach problem solving. *Arithmetic Teacher* 29,6.

Burns, M. 1985. The role of questioning. *Arithmetic Teacher* 32, 14–16.

Bybee, R. W. 1986. *Science Technology Society. 1985 Yearbook of the National Science Teachers Association.* Washington, D.C.: National Science Teachers Association.

Caldwell, J. H., W. G. Huitt, and A. O. Graeber. 1982. Time spent in learning: Implications from research. *Elementary School Journal* 82, 471–480.

Callison, P., R. Anschultz, and E. Wright. 1997. Gummy worm measurements. *Science and Children* 35(1), 38–41.

Campbell, J. 1992. Laser disk portfolios: Total child assessment. *Educational Leadership* 49, 69–70.

Cannings, T. R., and L. Finkel. 1993. *The technology age classroom.* Wilsonville, Oreg.: Franklin, Beedle, and Associates.

Cartwright, G. P., C. A. Cartwright, and M. E. Ward. 1989. *Educating special learners* (3rd ed.). Belmont, Ca.: Wadsworth.

Cegelka, P. T. 1988. Multicultural considerations. In. W. Lynch and R. B. V. Lewis (eds.). *Exceptional children and adults* (pp. 545–587). Glenview, Ill.: Scott, Foresman.

Champagne, A., R. F. Gunstone, and L. E. Klopfer. 1983. Naive knowledge and science learning. *Research in Science and Technological Education* 1(2), 173–183.

Charnpmmear, M., and B. Reider. 1995. *The integrated elementary classroom: A developmental model of education for the 21st. century.* Boston: Allyn & Bacon.

Chase, C. I. 1999. *Contemporary Assessment for Educators.* New York: Addison-Wesley.

Chiapetta, E. L. 1976. A review of Piagetian studies relevant to science instruction at the secondary and college levels. *Science Education* 60, 124–136.

Cliatt, M. J. P., and J. M. Shaw 1985. Open questions, open answers. *Science and Children* 23, 14–16.

Coble, C. R., and D. R. Rice. 1982. Rekindling scientific curiosity. *Science Teacher* 50, 2.

Cohen, E. 1991. Strategies for creating a multiability classroom. *Cooperative Learning* 12(1), 4–7.

Coie, J. D., K. A. Dodge, and H. Coppotelli. 1982. Dimensions and types of social status: A cross age perspective. *Developmental Psychology* 18, 557–570.

Collins, C. 1992. Thinking development through intervention: Middle school students come of age. In C. Collins and J. N. Mangieri (eds.). *Teaching thinking: An agenda for the 21st century.* Hillsdale, N.J.: Lawrence Erlbaum.

Collins, C., and J. N. Mangieri (eds.). 1992. *Teaching thinking: An agenda for the 21st century.* Hillsdale, N.J.: Lawrence Erlbaum.

Comstock, A. B. 1911. *Handbook of nature study.* Ithaca, N. Y.: Comstock.

Copi, I. M. 1978. *Introduction to logic* (5th ed.). New York: Macmillan.

Correro, G. 1988. *Understanding assessment in young children. Developing instructional programs K–3.* Jackson, Mississippi Department of Education.

Costa, A. 1985. *Developing minds: A resource book for teaching thinking.* Alexandria, Va.: Association for Supervision and Curriculum Development.

Craig, G. S. 1927. *Certain techniques used in developing a course of study in science for the Horace Mann elementary school.* New York: Bureau of Publication, Teachers College, Columbia University, Contributions to Education, No. 276.

Cuban, L. 1985. The "at-risk" label and the problem of urban school reform. *Phi Delta Kappan* 70, 780–784, 799–801.

D'Ignazio, F. 1994. Electronic highways and the classroom of the future. In T. R. Cannings and L. Finkel (eds.), *The technology age classroom* (pp. 632–638). Wilsonville, Oreg.: Franklin, Beedle, and Associates.

Danielson, C., and L. Abrutyn. 1997. *An introduction to using portfolios in the classroom.* Alexandria, Va.: Association for Supervision and Curriculum Development.

Davidson, J. L. 1982. The group mapping activity for instruction in reading and thinking. *Journal of Reading* 25, 52–56.

Dillon, J. T. 1982. The effect of questions in education and other enterprises. *Journal of Curriculum Studies* 14, 127–152.

Dixon-Krauss, L. 1996. *Vygotsky in the classroom.* White Plains, N.Y.: Longman.

Dodge, K. A. 1983. Behavioral antecedents of peer social status. *Child Development* 54, 1386–1399.

Dodge, K.A., G. Petit, J. McClaskey, and M. Brown. 1986. Social competence in children. *Monographs of the Society for Research in Child Development* 51, 2, serial number 213.

Dorr-Bremme, D. W. 1983. Assessing students: Teachers' routine practices and reasoning. *Evaluation Comment* 6, UCLA Center for the Study of Evaluation.

Drake, S. 1993. *Planning integrated curriculum.* Alexandria, Va.: Association of Supervision and Curriculum Development.

Dreyfus, A., E. Jungwirth, and R. Eliovitch. 1990. Applying the "cognitive conflict" strategy for conceptual change-some implications, difficulties, and problems. *Science Education* 74(5), 555–569.

Driver, R., and B. Bell. 1985. Students' thinking and the learning of science: A constructivistic view. *School Science Review* 67(240), 443–456.

Driver, R., and Erickson, G. 1983. Theories in action: Some theoretical and empirical issues in the study of students' conceptual frameworks in science. *Studies in Science Education* 10, 37–60.

Driver, R., H. Asoko, J. Leach, E. Mortimer, and P. Scott. 1994. Constructing scientific knowledge in the classroom. *Educational Researcher* 23 (7), 5–12.

Dunfee, J. 1991. Investigating children's science learning. *The Education Digest* 36, 5.

Ebel, R. L., and D. A. Frisbie. 1986. *Essentials of educational measurement* (4th ed.). Englewood Cliffs, N.J.: Prentice Hall

Ebenezer, J., and S. Connor. 1998. *Learning to teach science: A model for the 21st century.* Upper Saddle River, N.J.: Merrill.

Ebert, C., and E. Ebert. 1993. An instructionally oriented model for enabling conceptual development. In J. Novak (Ed.), *Proceedings of the third international seminar on misconceptions and educational strategies in science and mathematics.* Ithaca, N.Y.: Cornell University.

Eisner, E. W. 1994. *Cognition and curriculum reconsidered* (2nd ed.). New York: Teachers College, Columbia University.

Elementary Science Study. 1978. *Elementary science study materials.* New York: McGraw-Hill.

Engle, B. 1990. An approach to assessment in early grades. In C. Kamii (ed.), *Achievement testing in the early grades: The games grown-ups play.* Washington, D.C.: National Association for the Education of Young Children.

Farley, J. R. 1982. Raising student achievement through the affective domain. *Educational Leadership* 39,7.

Fauvre, M. 1988. Including young children with "new" chronic illnesses in an early childhood education setting. *Young Children* 43, 71–77.

Feldhusen, J. F. 1989. Thinking skills for the gifted. In J. F. Feldhusen, J. Van Tassel-Baskra, and K. Seeley (eds.). *Excellence in education for the gifted.* Denver: Love.

Field, J. 1997. Teaching science with broken pencils. *Science and Children* 34, 17–19.

Finley, F. N. 1983. Science processes. *Journal of Research in Science Teaching* 20, 1.

Fleer, M. 1992. Identifying teacher-child interaction which scaffolds scientific thinking in young children. *Science Education,* 76(4), 393–397.

Fogarty, R. 1991a. *How to integrate the curricula.* Palatine, Ill.: IRI/Skylight.

Fogarty, R. 1991b. Ten ways to integrate curriculum. *Educational Leadership* 49(10), 24–26.

Forgan, H. W., and C. T. Mangrum. 1989. *Teaching content area reading skills* (4th ed.). Columbus, Ohio: Merrill.

Forster, P., and B. A. Doyle. 1989. Teaching listening skills to students with attention deficit disorders. *Teaching Exceptional Children* 21(2), 20–22.

Fosnot, C. T. 1993. Rethinking science education: A defense of piagetian constructivism. *Journal of Research in Science Teaching* 30(9), 1189–1201.

Fox, P. 1994. Creating a laboratory. *Science and Children* 31, 4, 20–22.

Fraser, B. J. 1978. Environmental factors affecting attitude toward different sources of scientific information. *Journal of Research in Science Teaching* 15, 491–497.

Fraser, B. J. 1987. Classroom learning environment and effective schooling. *Professional School Psychology* 2, 25–41.

Fraser, B. J., and P. O'Brien. 1985. Student and teacher perceptions of the environment of elementary-school classrooms. *Elementary School Journal* 85, 567–580.

Fraser, B. J., R. Nash, and D. L. Fisher. 1983. Anxiety in science classrooms: Its measurement and relationship to classroom environment. *Research in Science and Technological Education* 1, 201–208.

Fredericks, A. 1992. *The integrated curriculum.* Englewood, Colo.: Teacher Ideas Press.

Friend, M., and W. Bursuck. 1996. *Including students with special needs: A practical guide for classroom teachers.* Boston: Allyn & Bacon

Gabel, D.L. (Ed.). 1994. *Handbook of research on science teaching and learning.* New York: Macmillan.

Gallagher, J. J. 1988. National agenda for educating gifted students: Statement of priorities. *Exceptional Children* 55, 107–114.

Gardner, H. 1985. *Frames of mind: The theory of multiple intelligences.* New York: Basic Books.

Gardner, H. 1991. *The unschooled mind: How children think and how schools should teach.* New York: Basic Books.

Gardner, H. 1993. *Multiple intelligences: The theory in practice.* New York: Basic Books.

Gardner, H., and J. M. Walters. 1985. *The development and education of intelligences. In Essays on the Intellect.* Alexandria, Va.: Association for Supervision and Curriculum Development.

Gauld, G. 1982. The scientific attitude and science education: A critical reappraisal. *Science Education* 66, 1.

Gega, P. C., and J. M. Peters. 1998. *Science in elementary education* (8th ed). Upper Saddle River, N.J.: Merrill.

Geneshi, C. 1987. Acquiring oral language and communicative competence. In C. Seefeldt (Ed.), *The early childhood curriculum, a review of current research* (pp. 136–151). New York: Teachers College Press, Columbia University.

Gertler, N. 1994. *Multimedia illustrated.* Indianapolis, Ind.: QUE.

Gherke, N. 1991. Explorations of teachers' development of integrative curriculums. *Journal of Curriculum and Supervision* 6(2), 107–117.

Giere, R. N. 1984. *Understanding scientific reasoning* (2nd. ed.). New York: Holt, Rinehart and Winston.

Gil-Perez, D., and J. Carrascosa. 1990. What to do about science "misconceptions." *Science Education* 74(5), 531–540.

Glaser, B. G., and A. L. Strauss 1967. T*he discovery of grounded theory: Strategies for qualitative research.* New York:Aldine.

Goffin, S. G., and C. Q. Tull. 1988. Encouraging cooperative behavior among young children. *Dimensions* 16, 15–18.

Gollnick, D., and P. Chinn. 1994. *Multicultural education in a pluralistic society* (4th ed.). New York: Merrill/Macmillan.

Good, R. G. 1977. *How children learn science: Conceptual development and implications for teaching.* New York: Macmillan.

Grace, C., and E. F. Shores. 1992. *The portfolio and its use: Developmentally appropriate assessment of young children.* Little Rock, Ark.: Southern Association of Children Under Six.

Haladuna, T., R. Olsen, and J. Shaughnessy. 1982. Relations of student, teacher and learning environment variables to attitudes toward science. *Science Education* 66, 671–688.

Haney, W., and G. Madus. 1989, May. Searching for alternatives to standardized tests. *Phi Delta Kappan* 684.

Hannafin, M. J. 1985. Keeping interactive video in perspective. In E. Miller (ed.), *Educational media and technology yearbook 1985.* Littleton, Col.: Libraries Unlimited.

Hart, D. 1994. *Authentic assessment: A handbook for educators.* Menlo Park, Calif.: Addison-Wesley.

Hartup, W. W., and S. G. Moore. 1990. Early peer relations: Developmental significance and prognostic implications. *Early Childhood Research Quarterly* 5, 1–7.

Hassard, J. 1990. *Science experiences: Cooperative learning and the teaching of science.* Menlo Park, Calif.: Addison-Wesley.

Hauser, W. 1996. Multicultural education for the dominant culture. *Urban Education* 31 (2), 125–148.

Hein, G. E., and S. Price. 1994. *Active assessment for active science.* Portsmouth, N.H.: Heinemann.

Holliday, W. G., H. G. Wittaker, and K. D. Loose. 1984. Differential effects of verbal aptitude and study questions on comprehension of science concepts. *Journal of Research in Science Teaching* 21, 143–150.

Howes, C. 1988. Peer interaction of children. *Monographs of the Society for Research in Child Development* 53, 1, serial number 217.

Hunkins, F. P. 1972. *Questioning strategies and techniques.* Boston: Allyn & Bacon.

Inhelder, B., and J. Piaget 1958. *The growth of logical thinking from childhood to adolescence.* New York: Basic Books.

Inhelder, B., and J. Piaget. 1964. *Early growth of logic in the child.* New York: Harper & Row.

Ireland, J. C., D. Wray, and C. Flexer. 1988. Hearing for success in the classroom. *Teaching Exceptional Children* 20(2), 15–7.

Jacobs, H. 1991. On interdisciplinary education: A conversation. *Educational Leadership* 49(10), 24–26.

Jacobs, H. H. 1989. *Interdisciplinary curriculum: Design and implementation.* Alexandria, Va.: Association for Supervision and Curriculum Development.

Johnson, D. D., and P. D. Pearson. 1984. *Teaching reading vocabulary* (2nd ed.). New York: Holt, Rinehard and Winston.

Johnson, D., and R. Johnson 1994. *Learning together and alone: Cooperation, competition, and individualization* (4th ed.). Needham Heights, Mass.: Allyn & Bacon.

Jonassen, D. H. 1991. Evaluating constructivist learning. *Educational Technology* 31(9), 28–33.

Jones, C. J. 1992. *Social and emotional development of exceptional students: Handicapped and gifted.* Springfield, Ill.: Charles C. Thomas.

Joyse, B., and E. Calhoun, 1998. *Learning to teach inductively.* Boston: Allyn & Bacon.

Kagan, J. 1980. Jean Piaget's contributions to education. *Kappan* 62, 4.

Karplus, R. (director). 1972. *Science curriculum improvement study teaching materials.* Chicago: Rand McNally.

Kauchak, D. P., and P. D. Eggen. 1998. *Teaching and learning: Research based methods.* Boston: Allyn & Bacon

Kelly, T. E. 1989, October. Leading class discussion of controversial issues. *Social Education,* 368–370.

Kepler, M. 1996. How to make hands-on science work for you. *Instructor* 105(6), 46–53.

Killoran, J. 1992, February. In defense of the multiple-choice question. *Social Education,* 108.

Kitano, M. K. 1989. The K–3 teacher's role in recognizing and supporting young gifted children. *Young Children* 44(3), 57–63.

Kitano, M. K., and D. E. Kirby. 1986. *Gifted education: A comprehensive view.* Boston: Little, Brown.

Kitcher, P. 1982. *Abusing science.* Cambridge, Mass.:MIT Press.

Kivalic, S. 1993. *ITI: The model: Integrated thematic instruction.* Village of Oak Creek, Ark.: Books for Educators.

Klein, E. 1989. Gifted and talented. In G. P. Cartwright, C. A. Cartwright, and M. E. Ward (eds.). *Educating special learners* (3rd ed.). Belmont, Calif.: Wadsworth.

Krendl, K. A., and D. A. Lieberman 1988. Computers and learning: A review of recent research. *Journal of Educational Computing Research* 4, 388.

Kubuszyn, T., and G. Borich. 1996. *Educational testing and measurement: classrom application and practice.* New York: HarperCollins.

Kuhn, D., E. Amsel, and M. O'Loughlin. 1988. *The development of scientific thinking skills.* San Diego: Academic Press.

Kuhn, T. S. 1970. *The structure of scientific revolutions.* Chicago: University of Chicago Press.

Kulm, G., and S. M. Malcom. 1992. *Science assessment in the service of reform.* Washington, D.C.: American Association for the Advancement of Science.

Ladd, G. W. 1988. Friendship patterns and peer status during early and middle childhood. *Journal of Developmental and Behavioral Pediatrics* 9, 229–238.

Lapp, D., and J. Flood. 1994. Integrating the curriculum: First steps. *The Reading Teacher* 47(5), 416–419.

Lapp, D., J. Flood, and N. Farnan. 1989. *Content area reading and learning.* Englewood Cliffs, N.J.: Prentice Hall.

Lawrenz, F. 1975. The relationship between science teacher characteristics and student achievement and attitude. *Journal of Research in Science Teaching* 12, 10.

Lawson, A. E. 1978. The development and validation of a classroom test of formal reasoning. *Journal of Research in Science Teaching* 15, 1.

Lawson, A. E. 1982. Formal reasoning, achievement, and intelligence: An issue of importance. *Science Education* 66, 1.

Lazear, D. 1991. *Seven ways of knowing: Teaching for multiple intelligences* (2nd ed.). Palatine, Ill.: Skylight.

Lee, K. S. 1982. Guiding young children to successful problem solving. *Arithmetic Teacher* 29, 5.

Lerner, J. W. 1989. *Learning disabilities* (5th ed.). Boston: Houghton Mifflin.

Lewis, R. B., and D. H. Doorlag. 1991. *Teaching special students in the mainstream.* New York: Merrill.

Lillie, D. L., W. H. Hannum, and G. B. Stuck 1989. *Computers and effective instruction.* New York: Longman.

Lilly, M. S. 1992. Labeling, a tired, overworked, yet unresolved issue in special education. In W. Stainback and S. Stainback (eds.). *Controversial issues confronting special education: Divergent perspectives* (pp. 85–95). Boston: Allyn & Bacon.

Linn, M. C. 1973. The effect of direct experiences with objects on middle class, culturally divers, and visually impaired young children. *Journal of Research in Science Teaching* 20, 183–190.

Lipson, M., S. Valencia, K. Wixon, and C. Peters. 1993. Integration and thematic teaching: Integration to improve teaching and learning. *Language Arts* 70 (4), 252–263.

Lockard, K. A., P. D. Abrams, and W. A. Many. 1987. *Microcomputers for educators.* Boston: Little, Brown.

Lonner, W. J., and V. O. Tyler. 1988. *Cultural and ethnic factors in learning and motivation.* Western Washington University Press.

MacDougal, J. D. 1996. *A short history of the planet earth.* New York: Wiley.

Maeroff, G. I. 1991, December. Assessing alternative assessment. *Phi Delta Kappan,* 278.

Manning, M. L., and L. G. Baruth. 1996. *Multicultural education of children and adolescents.* Boston: Allyn &Bacon

Martinello, M., and G. Cook. 1994. *Interdisciplinary inquiry in teaching and learning.* New York: Merrill.

Marzano, R. J., D. Pickering, and R. Brandt 1990. Integrating instruction programs through dimensions of learning. *Educational Leadership* 47, 5.

May, L. 1997. Developing logical reasoning. *Teaching Pre-K–8* 28(2), 22.

Mayer, D. A. 1995. How can we best use children's literature in teaching science concepts? *Science and Children* 33(8), 22–25.

Mayer, V. J. 1990. Teaching from a global point of view. *The Science Teacher* 57(1), 47–51.

McAnarney, H. 1982. How much space does an object take up? *Science and Children* 19, 4.

McCormick, L. 1990. Cultural diversity and exceptionality. In N. G. Haring and L. McCormick (eds.), *Exceptional children and youth* (5th ed.). Columbus, Ohio: Merrill.

McCormick, C. B., and M. Pressley. 1997. *Educational psychology: Learning, instruction, assessment.* New York: Longman.

McDonald, J., and C. Czerniak. 1994. Developing interdisciplinary units: Strategies and examples. *School Science and Mathematics* 94(1), 5–10.

McInerney, J. D. 1986. Scientific progress and public policy: Challenge to traditional values. In R. W. Bybee (Ed.). *Science Technology Society. 1985 Yearbook of the National Science Teachers Association.* Washington, D.C.: National Science Teachers Association.

Miller, K. W., S. F. Steiner, and C. D. Larson. 1996. Strategies for science learning. *Science and Children* 33(6), 22–25.

Miller, L. 1993. *What we call smart: A new narrative for intelligence and learning.* San Diego, Calif.: Singular.

Mokron, J. R. 1986. The impact of microcomputer-based labs on children's graphing. *YERC Technical Report* 2, 7.

Moore, R. W. 1982. Open-mindedness and proof. *School Science and Mathematics* 82, 6.

Myer, L. A., L. Crummy, and E. A. Greer. 1988. Elementary science textbooks: Their contents, text characteristics, and comprehensibility. *Journal of Research in Science Teaching* 25, 435–463.

Nachmias, R., and M. C. Linn. 1987. Evaluations of science laboratory data: The role of computer presented information. *Journal of Research in Science Teaching* 24(5), 505.

National Association for the Education of Young Children. 1988. *Statement on standardized testing of young children 3 through 8 years of age.* Washington, D.C.: Author.

National Association for the Education of Young Children. 1989. *Guidelines for appropriate curriculum content and assessment in programs serving children age 3 through 8.* Washington, D.C.: Author.

National Research Council. 1996. *National science education standards.* Washington, D.C.: National Academy Press.

National Science Teachers Association. 1964. *Theory into action in science curriculum development.* Washington, D.C.: Author.

National Science Teachers Association. 1992–1993. Science/technology/society: A new effort for providing appropriate science to all. In *National science teachers association handbook (1992–1993)* (pp. 168–169). Washington, D.C.: Author.

Olson, D. R., and J. W. Astington. 1993. Thinking about thinking: Learning how to take statements and hold beliefs. *Educational Psychologist* 28(1), 7–24.

Orlich, D. C., R. J. Harder, R. C. Callahan, and H. W. Gibson. 1998. *Teaching strategies: A guide to better instruction.* New York: Houghton Mifflin.

Padilla, M. J., and E. J. Frye. 1996. Observing and inferring promotes science learning. *Science and Children,* 33(8), 22–25.

Padilla, M. J., J. R. Okey, and F. G. Dellashaw. 1983. The relationship between science process skill learning and formal thinking abilities. *Journal of Research in Science Teaching* 20, 3.

Palady, L. G. 1978. *SCIS II sampler guide.* Boston: American Science and Engineering.

Pallrand, G. J. 1979. The transition to formal thought. *Journal of Research in Science Teaching* 16, 5.

Parke, B. N. 1989. *Gifted students in regular classrooms.* Boston: Allyn & Bacon.

Parker, S. P. (ed.). 1989. *McGraw-Hill dictionary of scientific and technical terms* (4th ed.). New York: McGraw-Hill

Parsons, A. S. 1988. Integrating special children into day care programs. *Dimensions* 16, 15–19.

Pasche, C. L., L. Gorrill, and B. Strom. 1989. *Children with special needs in early childhood settings.* Menlo Park, Calif.: Addison-Wesley.

Paulson, F. L., P. R. Paulson, and C. A. Meyer. 1991. What makes a portfolio a portfolio. *Educational Leadership* 48, 802–806.

Pearson, D. P., and L. Fielding. 1991. Comprehension Instruction. In R. Barr, M. L. Kamil, P. Mosenthal, and P. D. Pearson. *Handbook of reading research,* (Vol 2), (eds.), New York: Longman.

Pederson, J. E. 1993. STS issues: A perspective. In R. E. Yager (Ed.) *National Science Teachers Association (1939): The science, technology movement.* Washington, D.C.: NSTA.

Perkins, D. N. 1991. What constructivism demands of the learner. *Educational Technology* 31(9), 19–21.

Perrone, V. (ed.). 1991. *Expanding student assessment.* Alexandria, Va.: Association for Supervision and Curriculum Development.

Peterson, N. L. 1987. *Early intervention for handicapped and at-risk children.* Denver, Co.: Love.

Piaget, J. 1963. *The Psychology of Intelligence.* Totowa, N. J.: Littlefield.

Piaget, J. 1972a. *Judgment and reasoning in the child.* Totowa, N.J.: Littlefield.

Piaget, J. 1972b. *The child's conception of physical causality.* Totowa, N.J.: Littlefield.

Piaget, J. 1974. *The origins of intelligence in children.* New York: International Universities Press.

Piaget, J. 1975a. *The child's conception of the world.* Totowa, N. J.: Littlefield.

Piaget, J. 1975b. *The psychology of intelligence.* Totowa, N. J.: Littlefield.

Piaget, J., and B. Inhelder. 1956. *The child's conception of space.* London: Routledge and Kegan Paul.

Putnam, J. 1997. *Cooperative learning in diverse classrooms.* Upper Saddle River, N. J.: Merrill/Prentice Hall.

Ramirez, B. A. 1988. Culturally and linguistically diverse children. *Teaching Exceptional Children* 20(4), 45–46.

Raynes, M., M. Snell, and W. Sailor. 1991. A fresh look at categorical programs for children with special needs. *Phi Delta Kappa* 73, 326–331.

Reif, R. J., and K. Rauch. 1994. Science in their own words. *Science and Children* 31(4), 31–33.

Reynolds, K. E., and R. H. Barba 1996. *Technology for the teaching and learning of science.* Boston: Allyn & Bacon.

Rezba, R. J., C. Sprague, R. L. Fiel, and H. J. Funk. 1995. *Learning and assessing science process skills* (3rd. ed.). Dubuque, Iowa: Kendall-Hunt.

Ridley, M. 1996. *Evolution* (2nd ed.). Cambridge, Mass.: Blackwell Science.

Robinson, F. P. 1970. *Effective study* (4th ed.) New York: Harper & Row.

Rogers, R. E., and A. M. Voelker. *1970.* Programs for improving elementary science instruction in the elementary school; elementary science study. *Science and Children* 8, 1.

Rogers, R. T. 1987. The computer-assisted laboratory. *Physics Education* 22, 223.

Romney, E. A. 1971. *A working guide to the elementary science study.* Newton, Mass.: Educational Development Center.

Ross, M. E. 1997. Scientists at play. *Science and Children* 35, 35–38.

Rowe, M. B. 1974. Pausing phenomena: Influence on the quality of instruction. *Journal of Psycholinguistic Research* 3, 3.

Rowe, M. B. 1974a. Wait-time and rewards as instructional variables, their influence on language, logic, and fate control: Part one, wait-time. *Journal of Research in Science Teaching* 11, 81–94.

Rowe, M. B. 1974b. Relation of wait-time and rewards to the development of language, logic, and fate control: Part two, rewards. *Journal of Research in Science Teaching* 11, 291–308.

Rubba, P. A. 1987. Perspectives on science-technology-society instruction. *School Science and Mathematics* 87, 181–189.

Rubin, D. 1992. *Reading and study skills in content areas.* Boston: Allyn & Bacon.

Rubin, D. 1993. *A practical approach to teaching reading.* Boston: Allyn & Bacon.

Ruchlis, H. 1990. *Clear thinking: a practical introduction.* Buffalo, N.Y.: Prometheus Books.

Ruggiero, V. R. 1988. *Teaching thinking across the curriculum.* New York: Harper & Row.

Sanders, N. M. 1966. *Classroom questions: What kinds?* New York: Harper.

Santa, C. M., and D. E. Alvermann (eds.). 1991. *Science learning: Processes and applications.* Newark, Del.: International Reading Association.

Saul, W., and S. A. Jagush (eds.). 1986. *Vital connections: Children, science, and books.* Portsmouth, N.H.: Heinemann.

Scarnati, J. T., and C. J. Weller. 1992. The write stuff: Science inquiry skills help students think positively about writing assignments. *Science and Children* 29(4), 28–29.

Schlichter, C. L. 1983. The answer is in the question. *Science and Children* 19, 3.

Schneider, L., and J. W. Renner. 1980. Concrete and formal teaching. *Journal of Research in Science Teaching* 17, 6.

Schwier, R. 1992. *A taxonomy of interaction for instructional multimedia.* Paper presented at the Annual Conference of the Association for Media and Technology, Vancouver, British Columbia, Canada. Review in

Journal of Educational Multimedia and Hypermedia 3(1), 112–113.

Science—A Process Approach. 1979. *Curriculum materials.* Lexington, Mass.: Ginn.

Science Curriculum Improvement Study. 1970. *SCIS sampler guide.* Chicago: Rand-McNally.

Science Curriculum Improvement Study. 1980. *Curriculum materials-SCIIS.* Chicago: Rand-McNally.

Scott, J. (ed.). 1993. *Science and language links: Classroom implications.* Portsmouth, N.H.: Heinemann.

Sharan, S. 1980. Cooperative learning in small groups: Recent methods and effects on achievement, attitudes, and ethnic relations. *Review of Educational Research* 50, 241–271.

Shaw, J. M., and M. Cliatt. 1981. Searching and researching. *Science and Children* 19, 3.

Simpson, R. L., and B. S. Myles. 1990. The general education collaboration: A model for successful mainstreaming. *Focus on Exceptional Children* 23(4), 1–10.

Singer, H., and D. Donlan. 1988. *Reading and learning from text* (2nd ed.). Hillsdale, N.J.: Lawrence Erlbaum.

Slavin, R. E. 1989. Students at risk of school failure: The problem and its dimensions. In R. E. Slavin, N. L. Karweit, and N. A. Madden (eds.), *Effective programs for students at risk.* Boston: Allyn & Bacon.

Slavin, R. E. 1994. *Cooperative learning* (2nd ed.). Needham Heights, Mass.: Allyn & Bacon.

Smith, J. D. 1998. *Inclusion: Schools for all students.* Belmont, Calif.: Wadsworth.

Smith, N. B. 1969, December. The many faces of reading comprehension. *The Reading Teacher* 249–259, 291.

Smith, W. S. 1983. Engineering a classroom discussion. *Science and Children* 20,5.

Southern Association on Children Under Six. 1990. *Developmentally appropriate assessment.* Little Rock, Ark.: Author.

Stahl, S. A., and C. H. Clark. 1987. The effects of participatory expectations in classroom discussion on the learning of science vocabulary. *American Educational Research Journal* 24, 542–556.

Stahl, S., and B. A. Karpinus. 1991, September. Possible sentences: Predicting word meanings to teach content area vocabulary. *The Reading Teacher* 45, 35–43.

Stepans, J. I., B. W. Saigo, and C. Ebert. 1995. *Changing the classroom from within: Partnership, collegiality, and constructivism.* Montgomery, Ala.: Saiwood.

Stice, C., J. Bertrand, and N. Bertrand. 1995. *Integrating reading and the other language arts.* Belmont, Calif.: Wadsworth.

Suchman, J. R. 1962. *The elementary school training program in scientific inquiry.* Champaign/Urbana: University of Illinois.

Sumrall, W. J., and J. Criglow. 1995. The "scoop" on science data. *Science and Children,* 32, 6, 37–39, 44.

Suydam, M. 1982. Update on research on problem solving: Implications for classroom teaching. *Arithmetic Teacher* 29, 6.

Swartz, R., and S. Parks 1994. *Infusing the teaching of critical and creative thinking into elementary instruction.* Pacific Grove, Calif.: Critical Thinking Press.

Tiedt, P. L., and I. M. Tiedt. 1990. *Multicultural teaching: A handbook of activities, information, and resources* (3rd. ed.). Boston: Allyn & Bacon.

Tippins, D. J., and N. F. Dana. 1992, March. Culturally relevant alternative assessment, *Science Scope* 51.

Tisher, R. R. 1971. Verbal interaction in science classes. *Journal of Research in Science Teaching* 8, 1.

Tishman, S., D. N. Perkins, and E. Jay. 1995. *The thinking classroom: Learning and thinking in a culture of thinking.* Boston: Allyn & Bacon.

Tobin, K. G., and W. Capie. 1982. Lessons with an emphasis on process skills. *Science and Children* 19, 3.

Trollip, S. R., and S. M. Alessi. 1988. Incorporating computers effectively into classrooms. *Journal of Research on Computing Educations* 21(1), 70–81.

U.S. Department of Education. 1993. *Fifteenth annual report to Congress on the implementation of the Individuals with Disabilities Education Act.* Washington, D.C.: Author.

U.S. National Research Center. 1998. *TIMSS United States.* URL: http//www.ustimss.msu.edu.

van Ments, M. 1990. *Active talk: The effective use of discussion in learning.* New York: St. Martin's Press.

Vandercook, T., and J. York. 1989. A team approach to program development and support. In J. York, T. Vandercook, C. MacDonald, and S. Wolff (eds.). *Strategies for full inclusion* (pp. 21–43). Minneapolis, Minn.: University of Minnesota, Institute on Community Integration.

Vanderhoof, B., E. Miller, L. B. Clegg, and H. J. Patterson. 1992, March. Real or fake? The phony document as a teaching strategy. *Social Education* 169–170.

Victor, E. 1974. The inquiry approach to teaching and learning: A primer for the teacher. *Science and Children* 12, 2.

Villegas, A. 1991. *Culturally responsive pedagogy for the 1990's and beyond.* Princeton, N.J.: Educational Testing Service.

Vockell, E. L., and E. M. Schwartz. 1992. *The computer in the classroom* (2nd ed.).Watsonville, Calif.: McGraw-Hill.

Vockell, E. L., and M. Simonson. 1994. *Technology for teachers.* Dubuque, Iowa: Kendall/Hunt.

Vygotsky, L. S. 1962. *Thought and language.* Cambridge, Mass.: MIT Press.

Waldron, K. A. 1996. *Introduction to special education: The inclusive classroom.* Albany, N. Y.: Delmar.

Walker, J. L. 1988. Young American Indian children. *Teaching Exceptional Children* 20 (4), 50–51.

Watson, B., and R. Konicek. 1990, May. Teaching for conceptual change: Confronting children's experience. *Phi Delta Kappan,* 127–133.

Webb, N., and S. Farivar. 1994. Promoting helping behavior in cooperative small groups in middle school mathematics. *American Educational Research Journal* 31(2), 369–395.

Weiss, I. R., B. H. Nelson, S. E. Boyd, and S. B. Hudson. 1989. *Science and mathematics education briefing book.* Chapel Hill, N. C.: Horizon Research.

Welch, W. W. 1981. *What research says to the science teacher* (Vol. 3). Washington, D.C.: National Science Teachers Association.

Wertsch, J. V. 1984. *The zone of proximal development: Some conceptual issues.* In B. Rogoff and J. V. Wertsch (Eds.). *Children's learning in the zone of proximal development* (pp. 7–18). San Francisco: Jossey-Bass.

Wesman, A. G. 1971. Writing the test item. In R .L. Thorndike (ed.), *Educational measurement* (2nd ed.). Washington, D.C.: American Council on Education.

Wheatley, G. 1989. Instructional methods for the gifted. In J. Feldhusen, J. Van Tassel-Baska, and K. Seeley (eds.). *Excellence in educating the gifted.* Denver: Love.

Wheatley, G. H. 1991. Constructivist perspectives on science and mathematics learning. *Science Education* 75(2), 9–21.

White, E. P. 1982. Why self-directed learning? *Science and Children* 19, 5.

White, E. P. 1986. It'll be a challenge!: Managing emotional stress in teaching disabled children. *Young Children* 41, 44–48.

Wiggins, G. 1989, May. A true test: Toward more authentic and equitable assessment. *Phi Delta Kappan* 703–704.

Wiggins, G. 1992. Creating tests worth taking. *Educational Leadership* 49, 26.

Willis, S. 1995. Making integrated curriculum a reality. *Association for Supervision and Curriculum Development Education Update* 37(4), 4.

Wilson, L., D. Malmgren, S. Ramage, and L. Schultz. 1993. *An integrated approach to learning.* Portsmouth, N.H.: Heinemann.

Wise, K. 1989. The effects of using computing technologies in science instruction: A synthesis of classroom-based research. In J. D. Ellis (ed.), *Information technology and science education.* Columbus, Ohio: ERIC.

Woerner, J. J., R. H. Rivers, and E. L. Vockell. 1991. *The computer in the science curriculum.* Watsonville, Calif.: McGraw-Hill.

Wolf, D. P. 1989, May. Portfolio assessment: Sampling student work. *Educational Leadership* 46, 36–38.

Wolfinger, D .M. 1984. *Teaching science in the elementary school: Content, process and attitudes.* Boston: Little, Brown.

Wolfinger, D. M. 1994. *Science and mathematics in early childhood education.* New York: HarperCollins.

Wolfinger, D. M., and J. W. Stockard. 1997. *Elementary methods: An integrated curriculum.* New York: Longman.

Woodward, A., and D. L. Elliot. 1990. *Textbooks: Consensus and controversy.* In D. L. Elliot and A. Woodward, (eds.), *Textbooks and schooling in the United States.* Chicago: University of Chicago Press.

Yager, R. E. 1991. The constructivist learning model: Towards real reform in science education. *The Science Teacher* 58(6), 52–57.

Yager, R. E. (Ed.). 1993. *What research says to the science teacher: The science teacher: The science, technology, society movement* (Vol. 7). Washington, D.C.: NSTA.

Ziv, A., and O. Gadish. 1990. Humor and giftedness. *Journal for Education of the Gifted* 13(4), 332–345.

CREDITS

Index